Praise for *On Becoming a Teen Mom*

"An illuminating, inspiring, often heartbreaking investigation into the lifeworlds of teenage moms. The authors bypass stale moral panic agendas, instead creating space for the young women to speak their own truths, in their own words, while skillfully answering the forgotten question, who are these kids?"

Donna Gaines, author of *Teenage Wasteland* and *A Misfit's Manifesto*

"A revealing exploration of the complex reality and surprising diversity behind the stereotypes of teen motherhood. Mary Patrice Erdmans and Timothy Black combine personal life histories with rigorous argument to show how teen pregnancy in America is the outcome rather than the cause of impoverished neighborhoods, stressed families, and educational inequities."

Stephanie Coontz, author of *The Way We Never Were: American Families and the Nostalgia Trap*

"*On Becoming a Teen Mom* is a welcome counterweight to reductionist and pathologizing accounts of adolescent mothers. This book is a must-read for anyone who wants to get beyond pearl clutching and move toward supporting pregnant and parenting teenagers."

Jeanne Flavin, author of *Our Bodies, Our Crimes: The Policing of Women's Reproduction in America*

"*On Becoming a Teen Mom* offers one of the deepest investigations into teen pregnancy that I have seen. Until we begin to address issues systemically, the 'problem' of teen pregnancy and the real problems young mothers face will not go away. This book is a significant and important contribution toward that effort."

Wanda S. Pillow, author of *Unfit Subjects: Education Policy and the Teen Mother, 1972–2002*

"By interpreting common themes in the life histories of the many teen mothers they interviewed, these authors question the assumption that their futures were completely promising before they became young mothers, or that their early motherhood compromised their futures any further. We need to listen

to these young women, and policy targets need to be earlier, broader, and deeper than individual sexual, contraceptive, or pregnancy behavior alone."

Arline T. Geronimus, Fellow, Center for Advanced Study
in the Behavioral Sciences, Stanford University

"*On Becoming a Teen Mom* powerfully reminds us that any serious discussion of the causes and consequences of teen motherhood is incomplete if it fails to account for the larger social forces at play in girls' lives."

Lorena Garcia, Associate Professor of Sociology and Latin American
and Latino Studies, University of Illinois at Chicago

"The writing pulled me in—accessible, serious, straightforward. Once I started reading, I couldn't put down this compelling and disturbing book on the tragedy that is structural inequality."

Alisse Waterston, author of *My Father's Wars:*
Migration, Memory, and the Violence of a Century

"While the statistics about teen pregnancy tell one story, this book tells compelling stories about the multi-challenged lives of teen mothers. Mary Patrice Erdmans and Timothy Black have made a major contribution to the understanding of the intersection of teen pregnancy, family and community violence, and poverty in the United States. The voices of these teen mothers need to be heard."

John M. Leventhal, MD, Professor of Pediatrics,
Yale School of Medicine

On Becoming a Teen Mom

On Becoming a
Teen Mom

Life before Pregnancy

Mary Patrice Erdmans
and Timothy Black

UNIVERSITY OF CALIFORNIA PRESS

University of California Press, one of the most
distinguished university presses in the United States,
enriches lives around the world by advancing scholarship
in the humanities, social sciences, and natural sciences. Its
activities are supported by the UC Press Foundation and
by philanthropic contributions from individuals and
institutions. For more information, visit www.ucpress.edu.

University of California Press
Oakland, California

© 2015 by Mary Patrice Erdmans and Timothy Black

Library of Congress Cataloging-in-Publication Data

Erdmans, Mary Patrice, author.
  On becoming a teen mom : life before pregnancy /
Mary Patrice Erdmans and Timothy Black.
    p. cm.
  Includes bibliographical references and index.
  ISBN 978-0-520-28341-1 (cloth : alk. paper)
  ISBN 978-0-520-28342-8 (pbk. : alk. paper)
  ISBN 978-0-520-95928-6 (ebook)
  1. Teenage pregnancy—United States. 2. Teenage
girls—United States—Social conditions. I. Black,
Timothy, author. II. Title.
  HQ759.4.E74 2015
  306.874'32—dc23
                                        2014024489

Manufactured in the United States of America

24 23 22 21 20 19 18 17 16 15
10 9 8 7 6 5 4 3 2 1

In keeping with a commitment to support
environmentally responsible and sustainable printing
practices, UC Press has printed this book on Natures
Natural, a fiber that contains 30% post-consumer waste
and meets the minimum requirements of ANSI/NISO
Z39.48–1992 (R 1997) (Permanence of Paper).

*To Jean Baker, Angela Erdmans, and
James Louis Erdmans*

Contents

List of Illustrations   *ix*
Acknowledgments   *xi*

Introduction: The Backstory to the Baby   *1*
1. The Distraction   *8*
2. Young Young Mothers   *40*
3. Child Sexual Abuse   *77*
4. Violence against Women   *105*
5. Education   *143*
6. Contraception and Abortion   *176*
Conclusion: Getting beyond the Distraction   *217*

Appendix A: Listening to Life Stories   *227*
Appendix B: Tables   *236*
Notes   *239*
References   *285*
Index   *319*

Illustrations

FIGURES

1. Birth Rates for Teens Age 15 to 19, 1940–2010 / *13*
2. Birth, Pregnancy, and Abortion Rates for Teens Age 15 to 19, 1990–2008 / *14*
3. Percent of Children Born to Unmarried Women by Age of Mother, 2007 / *15*
4. Birth Rates for Teens Age 15 to 19 by Race and Hispanic Origin, 1991–2009 / *24*
5. Pregnancy, Birth, and Abortion Rates for Teens Age 10 to 14, 1990–2008 / *46*
6. Pregnancy, Birth, and Abortion Rates by Age Group, 2008 / *189*

TABLES

1. Characteristics of 16 Mothers Pregnant before Age 15 / *48*
2. Births by Age Groups, 1975–2010 / *63*
3. Percent of Mothers with Problems in Household While Growing Up / *119*
4. Educational Status at Time of Interview / *154*

5. Comparison of Mothers Who Dropped Out before the Pregnancy, Dropped Out after the Pregnancy, and Never Dropped Out / *157*

6. Percentage of Pregnancies Ending in Abortion by Age, Race, and Hispanic Origin, 1990 and 2004 / *210*

7. Characteristics of the Sample / *236*

8. Age of Mother at Time of Birth for Teen Births in Connecticut, 1998–2010 / *238*

9. Number and Rate of Births for Teens Age 10 to 14 by Race and Hispanic Origin, 1990–2010 / *238*

Acknowledgments

We are beholden to the teen mothers who shared their life stories with us. You are amazing women whose wisdom about life and how things work in society far outreaches our own understanding. We do not claim to have done you justice by writing a book based on your stories. Words on a page are not real life. It is thus, with humility, that we thank you for allowing us to examine your life stories and to grapple with some of the larger social issues that concern us.

This project has a long historical reach and we apologize in advance to anyone whose contributions we fail to recognize. We particularly want to thank those scholars who gave generously of their time to read an entire draft of our manuscript at a crucial phase of its development. These include Jamie Fader, Annette Lareau, John Leventhal, Michael Lewis, and Jean Malone. We are grateful to others who read parts of the manuscript at varying stages of the writing process, particularly Steven Adair, Sky Keyes, and members of our writing group in Hartford—Chris Doucot, Jerry Lembcke, Bill Major, Jim Russell, and Lucy Rosenblatt. Katha Pollitt provided Mary with encouraging feedback on the book prospectus at the 2006 Wesleyan Writing Conference. We also thank our reviewers Alisse Waterston and Wanda Pillow for their careful readings, and particularly their methodological and theoretical acuity. We are honored by the mindful attention that all these serious thinkers gave to our work, each engaging the topics differently from their own scholarly locations and lived experiences.

Many assisted us with the interviews, analysis, and administrative and technical work at the University of Hartford, Center for Social Research. We give a hearty thank you to Meredith Damboise, Kristina Dickinson, Madelyn Figueroa, and Bette Decoteau for their help throughout the project. Numerous others worked on particular segments of the research including Ron Albert, Erik Beach, Nicole D'Anna, Mary Ann Gonzalez, Nardine Justinien, Kevin Lamkins, Lauren LoBue, Scott Virgin, Matthew Walker, Denise Washington, and Sarah Zucker. We also want to thank the Family Support Workers of the home-visitation program who helped us gain access to the mothers we interviewed for this study. Finally, we thank Elizabeth Nalepa, Bradley Powell, Michelle Rizzuto, Kimberly Racut, Michael Slone, and Alicia Smith at Case Western Reserve University for their assistance in preparing the manuscript.

The life-story research was funded by the Children's Trust Fund, now a division of the Department of Social Services of the State of Connecticut. Of course, opinions, findings, and conclusions herein are ours alone and do not reflect the views of this or any other government agency. We are particularly grateful to Karen Foley-Schain for her leadership at the Children's Trust Fund, for her willingness to take risks to critically examine the statewide home-visitation program that she developed and directed, and for her encouragement and support of our research, public presentations, and publications.

Other support came from institutions that generously allowed Mary time to work on this whale of a project (we had over twenty thousand pages of interview transcripts). We thank Central Connecticut State University for the course releases they granted her in the early stages of data collection and analysis and for the yearlong sabbatical to start writing the book, and Case Western Reserve University for providing release time to revise the manuscript.

We also appreciate the work of Naomi Schneider at University of California Press who enthusiastically supported our book. We appreciate her knowledge and experience, as well as her openness and willingness to collaborate. A team of other experts at the press also helped us get this book through production and to the reading public, including Christopher Lura, Elena McAnespie, Jessica Moll, and Ally Power.

Lastly, Mary thanks her friends Julie Leff (1959–2013), Jean Malone, Nancy Tester, and Katie Voelker, who, over the long course of this project, challenged her logic and tempered her emotions by questioning her assertions. Their critiques motivated us to write in a style that was accessible to a general audience. We want them, and others like them, to understand why some young women become teen mothers.

The Backstory to the Baby

Diane, a twenty-one-year-old white mother[1] with a two-year-old daughter, saw a chain reaction in her life starting with what she called one bad choice:

> If I hadn't slammed the door, then I wouldn't have angered my mother, and we wouldn't have gotten in a fight, and I wouldn't have slapped her, and she wouldn't have kicked me out, and I wouldn't have gone to live with my boyfriend, and I wouldn't be pregnant. [sigh] And so, if I could change anything, I would say I wish I hadn't slammed that door.

And yet, several things put Diane on the trajectory to early motherhood before she slammed the door: she was failing high school, had been sexually abused as a child, and was angry at her mother for not protecting her. When she left home, she was 18 and had little money. She met a man on a bus, took a job at the fast-food restaurant where he worked, and soon moved in with her new "boyfriend," who was eight years older. He didn't like to use condoms because they didn't feel good and she didn't take birth control pills regularly because she didn't always have a prescription. Besides, "the pill makes me fat," she complained, and she was told she shouldn't take the pill if she was smoking and she didn't want to quit smoking. She figured she hadn't gotten pregnant yet, and even if she did, well, she always wanted a baby, so, "it might be a problem that it came too early, but no baby is really a problem."

After she became pregnant, her boyfriend started to physically abuse her. One night he ripped the phone out of the wall socket and threatened her with a knife; she screamed and a neighbor called the police. They were both arrested—her boyfriend went to jail and she was sent to anger management classes. She took out a restraining order and moved out on her own with support from the state. Living alone with her child in public housing and telling her life story to a researcher sitting in front of her with a tape recorder, she said, "I don't regret having my daughter"—but she wishes she hadn't slammed that door.

In this book we explain what happened before Diane slammed that door. This book tells the life stories of 108 racially and ethnically diverse mothers who were living in Connecticut when we interviewed them in 2002 and 2003.[2] Most of them were still teenagers and new mothers, and they talked about their lives before they became pregnant—what it was like growing up, going to school, and living in their neighborhoods. Their backstories place their young births in a biographic stream that winds through social and economic circumstances.

Teen mothers are not a monolithic group and the decision to have a child is not a one-act play. While each life story is unique, when we locate it within a set of social conditions, similar patterns cohere into identifiable trajectories. For example, victims of child sexual abuse often followed a well-trod path: sexual assault as a child, precocious and risky sexual behavior as an adolescent, withdrawal from school, abuse of alcohol and drugs, and finally pregnancy and early motherhood. The "goody-two-shoes" student took a different path to motherhood than the gang-affiliated street girl; the 14-year-old mother with a 26-year-old partner had a different relationship with the baby's father than the 18-year-old who had been dating her same-age boyfriend for several years.

Understanding teen births within a biography adds complexity to statistical snapshots—especially the "color" snapshots—that often demonize teen mothers. For instance, in 2013, The National Campaign to Prevent Teen and Unplanned Pregnancy reported the following in bold letters: "52% of Latinos will become pregnant at least once by age 20—compared to 3 in 10 teen girls overall."[3] Statistics like this tell us nothing about the lives of young Latinas, and unwittingly lend support to those who see the higher rate as an urban pathology that is contributing to a growing "Hispanic underclass."[4] Black teen mothers have been similarly maligned in the past and present. In 2013, the New York City Public Health Department led a shame campaign by placing public service announcements on trains, on buses, and at transportation stops that showed photos of frowning or crying black (and biracial) children saying such things as "I'm twice as likely not to graduate high school because you had me as a teen," and, "Honestly Mom . . . chances are he won't stay with you. What happens to me?" These statistics and campaigns support a national narrative that casts black and brown teen mothers as threatening the societal moral order, bankrupting public coffers, and contributing to high rates of poverty, incarceration, crime, and school dropout.

Ironically, and sadly, when teen mothers are defined "as a problem, rather than a people with problems,"[5] policies tend to focus on changing behaviors rather than addressing needs. For instance, the problem many poor teen mothers have is that they need money and resources; however, the 1996 Welfare Reform Act defined teen mothers as a problem because they used more state resources, and subsequently, this legislation restricted the very thing they needed most—money and resources. Being defined as a problem also stigmatizes teen mothers, which has its own negative consequences. For example, teenagers who feel ashamed may hide their pregnancies well into their third trimester, reducing prenatal care and jeopardizing the health of the child.

This focus on teen mothers *as a problem* distracts us from the larger social problems that wreak havoc in the lives of these young women. It is not enough, however, to expose the problems that precede their pregnancies. Certainly you will read about these problems in their stories—often painful narratives of family neglect, partner violence, parental substance abuse, and school failure. Centering their voices in this book runs the risk of bolstering stereotypes and symbolically impugning them with their own words. Instead, we intend to show that their problems are embedded in larger social forces, and that their struggles are related to their social locations. In this regard, we adopt a critical framework that attempts to explain their early births by analyzing how power and domination are structured through hierarchies of race, class, and gender. We begin with their individual stories, but then move outward to identify status hierarchies, public policies, institutional dynamics, national discourses, and systemic deprivation. We do this to disrupt oversimplified, predictive explanations of teen motherhood, and sensitize our readers to the lived experiences of teen mothers. In other words, we want our readers to hear Diane's voice, her efforts to make sense of her life; but we also want our readers to reflect on how sexual abuse, negative school experiences, and partner violence are lived within the parameters of a white, female, working-class life, and to understand their effects on her trajectory to becoming a teen mother.[6]

The goal of this book is to move the gaze away from the pregnant belly to the life events that preceded the early birth. We do so for two reasons. First, we want to expose problems causing distress in these young women's lives that often get lost in the glare of the public spotlight on "teen moms." Second, focusing on life events brings into stark relief the social circumstances in which they occur, and we want to suggest that addressing these social circumstances is crucial to transforming their lives.

In chapter 1 we examine how teen mothers have been constructed as *the problem,* and argue that this prevents us from seeing the more pressing problems evident in the backstories of young mothers' lives—systemic inequality rooted in patriarchy, poverty, and racism. In subsequent chapters we address these problems. In chapter 2, we focus on young mothers pregnant before they were 15, the "young young mothers" or "kids having kids." These teen mothers are the least likely to be prepared for motherhood, but they also represent less than 2 percent of teen mothers in the United States. In this chapter we look at issues related to their young age—parenting practices, sexual exploration, and statutory rape—to show how focusing on the bad parent, the overfertile Latina, and the predatory man distracts us from seeing problems associated with impoverished neighborhoods, racial stereotypes, and female subordination.

In chapter 3, we see that it does not matter whether girls are black, white, or brown—child sexual abuse has serious consequences for them all: it has a negative effect on school performance; it distorts a girl's understanding of herself, her boundaries, and her sexuality; and relatedly, it makes her vulnerable to teen pregnancy and birth. The silence that often accompanies child sexual abuse enhances the trauma as it buries the injury more deeply into the recesses of the survivor's consciousness, far from the scrutinizing eyes of the public.

Chapters 3 and 4 have some of the saddest stories in the book. The lives of these girls are mired in violence, deprivation, humiliation, and oppression. Chapter 4 focuses on violence in their households, communities, and relationships. Their stories show how violence shaped life chances and choices. When national and local social hierarchies place women in dehumanizing circumstances, motherhood provides a much-desired counterbalance as a valued identity. Giving birth to another human being is powerful. In these narratives, the mothers talked about how "the baby changed my life," which included coming off the streets, breaking drug addictions, leaving violent men, going back to school, or just staring at their baby's face to ease their depression.

Chapter 5 turns attention to education and focuses on young mothers who dropped out of school *before* they were pregnant. In these life stories, we identify the chronology of events that led to school disengagement and teen birth. Both domestic violence and child sexual abuse contributed to school failure, as did the problems of underfunded, racially isolated, underperforming urban schools in Connecticut. The common misbelief that teen births cause school dropout sidetracks us from tackling the more serious problem of cumulative school failure, particularly among poor urban students of color.

Finally, chapter 6 tells a story counter to the national narrative by focusing on the "good girls"—those with lives unencumbered by violence, trauma, and academic failure. These 15- to 17-year-old girls were doing well in school, had good relations with their parents, and were not exploited by predatory males. Their pregnancies were unintended. The questions we address in this chapter are about contraception and abortion: why did they not use birth control, why did they carry the pregnancy to term, and why did they keep the child? We look at two barriers to contraception: a national discourse that defines teen sex as risk behavior rather than normal desire, and gender inequalities that complicate intimate relationships.

We conclude by restating our main point. When we take the event that has become reified into a social problem—teen birth—and place it in its biographical and social context, we learn about inadequate household income, child abuse and neglect, poor education, violent households and relationships, subordinate gender identities, and silenced conversations. This full-figured social context helps us to see the silhouettes of gender, class, and racial inequality. Our task is to use their life stories to show how structural inequality shapes a biography and to suggest that the best way to help teen mothers is to confront these larger inequalities.

LISTENING TO THEIR LIFE STORIES

The young mothers in our study were recruited from a statewide home-visitation program for first-time mothers in Connecticut. We give an overview of the home-visitation program, research methods, and study population in chapter 1 and appendix A. We worked together with

program supervisors and home visitors across 15 program sites to identify mothers for the study.[7] Home visitors encouraged mothers to participate in the study and, if they agreed, their names and contact information were passed along to us. As we tell the stories of these mothers,
keep in mind that they were recruited from disadvantaged populations.
The mothers are not representative of all blacks, or Latinas, or whites,
or representative of the working class or marginalized poor more generally. They are a sample of a more disadvantaged population—but then,
so are most teen mothers.

In their life stories, these young mothers are trying to explain how
they became mothers. They tell their stories as a sequence of concrete
experiences that include slamming doors, slapping faces, and slitting the
tires of unfaithful partners. As sociologists, we tell a different story, but
a story that comes from two lengthy interview sessions and our professional lives as sociological storytellers.

The life story is not simply a chronology of what happened—this and
then that. It is a "story" that makes sense of what happened so that
"this" is connected to "that."[8] People anchor life stories around pivotal
events that give meaning to their present lives.[9] Motherhood is a pivotal
event in a woman's life and these mothers described this to us, in part
because they were in a home-visitation program for first-time mothers.
But they also described many other pivotal events—or turning points—
that created dramatic changes in their lives so that they talked about
"before" and "after" concepts of self.[10] For example, one mother, Bonnie, who was raped, said, "*after that* I started getting wild, doing drugs,
skipping school." In her life story, she also talked about an "aha" turning point that led to her recovery from drug abuse. She said she "woke
up" after her heroin-dependent aunt died of AIDS. Other mothers
referred to dramatic life events such as a serious accident, the death of a
sibling, or the incarceration of a parent as turning points. In this book
we examine these turning points or pivotal moments that preceded the
young birth.

Interpreting their narratives, we listened to not only the content, but
also the form—that is, *how* they talked about their lives. For instance,
the hidden, obtuse, indirect ways that stories of child sexual abuse
entered into narratives were instructive. Some used clinical terms, revealing a history of therapy; others used legal and medical words they mis-
pronounced; some cried while others presented the facts in monotone;
some slipped the abuse into the story but refused to elaborate, while others made it a prominent feature. We also listened to how they talked

about the pregnancy and analyzed what it meant, for example, when the baby suddenly appeared in the story ("and then I got pregnant") without any discussion of a relationship, growing intimacy, or contraception. We heard how the fetus was an "it" when they considered terminating the pregnancy and was referred to as "my baby" when they decided not to abort.

We begin each chapter with one or two life stories. These five- to 10-page first-person accounts are distilled from more than a hundred pages of transcript, and represent the important events, relationships, and circumstances in their lives leading up to the pregnancy. In the rest of the chapter, we then tell our own sociological story that identifies patterns, trajectories, and sociohistoric contexts in order to interpret their life stories. While life stories and their analyses invoke complexity— a responsibility that we try to honor in this book—the purpose of this research is to understand better how race, social class, and, in particular, gender inequalities shaped their lives. As such, we go back and forth between their concrete, first-person life stories and our interpretive, third-person analyses to show how structural inequalities are manifest in individual biographies.

We start with the life story of Ivalesse. In her story, patriarchy gets expressed in the violence she suffered at the hands of her father, a cousin, and her partner. Poverty is reflected in her underfunded school, violent neighborhood, and the fact that even though she worked constantly in the legal labor market, she remained poor. And racial and ethnic inequality is found in the backstory of colonization that sets the stage for circular migration between Puerto Rico and the US mainland and the high rates of poverty in Puerto Rican communities in Connecticut.

CHAPTER I

The Distraction

IVALESSE: "I HAVE TO DO FOR MY OWN"

Ivalesse was born in Connecticut, raised in Puerto Rico, and returned to Connecticut when she was 13, becoming pregnant two years later. The interview was conducted in a weave of Spanish and English. Ivalesse and her two younger brothers were adopted when she was young. Her adoptive mother had a ninth-grade education and her adoptive father finished sixth grade (she refers to them as her mother and father). At the time of the interview, Ivalesse was 20 and had two children. Her story illustrates many of the themes developed in subsequent chapters: strict parenting strategies, child sexual abuse, partner violence, impoverished and neglected neighborhoods, inadequate schools, and barriers to contracepting.

I was sexually molested when I was a child by a friend of my family. I had to be less than six years old. He used to molest my brother too. Every time that guy used to come, we used to hide each other. I haven't seen him for like so long and honestly I don't want to see him. I tried to black it out. It's like I put it to one side of my brain, decided I don't want to be bothered with that section; it's like I don't want to remember anything. What I want to do is, I want to forget.

* * * * *

My mother's really caring for her children, she's really loving, you know, she's there when you need her. She never turns her back on you no matter what. She's what we call the perfect mother because she, she's, she's everything. She's the head of the family even though we have my father.

My mother would never hit you, she talks and she lets you know you did it wrong. My father is the one that likes to hit. He's the one, if he gets out of control, he'll hit you with whatever he finds—one time he actually hit me with his hand and he had a big ring. He slapped me right on the mouth and I got cut. My mother's more of a calm person, she knows that hitting you is not going to solve anything. What it's going to get you to do is catch that anger, hold it inside so you're going to hate them.

My mother has to see what's going on with a situation, but my father, his word is the last thing. I used to clean the kitchen and mop the floor every single day, and my mother let me go out to a friend's house three streets away, and so one day I said, "I'm done with the kitchen will you let me go out with my friends?" My mother was like, "yeah sure it's no problem," but when [my friends] came to pick me up, [my father] didn't let me go. So, my mother wanted to give me a little more liberty, but him, no. I think that's one of the reasons I got my boyfriend and had my children, you know, I didn't have any liberty. I didn't have any privacy, [my father] is coming to check all your drawers, whatever you have there. And I don't think that was fair you know.

* * * * *

I'm in high school now; this is my senior year. I'm going to graduate as a CNA [Certified Nursing Assistant] and [with] my high school diploma, so I'll be able to get a job and then go on to college. The high school I'm at doesn't have books. They're so behind. They actually have come out in the papers that we're the worst school in Hartford. They don't have the supplies for the school, um, the teachers are, well, you know, high school is supposed to educate for two stuff in life: it's either to confront the real world outside the school, [or] for college—and we're not getting that type of education.

I'm a pretty good student, not an honor student, but a pretty good student. I was supposed to graduate last year but I didn't have enough credits, so the only reason I go to school is to get those three credits—math, USA history, and civil rights and biography—so I'll be able to get my diploma. That's all I really care about. My certification for CNA I'm done with.

I took general courses until my sophomore year. In my sophomore year, this teacher was doing a presentation about the Allied Health Group and one English teacher tells me, "You should get into the Allied Health. That'd be good for you, you have a kid and when you finish school you would be able to have a job and then if you want to go on, you would go to whatever college is here." It was not a bad idea. And actually, because that teacher, I have my CNA certification when I graduate.

I never dropped out. When I got pregnant [at age 15], I was in eighth grade for my daughter; then for my son I was in high school already, so I didn't drop out because they [my parents] were like, "If you drop out of school you aren't going to be anybody. You're going to be working in a factory and we don't want you to do that. We want you to go to college or if you don't go to college, just please finish school, things are going to be so much easier for you." So that's what I'm doing, I was like, hey it's true if I don't want to work in a factory when I just make what, $7.00 an hour at minimum wage. No. I prefer to have a job that pays well and, like, CNA is a job that so many people depend on you and it's in the health care. It's a pretty good job. Then you go to college and you get to be an RN. So those are the plans that I have right now. Just keep going. I have to do for my own, nobody else is going to do it for me.

* * * * *

Luis is my husband. [He is the father of both her children; they are not legally married.] He is in jail. This is his second time. He was in for 10 months; he violated the probation so he's back in again. He always calls or he writes. I go to see him like twice a week, depends what days I have off. He's in the Young Man's Institute and thank God it's not that far, but what I do is one day I bring his son and the other day I'll bring his daughter. So he gets to see them. His daughter actually gets to talk to him.

I met him at West Side Middle School. We were in seventh grade. He's older than me by a few months. In science class I noticed he was looking back and so one day he decided to ask me out. I started laughing. I was like No. And after that we started just being friends. We used to talk, we used to make fun of stuff. I think it was for his birthday, at school, I kissed him and after that I was trying to help him out with schoolwork and everything so he started coming to my house. I started showing him to my parents, you know, he was my friend and everything and then he asked me out and since then our relationship started. We used to do everything. We used to play like little children outside. We used to talk for hours. We used to get together in a group, all our friends and stuff like that. So it's been six years now.

* * * * *

I went to the doctor because I always had a regular period and he comes and tells me, "Well, you're pregnant." I started laughing in his face and I was like, "I'm sorry I'm not having any children right now, I'm too young." Luis was scared, he didn't know what to do, he didn't tell his mother. He didn't want anything to do with me, so um, after a while we started realizing, hey, this is no joke. It's like ok you have to be more mature and even if you're 15, you have to grow up years older and that's what I did. I was like okay this is no joke and I have to do it myself, and that's what I do. That's why I go to school.

My mother was crying, she was like, "How you could do this to me?" My father wanted to kill him [laughing]. After a while it changed. Hey there's nothing we can do. What's done is done. I think parents have their own faults because if you don't have communication with your children, I mean, how are you going to tell them what sex is all about. If you don't do that, they are going to find out on their own. I think that's what happened with us. I discovered everything on my own; I think that's one of the problems.

* * * * *

Hartford's not good. I just want a place where I can prosper and my children can move forward. Hartford doesn't have any jobs, they don't have programs for children. I don't have any neighbors. I live in a building that is next to the highway and I only had the factory next to me [laughs] and the people came to fight over here. The projects are there, and the police are always there. They burned a car or they stole a car or they take all the parts of the car. One time a girl fell asleep, the little boy knocked over the lamp, there were clothes on the floor and they caught on fire. One time it was a couple selling drugs here; they took them. Another man who lived by himself had problems with alcohol, he started a fire. And then another couple had a fight in the parking lot of the factory and they were talking, rubbing in each other's faults in each other's faces and I cannot sleep. Of all the places, they come here and I have to wake up at seven o'clock in the morning because I'm opening [at Walgreen's]. The police came and took them, they come here all the time. That's why I don't want to be here.

* * * * *

This month I started to cashier at Walgreens. It's only part-time because I go to school. I started working when I was 16, in a factory. That was a summer job only. I was a machine operator and maintenance [laughs] so I have tried everything. A job is a job, it doesn't matter how low it is or how honorable, it's a job. You can always earn a little money.

In Walgreens I get eight dollars an hour. I like it but you are always angry because you have to work with a lot of customers. The people yell at you, they fight, they think that everything is your fault. You try to be nice, try to have smile on your face, but sometimes you cannot. It's really different in a hospital, because in a hospital you give a smile to a patient that's sick, that person appreciates you way more than a person that you give a smile in the store, they don't care. So it's a real difference. I get more satisfaction in the hospital.

I think as long as you have a job, the more beneficial it is for you because then you're responsible, you're able to work. I don't ask nobody for money, I am the one who gives the money. I don't ask nobody for money I just try to make it on my own.

* * * * *

When I was 18 I got pregnant again so I had an abortion because I couldn't have another kid. When I got pregnant with my son [at age 20] that was the difficult part, you know, for [my parents] to still help me out. They haven't turned their back on me. So that's pretty good. I think I'm really fortunate to have my parents, you know, help me out.

If I could be young again I would try to take life slower, not to live it all at once, because I think that's what I tried to do. The boyfriend— that's normal—but having children—I should've wait, I should've.

HISTORICAL NARRATIVES, DEMOGRAPHIC
REALITIES, AND LOCAL CONTEXTS

On June 2, 2008, Nick Carbone, a 71-year-old former deputy mayor of Hartford, Connecticut, was brutally beaten by young street ruffians on his way to breakfast. Three weeks later, a photo of Carbone appeared on the front page of the *Hartford Courant*, his face still swollen and scarred, with an article identifying the factors that he believed "fueled urban violence: predatory lenders; teenage pregnancy; incarceration; the release of inmates into the city; failing schools and judicial systems." There were teen mothers—sandwiched between predators and criminals—listed as one of the "root causes of urban poverty."[1] A few months later, Bill Cosby made an appearance at the Legislative Office Building in Hartford and placed a number of social problems—burgeoning black incarceration

FIGURE I. Birth Rates for Teens Age 15 to 19, 1940–2010. Sources: Ventura, Mathews, and Hamilton 2001, table 1; Martin et al. 2012, table 4.

rates and an overburdened foster care system—on the shoulders of black teen mothers and absent fathers.

Why teen mothers? Where does this idea come from? Not, it would appear, from the numbers. Only a small percentage of teenagers are actually having babies. In 2008, 4 percent of teens 15 to 19 gave birth.[2] Nor has this rate been increasing. Beginning in 1991, the rate declined continuously until 2005, when the teen birth rate was less than half of what it was when it peaked in 1957 (see figure 1). And although the rate increased slightly in 2006 and 2007, it continued to decline in 2008 and by 2010 it was at its lowest in recorded history.

The decline in the teen birth rate is a result of fewer pregnancies, and not more abortions. Both pregnancy and abortion rates have been declining in tandem with birth rates (see figure 2). Abortion rates have declined steadily since the late 1980s, and the percent of pregnancies that were aborted declined from roughly one-third in 1990 to one-quarter in 2008.[3] In that year, only 7 percent of teens 15 to 19 had a pregnancy and the pregnancy rate was at its lowest since 1976.[4] So, where *is* the problem? Fewer teens are getting pregnant, fewer teens are having abortions, and fewer teens are having babies.

One reason for the concern is that, despite the decline, the US teen birth rate remains considerably higher than most advanced industrialized countries: three times the Canadian rate, seven times the Swiss and Danish rates, 11 times the Dutch rate, and even two times higher than predominantly Catholic countries like Ireland and Poland where abortion is illegal except under extenuating circumstances.[5] But then, the United States does not compare well with these countries on a number of measures—poverty, inequality, incarceration, medically uninsured, or infant mortality—and

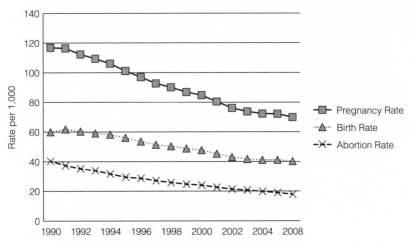

FIGURE 2. Birth, Pregnancy, and Abortion Rates for Teens Age 15 to 19, 1990–2008.
Source: Ventura et al. 2012, table 2.

these issues do not evoke the same moral outrage as teen motherhood. In short, teen birth rates are lowest in areas where there is less inequality and higher welfare benefits; and compared to other advanced industrialized nations, the United States has higher rates of inequality and lower levels of welfare support.[6] And, not surprisingly, higher rates of teen births.

Perhaps what underlies much of the preoccupation with teen motherhood is that most of the births are out of wedlock and represent what Senator Rick Santorum (R-PA) defined as "the calamity of illegitimacy in our generation."[7] At the peak of teen motherhood in the 1950s, about 80 percent of teen mothers were married; by 2007, over 85 percent were unmarried.[8] This upward trend in unmarried teen births started in the black community (bolstering narratives of black urban pathology); however, as sociologist Frank Furstenberg pointed out, "black women were only at the vanguard of a new pattern of family formation" since both white women and nonteens, especially women in their 20s, are now increasingly having children outside of marriage.[9] By 2007, 40 percent of all children in the United States were born to unmarried women and less than a quarter of these births were to teenagers (see figure 3).[10] On this issue, European comparisons do not set off alarms. In the same year, at least one-half of births in Sweden, Norway, France, and Iceland were to unmarried women.[11]

Despite this growing trend, unwed mothers are not equally distributed across class lines; they are more likely to have lower incomes and

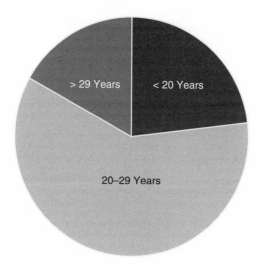

FIGURE 3. Percent of Children Born to Unmarried Women by Age of Mother, 2007. Source: Ventura 2009, figure 5.

less education.[12] Marriage is still considered the norm for college-educated, middle-income adults, and this contributes to the continuing negative attitude toward unwed mothers. In a 2008 national survey, two-thirds of the respondents believed that the trend in "more single women having children" was a "bad thing" for society.[13]

Perhaps another reason teen mothers attract attention is because they have been commodified in television programs such as *16 and Pregnant* and its sequel, *Teen Mom*. The emotional traumas that often accompany unintended pregnancies create drama that sells products. The commodification of "celebrity" crisis was blaring on one magazine's headline: "TEEN MOMS IN CRISIS" (all in caps with fire-engine yellow block letters). Underneath was written, "Accusations of neglect for Amber: 'The baby nearly fell out the window!'"[14] Stakeholders and the general public have suggested that there is a "craze" among high school youth because Hollywood has "glamorized teen pregnancy."[15] We find no evidence, however, of a "craze" in the declining teen birth rate. And while these programs may create celebrity for a few teen mothers, they do not glamorize their lives. These shows are morality tales, not fairy tales. In most episodes, the fathers of the babies leave or talk trash about the mothers; the pregnant teens get fat and argue with their parents; and once they have the baby, the programs are a reminder that a baby is a pooping and crying full-time responsibility.[16] In fact, studies have shown that teens and parents believe these shows depict a negative image of early, unplanned pregnancies, and one study even suggested that the show has contributed to the downward trend in teen births.[17]

Despite falling teen birth rates, we continue to expend state resources to prevent teen pregnancies, even during periods of fiscal crises.[18] A 2010 national survey found that nine in 10 adults and teens believed that teen pregnancy is an important problem.[19] And in the 2013 State of the Union address, President Obama followed in the footsteps of his Republican and Democratic predecessors by drawing attention to our need to "reduce teenage pregnancy." Should we anticipate that the concern will subside with time or will we continue to a have Teen Pregnancy Prevention Month every May? We have our doubts that the issue is going away because public preoccupation—or what Furstenberg calls "public obsession"—with teen motherhood is not about the empirical reality, but about political and cultural constructions of teen motherhood.[20] It is not the numbers but rather the interpretive frames through which the numbers are understood that matter—in others words, the preoccupation is not about teen mothers, but about what they have come to signify.

HISTORICAL NARRATIVES OF BLAME AND SHAME

Teen mothers have made their way into the public lexicon because they are perceived to be part of what Adolph Reed sardonically calls the "transmission belt that drives the cycle of poverty."[21] While the term "teen mother" is a descriptive term referring to the age of the mother, it has also become a marker of immorality, what Brett Williams describes as the "touchstone of pathology among the poor."[22] Where did this moral discourse originate and why does it continue? We identify three overlapping historical narratives of stigmatizing discourse.

The first is the *underclass* narrative that originated in response to a growing black urban population and ghetto uprisings of the 1960s. White, middle-class, native-born Americans have long feared the higher reproductive rates of undesirable populations; at the turn of the twentieth century, the undesirables included white immigrants as well blacks.[23] This changed in the second half of the twentieth century when poverty became more publicly associated with black urban ghettos that produced an even more negative, unsympathetic, and undeserving public disposition toward the poor, which became symbolized by the term "the underclass."[24] Gunnar Myrdal first used the term "under-class" in 1963, although it lacked a racial connotation and was instead rooted in structural unemployment and economic marginalization.[25] Herbert Gans traced the evolution of the term from the loss of its hyphen in 1964 to its initial transformation into a more behavioral and racial reference in a 1973 *Public Interest* article, to the cover of *Time* magazine in 1974 and then again in 1977, where its reiteration reached full transformation into a reference for unseemly black poverty.[26] The cover of the 1977 *Time* article described the underclass as a "Minority within a Minority," and estimated that somewhere between seven and 10 million black Americans fit a loose criteria that included juvenile delinquents, school dropouts, drug addicts, welfare dependents, looters, arsonists, violent criminals, *unmarried mothers,* pimps, pushers, and panhandlers.[27] It was not unlike Nick Carbone's commentary three decades later, where unmarried mothers were sandwiched between criminals and pimps.

It was Ken Auletta who solidified public use of the term in his now famous series of stories, first appearing in the *New Yorker* in 1981, where he provided a reformulated culture-of-poverty description of the black urban poor that emphasized behavioral pathologies. Auletta described the underclass as antisocial, deviant, welfare-dependent, and violent, with "bad habits" and a "welfare mentality."[28] Social scientists gave legitimacy to this public discourse, often unintentionally, with a language of "ghetto-specific culture," "black underclass," "dysfunctional" or "disorganized culture," and "tangle of pathology."[29] Illustrating the full reach the concept had acquired by the early 1990s and its implications for unmarried adolescent mothers, Harvard scholar Christopher Jencks subdivided the moral underclass into the jobless, the criminal, and the *reproductive* underclass.[30] Research foundations provided further legitimacy by funding grants on the topic.[31] By the 1990s, the term was in the public consciousness and teen births were woven into the presumed tapestry of pathology. As historian Linda Gordon writes, "teenage pregnancy often becomes a rhetorical surrogate for a more general 1980s discourse about single mothers, welfare, and the 'underclass.'"[32]

The second narrative is the *politics of blame and gain.* In the shifting post-Keynesian state of economic insecurity in the 1970s and 1980s, a conservative backlash mounted toward the achievements of the Civil Rights Movement and the aspirations of the Great Society. Blame was directed at black welfare mothers, irresponsible black fathers, and black street criminals, as well as at white liberals, who had presumably given license to immoral behavior and urban pathology through generous and unaccountable welfare legislation.[33]

In the 1960s, at the same time that the rate of unwed births began to increase in black communities, welfare rolls exploded as the War on Poverty along with the Civil Rights and Welfare Rights movements resulted in large numbers of black mothers, who had been denied public assistance in the past, gaining access to the rolls.[34] Daniel Patrick Moynihan was among the first to sound the alarm in his now famous 1965 report, where he asserted that "the breakdown of the Negro family led to a startling increase in welfare dependency."[35] Moynihan attributed the crisis in the black family to the structural unemployment of black men, but his thesis about the threats posed to the traditional family by black matriarchy had larger and longer-lasting implications. Moynihan suggested that strong, independent black women had destabilized the black family by emasculating black men and raising a generation of poorly socialized black male youth.[36] Essentially, Moynihan flipped a public switch in which racial oppression and structural unemployment were supplanted by the controlling image of the black matriarch and, subsequently, the welfare mother.[37]

Federal policies directed at lowering poverty rates subsequently became intertwined with family planning policies. In 1964 federal funds became available for birth control for low-income women and, in 1970, Title X of the Public Health Services Act included family planning services. Birth control was understood as a way of decreasing family size, especially among low-income populations. Increasingly adolescent girls were accessing these services and, in 1978, Title X was amended to articulate clearly that family planning services were to be available to all adolescents.[38] This was considered pragmatic legislation intended to stem the tide of teen pregnancy, unwed births, and increased welfare funding. Linda Gordon has suggested, however, that the "propaganda campaign" in the 1960s that raised concern about overpopulation in the United States and pushed for public assistance for birth control "incorporated much eugenic thinking, that is, emphasizing the high fertility rates of selected and allegedly less desirable groups." She provides examples of birth control campaigns that linked birth rates to urban crime and argues "urban crime was a *sotto voce* call upon racism."[39]

While the 1970s laid the conceptual groundwork for the black underclass, moralism replaced pragmatism in the 1980s and the dysfunctional black family became the lightning rod. As the economic crisis deepened at the end of the 1970s, conservatives went on the offensive, blaming liberals for a bloated welfare state that subverted traditional American values like hard work, self-sufficiency, and marriage—or, in other words, for creating the problems in black ghettoes and in single-parent families more generally.[40] Neither liberals nor conservatives contested the link between teenage pregnancy and poverty, but conservatives sought to control sexual behavior while liberals wanted to provide access to contraception. In this way, liberals were painted as the "permissive" politicians who encouraged immoral behavior (teenage sex outside of marriage) by providing access to federally funded contraception.[41]

Here was a political football that "the Gipper," Ronald Reagan, could run with to turn moral blame into political gain. Furthermore, the politics of blame narrative extended beyond the poor or black underclass to include War on Poverty elites, liberal reformers, and social engineers, who had failed to communicate to poor teen mothers that they should take a vow of chastity and invest in their futures through work and marriage. In 1981, soon after Reagan took office, the Adolescent Family Life Act (AFLA) was passed, which banned the use of federal funds for abortion counseling and promoted sexual abstinence initiatives for teens—the so-called chastity bill. In this discourse, promiscuity, irresponsibility, and poor discipline were placed at the center of the "teen mom problem."[42]

The blame to gain strategy has deeper historical roots. The politics of gain was an explicit electoral strategy developed by Republicans to lure white southern Democrats and white working-class northerners out of the Democratic Party. Goldwater planted the seed in his 1964 campaign, followed by Nixon's "southern strategy" and law and order campaign, which then culminated in Ronald Reagan's first presidential campaign, in which his subtle mastery of racially coded language won him the support of the so-called Reagan Democrats (the 22 percent that defected from the party to elect him). With paternalistic charm, Reagan argued that the Democrats had abandoned traditional values, such as the work ethic, a restrained sexual morality, religious conviction, and the nuclear family, and had instead become the party of big government that represented the special interest groups, by which he meant blacks, homosexuals, welfare recipients, criminal offenders, *unwed mothers,* and illegal immigrants.[43] Reagan's 1984 campaign slogan was a direct appeal to the white working class: "You haven't left the Democratic Party," he insisted, "the Democratic Party left you."[44]

Reagan's rhetorical mastery is even more astonishing when we consider that the teen birth rate had been in decline since 1960 and did not begin to increase until near the end of Reagan's second term. And yet, as Wanda Pillow points out, in the 1980s teen motherhood became synonymous with the black welfare mother and was constructed as an epidemic associated with poverty, immorality, and promiscuity.[45] General economic insecurity coupled with racial fear and changing family norms seduced a growing segment of the white population into believing these rhetorical messages.[46]

When birthrates to white mothers began to decline faster than birthrates to black and brown mothers, *Time* magazine, once again, marked the development. Just as it had run cover stories on the black underclass two decades earlier, in 1990 *Time* contributed to the moral panic with a front cover that displayed an American flag with the white stripes replaced with yellow, brown, and black stripes, and a caption below warning about "America's Changing Colors" with a question above: "What will the U.S. be like when whites are no longer the majority?" The blame for a changing America was directed at black and brown teen mothers, liberal welfare legislation, Civil Rights' elites, and the Democratic Party.

These allegations had their effects on the Democratic Party. In the 1980s, several of the more liberal candidates failed to get the party's presidential nomination—most notably, Ted Kennedy and Jesse Jackson—while the Party's moderately liberal nominees in the 1980s, Walter Mondale and Michael Dukakis, failed at the voting polls. By 1992, stung by the politics of blame and gain, Bill Clinton and the Democratic Party were fully on board with the prevailing conservative rhetoric, invoking the language of personal responsibility, three strikes and you're out, and the "epidemic of teen moms," which Clinton defined as a our "most serious social problem" in his 1995 State of the Union address.[47] Clinton did nothing to reduce abstinence spending, and between 1996 and 2006 over 1.5 billion dollars was spent on these programs.[48] In addition to AFLA monies, funding for abstinence programs was appropriated in welfare reform legislation in 1996, which also created stricter policies requiring that "programs may not in any way advocate contraceptive use or discuss contraceptive methods except to emphasize their failure rates."[49] While most conservatives and liberals support the teaching of abstinence, only a subset of extreme conservatives favors abstinence-only programs.[50] And yet, monies were appropriated for these programs as the blame for rising poverty rates shifted to the bellies of young mothers.

The third—and again overlapping—discourse is the *neoliberal* narrative embedded in the reorganization of the state and capitalism beginning in the 1970s. A series of economic recessions in the 1970s spelled trouble for economic elites, who had watched profit rates decline since the 1960s. The recession from 1973 to 1975 was indicative of deeper economic problems that more conventional Keynesian remedies were unable to resolve. Keynesian social democratic strategies emphasized the importance of the government in regulating markets, in establishing the parameters for capital and labor bargaining, in pumping money into a lagging economy through public investments, and in socializing the costs of preparing and sustaining labor needs.[51]

The neoliberal turn reenacted economic principles that existed prior to the New Deal and that had provided the basis for criticism of the New Deal through much of the post–World War II period. Neoliberalism was a return to principles integral to a dominant political and cultural narrative of America that championed self-regulating markets, individual freedom and self-sufficiency, entrepreneurship, and limited government.[52] Neoliberal policies resulted in the state deregulation of the economy, a downward restructuring of taxes, a retrenchment of welfare entitlements, a military buildup, and the privatization of the public sector. This political realignment and economic transformation dramatically increased social inequality as the redistributive function of the state was sacrificed to corporate profitability.[53] Moreover, it reinvigorated earlier twentieth-century preoccupation with the undeserving poor and resulted in a reorganization of the US welfare system that enhanced its authoritarian role.

Cutting public entitlements became a central part of the Reagan economic strategy—or perhaps more accurately, shifting these costs to the military and later to the drug war and prison expansion had the effect of increasing the repressive arm of the state apparatus for both foreign and domestic purposes. Within this context, teen mothers became not only too expensive, but a segment of the undeserving poor that the Great Society had unwittingly supported. In short, if young black and brown mothers continued to reproduce at rates higher than white mothers, and if they remained unmarried and welfare dependent, then the future of America was being compromised—its moral fabric along with its international competitiveness. The world had changed and the United States could no longer assume its economic dominance; instead, the role of the US government would be focused almost exclusively on capital accumulation at home and abroad. The public costs of assistance to the poor would be reduced by changing eligibility standards and reducing benefits, privatizing services, requiring that the poor meet behavioral expectations to receive benefits, and eventually supplanting entitlements with temporary support. These policies affected unmarried teen mothers.

The first mention of teenage pregnancy in a US legislative hearing did not occur until 1975, at the beginning of the transition to the neoliberal era and, ironically, amid a 15-year decline in teen birth rates.[54] Rapidly rising welfare rolls and projected welfare costs increased the scrutiny of young unwed mothers.[55] The Federal Office of Child Support Enforcement was established through legislation this same year to more aggressively identify fathers and pursue child support to reduce welfare eligibility and costs. The chastity bill mentioned earlier was passed in 1981, and was followed by 1984 legislation that attempted to reduce the welfare rolls by including the income of anyone residing in the household when calculating benefits. Further, this legislation required that states pass through $50 of child support to mothers, a portion of the money that the states had collected from fathers if their children received welfare benefits. The pass-through money to the mothers was provided as an incentive for them to cooperate more fully in identifying nonresidential fathers so that states could recover a greater share of welfare expenditures. The Family Support Act (FSA) passed in 1988 included specific language that targeted unwed teen mothers, *allowing* states to require formal residency with a parent, school attendance, and, for older teen mothers, work or job-training activities.[56] The culmination of these efforts, however, occurred under Democratic President Bill Clinton, when he signed the Personal Responsibility and Work Opportunity Reconciliation Act (PRWORA) in 1996.

The historical irony mentioned earlier was again apparent; the legislation was passed even though teen birth rates had been on the decline since 1991. Still, unwed teen mothers were at the center of this legislation, as were noncustodial fathers, and they were painted as a resource drain.[57] State incentives included in the FSA now became federal requirements: teen mothers younger than 18 *had* to live with a parent or in an adult-supervised home and were required to attend school or a training program in order to qualify for cash assistance. Like everyone else, the mother, once she turned 18, was subject to the five-year lifetime limitation on cash assistance established under PRWORA that ended cash welfare as an entitlement. This provision also allowed states to adopt shorter time limits, and Connecticut championed the cause, establishing the strictest time limit in the nation at 21 months. PRWORA also gave the states the option to eliminate the $50 child pass-through to the mother, a measure that 31 states adopted.[58] Finally, the preoccupation with unwed teen motherhood in PRWORA also included an aggressive campaign to prosecute men for statutory rape (an issue we take up in the next chapter).

All three of these narratives—the underclass, the politics of blame and gain, and the neoliberal narratives—stigmatized as they informed the public's understanding of teen births. They were distinct in their particular aims and objectives, their strategies, and the rationales that they employed, but it was the intersection of the three that provided a powerful historical discourse that deeply embedded teen mothers in public scorn and dehumanizing jeopardy. The reorganization of capitalism and the state, combined with the political strategies of both parties and the narratives of moral culpability directed at the urban underclass and "misguided" War on Poverty liberals, has placed vulnerable citizens—young low-income mothers and their children—in social and economic peril.

As Ann Phoenix wrote in her article on the social construction of teenage motherhood in *The Politics of Pregnancy*: "Once an issue (like teenage motherhood) has been defined as problematic, that definition gains its own momentum. Thus, negative findings concerning a minority of individuals are overgeneralized to include the whole group, and individuals within the group are considered only in relation to the problem status. The cause of the problem is couched in individualistic terms which result in victims blamed for causing the perceived problem."[59] In this political-economic-social context, the declining rates of teen motherhood become irrelevant. Even though teen births, pregnancies, and abortions have been decreasing for more than 20 years, the hierarchies of race, gender, and class drive the narratives.

BLACK, BROWN, AND WHITE: NUMBERS AND INTENTIONS

Leon Dash's book *When Children Want Children* documents the lives of six teen mothers in one of the poorest areas in Washington, DC.[60] While he provides a compelling picture of poor blacks living in an urban ghetto, it is only one snapshot of adolescent motherhood. Unfortunately, his account and others that focus only on black inner-city teen mothers reinforce the perception that the face of teen mothers is black. It is easier to define teen pregnancy and births as "epidemics" and "crises" in a tone that carries a moral note when they are perceived to be black and brown problems.[61]

The numbers tell a different and more complex story about teen motherhood, race, and ethnicity. First, given the argument that the US teen birth rate is a "problem" because it exceeds rates in other industrialized countries, it is important to note that the *white* teen birth rate in

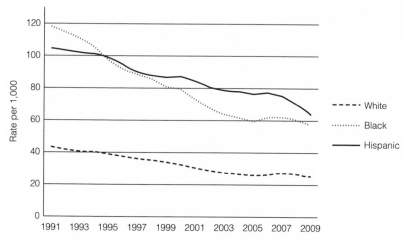

FIGURE 4. Birth Rates for Teens Age 15 to 19 by Race and Hispanic Origin, 1991–2009. Source: Martin et al. 2012, table 8.

the United States alone exceeds the rates in other countries.[62] Second, while blacks are more than twice as likely as whites to become teen mothers, in 2008, just under one-quarter of the mothers who gave birth before age 20 were black, one-third were Hispanic, and almost 40 percent were white.[63] Moreover, while birth rates have declined significantly for all teens, black teens had the steepest decline at 52 percent (see figure 4). In 1995, the Hispanic teen birth rate surpassed the black rate and has since remained the highest.[64] Connecticut mirrored these national trends, and in 2005 the Hispanic birth rate for teens age 15 to 19 also exceeded the black rate.[65]

In our national preoccupation with racial and ethnic differences, however, what is often lost is the relationship between poverty and teen births. For example, for Puerto Ricans, the fertility rate is similar to the general US population, but their teen birth rate is 25 percent higher.[66] Puerto Ricans are also one of the poorest groups in the United States, which suggests that for Puerto Ricans, poverty may play a significant role in early childbearing.[67]

Girls who grow up in impoverished neighborhoods, attend inadequate schools, and live in households with scarce resources are more likely to become teen mothers, regardless of whether they are black, white, or Hispanic.[68] Urban areas have higher rates of teen births because of concentrated neighborhood poverty; blacks and Puerto Ricans have higher rates of teen births because they have higher rates of poverty and they are more likely to live in areas of concentrated neighborhood poverty. But poverty also exists among whites living in small towns and isolated rural areas. And since four in 10 teen births are to white mothers, we need to understand adolescent motherhood as more than a black or brown inner-city problem, especially when black and brown faces become camouflage for larger problems and thereby make it easier to engage in narratives of blame.

Narratives of blame that single out black and brown communities tend to blame the culture in these communities for teen births, drawing on deeply embedded culture-of-poverty or underclass theses. In these instances, early pregnancies are construed as intended and part of the so-called cycle of poverty. In the opening pages of Dash's book, a young African American teenager tells the readers: "Girls out here get pregnant because they *want* to have babies. . . . *None* of this childbearing is an accident."[69] Dash reports that he "did not find a single incident in which procreation had been accidental on the part of *both* sexual partners."[70] He also talked to only six couples, but his well-written and widely read book provides support for the assumption that young mothers intend their pregnancies. When viewed this way, it is assumed that early childbearing is a cultural phenomenon. Dash, however, traces this culture back to slavery and postbellum black family structures in the rural South.

Taken out of historical or structural contexts, the "unwed teen mom" invokes racial stereotypes of young girls intentionally violating social norms, leaving them open to criticism and blame. References to single mothers or "welfare moms" are often signifiers for black and brown mothers and a culture of poverty that supports childbearing outside of marriage. While black women of all ages are more likely than white women to give birth outside of marriage, when controlling for poverty, these rates are not so dissimilar.[71] The bottom line is that in the United States, the unwed teen mother is white as well as black and brown.

White teen mothers have not been entirely impervious to media scrutiny. As we pointed out, shows like *16 and Pregnant* and *Teen Mom* have brought young white mothers into the conversation. And in 2008, rumors circulated about a group of girls—all white—at Gloucester High School in Massachusetts who made a pact to get pregnant. The framing of the issue, however, never reached the level of cultural attribution, as is more common when black and brown neighborhoods are involved. Instead, public concern hinged on the fear that the glamour and appeal of early motherhood had misled these impressionable teens—the so-called Gloucester 18.[72]

Culture is difficult to characterize because it is inseparable from structural conditions and because it is rarely monolithic; it instead comprises contradictory tendencies, logics, and dispositions, which are manifest in identities that are fluid and situational. Academic studies estimate that one-quarter to one-third of teenage pregnancies are intended.[73] And while studies report that some teens are pleased to be pregnant, this is different than having intended the pregnancy.[74] In general, most teens do not want to be pregnant, nor do their parents or "culture" encourage them to get pregnant.[75] In our study, only two of the 108 young mothers said that their mothers encouraged their pregnancies, and only 23 said that their pregnancies were intended or wanted. Most of the young mothers said they did not want or intend to get pregnant, and as you will soon hear in their stories, they were upset (as were their parents) when they first found out they were pregnant.

This issue becomes muddled, however, with young women in our study like Rachel, who was "shocked" when she learned she was pregnant even though she had been in a sexual relationship with her boyfriend for over a year and they had not been using contraception. Many others took the same "unintended" route—that is, they did not want to get pregnant and yet they did not take any precaution to prevent a pregnancy. Were they intended or accidental births or what Kathryn Edin and Maria Kefalas have described as "somewhere in between"?[76] Or what Katherine Trent and Kyle Crowder refer to as "more an unintended result of risky behavior than a result of rational choice"?[77]

Several scholars take issue with the notion of accidental motherhood. Kristin Luker points out that when middle-class professional women decide to postpone childbearing until they are older, this is seen as a career strategy, but "the actions of poorer and younger women are often thought of as accidents, rather than as efforts to cope with the same pressures using different resources."[78] Luker refers to Arline Geronimus, who argues that it is often a rational strategy for poor women in impoverished neighborhoods to have their children when they are younger and healthy, and when the child's grandmothers are also younger and healthy enough to support them.[79] To define the pregnancy as an accident confounds women's right to choose motherhood, and certainly deciding to carry the pregnancy to term and to keep the child rather than surrender it to adoption is no accident. This is part of what we try to explain in this book: For those who did intend the pregnancy, why did they? For the others, why not choose abortion or adoption as strategies to resolve an unintended pregnancy?

CLASS, GENDER, AND MARRIAGE

As the frames for viewing and stigmatizing teen motherhood suggest, the politics surrounding early births gather energy as a defense of the institution of marriage. Adolph Reed made this observation years ago when he asserted that "the concern is not even so much with teenage childbearing in general as when it occurs out of wedlock; to that extent the teen pregnancy issue is a subset of the out-of-wedlock birth issue."[80] Few elected officials would publicly disagree with the statement prefacing the PRWORA legislation: "Marriage is the foundation of a successful society."[81] Of course, with the out-of-wedlock birth rate around 40 percent and the divorce rate around 50 percent, the "foundation" would appear to be crumbling, which has created alarm among conservatives like Patrick Fagan at the Heritage Foundation, who argues that the "effects of the abandonment of marriage" for the child are "retarded cognitive development" as well as problems with "impulse control" and "warped social development." Further, he asserts, the "path to decent income is well known and traditional: complete school first, then get a job, then get married, then have children—in that order"; having a baby out of wedlock "derails" progress.[82] In 2008, the conservative wing of the Democratic Party, the Democratic Leadership Council, agreed with Fagan's comments when they asserted that the "root cause" of poverty and dependency is "unwed childbearing."[83]

Unwed teen mothers raise the hackles of elected officials and the public, who associate the early births with increased costs to taxpayers.[84] In 2001, California Congressman Wally Herger articulated this position: "Teen pregnancy cuts short the teen parents' opportunities to build a promising future, and puts their child at a fundamental disadvantage in so many ways. It means years of dependence for many struggling young families, which is a cycle that has repeated itself too often in recent generations. It is easy to see why preventing and reducing the incidence of teen pregnancy is absolutely critical to progress on welfare reform."[85] For conservatives like Herger, poverty and poverty-related problems are largely attributable to the decay of traditional family values, and a good dose of hard work, self-sacrifice, and religious faith would go a long way toward restoring the American family and solving problems like unwed adolescent childbearing.

Liberals, on the other hand, are more likely to focus on the opportunity structure and institutions that provide social mobility for low-income groups. If schools are effective, neighborhoods safe, housing decent, and medical care available, then low-income groups can work to improve their individual and family circumstances and begin to climb the proverbial income ladder. In this formulation, however, liberals tend to agree with conservatives that early childbirth is an obstacle to individual and family success, that it proscribes opportunities, inhibits social mobility, reproduces poverty, and betrays the standard pathway to success that Fagan describes: school first, then a job, then marriage, then children.

Implicit in both conservative and liberal scripts is that people should not have children until they have enough money to raise children without having to rely on state assistance (you can rely on parents or inherited wealth, but not the state).[86] This script assumes that, in the United States, everyone can acquire the resources they need to raise children if only they postpone childbearing, pursue education, and work toward individual achievement. In the past 30 years, however, the so-called opportunity structure has been torn asunder by dramatic increases in economic inequality, the redistribution of income and wealth upward, the retrenchment in public expenditures and social welfare, and the restructuring of the tax burden away from the wealthy and corporations.[87] Recent mobility studies indicate that movement across income groups, particularly at the higher and lower ends, has become more stagnant in the United States.[88]

Those embracing the "up and out" model of poverty ignore the "stickiness" of being located at the bottom of the income ladder. Focusing on opportunities can result in altering systemic barriers, and can lead, for instance, to making investments in human capital, but it can also focus the blame on individual behavior. The preoccupation with sexual behavior is a good example of the latter. In these instances, poor teens become morally culpable for their own poverty and the scorn of the public who see the "cycle of poverty" hinging on the behavioral choices of the poor. If they would only abstain, intones the right; if they would only contracept, preaches the left.

The assumptions about when to have children, encoded in a middle-class culture of aspiration and meritocracy, are problematic, to say the least, since large numbers of people at the bottom of the class structure cannot and will not ever achieve economic stability. If poor women have little chance of going to college, getting married, and securing a well-paying job, then the proscription to wait is a de facto statement to stop reproducing.[89] Of course, the idea that poor women should not procreate is not publicly stated this bluntly since it would violate civil freedoms.

And yet, this position is implicit in many arguments against teen motherhood, in taxpayers' fury about the poor, and in public sentiments that steal in under the cloak of "common sense": don't have children until you can afford them; two-parent families—father and mother—are better than one.[90] These statements ignore the economic and social context within which young women have babies, place the blame on the behavior of young men and women, and morally remind them that there is a right time and place to have babies—"right" according to middle-class lifestyles.

This classed and gendered message is racially encoded in our public policies. The push for welfare reform in the 1990s was reflexively a push against the "pathologies" of the urban "underclass," which, as we have seen, included teen motherhood and, we might add, father absence. The symbol of social decay and cultural licentiousness was not Bristol Palin, the daughter of the 2008 US vice presidential nominee, but the 16-year-old, unmarried, black or Latina mother. Scholars and policymakers, both liberal and conservative, want to know: "why are they having babies?" Yet no one asks middle-class women why they have babies. Middle-class women, married women, women of all races have babies because they want children—to give their lives focus, to provide an existential reason for being, to have someone to love and someone to love them, and, mostly, because they are women and that is what they are socialized to do and what their families and friends expect them to do, and what their bodies conspire with them to do.[91] Poor, unmarried, young women have children for the same reasons. Motherhood is a mark of achievement—not just for teen mothers but also for most women; it fulfills expectations and provides a source of status. Having a child completes a biological destiny—across class, gender, and race. No one challenges the natural desire for women and men to procreate; so, when discussing teen mothers, isn't it equally odd to ask why they want children?

THE ROLE OF SCHOLARS

Scholarly research is laden with correlations that associate early childbirth with infant mortality, low birth weight, low educational achievement, delinquency, incarceration (for boys), poor cognitive functioning and language skills, and child abuse and neglect.[92] Studies also assert that when compared to the general population, teen mothers are less likely to complete high school and find adequate employment, and are more likely to be poor.[93] These findings reach beyond scholarly journals and are reproduced in the media, at state legislative hearings, and by heads of public and private agencies seeking money to address these problems.

A smaller number of scholars, however, have argued that poverty may be more of a cause than consequence of early childbirth. Kristin Luker and Arline Geronimus were among the first to do so, departing from the more normative and conventional negative constructions of teen births. Disentangling the correlation between teen births and poverty, Luker argued persuasively in *Dubious Conceptions* that poverty generally precedes most early childbirth, while Geronimus added that childbearing for poor teens does not represent "irrationality and the abdication of personal responsibility" but instead "the struggle by the poor to work actively to fulfill the values of self-sufficiency, hard work and responsibility to children and elders in an environment that constrains and changes the available routes for attaining these goals."[94]

More recently, scholars who originally supported the belief that poverty and other related problems are negative consequences of teen births have reversed their positions. Most notably, prominent sociologist Frank Furstenberg, whose early findings demonstrated that having a child as a teen led to a variety of negative consequences, found that, as mothers aged, many of the consequences were not so devastating. He now agrees with Geronimus and Luker that the "the timing of first births among highly disadvantaged women is largely a marker of, not an important causal factor in shaping, the life course of low-income women and their children."[95] While many factors limited the life chances of the young women in his study, he no longer believes that having a baby was one of them—or, at least, it is not nearly as significant a factor as he once thought. With a critique of the field that includes himself, he writes that "early social science evidence greatly exaggerated the impact of early childbearing on mothers, and probably its impact on their offspring as well."[96]

Much social science research overstates the negative consequences of early childbirth because they compare teen mothers to peers in national surveys without taking into consideration preexisting conditions. Teen mothers are more likely to come from low-income families, stressful and violent neighborhoods and households, and poor school districts, so it is no surprise that after they have children they remain economically disadvantaged, in stressful environments, and poorly educated. And it is no surprise that when compared to the larger population on indicators of education, income, and health, the teen mother and her child come up short. However, when researchers control for preexisting disadvantages to get a better estimate of the real effects of the early birth, the negative consequences to the mother and child dissipate.[97] When comparing women who live in similar social and economic circumstances, young mothers do as well as (or as poorly as) those who delayed childbirth; moreover, some aspects of the adolescent mother's life may even improve after they give birth.[98] One example of this is education. While it is true that, compared to the general population, teen mothers have higher rates of school dropout, studies that examine more closely the sequence of events find that school disengagement usually precedes the pregnancy.[99] And studies that try to control for preexisting economic disadvantages find that teen mothers are as likely to complete high school (by diploma or GED) as their peers, perhaps because having a child becomes an incentive to stay in school or return to school.[100]

While the consequences of early childbirth for the mother are not as problematic as scholars once thought, neither are the negative outcomes for the children of teen mothers when studies take preexisting factors into account. Children of poor mothers have more problems than children of affluent parents, but behavioral, developmental, and health problems associated with early childbirth are also associated with poverty, violent neighborhoods, inadequate schools, family instability, emotional and physical stressors, and racism.[101] While scholars do not say there are no negative consequences to early childbirth, they now admit that the young age of the mother is not the most significant variable.[102]

Consistent with these positions, and with the arguments made more than two decades ago by Luker and Geronimus, we suggest in this book that the focus on the presumed, and often inflated, negative consequences of early childbirth is a distraction from more serious and related problems that precede the early births.[103] The life stories of the young mothers in our book challenge policy-makers like Congressman Herger, who believes that "opportunities to build a promising future" are cut short by an early birth. Instead, we argue, their opportunities were cut short by child sexual abuse, impoverished neighborhoods, undiagnosed illnesses, and inadequately funded schools—all of which preceded the early births. Every one of the costs of early childbirth to the mother, the child, and the taxpayer corresponds to the costs of an economic and social system that creates and exacerbates inequality. And while researchers point out that our teen birth rates, while declining, are still significantly higher than they are in comparable countries, it is also the case that the level of inequality in the United States is greater than in those countries.[104] The focus on adolescent mothers serves merely to distract us from more systemic problems that will not be solved by a campaign to prevent teen pregnancy.

In this book we move the gaze away from the belly and the baby carriage and, instead, take a wide-angle view of life events leading up to the pregnancy and delivery. The life stories of 108 teen mothers help us to understand what it was like growing up in their homes, schools, and neighborhoods. All of the mothers were under the age of 25 at the time of the interview. Their young age precludes any informative analysis of the consequences of early childbirth.[105] Our focus in this book, then, is on the antecedents to the early births, and in particular on the conditions of structural inequality as manifest in gender, class, and racial hierarchies.

PATRIARCHY, POVERTY, AND RACISM

Using a critical paradigm to understand how the organization of power and domination shaped the trajectories of these young mothers, we examine the grooves of systemic inequality, in particular, patriarchy, poverty, and racism. It seems odd, but many discussions about teenage pregnancy are skewed toward discussions of poverty and race, and overlook the distinctly gendered experience of inequality. Linda Gordon writes: "Teenage pregnancy, like many reproductive problems, is problematic largely because of the social inequalities it thrives upon and helps to reproduce. But these inequalities include those of gender as well as class and race, and if recognition of the first is suppressed, solutions are unlikely to be found."[106] While we begin here with a discussion of poverty, it is only because this concept is easiest to present as systemic inequality.

Poverty is more than simply a measure of income, despite the frequent public reference to a "poverty line." Poverty refers to systemic deprivation—a lack of material and social resources through which people exercise the freedom to create their lives. The markers of systemic deprivation include deteriorating neighborhoods that are regulated by interpersonal and structural violence; unhealthy environments that lead to chronic health problems such as asthma, hypertension, malnutrition, diabetes, obesity, and lead poisoning; underfunded schools that cannot serve as vehicles of economic mobility; and racial and class segregation that isolates and stigmatizes communities. Impoverished communities exist in both rural and urban settings, where people live "in" poverty. Poverty is thus a manifestation of economic and social inequality.

The conditions of poverty shape strategies for living, but the expectations of the larger society shape how those strategies are evaluated. Fertility-timing norms vary by class, but the expectations of the larger society are shaped by the norms of the middle class. In this worldview, having a child at the age of 16 appears irrational and irresponsible. These middle-class assumptions about when women should bear children overlook the realities of people living in poverty—where, as Geronimus found, infants born to mothers in their twenties are more likely to die than those born to mothers in their teens.[107] She argues that fertility-timing norms are established with resources and economic needs and pursuits in mind. In areas with high poverty and poor health indicators, a successful strategy is early childbirth within extended multigenerational families so that care for children is shared. Geronimus asserts that it may be the best practice for the child "if their birth and pre-school years coincide with their mother's peak health and access to social and practical support provided by relatively healthy kin."[108] And given what she has termed the "weathering" effect that poverty has on the health of its residents, women are healthiest when they are younger.[109]

While Geronimus's research has focused on extremely poor, black, urban areas (Detroit and Harlem), Linda Burton examines fertility-timing norms in a semi-rural community and also concludes that early childbearing is a life-course strategy in poor communities with few marriageable men or job opportunities. Shortened generations in poor communities make it practical for the child's grandmother (in her 30s) to parent the newborn, while the teen mother (who was often parented by her grandmother) takes care of her grandmother. An accelerated timetable for childbirth, Burton argues, is a rational response to the conditions of poverty.[110]

Patriarchy, like poverty, is a systemic problem. Just as poverty is not simply about income, patriarchy is not simply about men. Like class inequality and racial injustice, it is about power. Patriarchy is organized across and within institutions (for example, the family, the economy, the polity, and the media) and is manifest in disparate valuations of men and women as well as in formal and informal rules for behavior that limit opportunities for women by shaping the expectations that they have for themselves and that others have for them. For example, child care is still primarily the responsibility of women (even though most women are working outside the home), and child care is considered an individual responsibility and not a citizenship right. The routine talk about "working mothers" but not "working fathers" expresses different expectations for parenting. As Anita Ilta Garey points out, the dominant cultural model of working mothers assumes a dichotomous and contentious relationship between work and family, one that places women in no-win situations: they are seen as less committed mothers when they work, and less committed workers when they mother.[111] These expectations evolve from a system whereby work outside the home, traditionally done by men, is privileged over work done in the home, traditionally done by women. These cultural messages are encoded in a patriarchal system.

Similarly, patriarchy is the context in which unmarried mothers are demonized. Policy-makers and social scientists did not label teen births as an epidemic when the rate was at its highest in the 1950s and 18- and 19-year-old mothers were much more likely to be married (then it was the young marriage that was the problem). Today it is the absence of a man, both husband and father, that makes the early birth a problem. Sociologist Ruth Sidel argues that in the public's eye, a family without a man "is faulted as deficient, defective, disrupted, broken." She adds that an "ideology that defines any family without a live-in biological father as inferior, unstable and even harmful will make single mothers feel like outsiders and indeed encourage others to perceive them as beyond the pale."[112]

A focus on patriarchal structures rather than on depraved men moves the discussion of teen births away from blaming individuals. We examine systemic gender inequalities in our discussions of statutory rape, child sexual abuse, and interpersonal violence. Patriarchy contextualizes the gendered violence intertwined with sexual relations, gender performance, and power. How to be a woman can be shaped at the end of a violent slap or by the violation of unwanted penetration. Childbirth is then an articulation (volunteered, coerced, or forced) of womanhood.

Finally, as our earlier description of the overlapping narratives of blame suggests, no group of young mothers has been more demonized than black teens. Racism is oppression rooted in capitalism and white supremacy, manifest historically in systems of slavery and colonization, Jim Crow and urban ghettos, and contemporarily in interlocking institutions that create stratified patterns of inclusion and exclusion.[113] Racism is not about racists but about an organization of social relations, power, and opportunity. For example, in Connecticut, poor black and brown students are overrepresented in underperforming urban schools, while white and, to a lesser extent, black middle-class students thrive in well-funded suburban schools. When our attention shifts away from deviant teen mothers to the problems of underfunded and overburdened schools, we are confronted with the larger systemic problem of educational inequality undergirded by racial and economic apartheid. In the life stories of mothers who dropped out of high school before they had children, we see the cumulative effect of disadvantage that materialized in their failed transition from middle school into high school; and for those who stayed in school, we see the benefits of racial and economic privileges.

THE LIFE-STORY STUDY IN CONNECTICUT

The young mothers in this study were all participating in a home-visitation program for first-time mothers in Connecticut. As part of a larger assessment of the program, the life-story interviews were designed to help program leaders better understand their families.[114] We asked the young mothers to tell us what it was like growing up. They talked about their families, neighborhoods, school experiences, friends, and boyfriends. They told us how they found out they were pregnant and about their decision to carry the pregnancy to term.

As sociologists, we examine structural forces of systemic inequality that precede these early childbirths to understand why they had children when they were teenagers. Many of the mothers, however, used a personal responsibility frame to explain their behavior. Socialized in a culture of individualism and knowing that society disapproves of their early motherhood, they constructed self-blame and bootstrap-determination narratives. Some called themselves "lazy" and gave this as a reason for dropping out of school. Others talked about the need for "hard work" and "stepping up" to meet their "responsibilities." More than one mother said: "I was responsible enough to have sex; I can be responsible enough to raise the child."

In addition, many of these young mothers were critical of people who "suck off the state," but they also wished the state would act more efficiently, empathetically, and effectively. Most agreed with Ivalesse that state assistance "should be for people that need it. I need it because I earn honestly and it's not enough for me and for my children. The unemployment office can help because sometimes it's hard to find a job. The problem is that the majority of people do not have a car." But she also believed that "the government is at fault because they let the factories go. And it shouldn't be like that because we have to work, we have families to feed." Ivalesse was one of the few mothers who tied her own job opportunities to educational disparities, transportation problems, and deindustrialization. Others pointed the finger at themselves with statements like "I didn't get that job at Blockbuster because there was someone more qualified." The mothers wanted to become financially independent from their parents and the state—as Ivalesse said, "I have to do for my own"—but sometimes this made them more economically dependent on men or the streets.

Similarly, mothers complained about men but they did not talk about systemic gender inequality. There was general agreement among the young mothers that they were responsible for their children. In their minds there was a traditional gender division, where men were disciplinarians and providers, and women were caretakers—and they believed that this made sense biologically.

Appendix A provides an expanded methodological discussion about the interview procedures and ethics as well as the process of analysis and the construction of life-story vignettes. The 108 teen mothers in the study were ethnically and racially diverse with 36 non-Hispanic white, 36 Puerto Rican, 18 African American, 11 biracial, three other Latina (that is, not Puerto Rican), two West Indian, and two Asian mothers. This breakdown by race and ethnicity roughly reflects statewide births of teen mothers.[115] They were all living in Connecticut, with a little more than one-half residing in large and small cities and the others in towns and rural areas. The urban-rural divide also parted along racial lines: 83 percent of whites lived in towns and rural areas, and 85 percent of blacks and Puerto Ricans in small cities and urban areas.

From a distance, Connecticut has a high-earning, highly educated populace. At the time of the study, it was the wealthiest state in the union.[116] This image, however, masks stark conditions of inequality in the state, where poverty and racial minorities are geographically concentrated and income disparities are among the highest in the union. For instance, the capital city, Hartford, has one of the highest child poverty rates in the country: in 2006, 43 percent of children 17 years and younger lived below the poverty line, the sixth highest rate in the nation.[117] Teen birth rates follow accordingly, with Hartford leading the state in teen births (18 percent of all teen births in 2005).[118] Beneath the facade of prosperity, Connecticut exemplifies a state that has been torn apart by economic and social inequality in the past 30 years.[119] The stories we tell in this book are from the mothers who live in the shadows of wealth and prosperity.

The geographical organization of socioeconomic disparities in the state is even more pronounced when we include race in our analysis, illustrating social and economic conditions that are approaching what we may fairly call racial apartheid in Connecticut. The 2000 census reported that almost one-half of Latinos (45 percent) and blacks (49 percent) in Connecticut lived in the four largest—and poorest—cities, where 14 percent of the state population lived, while 78 percent of Connecticut towns were more than 90 percent white.[120]

The mothers in our study were recruited into the voluntary home-visitation program from birthing hospitals throughout the state. They were first-time mothers who were offered parenting support because they were identified as vulnerable, or "at-risk" of being bad parents.[121] Eligibility in the program required that the mothers meet a combination of factors that constituted a "risk" index. These factors included being young, poor, single, socially isolated, having less than a high school education, or experiencing family problems, poor mental health, a cognitive deficit, late or limited prenatal care, drug or alcohol abuse, or repeated abortions.[122] In other words, the women in our study provide a window onto a population of vulnerable teen mothers; but their situations varied, as some of the mothers were considered vulnerable only because they were young and single and had not yet finished high school, while others displayed a much greater breadth of problems. Table 7 in appendix B provides a demographic description of the sample.

The mothers in our study are younger than the national aggregate of teen mothers—another aspect of their vulnerability—with 60 percent younger than 18 when they had their first child, roughly two times the national and state averages (see table 8 in appendix B for state data). Many of their life trajectories were punctuated by child abuse, domestic violence, and substance abuse. Only 15 girls grew up with both original parents, and one-third were currently living in blended families. More than one-third had no contact with at least one of their parents as a result of death, incarceration, or abandonment.[123] Many, but not all, of the mothers came from educationally impoverished families (over one-half of the babies' grandparents had not completed high school, but one-half of their grandmothers had some postsecondary education). Some grew up in families that were desperately poor, but most were just-getting-by working class. A few were stable working-class immigrants, others were working-to-middle-class climbers, and a few were middle-class sliders destabilized by divorce and alcoholism. Less than one-quarter of the mothers grew up in areas of concentrated poverty, and even there, some lived in households that were relatively stable economically and emotionally. Education interacted with family income and neighborhood so that the poorest families had the least education and lived in the most impoverished neighborhoods.

Studying a vulnerable sample of young mothers is useful because they resemble the population of teen mothers nationally, who are more likely to be poor, to have experienced sexual violence, and to have done poorly in school; however, having chosen a vulnerable population, we risk reproducing stereotypes about adolescent mothers. Their struggles may invite moral contempt and reductive interpretations. We counter this telescopic tendency with sociological storytelling that widens our focus to include an analysis of the social structures and larger forces of inequality that cradle their backstories. Moreover, the mothers in our study represent considerable diversity in race and ethnicity, geographical location, family stability, life experiences, and even age when we consider the differences between young adolescents and older teen mothers. We remind readers that even within poor communities and vulnerable families, the majority of young girls do not become teen mothers and life experiences do indeed vary. The Puerto Ricans in our study are no more representative of a Puerto Rican culture than white teen mothers are representative of white culture.[124] This is why chapter 6 is important, where we discuss the narratives of 15- to 17-year-old girls with high academic achievements who were not troubled by violence and abuse. These stories of the black, white, and brown "good girls" challenge stereotypes about teen mothers and call into question dismal deterministic life-course predictions often associated with early motherhood.

At the time of the interviews, roughly two-thirds of the mothers were still teenagers who had only one child under the age of two years. Their young age influenced the tone of their life stories. Some mothers articulated their feelings and perceptions well, and detailed stories tumbled from their mouths in long full paragraphs. Many of these "talkers" were simply good storytellers with interesting stories to tell. Others had childhoods that had been heavily managed by the state—child protective services, foster homes, psychiatric institutions, detention centers, courts, jails—and they appeared to know the routine of reporting their scripted stories to people who asked, which made them deft at telling facts while hiding meaning. A small number had received enough psychotherapy to not only tell their life stories but analyze them as well.

At the other extreme were the reluctant narrators. One 14-year-old defiantly answered in monosyllabic yeah/nah, shoulder shrugs, and the

"I dunno" mantra of a sulky adolescent who distrusts adults. A few mothers' cognitive and emotional impairments limited their language. Some mothers were unwilling to revisit painful memories and were reluctant to offer more than the skeleton of an abuse narrative. And finally, a few mothers appeared to be under the influence of drugs (prescription and otherwise) and were a bit groggy during the interview.

The voice of the mother is a reflection of gender and class, race and ethnicity, personality and biography, and mind and self.[125] It is also a reflection of the interview performance—the telling of one's life story to another person. We encourage readers who are interested in the methodological issues related to the interview context (characteristics of the interviewers, descriptions of the setting, and issues related to intersubjectivity) to read appendix A. For others, it is important to remember that the life story is a constructed performance, not an absolute set of facts, and these particular storytellers were telling stories not only of their lives, but also of the creation of a new life.

CHAPTER 2

Young Young Mothers

GLADYS: "I'M KIND OF LIKE THE CINDERELLA"

Gladys was one of the youngest mothers in our study—pregnant at the age of 12. The father of the baby was 17, and though he could have been prosecuted for statutory rape, no charges were brought against him and Gladys did not describe herself as a victim. Born in Jamaica, Gladys moved to Connecticut when she was in grade school. She returned to Jamaica in the summers, living within a large extended family in a rural area. In Hartford, she lived with her aunt, who was a strict guardian, and her grandparents.

[My father] was really good with me. He always loved me, made sure I had the things I needed. Back in Jamaica, my father and mother separated and then he found his new wife and he came up here. Me and him are not that close now because I didn't really get along with his new wife and his new family. They're nearby but we're not that close. My aunt bought this house so I moved here, and then my grandparents came up from Jamaica like a year after.

My grandfather was usually working and he would just come home on weekends and my grandmother was always home. [My aunt] was working from three to 11 so sometimes I would just get a glimpse of her 'cuz I go to school and by the time I'm home she's leaving.

[My grandmother] is very sweet, very sweet. She loves to cook. [laugh] She's fun to talk to, especially when she talks about what it was like when

she was a kid. She's funny, [laugh] like she always has a comment for certain things that you say and it just always gets you to laugh. She's been with me mostly through everything. [My grandfather,] he's just the same. He's excellent. He's very quiet but he will speak his mind when push comes to shove. He'll let you know what he's thinking. Otherwise from that, he's very, very sweet, and loving too, especially with his great-grandson, my son.

* * * * *

When I came up here I started the third grade. I stayed back one year [in fourth grade], but after that I didn't want my friends to go on again without me so right now I'm an A-B student.

I really have a lot of nice friends. They always want me to come and sleep over, but my aunt will always say no. My aunt wouldn't let me go anywhere. I'm always pent up in the house. The school has a lot of programs but each time that I would ask my aunt for something, the answer would always be no. If I wanted to go somewhere, no, no, no. "No!" I would get in trouble just for going outside. "Where have you been?" Dah-da-da-da-da! So after a while I just didn't ask.

Every time my aunt would argue with me, she would say she doesn't want to have nothing to do with me and it was "I don't care about you." Me and her just aren't that close. With my cousin she's totally different. My cousin is her princess. So, I'm kind of like the Cinderella. So whenever she says dishes and like housework, she expects me to do 'em and she starts cussing and saying, "Oh, this child is no good and she doesn't do anything I say." She would curse at me and that just shut me down, it made me feel so bad. I wanted to curse back at her but I never did. I felt angry. I kept everything inside until one day I exploded. [laugh] I cursed at her. She was saying I was disrespectful, I was ungrateful and she just kept on like that. Ugh. [big sigh]

Half the reason why I got pregnant was because my aunt. I got the guts to ask her if I could go to this graduation party for the eighth graders and she said No and that just really ticked me off and I stayed [after school for the party] and came home 11 o'clock. After that she was just so upset with me we never talked. So I was basically left to do what I want [that summer]. [My aunt] worked at a live-in job and my grandmother was in Jamaica and there was only my grandfather and he would work every other night and has a job during the day, too, so during the day it was just me and I wasn't gonna stay at the house.

I went out each day [to see] Carl. At first we were just friends and we were just messing around and everything. We'd go to the park and play basketball. It wasn't like I spent a whole lot of time with him. I'd say about a good six months I knew him but it was mostly like hours and hours on the phone. And then, during the summer, after the party, I be just left by myself, and I went back to his parents' house and we just hang out together and watch movies and everything. It was [whisper] just right down the street, right down there.

* * * * *

[My aunt] sent me back to Jamaica. I went down pregnant and I didn't know it and then I ate spicy food and started throwing up. My mom wasn't all that upset [that I was pregnant] because she was saying it didn't happen down there. When I came up here my grandmother and my grandfather didn't say anything. Nothing, no bad comments, no good comments, nothing. [My aunt] was completely silent. She didn't really say anything about it.

At first, I was like, "No, I didn't want it." I was knowing how my aunt is and I thought she was gonna be so upset with me so at first I was thinking abortion. Then after I started going to the hospital, a social worker started talking about all different kind of options, so I was thinking about adoption. After I had my son, I just couldn't go through with it 'cuz it was just too hard.

I didn't really want Carl to know. He had just started working down at the grocery store, so I walked in one day with my cousin and she said, "Why is that guy staring at you?" I was like that's the baby's father. She was like are you gonna tell him? And I was like, "No, I don't want nothing." She was like I'll say something to him. So she went up to him and was like, "I think Gladys might be pregnant with your baby." He kind of just looked at me and that was basically it. He didn't say it's not mine. He didn't say it's his. He didn't say anything. He just looked at me and then he went on checking groceries.

LUANNE: "HE SAID IF I DIDN'T DO IT HE WOULD NEVER TALK TO ME AGAIN"

Luanne gave birth on her fifteenth birthday. She lived in a stable working-class neighborhood in a two-story house that her family owned. Both her mother (British white) and stepfather (African American) worked full time, and her biological father (African American) maintained a strong presence in her life. Luanne's neighborhood was racially mixed and in the late afternoons when we interviewed her, young children and older teens played outside on the streets.

I'm called Mulatto. Or you can say African American. This kid in school the other day thought I was Mexican or Puerto Rican and I told him, "No, I'm Mulatto." And he goes, "What's Mulatto?" I told him it was black and white. He went, "Isn't that African American?" I said, "Yeah, but you can also use Mulatto." I don't know where it came from. My mom's just white, she was born in England.

My dad used to beat my mom. I don't really remember but I remember it was bad. They sent me [to counseling] because I wouldn't talk to nobody. My stepfather moved in when I was seven. I don't like him, I think he's mean. I don't think he likes me because he doesn't like my dad and I look like my dad, but he likes my sister because she doesn't look like my dad. I have tanned skin and my sister looks white. She looks like my mom. She has blonde hair and blue eyes and I have my dad's color hair. I have like curly brown hair and I just have his features—so he doesn't like me. He yells at me all the time.

I lived with my dad in sixth grade, during the summer. He's strict. He never let me did nothing. I had to stay in the house, I could only use the phone for like a half an hour. I can't have any friends over there. He's just an idiot, I don't like him. He said I wore rags. He said he was going to rip them off me and use them to wash the car with. I don't talk to him about my boyfriends because he's like, "I don't like any boys you go out with." Every time I say something about a boy he yells and gets mad, he just doesn't like me going out with them.

My mother has to know everywhere I go and my stepfather has to know every detail, "Where you going, how you getting there?" And I get an attitude and get in trouble—like two weeks' punishment, no phone, no nothing—for being late coming home from a friend's house or not telling them where I was or not doing homework when I was supposed to.

* * * * *

I don't like school. I don't like sitting there for a long time and I just really don't like going. I used to do track. I have a whole bunch of trophies for winning because I was the fastest in my school. I played basketball for a year in sixth [grade]. I got into middle school and I started hanging out with a lot of my friends and I was not interested anymore.

I met Johnnie [the father of the baby] at my friend's house. I was going to her birthday party and he lives right next to her. I didn't know who he was and I was getting out of the car and he chased me into her house. And then we just became friends. We didn't do nothing. We talked on the phone. That's it. He could never go to a dance because he was always suspended or he had detention or something.

He's my same age. He didn't like my friends. He said they're too preppy for him. He hangs out with all the thugs. He's Jamaican and Mulatto and he wears his hair in braids. He's really skinny. He wears those big clothes. He wears bandanas. He has like long eyelashes and these kind of great big eyes—they're not too big but they're big. I like him but I don't like him. When I met him he was nice, but I think he's a jerk. I don't like him anymore. I think he just wanted to go out with me and he started being a jerk, and his true colors starting coming.

He was a drug dealer. Everything—crack and cocaine, and all that other crap. I didn't really want to mess with that stuff [laughter] because I have heart problems and if I even tried, I'd probably have a heart attack. I just stay away. He carries a switchblade knife in his pocket. He says, "just in case." I don't know, it's probably for me. [laughter] He'll probably kill me.

* * * * *

It was my first time. He said if I didn't do it he would never talk to me again, so I did it. And then I have a baby. I don't know what happened. He's an idiot. He probably poked holes in [the condom] because at school all the boys made a bet how many girls they can get and out of all them girls they had to poke a hole out of at least one; and I didn't know it until after I got pregnant. And then all the boys started to talk to me saying, "Oh, you know I made a bet" and everything else. The one that had sex with the most girls won—or won something—I don't even know what they won. But I didn't know that until after or I would've never done it.

I didn't want to tell my mom [I was pregnant] so I hid my tampons behind my TV [laughing] and I came home from school and she had them on the table and she started screaming at me and then she [bought me] a pregnancy test and it said I was pregnant. And then she wanted to make sure—she brought me to the hospital and they took one and it said it wasn't. And then we waited and I was like throwing up and everything and we took another one and I was pregnant.

My mom was crying and she said it was my decision and she said that she would support me and everything. And my stepdad punched a hole through the wall. We were all together and he just went off, started punching things and his fist went right through the wall. He just likes to yell, he thinks he's the king of the house. He yells at everything.

And my dad said he didn't want to talk to me anymore. He said he was going to get a lawyer so I can have an abortion, but I don't believe in abortion because it was a mistake and everything, but I think if you have a baby that you should let it live because it wasn't the baby's fault, it was your fault, so you have to live with the consequences. I don't believe in abortion. I really don't. My whole family doesn't. A lot of my friends believe in abortion, and a lot of my friends don't. I just made a choice by myself. [My dad] accepted it and then he used to take pictures of my stomach as I grew and he put them in an album—and when he was born he loved him. He loves to hold him.

Johnnie don't care. I told him when I found out and he yelled at me and smacked me across my face and shoved me against the locker. He thought I was lying. I ran into the bathroom so he couldn't follow me and then he went right in and started like hitting me. He got suspended.

He seen [the baby] when he was like a week old. I haven't talked to him ever since then. He threatened to shoot me and he's violated his probation. He always used to call my house and threaten that he's going to take the baby and a whole bunch of stuff. I was crying 'cause he said that he could be there in five minutes and he was going to be outside of my house with a gun to kill me. He always used to drive past my house and look in my windows. I called my mom and I started crying. And she called the cops. He got caught in a drug raid, I think. I don't know the rest because I don't talk to him. He's in detention.

DISTRACTING DISCOURSES: PARENTAL NEGLECT, HISPANIC FERTILITY, AND PREDATORY MEN

We begin our analysis with a chapter that evokes one of the public's worst fears: 13- and 14-year-old girls getting pregnant and having children. Their young age raises concerns about the parenting capabilities of mothers who, in many ways, are still children: they cannot apply for state assistance, cannot get a driver's license, and may even have the same pediatrician as their children. These young young mothers are less likely to receive adequate prenatal care and more likely to give birth prematurely to children with lower birth weight who have a higher risk for disability, disease, and death.[1] We share the public's concern about this population of young young mothers, but hasten to add that this

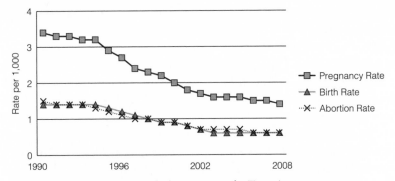

FIGURE 5. Pregnancy, Birth, and Abortion Rates for Teens Age 10 to 14, 1990–2008. Source for Pregnancy and Abortion Rates: Ventura et al. 2012, table 2. Source for Birth Rates: Martin et al. 2012, table 8.

group of "kids having kids" is quite small—in 2010 only 20 children were born to mothers under 15 in Connecticut.[2] Nationally, birth and pregnancy rates for this age group declined by more than one half since 1990 (see figure 5). Even in 2006, when the birth rate for teens 15 to 19 increased for the first time in 15 years, the rate for the youngest age group did not.[3] By 2010, only four out of 10,000 girls ages 10 to 14 years gave birth in the United States.[4]

Population studies report data on teen births by the age group 10 to 14, but in this chapter we include mothers who became pregnant at age 14 even when they gave birth at age 15. Among the 108 teen mothers we interviewed, 16 mothers were 12 to 14 years of age when they became pregnant; of these, seven were younger than 15 when they gave birth, and Luanne gave birth on her fifteenth birthday.[5] Toward the end of this chapter, when we turn our attention to statutory rape, we discuss stories of mothers who were sexually active before the age of 16. Eleven mothers in our study were in relationships at the time they became pregnant that violated statutory rape laws in Connecticut (they were under the age of 16 and the partner was more than two years older), and of these, seven were young young mothers who became pregnant before age 15. The mothers in this chapter were also quite young when we interviewed them; only three were older than 16. Their young age is a reminder that this book focuses on the antecedents rather than consequences of early childbearing.

The young young mothers grew up in homes with less violence than the middle and older teen mothers: just under one-third grew up in homes with domestic violence or child abuse compared to almost one-half of the other mothers.[6] Their economic backgrounds ranged from low to lower-middle income, and neighborhoods varied from poor to stable working-class. Only three were living with both original parents; all but one of the mothers received Women, Infants, and Children (WIC) benefits; and they all received state health care assistance for their children. In this subgroup there were slightly more Puerto Ricans than in the overall sample. None of the mothers had graduated from high school: 10 of the mothers were still attending school at the time of the interview, and the six others had dropped out. The mothers' relationships with the fathers of their children varied from marriage to no involvement; and the relationship between the father and his child mirrored his relationship with the mother. (See table 1.)

In this chapter, we challenge three common explanations for very young births—poor parenting, higher fertility in Latino communities, and predatory men—arguing that, while there is some truth in all three explanations, they largely exaggerate and distort the issues. The first is that young births are a result of inattentive or permissive parents. In contrast, many of these young mothers spoke about parents and guardians who were characterized as being strict and overprotective. Exploring these narratives, we show how poverty and immigration influence parenting styles, disposing parents to use more restrictive rules in efforts to protect children from unwanted street influences.

Second, we examine the public narrative that young Latinas are giving birth at extraordinarily high rates and producing a new underclass in the United States. We analyze these trends, focusing on Puerto Ricans and Mexicans, and argue that, while poverty certainly contributes to young motherhood, birth rates have decreased considerably, that support from extended families is common, and that education, work, and marriage are aspirations they share with mainstream America. We assert that focusing on the small number of early births distracts us from addressing larger socioeconomic issues that contribute to the creation of intransigent poverty, such as structural unemployment and hypersegregation.

Third, we challenge the predatory man thesis that underscored ramped-up statutory rape laws in the 1990s.[7] We show how these laws and their enforcement were linked to welfare reform initiatives. Acknowledging that young teens are more vulnerable to sexual exploitation, we refocus the discussion by arguing that consent and predation are shaped by larger gender inequalities that lead to unwanted sexual

TABLE 1   CHARACTERISTICS OF 16 MOTHERS PREGNANT BEFORE AGE 15

Name	Race/Ethnicity	Place of Birth	Age MOB	Age FOB	Relation w/FOB	School Status	City Size	Family Structure
Keisha	Black	South Carolina	14	37	Not involved, warrant out for his arrest	Enrolled: high school	Town	Single, never married
Nona	Laotian-American	Massachusetts	14	15	Some contact, friends	Enrolled: night school	Town	Original two parents
Susan	White	Connecticut	13	18	Some contact, incarcerated	Enrolled: high school	Town	Divorced, live-in partner
Gladys	Jamaican	Jamaica	13	17	Not involved	Enrolled: middle school	Urban	Never married, father married someone else
Ana	Mexican	Mexico	14	19	Married	Not enrolled: eighth grade highest	City	Original two parents
Paloma	Puerto Rican	Puerto Rico	14	16	Cohabitating	Enrolled: school for teen mothers	Urban	Divorced
Carla	Puerto Rican	Puerto Rico	14	30s	Not involved, police investigating statutory rape	Enrolled: high school	Urban	Divorced, live-in partner
Danielle	Puerto Rican	Connecticut	15	15	Cohabitating	Not enrolled: eighth grade highest	Urban	Divorced

Name	Ethnicity	State	Age		FOB involvement	School	City size	Family structure
Donna	White	Connecticut	15	16	Not involved	Enrolled: high school	Town	Original two parents
Rosa	Puerto Rican /White	Puerto Rico	15	17	Not involved, incarcerated	Not enrolled: eleventh grade highest	Urban	Divorced, remarried
Virginia	Puerto Rican	Connecticut	15	15	Cohabitating	Not enrolled: ninth grade highest	Town	Divorced, remarried
Nita	Puerto Rican	Puerto Rico	15	18	Some contact, lives out of state	Enrolled: high school	Town	Original two parents
Luanne	Black/White	Connecticut	15	15	Not involved, incarcerated	Enrolled: high school	Town	Divorced, remarried
Lark	Puerto Rican /Black	Connecticut	15	15	Not involved	Not enrolled: tenth grade highest	City	Divorced
Christina	Puerto Rican	Connecticut	15	17	Not involved	Enrolled: high school	City	Divorced
Athena	Puerto Rican	Puerto Rico	15	27	Not involved	Not enrolled: eighth grade highest	Urban	Divorced

Age = age at time of birth.

MOB = mother of the baby; FOB = father of the baby.

City size: Urban >100,000; City 50,000 to 100,000; Town <50,000.

relationships and pregnancies. Blaming men is not going to solve these problems, but it does create another reason to put men in jail, usually poor black and brown men.

EARLY SEXUAL BEHAVIOR AND PARENTAL SUPERVISION

While the sexual liberation movement beginning in the 1960s relaxed sexual mores, most Americans still believe it is wrong for young teens to have premarital sex.[8] Sexual behavior for young teens rose through the 1980s, but began to decline in the mid-1990s; today roughly one in 10 females report having sexual intercourse before age 15.[9] The decline among young teens is important because their risk of pregnancy is greater than older teens (who are more likely to be educated about sex and to use birth control).[10] Moreover, girls who have their first sexual experience before age 15 are more likely than older teens to experience coercive sex (not rape, but not voluntary).[11] They are also more likely to have had their first sexual experience with someone who was four years or older than them.[12]

Examining large data sets, social scientists have identified demographic and social characteristics correlated with sexual activity and teen births. Girls at risk of early and risky sexual behavior (multiple partners, no contraception) are more likely to live in impoverished areas and to have lower school expectations.[13] They are also less likely to live with both original parents and more likely to have parents who exercise less supervision and fewer controls; their parents tend to have lower educational achievement, higher rates of unemployment, and more criminal arrests.[14] Not surprisingly, girls who use drugs and alcohol, belong to gangs, run away from home, and are truant or perform poorly in school are also more likely to engage in early and frequent sex.[15]

Examining the life stories, we did see incidences of poor parental supervision and fewer behavioral controls (like curfews and homework schedules), but this usually occurred in households where fathers and mothers were physically or relationally absent as a result of death, incarceration, physical or mental illness, drug addiction, migration, or abandonment. In households where parents or guardians were present and parental supervision was apparent, the mothers were more likely to describe harsh rather than permissive parenting. In fact, in 23 of the life stories, the young women described a primary caretaker (parent, step-parent, grandparent, or aunt) as "strict" or "controlling," while only seven included a narrative of caretakers who did "not set boundaries" or were "not attentive."[16]

This strictness can be a response to various factors including unsafe neighborhood conditions that lead parents to protect their children from unwanted influences by not letting them play outside of the home, a finding supported by numerous scholars.[17] Ivalesse, whose life story opened the book, said that she planned to keep her children close to her and engaged in sports and dancing "so they have less time for the streets," where fights occurred regularly in the parking lot outside her apartment. Keeping children close to home and away from the streets can also represent the attempts of immigrant parents to shelter children in a new country where norms and practices can differ greatly from the home country. This storyline was present in Gladys's narrative at the beginning of this chapter, where she described herself as the Cinderella living with a mean aunt. They lived in a stable working-class urban neighborhood that included an aging white population as well as new European (Albanian and Slovenian) and West Indian immigrants. Her neighborhood, however, abutted a mostly Puerto Rican neighborhood with high rates of poverty and crime, and the school she attended drew from both neighborhoods. Her aunt worked from three to 11 in the evening and was not home to supervise Gladys, but she did set down strict rules that Gladys was to come straight home from school and could not attend extracurricular events.

While we did not interview Gladys's aunt, we suspect she may not have been as mal-intended as Gladys described and speculate that her aunt was reacting to what she viewed as unsafe neighborhood conditions. The efforts of her aunt to be a good guardian were complicated by the different parenting rules that Gladys's mother applied when she was in Jamaica. Comparing her urban home in Connecticut to her village home in Jamaica, Gladys said:

> When I'm up here I'm cooped up and when I'm in Jamaica it's kind of like a bird getting out of a cage. I remember when I went down there the last time, I went out for the whole night with my cousin and nobody really even cared. They knew I was going out. They didn't really ask but I was just saying that I'm going out. And I went out, I enjoyed it, came home at five in the morning, slept over my cousin's and it was nothing. Up here now if I ever do that, I would be in so much trouble. Down in Jamaica it's like they know everybody, basically, they have an idea of where you're going.

Styles of parenting differed depending on the context—in the familiar surroundings of her Jamaican village, Gladys was allowed more freedom than in her urban US neighborhood. She emphasized several times in the interview that despite the freedoms permitted in Jamaica, her pregnancy occurred in Connecticut. Moreover, she clearly defined the pregnancy as part of a stream of actions that included strict rules and subsequent rebellion when she attended an eighth-grade graduation party and later that summer snuck over to the house of a boy who lived in the neighborhood, which led to her first sexual encounter and pregnancy at the age of 12.

Parental strictness and adolescent rebellion were also themes in Nona's story. Nona was the daughter of Laotian immigrants and lived in an extended family that included her parents, paternal grandparents, and her father's *amah* (nanny) from Laos. She lived in a family-owned duplex and her uncle's family lived in the other half. None of the factors that large studies find to be correlated with risky sexual behavior was present in Nona's family life—she was raised by her original two parents and lived in an economically stable neighborhood, in a lower-middle-income family with high educational expectations (her older brother was attending a four-year college at the time of the interview). The conflict in her childhood revolved around her parents' rules. Nona said she "argued a lot" with her parents because "they're strict":

> They used to let us do things with my aunts and uncles and my cousins, but only with the family. When it came to like doing things with our friends, they didn't really want us to do it. Friends could come over but we couldn't go to their house. They started letting us go out and stuff like when we were nine but as soon as I hit like 11 years old I was back stuck in the house again. There was like a two-year period where I wasn't allowed to go certain places, I couldn't stay at my friend's house. I barely could talk on the phone because they were always strict about the phone. "You're on the phone too long. What are you guys talking about on the phone?" My life was mostly in the house playing games and watching TV with my cousins and my sister and my brother. I don't like staying in the house and be like a prisoner. [laugh]

Nona resisted by sneaking out at night and became part of a marginalized group of students at her high school. At 14 she had a child; the father of the baby was the same age. She described the relationship in platonic terms, saying they "went to school together" and "hung in the same crowd." Nona did not want to be pregnant and hid it until she was almost six months along. When we asked her if she would raise her son similar to how she was raised, she said: "I don't want to raise him that way because when we was little we wasn't able to do nothing. I want him to be around people. I want him to be able to play sports. I don't want him to be stuck in the house like I was."

Nona's and Gladys's stories about early sexual behaviors and their unintended pregnancies illustrate how social contexts may influence parenting styles, but in their cases not toward permissiveness, but instead toward strictness. In their stories, we hear how supervision was intertwined with neighborhood conditions and migration. In the following section, we provide an example of what could be characterized as permissive parenting; but again, we examine the parenting strategy within a social context.

THE PRESUMED CRISIS OF YOUNG LATINA BIRTHS

As Latino immigration has surged in the past 40 years, concerns about fertility rates among the newcomers have also increased. This is nothing new; high fertility rates among immigrant groups have historically provoked nativist reactions, usually framed as a concern with demographic changes, increased welfare expenditures, or threats to the moral and social order of America.[18] Using more contemporary language, scholars and politicians express concerns about the creation of a new Latino underclass, identifying pathologies that are often attributed to the black urban poor. They assume that teen motherhood and father abandonment have become normalized and intermixed with school dropout, joblessness, substance abuse, and criminal behavior. Research then focuses on young Latinas as a population "at risk" for early childbirth.[19] Explanations for this usually identify the cultures of Latino groups, ranging from the *culture* of the country of origin where unwed early births and high fertility patterns are considered normative (for example, Mexico) to *cultural* adaptations to the conditions of neighborhood poverty (for example, Puerto Ricans).[20]

Heather Mac Donald from the Manhattan Institute illustrates this focus. In her 2006 article titled "Hispanic Family Values? Runaway Illegitimacy Is Creating a New U.S. Underclass," Mac Donald asserts that Hispanics are bringing "Third World levels of fertility to America" along with social pathologies associated with single-parent households, including "more juvenile delinquents, more school failure, more welfare usage, and more teen pregnancy."[21] Mac Donald cites high fertility rates among unmarried Hispanic women and Hispanic teenagers. Then, using interviews with social service professionals in California, she pieces together a profile of very young mothers, 14 and 15 years of age, and quotes one worker at an adoption agency who believes that it is "considered almost a badge of honor for a young girl to have a baby." Mac Donald notes that, on the one hand, it is the "tight-knit extended family" that "facilitates unwed child rearing," allowing for family members to "make up for the absence of the baby's father." On the other hand, she offers some of the worst examples of family crisis and dysfunction (incest, rape, child abuse, substance abuse, early school withdrawal, and welfare dependency). She sees the family pathologies and intergenerational poverty as "an echo of the black underclass," and yet she sees a difference in that Hispanic mothers and "absent fathers" work, "despite growing welfare use." She concludes by suggesting that academics are "not attuned to" these issues and quotes another worker who quips that the illegitimacy rate will "continue to grow until we can put birth control in the water."

Mac Donald's argument resonates with the underclass and neoliberal narratives used to demonize black and brown mothers for undermining, if not threatening, the morality, the governmental budget, and the future competitiveness of America. These explanations fit well into a narrative of blame that views the poor as morally culpable for their own poverty. In our study, it is not difficult to find examples that are similar to the ones that Mac Donald profiles to illustrate the pain and destructiveness that exist in marginalized communities, but we try to explain these personal struggles in their social contexts as part of our endeavor to understand (rather than morally condemn) teen mothers. Although the following life story of Danielle will no doubt provide grist for Mac Donald's mill, it is important to look beyond the politics of blame to see the complexity and social complicity that infuse her story with meaning.

Danielle was pregnant at 14 and had two more children before she turned 20. She was born in Puerto Rico and came to Connecticut with her mother and two younger brothers when she was seven. Aside from her father's infidelity, which precipitated the family move, she reported no problems in her family. At the time of the interview, Danielle was 20 and had been in a relationship with her partner, Javier, the father of her three children, for seven years.

Danielle met Javier in middle school. She was living in a dense Puerto Rican neighborhood in Hartford in a three-story brownstone apartment with her mother and two brothers on the second floor, her mother's friend above her, and Javier and his family below her. According to the census, she lived on a block where Spanish was the primary language spoken at home, and she confirmed that her neighbors, friends, and classmates all spoke Spanish.[22]

Javier was her same age and part of her circle of friends. She was in sixth grade when she "became his girlfriend." A year later she was pregnant. They were surprised about the pregnancy because when Javier was born there were complications and "he had problems in his private parts. The [doctors] told him he wasn't going to be able to have children. Since I had been with him for a whole year having sex and I never got pregnant, he thought he wasn't going to be able to have kids, so when I got pregnant he said that it was about time [laughs]."

There is no evidence that Danielle's family expected her to become pregnant, or that her early birth was normative, but it was clear that her family and friends did not stigmatize her when she became pregnant. Danielle stated: "These are my father's first three grandchildren, he took the news just fine since he wasn't going to be raising them or anything, so did my mother." Danielle, however, was surprised and afraid: "I was still too young; I didn't know how to have a baby. But even when I had this one [her third child], I was still afraid [laughs]." Danielle and Javier moved into their own apartment, but they always lived near her mother and mother-in-law (even though all three households moved frequently). She said her mother "would come to see me, everyday, and she would always bring me things."

Danielle was in eighth grade when she had her first child. She finished up the semester at home because of a fight with another female student: "This girl that was always starting trouble and I was going to fight her, so they sent me to the office and [the principal] told me that he was going to take me out of school until I gave birth." She gave birth in December, tried to get back into school when her baby was only one month old, but, she said, "those girls started problems with me again and we started arguing and all that and the principal told me that he was going to give me a week's suspension, so, I told him that was fine, then [laughs] I told him to keep his school that I wasn't coming back anymore. And I never went back to school." Danielle was on the margins at school before she became pregnant. Spanish remained her primary language, she was often in fights with other girls, and she did not have the academic skills to complete school. She tried to get a GED certificate, but did not pass the exam.

Javier also quit school during the first pregnancy and started working (first painting apartments and then in a warehouse), and he has worked ever since. "He works a lot," Danielle said, but he also spends time playing with and caring for their three children "from the time he gets home from work at four until he goes to sleep at eight or nine." Despite his steady work (she has never worked outside the home), they qualified for state assistance (food stamps, WIC, and Medicaid). They also received support from their mothers and Javier's sisters. At 15, Danielle was young to have a child, but the lifestyle that she and her husband embraced—working and raising a family—provided them with respectability.

With one exception, all of the youngest Puerto Rican mothers (including those of mixed heritage, Rosa and Lark) and the one Mexican mother lived in supportive, close-knit, extended families. Their families were extended horizontally and vertically, living near mothers and fathers, grandparents, mothers-in-law, aunts, uncles, sisters-in-law, and sisters. Almost all of them lived in Spanish-speaking areas of concentrated poverty in urban communities or small cities. In poorer communities, where the nuclear family is neither the real nor the ideal form, shared responsibility organized through family ties creates intergenerational kinships and the conditions for young girls to carry an unintended pregnancy to term rather than choose abortion.[23] Even when family members agreed that it would be better for the young girl to wait a few years, and even when they got angry with her for getting pregnant, they nonetheless supported the young mother.[24] In Danielle's case, her mother visited her daily: "She always brought me something and she would tell me it was for when I got cravings."

Family support, however, should not be mistaken for encouragement or a cultural norm. In a national study conducted with Latino teens and their parents, 84 percent of teens and 91 percent of their parents saw college and career as the "most important" goals for them, and three-quarters of the teens believed they should be married before they start a family. In this survey, however, only one-third of the teens thought that "being a teen parent would prevent them from reaching their goals," while almost one-half said that "being a teen parent would simply delay them from reaching their goals."[25] The survey suggests that while education and marriage are important values, an early birth is not perceived as a career-altering event.

At 15, Danielle and Javier were young to be parents, and while the larger society defines this early childbearing as deviant, even pathological, their immediate community provided support to help them raise their children. Did having a child at such an early age prevent Danielle from reaching her educational goals? We cannot answer this with certainty, but we do know that before she ever became pregnant Danielle was disengaged from school. She had a history of suspensions for fighting, and she had problems academically, in part because of the fighting, suspensions, and limited English-language skills (issues we discuss in chapter 5). She lived in a poor, insular, Spanish-speaking urban neighborhood where the majority of residents had not finished high school and met household needs with formal and informal work, government assistance, and familial support. Having children may have delayed her entrance into the low-wage labor market, but we speculate that having a baby did not likely change her trajectory. Danielle embraced a life that made sense to her within these conditions and actively worked to achieve working-class respectability by maintaining a separate apartment, raising her family (cooking and cleaning and child care), and living in a committed, cohabitating relationship with a man who had a strong work ethic.

THE WHITE RACIAL FRAME

Heather Mac Donald would most likely *not* disagree entirely with our analysis. After all, she points out in her article that Hispanics are likely to raise children in extended households and to work. She also notes that this did not decrease their need for public assistance, as Danielle's story again illustrates. Mac Donald would likely disagree, however, with our assertion that early births are not culturally normative. Citing statistics for 2003, she points out that the Mexican teen birth rate is 93 (per 1000 teens age 15 to 19), higher than black teens (65), and much higher than white (27) and Asian teens (17)—and much, much higher than teen birthrates in Japan (4), Italy (7), and France (10). Mac Donald concludes from these data that we "have a recipe for unstoppable family breakdown."[26] She focuses on Mexicans because they are the largest Hispanic immigrant group, but she paints with a broad brush, suggesting that *Hispanic* unwed teen birth rates are creating a new underclass.

Population data help to discern trends and identify demographic characteristics, but the language of statistics can be misleading and inadvertently reinforce existing stereotypes. It is not that the statistics are wrong, but how they are interpreted becomes a problem. Statistical profiles that reflect racial and class inequality are sometimes interpreted within what Joe Feagin refers to as the "white racial frame," a cognitive and emotional organization of racialized stereotypes, metaphors, dispositions, and inclinations.[27] Within this frame, the consequences of racial inequality, scientifically formulated, can nonetheless be easily attributed to the moral, cultural, and sometimes even genetic characteristics of oppressed racial groups. For instance, the statistical reality of higher teen birth rates for blacks and Hispanics might lead some to conclude that these behaviors are attributable to parental failure or cultural dysfunction within black and Hispanic communities, a point that Mac Donald goes to great length to make in her article. However, the teen birth rate she reported in 2003 for Hispanics in the United States was already dropping.[28] Mac Donald acknowledged in her article that the national teen childbearing rate had been in decline for 12 straight years, but nonetheless used this as a backdrop to interpret the higher Hispanic teen birth rate as an indication of Hispanic family breakdown and dysfunction.

The white racial frame that Mac Donald applies to her statistical profile is also evident in her reference to the Hispanic family or culture and the creation of a new Hispanic underclass. There is of course no such thing as a Hispanic culture. Hispanic is not a racial group, even though within the white racial frame it is treated as one. "Hispanic" is an umbrella term that refers to a large number of ethnic and national groups. Mac Donald focuses on Mexicans because they are the largest group in the United States, but Mexicans, Puerto Ricans, Cubans, and other Central and South American groups are quite distinct in their histories and cultures, and in their teen birth rates. For instance, in 2010, the Mexican birth rate for teens age 15 to 19 was 55 (per 1000), compared to 44 for Puerto Ricans and 24 for Cubans.[29] Any inference that is made from an analysis of one of these ethnic groups to a Hispanic culture or underclass is a "browned" red herring.

Returning our attention to young young mothers, we also can see how the white racial frame operates here. Mac Donald suggests in her article that very young childbearing is a norm in the Mexican community, a model that reflects "Third World" fertility trends and is characteristic of the mothers of young teen mothers, establishing an intergenerational cycle. Data can be presented in such a way as to reinforce these assertions. Nationally, Hispanics have higher fertility rates, as Mac Donald points out, and higher rates among young young mothers (under 15). Of course, part of the explanation for pregnancy outcomes is related to decisions regarding abortions, and Hispanics have the lowest abortion rate nationally, with around one-third under age 15 terminating their pregnancies in 2004 compared to roughly one-half of black and white teen peers.[30] Nonetheless, Hispanics and blacks have significantly higher teen birth rates than whites. Despite a precipitous decline in black and Hispanic birth rates since 1990, for teens 10 to 14, in 2010, the black birth rate was still five times higher and the Hispanic rate four times higher than that of their white peers (see table 9 in appendix B). Connecticut data yield similar patterns. Between 1998 and 2006, over one-half of mothers under age 15 in Connecticut were Hispanic, while Hispanics represented only 9 percent of the state's population in the 2000 Census (but 40 percent of Hartford's population).[31] And in 2008, 80 percent of births before age 15 were to black and Hispanic girls.[32]

Reported this way, these data reinforce arguments made by Mac Donald and others who emphasize family dysfunction, cultural pathology, or a reproductive underclass in black and brown communities. However, let's consider these same data another way.

Having a baby before the age of 15 is an extremely rare occurrence in all communities. In 2004, there were 2,827 births to black mothers under age 15 across the nation, out of around 1.75 million black girls ages 10 to 14.[33] And having a baby at that young age has become rarer in recent years. In 2010, the number of births to black mothers under 15 dropped to 1,573, and the rate of black births among this same age group has declined 80 percent since 1990 (see table 9 in appendix B). Nationally, in 2010, six-hundredths of 1 percent of Puerto Rican girls gave birth before the age of 15. Among Mexicans, the rate was eight-hundredths of 1 percent. For blacks, it was one-tenth of 1 percent.[34]

Another way to understand these statistics would be to consider these birth rates in relation to poverty rates. Based on the 2000 census, for instance, Connecticut had the highest per capita income in the country, but also some of the poorest cities, including Hartford, the second poorest city in the United States at the time. The statewide child poverty rate was 11 percent, but poverty was nearly four times that rate in Hartford (41 percent).[35] Further, the Hispanic child poverty rate was seven times and the black rate six times the rate of white child poverty in the state.[36] These differences line up with differences in teen birth rates.

Considering these high poverty rates, the births to black and brown young mothers do not look so pathological. In 2004, there were only 11 births to the 15,009 black girls ages 10 to 14 living in Connecticut, and 24 births to 17,287 Hispanic girls, far less than 1 percent for each group. In that same year, in Hartford, where more than three-quarters of the population is black or Hispanic and the child poverty rate is among the highest in the country, there were 12 children (10 Hispanic and 2 black) born to 10- to 14-year-old girls.[37] While this represents 30 percent of all births in the state to this age group, it is less than a baker's dozen.

We could, however, focus on the fact that in 2004 only one white girl in 85,861 gave birth at this age, or that between 1998 and 2006 only 8 percent of the mothers in Connecticut who gave birth before age 15 were white (n = 37), and only four of the white mothers lived in one of the four major cities.[38] Instead, we prefer to point out that (1) there is no widespread pattern or epidemic of young young births in any of these racial or ethnic groups; (2) there is no culturally deviant pattern if less than 1 percent of the group is having babies; and (3) given the conditions of poverty in which many black and brown families are parenting, the rates of births among this most vulnerable age group of girls would suggest that most parents and caregivers are *effectively* negotiating the dynamics that might lead to teen births.

The most unfortunate consequence of the white racial framing of statistical trends is that it often ends the conversation with a shake of the head and pointing of the finger at a Hispanic or black "underclass" instead of initiating a conversation about inequality and the social mechanisms of persistent poverty. For example, why is it that Javier cannot earn a living wage so that his family does not have to rely on state support? Why are Puerto Ricans concentrated in poor neighborhoods in Hartford? How is it possible that a city in the wealthiest state in the United States is annually listed as having one of the highest child poverty rates in the nation? Focusing on the 12 young young mothers in Hartford distracts us from these much larger questions that affect tens of thousands of citizens in Hartford and other similarly economically depressed areas in this country.

* * * * *

We turn now to the third distracting discourse surrounding births to the youngest teens. In addition to narratives about poor parenting and hypersexualized Latinas, a third explanation is predatory men. Here again we walk a tightrope as partial truths get converted into a blinding thesis with deep moral overtones that distracts us from more serious systemic issues of gender, class, and racial inequality.

MALE PREDATION AND STATUTORY RAPE

> Virtually no one endorses statutory rape laws without some hesitation or qualification. At the same time, however, virtually no one recommends abolishing the crime of statutory rape outright.
>
> —Legal scholar Michelle Oberman[39]

Statutory rape laws, which today are gender neutral, vary by state and usually include two components: the age of the victim (age of consent) and the age discrepancy between the victim and the perpetrator (age span).[40] The age of consent ranges from 14 to 19, but two-thirds of states have 16 as the legal age of consent (including Connecticut), meaning that a victim of statutory rape must be younger than 16.[41] In addition, 43 states have age-span provisions ranging from two to six years with three to four years being the most common, and five years being seen as the most reasonable by legal scholars.[42]

In the life stories, 11 of the 21 mothers women who gave birth before age 16 had partners who violated statutory rape laws in Connecticut. At the time we collected the life stories, statutory rape was defined as second-degree sexual assault when the perpetrator was at least two years older than a victim between ages 13 and 15.[43] If convicted of statutory rape, the minimum sentence was nine months with mandatory inclusion in a sex offenders' registry. If the victim was younger than 13, the charge could be upgraded from a misdemeanor to a felony and the perpetrator could be imprisoned for up to 10 years.[44]

It was not until the 1990s that statutory rape became defined as part of the problem of unwed teen births.[45] It bubbled to the attention of policy-makers for fiscal reasons. Starting with the assumption that teen mothers use more state assistance over a lifetime than nonteen mothers, officials made sweeping changes to harshen statutory rape laws. The 1996 Personal Responsibility and Work Opportunity Reconciliation Act (also known as the Welfare Reform Act) mandated that states and local jurisdictions "aggressively enforce statutory rape laws," and the Justice Department was given $6 million to research the "linkage between statutory rape and teenage pregnancy, particularly by predatory older men committing repeat offenses."[46]

Following this legislation, some states revised their statutory rape laws; others took efforts to enforce existent laws. Revisions included raising the age of consent, designating mandated reporters, conducting public relations campaigns to raise awareness, and making penalties harsher.[47] Laws already on the books included "fornication statutes" (laws banning sex between unmarried people), which were selectively enforced for teenagers because, as one Idaho prosecutor argued, "children having children imposes a heavy burden on society."[48] Other states required mandatory reporting of statutory rape law violations when the teenager became pregnant.[49] In Connecticut, Senator Lieberman suggested that in order to receive Medicaid, women had to identify the father, which would effectively identify offenders.[50]

The get-tough-on-men program in Connecticut was kicked off with a $250,000, two-prong advertising and education campaign. The first included billboards in the minority-populated cities of Hartford and New

Haven picturing a silhouette of a man behind bars and the slogan "Rob the cradle and get yourself a brand new crib." The second included posters in schools and community centers with the message: "He's not just breaking your heart. He's breaking the law." These graphic portrayals matched the hard-hitting language of Governor John Rowland, who made it clear that "statutory rape is a felony with guaranteed prison time."[51]

It bears repeating that the motivation for these get-tough campaigns was to lower welfare and health expenditures.[52] Senator Lieberman argued that "by focusing on the problems of teen pregnancy and statutory rape . . . we are economizing our future welfare expenditures and improving the lives of poor children."[53] He noted that a "remarkable percentage of babies born to teenage mothers have been fathered by men who are considerably older" and the only thing "Washington" can do about this is to "encourage" state attorneys "to be very aggressive in working with welfare authorities to once again take statutory rape as a serious crime and to prosecute it, understanding that this is *done to deter adult men from committing a sexual act that will result in a child born to poverty.*"[54]

The 1996 welfare reform legislation connected the breakdown of the two-parent family to burgeoning welfare expenditures, and teen mothers were easy culprits because the vast majority were unmarried and used more welfare over the course of their lifetimes. Policies that aimed at lowering teen births and welfare expenditures had a one-two moral-fiscal punch that appealed to both Democrats and Republicans.[55] Eva Clayton (D-NC) said that preventing teen pregnancy will "save us money in the long run" and Rick Santorum (R-PA) stated that teens should "not be getting more money for having more children out-of-wedlock."[56] The knockout punch was the legislation that incriminated men: "An effective strategy to combat teenage pregnancy must address the issue of male responsibility, including statutory rape culpability and prevention. The increase of teenage pregnancies among the youngest girls is particularly severe and is linked to predatory practices by men who are significantly older."[57] As Carolyn Cocca bluntly states in *Jailbait,* this legislation is based on the assumption that "statutory rape leads directly to teen pregnancy, it is caused by predatory sexual criminals, and it costs a lot of money."[58] It was a brilliant narrative: lock up slimy men, lower immoral teen births, and reduce unwanted welfare spending.

This narrative was supported with "scientific data" such as (A) "in the late 1980s, the rate for girls age 14 and under giving birth increased

TABLE 2   BIRTHS BY AGE GROUPS, 1975–2010

	1975	1980	1985	1990	1995	2000	2005	2010
10–14	12,642	10,169	10,220	11,657	12,242	8,519	6,722	4,497
15–17	227,270	167,789	165,630	183,327	192,508	157,209	133,191	109,173
18–19	354,968	353,939	299,696	338,499	307,365	311,781	281,402	258,505

Sources: Kost, Henshaw, Carlin 2010, tables 2.2, 2.3, 2.4; Martin et al. 2012, table 2.

26 percent"; (B) "almost 70 percent of births to teenage girls are fathered by men over age 20"; and (C) "a majority of such mothers have histories of sexual and physical abuse, primarily with older men."[59] The evidence, however, was flimsy and built on dubious statistical formulations. Between 1975 and 1995, there were both increases *and* decreases in the number of births for girls 10 to 14. When reported as a percentage, these changes may look large, but the numbers were small to begin with, so a 26 percent rate increase in the late 1980s amounted to less than 1,500 births—hardly the numbers necessary to bust welfare expenditure. (See table 2.) Legislation seeking to lower welfare expenditures by lowering the number of births to teens under 15 was farcical.

The second point—that two-thirds of children born to teen mothers were fathered by men older than 20—relies on data highlighted in the 1994 Alan Guttmacher Institute (AGI) report *Sex and America's Teenager* that echoed through both chambers of Congress but has since been soundly critiqued.[60] First, two-thirds of teen births are to mothers who are 18 and 19, so a father over 20 is not unusual. Second, Laura Duberstein Lindberg and her colleagues at the Urban Institute took a closer look at the research reported in the AGI report and calculated that only 8 percent of teens age 15 to 19 had babies by men who could have been prosecuted for statutory rape, concluding that "the enforcement of statutory rape laws won't be the magic bullet for eliminating teenage pregnancy."[61] Moreover, the number of teen mothers who have babies fathered by men older than 20 was declining (with a corresponding rise in the number fathered by teens).[62]

Congressional members ignored these critiques and trends as they pushed through the welfare reform legislation.[63] Michael Males, one of the authors of a study (mis)used by policy-makers to bolster the "get tough on male predators" argument, was outraged by these shenanigans and spoke out saying: "I would like to take the press and horsewhip them for the way they let politicians take the numbers and hype them."[64]

And hype them they did, as many elected leaders took on the role of both moral entrepreneur by expressing concern for innocent girls and fiscal conservative by proposing to lower welfare expenditures.[65]

The third point made in the legislation concerns the large number of teen mothers with histories of sexual and physical abuse. We strongly agree that this is an important issue, and we address child sexual abuse and gender violence directly in the following chapters. While this concern for young women is laudable—and a key reason why most people believe there should be laws to protect girls from sexual predators—we again remind readers that these enhanced statutory rape laws were part of a national debate on welfare reform. They were not part of a national discussion on violence against women. Nonetheless, they helped shift the discourse on teen mothers from "demonization ('the welfare queen') to victimization ('the exploited teen')."[66] In this logic, the "predatory male" became "public enemy number one."[67]

Shifting the Blame

If, as the data suggest, this legislation was not an efficient, effective, or rational strategy for lowering welfare expenditures, why was it articulated this way? Reducing welfare costs has been a key initiative among lawmakers since the mid-1970s, and focusing on fathers, child support, and unwed teen mothers has only increased in intensity since that time. It is difficult, however, to distinguish the preoccupation with governmental costs from the moralistic discourse that blames many of America's problems on early unwed motherhood and predatory men and, as the billboards placed in minority communities suggest, that locates this problem in poor minority communities. This formulation associates the problem of teen motherhood with an urban underclass, impugns black and brown men as oversexed predators, and plays well among voters who believe their flatlined wages were being wasted on supporting immoral childbearing practices and irresponsible fathers. Lowering the costs of welfare may have been part of the motivation, but narratives of blame and shame placed politicians like Joe Lieberman in the limelight, where he could brandish a moral identity that appealed to both sides of the aisle in Washington. This moral trump card was used at the local level as well. Ramon Rojana, Hartford's city health director, argued in 2004 that they needed to "enforce statutory rape laws" because there are "a lot of males preying on young girls."[68]

When campaigns whip up policy built on public fears rather than empirical reality, the result is often misguided laws and discriminatory enforcement.[69] Like crack cocaine laws, the consequences of these morality-fueled statutory rape laws came down harshest on the shoulders of the poor.[70] When statutory rape laws are enacted to lower teen births and subsequent welfare usage, it is de facto applied more often against the poor who apply for state assistance.[71] Further, when health care providers and state workers are mandated reporters, neither the parent nor the minor has to be involved for the state to bring charges.[72] Not only are poor women more likely to come to the attention of state authorities when they get pregnant, but prosecutors often see them as a part of the overproducing, undesirable reproductive underclass.[73]

Middle-class men are less likely to be charged with statutory rape because middle-class girls are more likely to use contraception and to abort, eliminating telltale signs of statutory rape.[74] They are also less likely to have mandated reporters like social workers and probation officers in their lives, allowing them to keep their behavior hidden from the eyes of the state. Furthermore, it is at the discretion of the local prosecutor to decide who is charged.[75] Evidence suggests that prosecution is more likely when the girl is perceived as coming from a "good home," and perceptions of "good homes" are influenced by race and class.[76]

Clear cases of predation often involve a status distinction (for example, teacher and student, doctor and patient, probation officer and juvenile offender) as well as an age difference. With teen mothers, however, there is not usually a status distinction, only an age difference, and even then, the majority of offenders prosecuted are not older men, but teenagers.[77]

Age alone is not a good indicator of predation for teen mothers, especially because most partners are less than five years older.[78] Moreover, studies have found that older partners are more likely than same-age partners to be cohabiting with or married to young mothers, and they are more likely to be better emotional and financial providers.[79] The point is, age differences alone do not constitute predation—older partners are not all predators exploiting innocent girls. In many cases, the teen mother does not want her partner charged because she does not see him as a predator but a partner. Even social service providers are reluctant to pursue statutory rape charges because of the potential damage it brings to the father-child relationship.[80]

In our own study, in seven of the 11 statutory rape cases, the teen mother described being in a close relationship with the older partner. These mothers (and their families) did not define the sexual act as rape or exploitation, and expressed no desire to prosecute the fathers. In fact, it was usually the opposite—they needed the fathers for support. And they needed to protect them from state agencies that wanted to fine them or send them to jail.

Violence and Victimization: Why Statutory Rape Laws Are Important

While the numbers are small and have a negligible impact on welfare expenditures, the exploitation of young girls is nonetheless deplorable. Studies have found that for most girls who have sex before age 15, the sex was not voluntary; in one study, three-quarters of the girls said they had sexual intercourse that was not voluntary.[81] Young teens also have more unhealthy relationships with older men, more difficulty negotiating safe sex, and more negative consequences as a result of these relationships, including suicide, substance abuse, and pregnancy.[82] Studies have also found that young girls who partner with older men (five years or more) often have other forms of gendered violence in their life histories such as partner violence and child sexual abuse.[83]

In several of the life stories, we saw how early exposure to violence was entangled with statutory rape. Of the 11 girls in our study whose child was the result of statutory rape, six of them had been sexually abused as children. In Carla's story, the child sexual abuse and statutory rape co-occurred. When Carla became pregnant at age 14, her 19-year-old boyfriend was arrested for statutory rape. When the paternity test came back negative, she said, "the detective asked me if I know who it was and I told him" about her mother's boyfriend, who had been raping her regularly since she was eight years old. We take up the issue of child sexual abuse and early childbirth in the next chapter.

For the remainder of this chapter, we want to argue that the problem with statutory rape laws is the problem of adjudication without social change. Adjudication is itself difficult because of the complicated issues regarding consent and predation that make the scope of statutory rape laws too wide (thereby circumscribing sexual freedom and penalizing sexual behavior) and yet not wide enough (because they do not, and cannot, address more insidious forms of predation that arise from systemic gender inequality). Placing the burden on the courts to address what are much larger issues of gender inequality leads to criminalizing the issue, often selectively and discriminatorily, without adequately addressing the source of the problem.

Complicating Stories of Consent and Predation

Michelle Oberman writes that statutory rape laws are both "protective and unquestionably legitimate" as well as "patriarchal and undeniably pernicious."[84] These laws can both restrict freedoms and fail to protect girls because the one-size-fits-all legal definitions of consent and predation are based on chronological years, while the practice of consent and predation is more complex. The practice (or sex) takes place on a field of gender inequality that makes it difficult to codify predation and consent into law because, as Kate Sutherland notes, the definition of consensual sex can "allow for considerable violence and coercion."[85]

Legal scholar Jennifer Drobac argues that in order to give consent a person must "have the cognitive ability to reason about the choice" and thus "ignorant cooperation does not indicate consent."[86] Who determines cognitive ability? With age of consent laws, the state does; with interpretation of consent, the courts do. And yet, children move through adolescence at varying speeds, and consequently not all teens below a certain age lack the "cognitive ability" to give consent.[87] This is where statutory rape laws can be pernicious. The misappropriation of the law can arguably occur in cases of mature (but underage) girls. In our study this was evident in the relationship between Maggie and her partner Jimmy (whom we also interviewed).

Despite the six-year age difference, Jimmy looked and acted younger than Maggie, who described how she manipulated both her mother and Jimmy at the beginning of the relationship.

> When I got involved with him he was 20, but he didn't know I was 14. I've always looked older and always been more mature, so I told him I was 17, and I told my mom that he was 17. So, meanwhile, he doesn't know that I'm 14 and my mom doesn't know that he's 20 and we're seeing each other for six months. And then the truth came out 'cuz my birthday came up and he thought I was turning 18. But by then we'd already been going out for six months. I lost my virginity to him and he's the only person I've ever had sex with.

In this context, it seems absurd to criminalize Jimmy's behavior, and no one did. Maggie's mother did not bring charges, state monitors (mandated reporters) were not involved in their lives, and the sign of sexual intercourse (the pregnancy) did not appear until she was 16. Further, they are both white, so there was no racial transgression as in the case of Susan, whose story we tell later.

The conundrum is establishing the line between protection and punishment, between a person's right to choose when to have sex and the ethical drive to protect the vulnerable. Statutory rape laws don't just protect young people from older predators; they also take away young adults' right to decide.[88] Legal scholars Sharon Elstein and Noy Davis suggest one solution is for cases to be adjudicated not on age (or age span) alone, but on "the maturity level of the girl and the man (i.e., their emotional rather than chronological ages); whether prosecution is in the best interest of the girl and/or their offspring; and whether the male has engaged in these relationships serially."[89]

On the one hand, Elstein and Davis make a persuasive argument: without a case-by-case consideration, statutory rape laws become the long arm of paternalism that denies mature girls the power to decide when to have sex and with whom. On the other hand, a case-by-case solution gives the courts a lot of power to interpret cases with jurors who may have sexist and racist views. Regarding gender, evidence suggests that jurors do not like these cases because they often do not see the man as "at fault" and they have a problem criminalizing what they define as normal teenage sexual relations.[90] Oberman argues that courts can reflect the cultural double standards regarding sexual behavior, where girls are still defined as "loose" in many courtrooms and where "non-virgin girls do not need or merit protection of statutory rape laws."[91] As for race, jurors may have racialized images of predatory men, who, as we have seen, have been the target of public campaigns (in black and Latino neighborhoods) to reduce welfare costs.

Despite the reluctance jurors have toward these cases and the persistent gender double standards, one study found that when a case came to trial, jurors convicted men in three-quarters of the cases and treated those convicted as sexual offenders (recommending treatment as well as registration as a sexual offender).[92] Men prosecuted are more likely to be racial minorities, even though studies have found that the age differences between teen mothers and their partners are similar across race.[93] Some legal scholars have suggested these laws unfairly prosecute Latino men, whose culture is presumed to condone "relationships between girls and older men."[94] Others argue that these laws target poor minority women, who are more likely to come to the attention of the state when they carry their pregnancies to term.[95] In order to bring about a charge of statutory rape, it first has to be known to authorities (or parents), and a minor has no reason to prosecute if they believe they are in a consenting relationship. In these instances, parents can bring the case to court but teens often refuse to testify against their partners.[96] It is easier to prosecute when there is evidence, such as a pregnancy or baby, or when the district attorney brings the case based upon state mandated reporters.[97]

Still others point out that the laws are most likely to be applied when the sexual relationship deviates from racial or age norms. When two white, heterosexual, middle-class teenagers who minimally violate the age span have sexual intercourse, they are not likely to be prosecuted.[98] But when there is an age or racial mismatch—a 14-year-old girl and a 25-year-old man, or a white girl and a brown or black boy—the risk for prosecution increases. Of course, public campaigns that associate statutory rape with contributing to higher welfare expenditures and place their billboards in poor black and Spanish-speaking neighborhoods can get into the consciousness of judges and jurors.[99]

In our study, of the 11 cases of statutory rape, five perpetrators had been charged or were under investigation. In three of the cases under investigation, the male was much older, in his late 20s or 30s. The fourth case involved two Puerto Rican teens—she was 14 and he was 17—and the charge was brought when her family applied for state assistance and she was required to name the father (he was living in another state at the time of the interview to evade the charges and the young mother planned to join him). The fifth case was that of Susan and Gabe, the only one that had been prosecuted by the time of the interview. Gabe was a 17-year-old, dark-skinned Puerto Rican from Hartford and Susan was a white 12-year-old who lived in a small city 20 minutes away. She said that the day she gave birth to Jeremy was the last time she saw Gabe:

> They arrested him the very next day—locked him up for statutory rape. He has two years. I've talked to him when I'm over his mom's house and he calls or he'll write me a letter and I'll write him a letter. [His mom] takes Jeremy to see him in prison because I am not allowed to. Not until I turn 16.

Susan did not portray herself as a victim. She narrated her story with a defiant persona as she described being on probation for "running away and fighting," but also with a school girl's pout that Gabe spent more time playing video games with her brother than with her. "I'm like, okaaaay, I'm supposed to be your girlfriend but you're spending time with my brother [laughs]." She did not describe Gabe as an older man, but instead as a teenager who wrestled with her brother in the family living room and went to concerts with her. Susan did not report that she was coerced into her sexual initiation or that she would have preferred that it had not happened. While the state defined Gabe's behavior as criminal, she did not.

Susan attended all of Gabe's court appearances and complained about the public defender's poor preparation for the trial and the state's role in his arrest. The Connecticut child protective agency had been involved with her family since Susan was three, when her mother voluntarily surrendered the children to the state. Susan had a close relationship with her family's social worker—in fact, she was the godmother of her child—but she was also the person who was required, by the state, to report the liaison, that is, the statutory rape.

In sum, the problems created by statutory rape laws reflect the complexities concerning the sexual behavior of young girls. On the one hand, we want to protect girls from exploitation; on the other, we do not want to deny girls the freedom of sexual expression. A law based on chronological age alone does not work. Efforts to criminalize the problem, as necessary as that may be, will have only limited effects without broader initiatives that address the core problem. What makes adolescent girls vulnerable to statutory rape is the organization of gender inequality, in others words, patriarchy. Moreover, the criminalization of the problem leaves the selection, prosecution, and judgment to an institution that is integral to the organization of the racial order in the United States. Perceptions of "the problem" are viewed—consciously and unconsciously—through a socially constructed racial lens that is consistent with the framing of the problem of teen motherhood. More effective strategies would address the larger issue of male sexual entitlement, which is hardly a matter reserved for low-income groups. We need to think about how to bring about social change and not just behavioral change.

The Problems of Adjudication without Social Change

Statutory rape laws can have the unintended consequence of attenuating male predation that occurs outside the defining parameters of the law. For instance, instead of being charged with the more serious crime of rape, predators could be charged with the misdemeanor of statutory rape. Cocca argues that statutory rape laws leave many teenagers "open to coercion that is not recognized as meeting the legal definitions of forcible rape"—for example, girls who were drinking.[100] In our study, Celina tells us about a relationship with an older "cool" drug dealer in the neighborhood when she was 15: "All the girls used to go crazy over him and he had eyes on me. I was all happy and stupid. I feel like an idiot now. So stupid." She admits she consented but argues in hindsight, "He was 26. That is rape!" According to the law, it was statutory rape.[101]

Moreover, coercion can and does exist between same-age peers.[102] Luanne tells us how she was a victim of a high school contest among boys to see who could "score" with the most girls (and pricking holes in the condoms was part of the prank). The boy's behavior was predatory but not prosecutable under the statute. Though she was 14 when she became pregnant, he was under the age of 16.

Statutory rape laws cannot address the gendered context of sexual negotiation. Male predation is an extreme version of a sexual ritual that is a performance of masculinity and femininity. Performances of collective masculinity illustrate the underlying scripts that encourage, sanction, and validate male domination of and entitlement to female bodies. Luanne's story exemplifies this when the boys at her school turned sex into a competitive game of "scoring." But Luanne's story of predation is not unique. There are similar cases across all regions of the United States, in urban, suburban, and rural communities. In one well-publicized case in a California suburb, a group of roughly two dozen boys, mostly white, who referred to themselves as the Spur Posse, created a game to see who could have sex with the most girls—it did not matter whether the girls consented or not, if they "scored" the boys received a point.[103]

There are many other examples of collective masculine performances that occur in male-dominated institutional spaces, such as the military, fraternities, and athletic teams.[104] And of course, if we broaden our scope even larger, we see that the organization of power within institutions can lead to sexual predation that is shaped by positions of domination and subordination and an associated sense of entitlement and impunity. For example, Cordelia told us how her corrections officer assaulted her when she was 14. She described walking to her cell with her hands cuffed behind her back, when the correction officer "put his penis in my [hands]."

> I was like, What the fuck! I told him, "Take it away from me 'cuz I'm gonna hurt you!" He didn't listen! He kept going like this, like I wasn't gonna do nothing! I swear to God! I squeezed it really hard with both my hands, yo! [laugh] Like this, just my nails was on his like this, real hard! "I told you not to do it because I'm not gonna get down with you like that." Yo, I got a year-and-a-half more to do [in the correction facility]. I told the counselor. Nobody helped me. Can you believe nobody helped me on that? Never, never, never helped me. He's probably doing it to other girls right now, you know what I'm saying. It's like a cult, you know, a cult!

Did she mean a cult of masculine domination? And did her repetition of the word "never" refer to the silence that surrounds these abusive behaviors which allows men to continue to hurt, humiliate, and violate women? Stories like Cordelia's point to a problem much larger than the narrow application of statutory rape laws suggests, and often they have been met with institutional silence or cover-up that serves to keep our gaze misfocused on poor minority communities.[105]

The other side of sexual negotiation and the performances of masculinity and femininity invokes female agency, or perhaps the concern with female complicity in their victimization. Many girls "voluntarily" participate in their first sexual experience even though they feel "ambivalent" or "negative" about their participation.[106] If we return to the California Spur Posse, only one of the eight boys was prosecuted because, for all the others, the district attorney defined the sex as "consensual."[107] Curious reporters—rather than the prosecutors—asked the boys how they managed to lure so many girls into having sex with them. "The boys responded that they were particularly good at an activity they called 'hooking'— their name for the practice of attracting girls through flattery. The boys described their 'hooking' techniques as consisting of approaching a girl and telling her something along the lines of the following: 'Oh—I'm in love,' or 'Let's just cuddle,' or 'Want to go for a walk?'"[108] This "game" can be played because we live in a society where women gain status in relationships with men, and men gain status from having sex with women. Teen boys receive the message that they are expected to have sex and girls receive the message that they are supposed to look sexy and attract boys.[109] These messages create the script for Luanne's pregnancy or the girls preyed upon by boy posses around the United States.

Statutory rape laws cannot address these forms of predation that are less visible and that are embedded in systems of gender inequality that overvalue men and undervalue women.[110] Michelle Oberman goes as far as to question whether "consensual sex" can even exist in a "society premised upon the sexual, social, and economic subordination of women." She writes: "Modern statutory rape laws lose sight of the considerable coercion, violence, and ambivalence in 'consensual' teen sex. Even between age-mates in a situation of apparent social equality, power may be too vastly imbalanced that evidence of verbal consent does not reveal the true nature of a teenage sexual encounter."[111] Consent must be considered within the context that, for women, "from the time they were infants, the entire force of the universe is bent upon insuring that they partner with men."[112]

Typically, the way in which these issues get addressed is to focus on the self-esteem of girls.[113] Low self-esteem is considered a salient feature in why girls say yes when they mean no, or why they assent or acquiesce to having sex when they do not want to have it. Carol Gilligan and other experts on the psychosocial development of adolescent girls show the mechanisms by which society shapes self-confidence, body image, and assertiveness during adolescence.[114] High self-esteem may decrease the likelihood that she will succumb to coerced sexual relations; however, reducing gender inequality to psychological characteristics redirects our gaze from gender hierarchies that shape choices. Oberman argues that any "girl who wants males to find her attractive, who wants acceptance and popularity, might reasonably consent to sex with a popular boy, with multiple popular boys, or with any partner who can persuade her that she is attractive and desirable."[115] The situational dynamics of male entitlement and virility and female attractiveness and validation get played out in adolescent sexual relationships, but these dynamics are rooted in societal definitions and cultural practices of masculinity and femininity and in the imbalance of power between men and women.

The general cultural framework that increases female vulnerability to sexual victimization is even more apparent when life circumstances disrupt normally protective structures. For instance, in several life stories, girls escaping male violence and predation in their homes became homeless, which put them at much greater risk to male predation when they became sex workers or part of the drug economy in order to support themselves. Lilly was a young mother whose life choices were shaped by both gender violence and poverty. An "older boy in the neighborhood," in the presence of others who stood by and did not help, raped Lilly when she was 10. After the rape she began "going crazy," attempted suicide, and spent the next few years in and out of institutions. It was in this vulnerable condition that, at age 15, she began having sexual relations with 23-year-old Rafael (although she did not have her first child until she was 16). During her second pregnancy with Rafael, he beat her so violently she was taken to the hospital. He was arrested but Lilly dropped the charges and her mother posted a $5000 bond to get him released (which he paid back). Despite the age difference and the abuse, Lilly described Rafael as a provider, not a predator. When he was around (he often traveled to the Dominican Republic, where he had other children), he gave her "$1000 a month." She also said he bought the children bedroom furniture, clothing, "whatever they need all I gotta do is call him. He take care of his kids." By this, she meant "all" of his children, those he fathered with her as well as with other women.

Both gender violence and poverty are integral to understanding Lilly's story. While the early sexual abuse may have disposed her to partnering with an older man (a point we develop more fully in the following chapter), her poverty deepened her vulnerability and kept her dependent on this violent man.[116] While linked to child sexual abuse and poverty, her story is framed by male entitlement and female subordination.

Finally, racial hierarchies deepen female vulnerability. When beauty gets constructed within a racist system that favors white physical features, the objectification of black women at the bottom of the hierarchy can increase predation and impede sexual negotiation. Shades of skin color get folded into the meaning-making processes of status, vulnerability, and acquiescence. This is evident in Luanne's description of the value of her appearance when she says her stepfather doesn't like her because she has her father's African American features—dark skin, curly hair. Luanne would probably be marked on a survey as having "low self-esteem," but her understanding of herself is derived from a racial hierarchy that values blue eyes, blonde hair, and light skin, and a gender context that leads her to believe she will be popular and attractive if she has a boyfriend. She succumbed to the advances of Johnnie when she was a freshman in a new larger school, a transitional year that creates uncertainty and self-doubt for many adolescents as they navigate new friendship networks, elevated academic expectations, and unfamiliar serpentine hallways.

When consent and predation are understood in the larger contexts of racism, poverty, and patriarchy, we see how statutory rape laws can both overreach and underreach in their goal of protecting innocent children from sexual predators. Statutory rape cases are often difficult to discern, interpret, and adjudicate. Moreover, while better judicial discretion and oversight may indeed be needed to mitigate the varying circumstances of these cases, judicial discretion has often failed poor men and men of color in courtrooms. When we combine the limited effectiveness of statutory rape laws in lowering adolescent sexual activity and the narrow scope of predation as defined strictly by age differences, with harsh penal consequences like imprisonment and registry as sexual offenders, we see that these laws have done little more than put a poor minority male population at risk while doing little to lower the vulnerability of girls.[117] When there is social injustice, as there is in our society where women are devalued and vulnerable to male predation, attempts to correct the problem must include both social change and legal change. Courts punish behavior; they do not change social conditions.

CONCLUSION

In this chapter we focused on the youngest teen mothers—the most vulnerable and, in many instances, the true "kids having kids." While public concern for these mothers and their children is important, this group of mothers is numerically small—and yet, they have become iconic. In the course of writing this book, we met public defenders, elementary school teachers, social workers, neighbors, and colleagues who told us about some personal experience with a young 14-year-old black or brown mother, whom they described as a stand-in for a culture (Latino, ghetto) and the entire population of teen mothers. It is worth repeating: six in 10,000 Puerto Rican girls, eight in 10,000 Mexican girls, and 10 in 10,000 black girls ages 10 to 14 gave birth in 2010 in the United States. And not only is this group small, it is getting smaller.

The myths we attempted to debunk in this chapter are that parents, Hispanic culture, and predatory men are "the problem." In doing so, we do not suggest that the parents of the teen mothers in our study are not part of the picture, but that the picture is more complex and worthy of a serious discussion that does not get whittled down to good and bad parents. Parenting is done within a milieu that defines options and evaluates behavior. For instance, families with few resources (material or social) may require long work hours or evening and weekend shifts that result in children being left without supervision for extended periods of time. Further, parents raising children in unsafe neighborhoods and immigrants raising children in unfamiliar cultures may try to protect their children by restricting their activities and friendships outside the home. In turn, this may backfire when children enter adolescence and seek autonomy from their parents through rebellion.[118] Similarly, understanding high birth rates among some Latino groups requires that we avoid a discourse of blame that feeds stereotypes and exploits fears, and that we do not make up terms like "Hispanic culture." Instead, it behooves us to document and evaluate trends accurately and to explore how a community can support early childbirths even though it does not promote them.[119]

The blame-men theories are most often invoked in discussions of the youngest teen mothers. It is easy to become morally outraged over cases of male predation where a much older man takes advantage of youthful innocence. These atrocities, however, can create moral panics that lead to misinformation, distortions, and misguided laws.[120] In the debates leading up to the 1996 PRWORA legislation, Eva Clayton argued passionately for a society that cared for its children, outlining the need for Food Stamps, Title I educational funds, and even a livable wage, but she used this as a preamble to advocate for "enforcing States' statutory rape laws" to break the "intergenerational cycle" of teenage pregnancy and poverty.[121] As we have shown in this chapter, these claims were based on misrepresented data, and while they would not have made a dent in welfare spending, they did reinforce a narrative snowballing in the 1980s and 1990s that demonized the so-called black and brown underclass. Moreover, these campaign strategies played well at the polls and shaped the careers of political moral entrepreneurs like Senator Joe Lieberman in Connecticut. District attorneys were encouraged to more aggressively enforce statutory rape laws, while mandatory reporting requirements increased scrutiny, most often in poor racial minority communities. Ironically, the application of these laws sometimes led to less father involvement, to fewer family resources, and even to the breakdown of the family. As Richard Delgado asserted, "statutory rape laws are one of the worst ideas that the family-values crowd has produced in years."[122]

What is unfortunate about these developments is that they have turned a very important issue—the exploitation of young girls—into yet another instrument for criminalizing black and brown young men, restricting the sexual freedom of young women, and cutting funding to the poor. Rather than blaming parents, Hispanic culture, or men, we think our attention should be focused on such things as unsafe neighborhoods, high rates of urban poverty, and systemic gender inequality that robs women of their ability to say no at any stage of the sex dance and makes them willing to barter their bodies for social status. In other words, adjudication efforts will not work unless they occur within a broader initiative for social change. As Valerie Small Navarro, at the American Civil Liberties Union in California, points out, we need to be "willing to invest time and money in women, not incarcerate men."[123] But unfortunately, as Mary Margaret Wilson, with the New York Council on Adolescent Pregnancy, explains, "People don't want to look at bigger things like poverty and racism."[124] And, we would add, patriarchy.

CHAPTER 3

Child Sexual Abuse

ALISHA: "I'M OLDER THAN DIRT INSIDE"

Alisha was a 19-year-old African American mother of a three-year-old son, Gareth, and the victim of physical and sexual child abuse and multiple rapes. She linked the violence that permeated her narrative to subsequent suicide attempts and poor mental health. She grew up in a large extended family, but her mother and father were mentally and physically absent for long stretches of time because of addictions and incarceration. As the title of her story suggests, she felt that the social trauma of poverty, sexual abuse, and other personal tragedies had aged her prematurely. Scarred by violence, she didn't expect to live past the age of 23.

My grandmother, my grandfather, my mother, my sister, my aunts, and my uncles lived in one big house. My mother lived on the third floor. My grandmother was on the second floor and she just loved me. She just took care of me. My mother has eight kids, and my father has four of us. When I was born he was in jail. When I was six, he was in jail. I first met him when I was like 10, he'd just got out of jail. He's in jail now [because he] shot his girlfriend in the butt. He's a jerk.

My father was a crackhead. My mother was a crackhead. I remember it looked like a light bulb in her mouth. I asked her, "Ma, how do you light that light bulb with your mouth?" Then she finally told me that that was a crack pipe. I don't want to talk about her. Her husband raped me. *That's why he's in jail now. And she's upstairs sleeping so we're just gonna leave it at that. She's been clean 14 years [now]. She's a good grandmother.*

My sister's father used to beat me and my mother. I got a big mouth. I talk a lot of junk so I'd get beat up for it. Hit me with belts, bats, shoes, hangers. Punch me, slap me. He hit me in the head with something so hard the [Department of Children and Families (DCF)] report says, "the impact was as if she was thrown out of a second floor window." I [was] four or five, I don't know. Nobody going to talk about it, so I don't know the whole story.

I was raped a couple weeks after I turned 15. I never told. I was always scared. I didn't know who he was. I knew the house but, I don't know, that was my first time. I was coming home from a party. This old guy in the window started talking to me, "Come up here." And I'm like, "No, what's the matter with you?" He just pulled me in the house. I was scared. I said, "No," and I cried and I fought him but, at the same time, I was like, "This is supposed to hurt. How comes it doesn't hurt?" He was old, in his fifties he looked like. That's why I like older guys.

He choked me and smacked me up a couple of times. Asked me if I wanted some drugs. "Nothing," I said, "No, I just want to go home." And then he let me go. I went to my teacher's house but I was too embarrassed so then I went to the pay phone, like three o'clock in the morning, I kept hanging up on her. Then there was a shootout at the pay phone and I just stood there while they were shooting. I wanted to get shot. I was like, "Just shoot me." Then I just went home, stripped, and went to bed.

The next day I told my teacher. She told me that it happened to her when she was younger, so we kind of clicked there and we're still friends to this day. I told my friend who is a cop and he just happened to be a snitch, and he told my mother—and it went from my mother to my grand-mother, and my grandmother told my grandfather, my grandfather told my aunt, my aunt told my sister. And then everybody said I had AIDS. So, after that, I found out you just don't tell your family your business.

I ended up having to go to the hospital and stuff. I never told who he was. When I went to the hospital, they gave me this big fat man [the therapist] and he touched my leg. You don't do that. If somebody's got raped, you don't give them a guy therapist and the guy don't come up in your face touching on your stuff. I'd feel be violating all over again.

That's when I first started mutilating. Burning and cutting. They figured if I went to a therapist I would stop. He diagnosed over two pages worth of mental illnesses. I don't believe I have them. Post Traumatic Stress—that's going to come with the lifestyle I have, so I claim that one—but you know that Borderline Personality junk, they just be throwing stuff out of their mouths.

Everybody in their own way mutilates their self. It's self-mutilation whether you smoke cigarettes or you comb your hair where it's extremely nappy and it's hurting your head, or you overeat. It's all self-mutilation, you know. I met one good doctor who thinks this is almost a way of therapy. It's not one of the normalest things to do, but he's not going to call me crazy and admit me for it because he understands it.

I like pain. You can't do anything that really will hurt me. I can get smacked, punched in the head, somewhere—but it's not going to hurt. It's going to just be like "ouch" for a minute, brush it off, and I'll be better. 'Cause I didn't get beat up like normal kids, like with a little switch, pop on a leg. We got beaten with household appliances; my father beat me with everything that he could find in the room.

* * * * *

When I met Samuel, I was 15, he was 38. I like them older; boys my age disgust me. He grew up with my father and he had a crush on my aunt when they were kids. I told him I was 23. I told him I was a social worker at the Middle School and he believed me. He's my first boyfriend.

Then Samuel and I became intimate. He would smack me but I don't care because he's like a little girl. That's what I tell him to his face, "You're like a woman. My mother hit me harder than that." The first time he ever hit me, I just started to cry. I couldn't believe he did it, and then I just started laughing and that scared him. That scares anybody.

Then Samuel left town and this African guy raped me. This was at the store around the corner. He liked my friend 'cause she looked African. He asked me to come into the store and call her. So I called her and once he seen she wasn't coming he just locked the store down. And he did it there. He walked. His brother had just died and he was leaving the country, going back home.

I was just going into my tenth-grade year. I got sick for like three months. I called my doctor and I was like, "We got to talk 'cause I'm kind of pregnant." She tried talking me into an abortion. I was like, "I don't believe in those."

I got scared so the hook was tell Samuel that Gareth was his. So I told him and he was like, "Okay, we can deal with this," thinking that he's dealing with a 23-year-old woman with a job and a college degree. So like a few minutes after I told him I was pregnant I said, "And you know what? I'm only 18."

"You're 18?"

"Well, what if I told you I was 17? What if I said I was 16? What if I'm 15?" He hung up on me and then he called me back crying, "How could you do this to me?" You saw what you wanted to see. You wanted to see a 23 old woman in front of you, so that's what you're seeing. You didn't see the little girl that was sitting before you—I wore baggy jeans, my hair in cornbraids. I never seen a 23-year-old woman wear her natural hair in cornbraids and not be able to have phone calls at a certain time.

The baby was born real sick, so I just told him the truth. I was like, "You know, you're not a father and I don't want you in my life no more and you can get out. And if he's going to die, then he'll just die having me as his parent. You don't need two parents."

The doctor that's like my gyno now made me love him 'cause I didn't like him. I was like, "God if this baby looks anything like [the father of the baby], I'll give him away." So when Gareth was born, he was black. He wasn't breathing. I was looking at the dark skin. So I was like, "Nope," and I just laid down and went to sleep and they revived him and brought me this yellow skinny baby and I was like, "I'll keep him." But the next day, I didn't want him. I was 16. I had never wanted a kid anyway. I had no job, no nothing. It took me a whole month before I could change his diaper. It made me puke every time and I got depressed because I thought I didn't love him.

* * * * *

A lot of people say I'm crazy. Some people say I'm stupid. I know I'm smart. I don't see myself living past 23 and I've always been like that ever since the time I was a little kid. Not that I want to die, it's that I'm going to die. I've dreamt about me being dead at 23.

DEIDRE: "TO THIS DAY, THEY SAY IT'S NOT TRUE"

Deidre was a 22-year-old Puerto Rican mother with a daughter almost five years old. As a child, she was raped and molested by several men in her extended family. Her family did not believe her when she told them about the abuse. In response to the sexual violence, she developed a tough persona that helped her survive on the street and in her family. The father of her child was similar in age, and while initially kind and supportive, he later became physically abusive.

I just remember [my mother] giving me away for her boyfriends. When I was three years old, DCF took me 'cause my mother left me in the house with a minor. Then she got pregnant and left to New York. She gave me up to my [paternal] grandmother. My other sisters and brothers went with my mother because we got different fathers—they didn't have no choice but to go with my mother 'cause their father was in jail and they didn't know their grandparents or anything.

I had my grandfather, my eight uncles, and my aunt. I used to like it 'cause I was the only granddaughter. I used to live right there on Plum Street with my grandmother. Well, it was good memories there until one day my grandmother went to work. She started working in a restaurant and I got up one day and I thought I was by myself so I ran outside and then my uncle seen me, one of my youngest uncles, he's almost my age, he seen me and he said, "come on, come upstairs we'll be together, whatever, I'll watch you." And he took me down in my grandmother's room and raped me.

I was nine or 10, I'm not sure. Probably even younger. I ran out the room and went to the bathroom. I tried to use the bathroom but I couldn't, so I ran to my grandmother's job and she asked me what happened and I said nothing. After that, years passed and I was like 12 years old and we moved to Holder Street and it happened again, my same uncle. He was 16, I think. It was only the two young ones, the twins, me, and my aunt, so we had a three bedroom. It was in the house, in my room, but it was at night and I didn't scream, I didn't yell, I didn't do anything.

So then after that happened, like a week later, my grandfather came in the bathroom when I was taking a shower and he said that he was gonna sit down and make sure he sees me washing myself and he molested me. My grandfather!

I didn't tell my grandmother until after it happened the second and third time, that's when I opened my mouth and I told one of my cousins and my cousin told my grandmother and then my father came down from Maryland and they put me in the room and they asked me and I said, "Yes, it's true, it's true," and they kept on telling me, "No, no," and I said, "Okay" and I just left it like that. To this day, they still say it's not true, but I know deep in my heart and God knows what happened.

Then when I graduated from sixth grade that's when I moved with my father for a year. It was because my baby sister's father had also molested me—he offered me money to like show him my body, 'cause like I was 13, but I had the biggest breasts. Since I was nine, I had the biggest breasts of the whole school—and I was scared—they used to call me torpedoes.

I went to my mother's house for a weekend 'cause it was by court. I had to go every weekend and one weekend that's when it happened. He was picking me up from my grandmother's house to take me to my mother's house. I remember coming out of one of those [highway] exits and that's where it happened, and then he gave me money. He told me to take the money, if not he was gonna do something, whatever, whatever, and I took the money.

I told a friend of mine because in those days we used to make our own gang, our own child gang, and we used to have a certain adult and tell them everything. So, that was my best friend's cousin, the only adult we ever trusted. I told her and she went, the day of my [sixth-grade] graduation, she went to my grandmother.

So when that happened my grandmother sent me to my father 'cause my baby sister's father is a King, he is one of those gang members. And they thought that something was going to happen because that's violation of their colors no matter what colors you have. They would kill him themselves because you don't do that to your daughters or stepkids or nothing 'cause that's family.

But my mother don't believe that. She never believed that he did that to me. My grandmother didn't believe that my grandfather did that to me, or my uncle. [My aunt] was the only one who believed me but I told her not to say anything to the cops or anything 'cause I didn't want the family to look at me like I did wrong.

Now [my stepfather's] in jail, but not for what he did to me. He's in jail for being a gang member and what he did to my sister and to my brother. The same thing. [My brother and sister] stayed quiet like me. They never said anything. They started saying stuff when he went to jail for gang stuff. That's when they started telling my mother and my mother still didn't believe it but they kept telling her, they kept telling her and my mother believed them. But, till this day she don't believe me, the oldest one, the one that made her a mom. She never believed me.

* * * * *

We're party people, you can put it like that. Our family is party people. We all get along, we love each other, you know, and till this day I go through what I've been through with my uncle or whatever and he knows what he did but I still go party with him. My uncle could tell me that "this bitch is bothering me" or whatever, and I'm just, "okay, I'll be there in two seconds." We're like that, you know. It's like we're brothers and sisters instead of uncle and niece because my grandmother was the one that raised me. Even though he did what he did to me, it's like I blocked everything, 'cause if I don't block it, I won't be able to live my life. I still think about it but I don't stress it as much.

Practically all of [my uncles] went to jail for fighting with their wives or whatever. Not all of them, but mostly all of them. In and out, in and out, but it wasn't for major things.

* * * * *

I went to so many schools. I was always out in the streets; not in gangs, not fightin', but dealing drugs, stealing from clothing stores, stealing from grocery stores, stealing cars, bringin' 'em to New York, and coming back with drugs in a different car. The car in New York, they sell it down here. I was a bichote.[1] I used to spend it on everybody else but me. That's how I was. I used to live right there with my uncle, but nobody knew. I was the quiet type. Everybody still thinks I'm the quiet type. I used to sell marijuana, crack. I used to sell cocaine. I used to sell the needles. I used to sell beer. The only thing I didn't sell was my body, but I used to sell everything else.

All this started happening when my stepfather molested me. That's when I started going crazy and started selling and hustling and being out in the street all the time and always shoplifting—but I would never get caught. I'm too good for that to tell you the truth. I was just always by myself. I never had friends. I don't believe in friends 'cause friends backstab you. I had associates. That's how I was raised.

I dropped out in the ninth grade. I liked the streets too much. I was with my boyfriend at that time. Part of the problems [with school] is just growing older and I'd be like, "I don't know this, I don't know that," but I know I'm very smart. I was never in special ed; I'm too smart for that. In the beginning I was getting As and Bs. I played everything—baseball, basketball, football, anything that any guy could touch me.

I was really back and forth on the streets until I met my baby father and he helped me a lot. He took me off the streets. In relationships you always have good and bad, you know, so you can't say it was perfect. He's mean. He's nice but he's mean. He's like me, that's why we probably don't get along—'cause, like, I'll be nice, but when you mess with me or something, I can kill somebody.

He was the only one that believed me [about the sexual abuse] right from the beginning. I told him I didn't feel comfortable to have no sexual relationship because of this. And he was like, "I'll wait until you're ready, I'm not gonna force you to do anything," and like a year later that's when I did and I came up pregnant, the first time, so. I didn't know nothing. It was like he showed me everything about sex. He was 19; I was 17 that first night we got it on.

I didn't know [I was pregnant] till I was five months. I went to my friend's house; she was having a little get-together. I was drinking and smoking and all of a sudden I started throwing up 'cause I couldn't stand the smoke or cigarettes. When I went to the hospital the next day they said I was five months pregnant—I was like "what!"

All the abusing-type shit started happening when I got pregnant. He was so cold and would always come home in a bad mood. After my daughter was born, he was abusive, like verbally at first, then hitting me, right after my daughter was born. He just hit me. But it wasn't to a point to hurt me. Even though it hurts you but it wasn't no point that I had to go to the hospital.

* * * * *

My social worker they tell me I need counseling because of what everything happened, but I don't know where and how, and I'm scared to go by myself so I haven't called. She asked me if I had anybody close to me that would help me and I told her, no, 'cause I don't conversate with nobody. I'm not close to my mother and I'm not close to my father, I'm not close to nobody. I stay to myself. So she asked me to see if I could find somebody that I can trust to take me and I said, "Yeah, yeah whatever." I haven't called or nothing, so. She said I'm gonna be in the hospital soon over a heart attack and stress. She said I have to get help before I go out of it—either go crazy or with heart problems.

I feel, deep inside I know I need help, it's just I don't know how to get help. I had spoke to this lady, she reads the [tarot] cards. She's like [pause] I need to get help before they take my daughter away.

WHAT THEY TELL YOU TO FORGET

> Honestly, I wish I could tell you but I tried to block it out. It's like
> I put it to one side of my brain, decided I don't want to be
> bothered with that section. I want to forget.
>
> —Delores, 19-year-old Puerto Rican mother

> It just brings back really bad memories and I've had a really
> rough morning and I kind of want it to get better. I don't want it
> to get worse.
>
> —Betsy, 19-year-old white mother

> I'd rather just kind of forget about it. I mean, it's something that
> happened but there's nothing I can do to change it.
>
> —Erica, 17-year-old white mother

Child sexual abuse was not something these young mothers wanted to talk about nor something we were expecting to hear.[2] Our interviewers were often as uncomfortable with this life event as the mothers. We did not set out to learn about child sex abuse; yet, many of the young women lived biographies mired in childhood pain and sexual violation. As we were piecing together the strands of traumatic stories, we noticed that the public's inclination to identify the moral failings associated with teen births seldom included the egregious incidences of child sexual abuse. Humiliation, family privacy, and cultural taboo work to obfuscate the complex biographies that twist through the experiences of early sexual abuse to the delivery rooms of young mothers.

Our determination to illustrate the often overlooked association between child sexual abuse and adolescent motherhood, however, runs the risk of blaming already fragile families. Mothers trusted us with their stories, and we have a responsibility in how they are represented. Deidre's story conveys not only instances of serial pedophilia, predatory older men, and incestuous violations, but also family instability, unprotected children, physical child abuse, and drug addiction, which carry the stinging judgment of bad parenting. By telling us their stories of personal violation, these young mothers opened the doors of their homes to let us see behind the thick walls of family privacy. Given this, we have three qualifications to make about these representations.

First, in our efforts to tell the backstory of adolescent motherhood, we acknowledge that we do not know the backstories of the others we are writing about—neglectful parents, violent men, drug-dependent family members. What are the biographical experiences that shaped their lives, the undisclosed junctures of pain, humiliation, or rage cast within the shadows of class exploitation and racism that constitute their own trajectories? While we cannot answer this question, it should serve as a reminder that our gaze is incomplete since we have only the young mothers' constructed stories and not those of their abusers. This is particularly important because child abusers have often been abused themselves.[3]

Second, the horrific abuse told by these mothers can steamroll our senses and prevent us from seeing the moments of redemption, forgiveness, and kindness embedded in their stories as well. Alisha told us that her mother had been clean from drugs for 14 years. Deidre will never forget what her similarly aged uncle did to her, but she saw him as an ally in neighborhood conflicts. Their childhood stories were laced with contradictory experiences and emotions that provide us with a complex profile of human experience.

Finally, in this and the next chapter, we may unwittingly leave readers with the impression that violence is a typical part of life among the poor. While some communities may be more vulnerable to interpersonal violence than others, it would be a mistake to conclude that violence does not occur in more privileged households and communities, or that it is typical of poor households. Moreover, because some of our discussion focuses on black and brown families, the stories we disclose can reinforce white racial frames for interpreting these issues. As social scientists, this poses a significant challenge. On the one hand, we feel a responsibility to bring attention to issues of gender violence; on the other, we acknowledge that our representations can be misused and decontextualized.[4]

The politics of representation is a tricky issue because bearing witness to and exposing unnecessary pain and misery is a practice intended to inspire moral outrage and political action, and yet these representations folded into different interpretative frames can result in voyeuristic feasting and moralistic victim blaming. This is particularly of concern in this chapter, since it is easy to provoke the ire of the public on the issue of child sexual abuse. There is probably a no more despised category of human beings, as illustrated by our ramped-up sex crime registries that have cast a large net over a range of behaviors, including cases of statutory rape discussed in the last chapter.[5] Child sex offenders occupy the bottom of any status hierarchy, even in prisons where they are considered the most depraved group and are frequently targets of violence. To address the problem of representation, we remind readers that child sexual abuse is a type of violence that occurs in all racial, ethnic, and social class communities; that it is a structural issue integral to the social organization of patriarchy and expressed as male entitlement to younger bodies for sexual pleasure and domination; and that patriarchy crosses racial, ethnic, and class lines.

Our national response to child sexual abuse is complicated—it is variously ignored and denied as well as demonized and sensationalized. It is both cloaked in secrecy and splattered across the headlines of newspapers. We have begun to publicly recognize the manifestation of child sexual abuse within some of our most honored institutions, mostly due to media exposure of abuse within the Roman Catholic ministry. But the Roman Catholic Church is not alone. Other professions and institutions have hidden abuse and the abusers under the pall of male dominance and class status. For instance, Dr. George Reardon, chief of endocrinology at St. Francis Hospital in Hartford, was in practice for more than 30 years, during which time he was accused of, but not charged with, sexual misconduct with children numerous times. He finally resigned from his position in 1993. Nine years after his death, a large collection of child pornography slides—hundreds of slides he took under the guise of a research project—was found in his former home, confirming the accusations of his victims. Only now are their stories being told, printed, prosecuted, and, most importantly, believed.[6] Silence, denial, social status, and institutional prominence combine to produce layers of power and violence that are difficult to see and uncover.[7]

The hidden-in-plain-sight nature of child sexual abuse should prompt us to be vigilant in looking for signs of abuse we do not want to see, but it can also lead us to see evidence that is not there. Child advocates have worked sometimes too aggressively to apprehend abusers, while the tabloid trials of questionable ritual sexual abuse cases at day care centers—Fells Acre Day Care Center in Malden, Massachusetts (1984), McMartin Preschool in Manhattan Beach, California (1984), Little Rascals Day Care Center in Edenton, North Carolina (1988)—have left some people skeptical. Groups like the False Memory Syndrome Foundation and Victims of Child Abuse Laws (VOCAL) mobilized in the 1980s and 1990s to temper the movement to expose and prosecute child sexual abuse, claiming the movement was overzealous and often based on invalid "recovered memories" that had become the handiwork of professionally ambitious therapists and, according to VOCAL, part of an anti-male agenda more generally.[8]

On this issue of too many false positives, we rely on the judgment of David Finkelhor, a sociologist at the University of New Hampshire and pioneer in the study of child abuse since the 1970s. Amid the political storm of the 1990s, Finkelhor conducted a comprehensive review of substantiated and unsubstantiated reports of child sexual abuse and retrospective studies of offenders. He concluded that people were more likely to conceal than fabricate, and that, in general, child protective services were "balanced" and the criminal justice system was "tempered rather than hysterical."[9] Because even the allegation of sexual abuse is irrevocably damaging to the accused, Finkelhor found that authorities were more likely to err on the side of caution, suggesting that the public preoccupation with false accusations is largely unwarranted.

PREVALENCE AND INCIDENCE OF CHILD SEXUAL ABUSE

Because of the silencing, measuring the extent of the problem has its challenges. Child sexual abuse metrics are reported as either incidence or prevalence. The incidence of child sexual abuse refers to the number of new cases each year that are reported, investigated, and substantiated by state child protective authorities. In 2009, the US Department of Health and Human Services documented 65,700 new cases of child sexual abuse that were confirmed by child protective authorities.[10] However, this figure greatly underestimates the true occurrence of child sexual abuse because it only includes cases in which the perpetrator is a family member or caretaker and because most cases of child sexual abuse are never brought to the attention of state authorities.[11]

The prevalence of child sexual abuse is determined through self-reported surveys or structured interviews in which respondents are asked about childhood occurrences of sexual abuse in their lifetimes. Consequently, the prevalence is much higher than the incidence, but both are sensitive to definitional criteria.[12] Studies that use more restrictive definitions, like genital contact or penetration, report prevalence around 3 to 9 percent, while broader definitions that include noncontact abuse range from 24 to 32 percent of adult women.[13] In Frank Putnam's 2003 review of child sexual abuse studies, he found that abuse rates in community samples typically ranged from 12 to 35 percent for women and from 4 to 9 percent for men.[14] Studies indicate that girls are at a much higher risk of sexual abuse: usually they are two and a half to three times more likely to be abused, although mental health professionals have also been found to be more reluctant to ask boys about childhood sexual abuse.[15] The overwhelming majority of offenders are men—law enforcement and self-reported data suggest that 90 percent are male and most of the abusers know their victim (roughly half are acquaintances, while family members are an estimated one-quarter to one-third of offenders).[16]

Of all types of child abuse, sexual abuse is the most likely to occur across social class and racial and ethnic groups. Confirmed state reports in 2008 indicated that more socially disadvantaged groups had higher rates of victimization.[17] Disparities in incidence rates, however, are likely to result from disadvantaged groups being exposed to more state surveillance by social workers, home-visitation professionals, and the courts. Research studies using prevalence rates are inconclusive on group differences. For instance, Frank Putnam's 10-year review of studies concludes that "race and ethnicity do not appear to be risk factors for CSA" and that "community survey studies find almost no socioeconomic effects."[18] Douglas and Finkelhor's review differs slightly. They suggest that findings on race and ethnicity are mixed and inconclusive and that a few studies have found socioeconomic effects.[19] These researchers agree, however, that sexual abuse is the least likely form of child maltreatment to be related to income, race, and ethnicity.

SHADOW NARRATIVES OF ABUSE

When we began our study, child sexual abuse was not in our lexicon of social problems. We knew we were interviewing young mothers who had been identified as "vulnerable" or "at risk," and yet in our 20-page interview schedule we did not have even one probe that explored child sexual abuse. The home visitation program's intake questionnaire also did not have any specific questions about child sexual abuse. Both the intake questionnaire and our interview schedule asked and probed about child abuse and neglect in general. We also probed for physical abuse when asking about child disciplinary practices, and we had direct prompts for domestic violence. But we did not ask if they had any unwanted sexual experiences as children. And yet, even without direct probes, a quarter of the women mentioned that they were molested or raped before the age of 16 or before they became pregnant, whichever came first. This became our definition of child sexual abuse—a conservative measure that most likely underestimated the prevalence of child sexual abuse among the young women we interviewed. And yet, the percentage of young mothers in our study who drew our attention to the issue was considerably higher than what is reported in the general population, reinforcing the link made by many researchers between child sexual abuse and adolescent motherhood.[20]

In our study, 27 mothers reported 45 acts of molestation and rape: 10 girls were abused by multiple perpetrators, 14 girls had been raped, four of them multiple times by different men. We did not include statutory rape as a form of child sexual abuse nor did we include date rape, though this happened frequently to some of the victims of child sexual abuse.[21]

Were they telling us the truth? We had no way to verify their stories; however, the information was provided voluntarily and the way they told their stories was convincing. Like the specialists in the field, we were persuaded that these women were more likely to hold back than to make up the abuse. The story of sexual abuse was never the centerpiece of their life stories. It was more often mentioned as an aside, an afterthought, or an explanation for why they moved from one city to another city. "Oh yeah, and then I was raped," one mother slipped into her story but then went silent. "That happened in my past, but I'm living in the future." Some never said exactly what their father or uncle or stepfather did, only that his behavior "was inappropriate." Most of the time when the young mothers hinted or mentioned they were abused, the interviewer asked her to elaborate, but not always. Interviewers were not as comfortable probing the topic of sexual abuse, especially incest, as they were probing more neutral topics like child care or employment.[22]

The shards of sexual abuse were scattered throughout the interview, told to us in piecemeal images or scenes, the way that victims often remember trauma. It remains in their memory as light on a rug through a living room window, a hand in the car on a highway exit ramp; it gets mixed with the smell of McDonald french fries or a bigger, smelly body crawling into bed in the dark of night, transforming the security of warm blankets into the trauma of penetration. Their memories are vignettes, not whole stories. They do not even try to make sense of the story because child sexual abuse often does not make sense to them. Cassandra tried to describe this:

> I don't even know, I don't remember, all I remember was that I was on the bed and the dude came to the bed, started like rubbing his shit on my, my, um, vagina and shit with my pants up and then he pulled my pants down and started rubbing it on my panties and I was like, I was like five, six, seven years and all I remember is the dude is, um, looking like my real father. And I remember when my mother came through and I remember the Wonder Bread was in the bag, it was like poking up, and I was like, Ma, where you was at? Mom, where you was at? He did me dirty Ma, he did me dirty and she was like what are you talking about and blah blah blah and right there it stop. I was so young and I don't remember and I don't got nobody that was there.

Cassandra had sharper memories when she was older and it happened again—but these were memories she would rather not have. "I just want to forget," she told us.

This was a phrase we heard repeatedly from survivors. They saw no value in remembering. "I talked to a couple of counselors about it," one rape victim said, and then added: "It's something I really don't like talking about." Because they tried to forget, could not remember, or were told to forget, their stories of child sexual abuse narratives were shadowy, oblique, and spotty. They were silenced by skepticism, silenced by shame, silenced by self-preservation, and silenced by the intensity of the denial from those around them.

We wonder how the work done by feminists in the 1960s and 1970s to "break the silence" and the ensuing growth in media attention, therapeutic practices, support groups, research, and state child protective services could seem so irrelevant, as if the chorus of survivors' voices 50 years ago was still struggling to be heard. Consider, for instance, the following quotation taken from the proceedings of the 1976 International Tribunal on Crimes against Women in Brussels: "Every woman is a potential victim of rape: little girls, adolescents, single women, married women, middle aged women—and even dead women. . . . Women live in terror of rape from the most tender age. An incredible number of children are victims of sexual aggression even in their own families or from relatives . . . from childhood on, every woman, as a potential rape victim, is made to feel guilty and is accused of provocation." [23] Thirty years later, women are still vulnerable and still struggling to speak and be heard. And we are still learning to listen and understand. When we listen to the life stories of the teen mothers who were sexually abused, those with horrific stories like Alisha and Deidre, the wrecking ball in their lives was not an early pregnancy, it was gender violence.

FROM SEXUAL ABUSE TO EARLY MOTHERHOOD

The path from sexual abuse to early motherhood is not one all victims walk. And they don't always walk it the same way. The stories of Kate, Laura, Tameka, and Bethany represent one well-trampled route: sexual assault as a child, precocious and risky sexual behavior as an adolescent (more partners and less contraception), failure and withdrawal from school, abuse of alcohol and drugs, violent (and older) partners, and finally pregnancy and motherhood. In this trajectory the trauma is externalized as delinquency and oppositional behavior.

Kate is white. She lived in subsidized housing with her mother and brother who was recently released from the hospital, where he was recovering from a gunshot wound. During the interview, her 15-month-old son wandered around the living room, eating Cheese Doodles. The house was clean with older furniture a bit ripped and worn. Kate was heavy set, with long light-brown hair and a rough demeanor. She had a nose ring, a pierced tongue, and a vocabulary peppered with expletives. She smoked throughout the interview and her mother sat beside her on the couch while she talked.

Kate moved out of her mother's house at the age of 16, she said, "'cuz I wanted to be with somebody [my mother] didn't like. The baby father. She couldn't stand the sight of him."

Mother: Tell her why.

Kate: Because of what he went to jail for.

Mother: What did he go to jail for?

Kate: Because everybody thinks that he raped this girl, which, it was *not* rape. They all just had sex with her. A lot of them had sex with her but don't

Mother: [interrupting] She was a minor and they all had their turn with her and hurt her. I'm supposed to let my daughter see someone like that?

Kate: That did not hurt that girl! Her mother's the one that called the police. See, don't nobody know the story. I know exactly what happened that day; I know the story.

Mother: She was raped, Kate.

Kate: Yeah, because of the simple fact that if you had seven people running into you in one day, your crotch is gonna look like you've been raped. She had seven boys run into her, which they don't know; they think just five—her boyfriend and the other four. That's where there's a lie. My crotch is gonna be messed up if I had two men running me in one day or three men. I mean just imagine, all different sizes and everything else running into you, yeah, I'm gonna look like I got raped, too, but her mother's the one that called rape, that little girl didn't. Her boyfriend was the first one to have sex with her, and then my boyfriend—my baby father—was the one to have sex with her, and then these other boys.

The interviewer was as puzzled as her mother that Kate did not see seven men having sex with a young girl as wrong.

Earlier in her story, Kate said the reason her family moved to Connecticut was "because my father was molesting his girls [her and her sister] and beating on us all the time. Mentally and physically he just tore us apart." Kate repeated kindergarten that year "because education-wise, I was just so messed up over it and we had just moved from Utah." In grade school, she "started having these sex fiends," and her problems snowballed in middle school.

> I was known to take girls' boyfriends. That's why I don't have friends now, 'cuz I was, you know, I was pretty. I wasn't that big then. Maybe in eighth grade I started getting a little bit chunky but I was not that big then and I was just known as either a whore or having sex with older men.

Kate's mother said she was having "problems skipping school and then I found out she was smoking marijuana, sneaking boys around, you know." When the interviewer asked her why she and her best friend were skipping school, Kate said:

> 'Cuz we are boy lovers. We love boys. We wanted to get high all the time. And we just found it so cool that, that we would sit here and leave school and laugh in people's face because we left school, we can just walk right off the property, right from the front door out to the parking lot where nobody would think that anybody would walk out through, and we did. And we waited right down the street and we caught onto the bus and we went [downtown] and we did whatever, but the most we did was getting high.

Her in-your-face opposition was not just about skipping classes but also about reclaiming power: "My best friend, we were like Bonnie and Clyde." While Kate talked with bravado about this rebel image, her mother told us that Kate began to change in "junior high, when you started liking boys, and the [school] work became too difficult. She got wild on me and then you missed so many days and that was why you were expelled." When asked directly about her school performance, Kate talked about the difficult high school curriculum, and then casually mentioned that she had "ADD" and was placed in "special classes" in middle school. In high school she could not keep up with the schoolwork and the social scene was unpleasant, so she and Clyde began skipping classes and smoking pot.

Kate was not doing well in school *before* she became truant and started using drugs. And before that, her father—who was never prosecuted—sexually abused her.

In an attempt to resolve some of her problems, Kate switched schools at the beginning of ninth grade, but then dropped out before the school year ended. That summer, she moved in with her boyfriend, who was five years older and "a little" abusive, Kate said. "He just like hooked me a couple times, socked me, pulled my ear. Last time he hit me, I was like three months pregnant." When the pregnancy test read positive in

September, she said: "I was happy. We were trying to make a baby." By the time their baby was born, the father of the baby was on trial for gang rape and Kate was 16 years old.

Another white mother, Laura, had a boyfriend serving a sentence for gang rape and murder. Laura was also sexually abused as a child, failed school, and had a violent older partner. Her destructive behavior began after she was raped at age 13, which left her pregnant. She miscarried. That year, she was also held back in school because of poor grades. The next few years, she lived at a residential school facility where she was in smaller classes and received special attention. In tenth grade she was mainstreamed back into the regular system and shortly after that became pregnant. As we describe in more detail in the next chapter, her violent boyfriend "slammed" her into a wall causing her to miscarry. She said, "then it was like everything went into a tailspin. I quit school. I ended up moving out, screwed around for a couple years, um, was into the whole drinking thing, getting into bars under age, getting served under age." Her tailspin began with the rape and she crashed as a 17-year-old mother.

Tameka was raped at age 12—the second time in her young life. She received no counseling for either rape. Soon after the second rape, she dropped out of school, began abusing drugs, and became a stripper. At age 17, she said: "I've been through a lot." It was as if she had lived "39 years: I've been through so much." She was living on the streets at the time she became pregnant. Bethany also ended up on the streets, with a drug addiction, two children, and a history of violence. We tell both of their stories at the beginning of the next chapter; they are two of the seven mothers who had been sexually abused as children and had a life story of violence that included sex work and substance abuse. Bethany said, "I drank every weekend, I mean drink to the point where I couldn't stand up. I kinda had to just, like, forget about it. That's pretty much what I did. I never went to counseling for it. I just stuffed it away and, you know, I was just extremely depressed."

A second trajectory also emerged in our analysis of the pathways from sexual abuse to young motherhood and is represented by Deidre's story, which introduced this chapter. On this route, the violence reverberates inward. The signposts in their narratives were mental illness, self-destructive behavior, and partnerships with older and often abusive men. The trauma became manifest in self-mutilation, eating disorders, depression, and acute psychosis.[24] Negative self-perceptions and poorly defined boundaries made these victims of child sexual abuse vulnerable to predatory men. Their older partners were often abusive, and, in this way, the violence of the initial trauma was repeated. This is one rationale for statutory rape laws—predators can more easily exploit traumatized girls. For example, in the previous chapter, we mentioned Lilly, who was raped when she was 10 years old by an 18-year-old man who was brought to her house by a group of her friends when her mother was not at home. During the rape, the man hit her with a BB gun and she was knocked unconscious. Her mother found her on her bed in a pool of blood and took her to the hospital. Shortly after the rape, she said, "I just started going crazy." She spent at least a year and a half at a psychiatric hospital and another year living in a residential treatment home. She was released when she was 15 years of age. Shortly after this she started a sexual relationship with a physically abusive 27-year-old drug dealer who was already the father of several other children.

Alisha, whose story precedes this chapter, said that she started self-mutilating after she was raped. Her depression, drug abuse, and abusive relationships also began at this time. She tried to commit suicide four times and ended up in a state hospital:

> They wanted me to stop mutilating myself [burning and cutting] and they figured if I went to a therapist, I would stop. I haven't done it since Valentine's Day, but that was a special circumstance and that wasn't really self-mutilation. That was just me taking it out on myself instead of going to hurt somebody else. It was just do it or kill him or kill her. I just did it, get it out of the way, get the anger off my chest.

Delores, who was raped when she was 10 years old, also inflicted violence on herself:

> I told [my parents about the abuse] the first time I tried to kill myself—I was 12—but they really didn't believe me. I was hospitalized then for a year because like me being sexually abused, me telling my parents, their not believing me, their coming in and out of my life, and the time my mom abandoned us in Puerto Rico, you know, the drama that my baby father put me through while I was just a child, you know, all that just affected me so bad where I developed a whole world inside of my head. You know, that I wouldn't let nobody enter so nobody would hurt me.

After she was released from the psychiatric institution, she returned to the violently abusive partner and had his baby.

In the life stories we saw these two (not totally distinct) trajectories of the sexually precocious and the psychologically disturbed. The first pattern included early and risky sexual behavior, oppositional behavior, substance abuse and older partners, and the second, mental illness, self-destructive behaviors, and older violent partners. Both trajectories included school failure preceded by poor academic performance. As Kate says about being sexually abused by her father, it messes you up "education-wise."[25]

We are not isolating sex abuse as the cause of teen births. In each of these trajectories there were contributing factors that were related to the abuse, such as chaotic homes, truancy and delinquency, alcohol and drug abuse, depression, and negative self-image. Other girls exhibiting some of these characteristics, but not sexually abused as children, may also become adolescent mothers. However, when we compared teen mothers in our study who had been sexually abused to nonabused teen mothers on a range of problems, it was apparent that sex abuse had profound effects on these young girls. In our sample, those sexually abused were more likely to have suffered from a mental illness (56 percent versus 23 percent), to have abused alcohol or drugs (52 percent versus 16 percent), to have dropped out of high school before pregnancy (44 percent versus 33 percent), to have been victims of statutory rape (22 percent versus 5 percent), and to have had abusive partners (63 percent versus 35 percent). It is important to remember that these comparisons are within a sample of disadvantaged women, suggesting that child sexual abuse compounds preexisting oppression and can lead girls to come undone.[26]

THE UNIQUE TRAUMA OF SEXUAL ABUSE

Certainly, not all sexually abused girls become teen mothers, nor are all teen mothers sexually abused, but the abuse does cluster with other problems and the life stories help us to see the process or ways that child sexual abuse can be linked to adolescent motherhood. Social science researchers have plowed this ground well. Studies have found that the factors that put children at risk of sexual domination also increase their risk of becoming young parents. For example, lack of supervision or poor parent-child communication makes children more vulnerable to perpetrators, less likely to be informed about sex, and more at risk to peer influence (for example, staying out late and mixing hormones and alcohol). Children from emotionally bankrupt homes crave affection, making them prey for exploitative play.[27] While these conditions make girls more vulnerable to sexual victimization, there is also something unique about the *trauma* of sexual abuse that puts girls at risk of early childbirth.

David Finkelhor and Angela Brown conceptualize the experience of child sexual abuse in terms of four trauma-causing factors: "traumatic sexualization, stigmatization, betrayal, and powerlessness."[28] First, because the abuse is sexual, the manifestation of the trauma is often sexual in nature and may include promiscuity, precocious sexual activity, prostitution, sexual dysfunctions, and aggressive sexual behaviors, as well as phobic reactions to sex.[29] The sexual abuse influences a young victim's understanding of what constitutes a healthy sexual relationship. According to developmental psychologist Judith Musick, the trauma leads to confusion about appropriate sexual behavior, misconceptions regarding acceptable sexual norms, and an inability to differentiate between sex, love, and caregiving.[30]

Second, the stigmatization that accompanies the assault can distort a child's self-image and lead to self-destructive behavior rooted in self-loathing—eating disorders, substance abuse, mutilation, and suicide.[31] Third, when the abuser is someone they trust, or when someone they trust does not protect them from the abuser, the victim feels betrayed. This betrayal is intensified if the parent or guardian does not believe their reports of abuse (or if they are the abuser). This betrayal can lead to mistrust and get expressed as problems with intimacy, in which they are unable to discern between healthy and unhealthy relationships, making them more vulnerable to abusive relations with older men.[32] In our total sample, 17 percent of the teen mothers were with partners who were at least five years older than they were; however, in the subsample of sexually abused teen moms, this doubled to 37 percent.

Finally, sexual assault can distort a child's sense of control, leaving her in a passive modus operandi where she feels pulled along by things that "just happen" and less able to direct the course of her life.[33] Musick writes: "The victimized girl learns ways of thinking about men and sex that interact with emotional vulnerability to make her highly prone to repeated victimization. She learns patterns of passivity and helplessness in relation to men."[34] She argues that the "invasion of her body" is what leads to feelings of powerlessness, especially repeated violation, which she defines as "a kind of brainwashing. It saps the will, destroys self-efficacy, and leads to the perception of the self as a victim."[35] The revictimization was evident in the life stories. Of the 27 girls who reported abuse, 19 of them had been abused more than one time (sometimes the abuse lasted for years) or by more than one abuser. And as noted earlier, almost twice as many of the child abuse victims had physically abusive partners when they were older. The multiple victimizations and clusters of violence are mechanisms of patriarchy, a system of male domination, which is, in this instance, expressed in literal terms as the male body physically asserting power, privilege, and domination over women forced into submissive, subordinate relations.

While reading the life stories, several motifs emerged as narrative arcs that characterized, explained, and connected their life events: the Tara motif ("everything will be better tomorrow"), the Boot Strap motif ("I can do it on my own"), the Whitewash motif ("everything is just fine"), and the Passive motif ("things just happen to me").[36] Eight of the 108 life stories had a strong Passive motif that was often characterized by the teen mother defining herself as someone with little ability to change or direct her life. Of the eight with a Passive life-story motif, five of them were victims of child sexual abuse (and four of the five were white). Michelle, who was abused as a child and then later raped by men she was partying with, said, "I just think I was very vulnerable and that's why all this stuff happened to me, 'cuz I wouldn't like put up a fight."

When these four traumatic dynamics of sex, shame, betrayal, and powerlessness merge in the life of an adolescent girl—a time when young people are forming a core concept of self, establishing boundaries that make clear distinctions between self and other, and participating in give-and-take peer relations—it is easy to see how teen pregnancy and births become more likely. The lowered self-esteem and feelings of mistrust, betrayal, and loss of control all complicate normal adolescent challenges.[37] Negotiating sexual relations is difficult enough for confident, healthy adolescents. It requires a strong 15-year-old girl to initiate contraceptive use or say "no" to persistent compliments and pleas. Sexual abuse compromises this strength and undermines confidence.[38] Understanding the trauma created by child sexual abuse helps contextualize the link between self-esteem and risky sexual behavior (or teen births). If we want to improve self-esteem, we can start by tearing through the cloak of silence that surrounds child sexual abuse and helping girls to heal.

THE CLOAK OF SILENCE

Child sex abuse victims are not powerless, even though they have been robbed of power. They can fight back, redefine the situation, rewrite the narrative, and define themselves as survivors and not victims.[39] When victims take action against the perpetrators, it helps them to reclaim power and mitigate the damage. But it is not easy, and the first step requires breaking the silence. Unfortunately, most sex abuse victims do not report the abuse.[40] This is one of the more sobering findings in our study. Forty years after the women's movement educated us about rape and child sexual abuse and initiated a panoply of local and national efforts to support survivors, challenge patriarchy, redirect internalized oppression, and "break the silence," incest and sex abuse are still shrouded in secrecy.

In our study, only 12 of the 27 girls told someone about the abuse immediately or shortly after it happened. Victims were silent for a variety of reasons. First, the sexual nature of the abuse created shame and a sullying of the sexual self. For instance, Alisha's abuse led to the rumor of her having AIDS and she learned her lesson to keep silent.[41] Second, some were afraid that others would be angry with them for what happened—especially when the abuser was an acquaintance. Michelle said: "When I was five in my daycare I got molested by the babysitter's son for about a year. I didn't tell anybody till I was like 12 'cuz I was so scared, you know, when you're young you're scared that everyone will hate you." Deidre, who was raped by her cousin twice, told her aunt "not to say anything to the cops or anything 'cause I didn't want the family to look at me like I did wrong." Third, girls were reluctant to tell because of family loyalties. In our study, more than half of the 45 perpetrators were family members (fathers, stepfathers, grandfathers, uncles, cousins, and a foster brother) and another quarter were friends of the family. Jackie said, "I didn't say nothing to nobody 'cuz that's my father's brother. I didn't want to start a big problem so I kept my mouth shut." It is not just the abuser they were protecting, but the family name, family members, and themselves.[42] Finally, girls didn't tell because they didn't think they would be believed. LaRonda, who was abused in four different foster homes, said she stopped reporting the abuse because "if you get raped too many times, they stop believing you."

While less than one-half of the girls told a family member or friend about the abuse, with little variation by race or ethnicity, only the white girls were believed. Black and Puerto Rican girls either were not believed or were simultaneously accused of being responsible for what had happened, a finding that is consistent with other research.[43] Jesenia told her family that her 30-year-old cousin molested her repeatedly from the age of three until "like nine years when one starts to, already starts to, you know," menstruate. When she told them, "they didn't believe me, so they left the thing like that, like I was a liar." Cassandra said her mother had been out "clubbing" and left Cassandra home with "this white dude who was a pig" who molested her. When her mother came home, she told her but "she was drunk that night and never believed me." Kim also tried to convince her family that her cousin was molesting her, "but they was always, 'Stop lying, you're fibbing and telling stories.'" And when Jackie finally told her parents about her abusive stepuncle, her mother believed her but "my father didn't believe me. He said I'm lying 'cuz he didn't want to believe the fact that his brother would do something like that, so he didn't believe me."[44] This denial intensifies the devastation of the crime.[45] Laura Codes, director of policy and advocacy at Connecticut Sexual Assault Crises Services, has noted that "survivors have to survive the assault, and then they have to survive the response from people, and that's a huge part of recovery."[46]

Who discloses and who is believed occurs at the intersection of family, race, ethnicity, and social class. Whites may be reluctant to disclose because of the privacy and privileges that the nuclear family has historically provided to them.[47] For families of color living in impoverished neighborhoods, however, a general lack of trust in the criminal justice system and child protective agencies to handle incidents judiciously and fairly may make them less likely to bring this attention to these agencies.[48] Among low-income families, a lack of resources may inhibit the prospects for prosecution and recovery. In these circumstances, handling the issue internally is preferable to involving institutional authorities. This is particularly relevant in Puerto Rican communities, where *familiso,* or the subordination of individuals to the needs of the family, prevails.[49] Further, we should note that differential institutional treatment and varying cultural reactions and strategies have made interracial coalitions to address violence against women (including sexual abuse) difficult to create and sustain, especially when the leadership of these movements is white.[50] Disclosures can mean different things to different people, and white insensitivity to this issue has historically been problematic, if not divisive.

Carol Ronai, a sociologist and survivor of child sexual abuse, has used auto-ethnography to write about child sexual abuse—a point of view simultaneously intimate and academic. She argues that breaking the silence is imperative to both individual recovery and public efforts to reduce the prevalence of this atrocious crime. Because the public and the private interact, the individual will suffer in private as long as the public refuses to address this issue: "Incest must be made a public concern so that victims are no longer saddled with the stigma, guilt, and shame associated with the experience. . . . If it becomes extremely common to discuss sexual abuse without shame, there is improved chance for children to come forward when it is happening to them."[51] Public awareness about the social problem is as important as therapy for the victims.[52] Without public dialogue, the personal trouble does not become a social issue.[53]

WHO GETS PROSECUTED, WHO GETS THERAPY

By naming the perpetrator and taking action against him, the young girl can begin to restore the balance of power. Too often, however, no action is taken even when the young girl is believed.[54] In our study, only two of 45 perpetrators were prosecuted and sentenced to prison; a third perpetrator was being prosecuted at the time of the interview (in this case the victim was not believed by her mother but she was believed by the authorities). In one case the victim reported the assault to school authorities and the perpetrator was expelled from school, but it is unclear if he was prosecuted in a court of law. Two of the victims who reported the abuse moved away from the perpetrator, but the assault was not reported to any authority. For example, when Diane, who was being abused by the father of her mother's boyfriend, finally told her mother (who was at the same time being physically battered by the boyfriend), her mother "packed everything up that next month and we moved. I was just basically told to just forget about it. I was just told, you know, we're not in the same state—don't worry about it."

Therapy is as important for the victims as prosecution. Early feminist efforts to address sex abuse advanced lay therapy as a mechanism for addressing internalized oppression. The intention was to liberate survivors, but also to raise consciousness about patriarchal patterns of domination. As the framework for understanding sex abuse became medicalized and criminalized in the 1980s and 1990s, broader social change initiatives were dropped in light of efforts to focus on the survivor's coping and adjustment needs and to prosecute offenders.[55] Nonetheless, some of the early initiatives to undo internalized oppression have survived in current practice. Judith Musick, for instance, argues that talking about the abuse in support groups helps the victim to break the offender's "psychological hold over her, to loosen the grip of the unacknowledged pain of her past on her current thoughts and actions."[56] It gives her confidence, and a confident woman is less likely to abuse drugs, drop out of school, and tolerate abusive partners. In addition, therapy helps to release the psychic energy needed to keep the images repressed. Repression drains cognitive energy and interferes with the ability to concentrate (which interferes with school). Speaking out about the abuse, being believed, taking action against the perpetrator, and receiving treatment all help the victim regain power after she has been violated.

Today, therapy has been reduced to state or private insurance–funded counseling sessions that focus on individual adjustment, removing the issue from the social world and placing it behind the closed doors and partially drawn blinds of counselors' offices. Only three of the 27 victims received counseling specifically related to the sexual abuse. Another 13 victims received some counseling later in their lives that was initiated for other reasons (such as drug abuse, truancy, mental illness, or suicide attempts), during which their experiences of child sexual abuse emerged. The counseling they received was often short and generally inadequate. Mollie, a 15-year-old white mother, raped by a stranger when she was 11, received six months of counseling. "It was free," she said. But was it enough? we asked. "Is there enough time for anyone [laugh] for that?" she replied. Who knows how much is enough, but most would say more than six months.

Competent professionals can certainly help the recovery. Mollie was one of the few girls who told someone, was believed, and then prosecuted and convicted the perpetrator. Mollie was also one of the few mothers who had some class privilege and the resources to receive counseling. Michelle did as well. She talked about her process of recovery that began with breaking the silence:

> I told my cousin [about the abuse] and she like laughed at me, so that was like really bad, and then she made me tell my mom, which is good. So we talked about it and she said, do you want to do anything? I said, "no, whatever," so then I did those drugs and whatever, had to get that out of my system. When I was 15, my friend and I went to this party with a drug-dealer friend that I knew, to this hotel party, which wasn't safe for me to go to at all and I got raped by two men. It was just so normal, so normal—I know, it's not normal, but to me.

A few months after this rape, she started a relationship with Mark, her 23-year-old boss at a fast-food restaurant. "At that point I was getting old enough where I was like, hey, wait a second. This doesn't happen to normal people." With the support of Mark, she sought out therapy:

> I was about 16, which is when we started dating. I decided I wanted to go to therapy and he helped me and encouraged me into doing that because he knew I needed it. I didn't really ever totally tell everybody everything, you

know. I just did drugs to like suppress it. I totally put it away in the box that we all have. Mark kind of encouraged me to go to therapy and I was like, okay. The first session I didn't really like it, so I stopped going and then I went back like three or four months later and it was great. It totally helped me, which I should be in therapy now, it did really help me. It made me not so [pause] angry about everything. I knew it wasn't my fault. I knew that all the people in my life must have had something wrong with them to do something wrong to me.

Michelle tells us how she moved from a position of victim and a pattern of revictimization to one of survivor through the process of disclosure, support, and talk therapy.

CONCLUSION

Despite significant efforts made by feminists in the 1960s and 1970s, by nonfeminist activists who joined the movement to address child sexual abuse in the 1980s and 1990s, and by state and institutional authorities in the 1980s and after, the silence surrounding child sexual abuse persists. The pain and violation that mark the lives of so many women in our study and in the population more generally propel survivors along a variety of different trajectories. One of these trajectories is adolescent motherhood. Certainly, not all, or even most, teen births stem from child sexual abuse, but many do, and a discussion of early births needs to acknowledge and address this.

With the legislation, funding, interventions, and publicity that have been mobilized over the past 40 years to address child sexual abuse, the cloak of silence has been partially pulled back. But as stories about abuse come to the attention of the courts and newspaper reporters, what is painfully evident is how many victims suffer in silence for decades. The prosecution of not just the perpetrators but also the institutions that shelter the criminals may help more victims come forward to report the abuse. The sentencing in 2013 of an unlicensed Hasidic therapist from an Orthodox Jewish community to 103 years in prison for the sexual abuse of a girl who was 12 years old when the attacks began should send the message, as State Supreme Court Justice John G. Ingram said, "to all victims of sexual abuse that your cries will be heard and justice will be done." In the same breath, however, he noted that it took "bravery and courage" for the victim to come forward.[57] Unfortunately, shame still silences many victims, so for every victim that comes forward there are dozens that remain in the shadows.

While steps have been taken to prosecute abusers, the social vulnerabilities of women generated through patriarchy and poverty have been largely ignored. As Nancy Whittier describes, states select from social movement platforms to create new policies and practices and, in the case of child sexual abuse, have advanced a framework for understanding sex abuse that deemphasizes the need for broader social change. As such, she argues, these "selection processes meant that the more radical elements of the movement, such as its critique of the patriarchal family or of children's powerlessness, never made it into official policy or procedure."[58] Instead, responses to sex abuse have been constructed in terms of individual pathologies, family dysfunction, survivor coping strategies and treatment, offender treatment, parenting adjustments, stricter prison sentencing, and mandatory offender registries. Lost in the shuffle is a larger analysis of social inequality, power, and domination. Sexual abuse is about patriarchy—the culturally embedded belief that seeps into both the male psyche and institutional routines that allow men the feelings of entitlement to others' bodies (young girls or young boys) for their pleasure.[59]

Social inequality is measured not only by distributions of income and wealth, but also by the distribution of suffering. Certainly, suffering is a part of living that no one escapes, but the resources to protect ourselves against suffering are not evenly distributed, and the suffering in silence that occurs among more socially vulnerable women is a systemic issue. This is nowhere more evident than in our analysis of violence in the lives of these young mothers, the issue that we turn to next.

CHAPTER 4

Violence against Women

Bethany, a 24-year-old white woman with two children, had her first child when she was 18. At the time of the interview, she was living in a residential drug treatment program with her second child. Her parents were divorced, but they remained active in her life. They both had some college education and Bethany grew up in economically stable households. Along with the other young mothers in this chapter, her narrative is a comingling of violence and drug addiction.

My parents were divorced when I was like two. I remember my dad was kind of a hippie. He took care of the family but my mother was real straight, straight edge. She sold cars but then she went to school to be a social worker. She supported us well, but being that she worked a lot I was left to take care of my little brother. My father was more of a partier, but he maintained a job, he worked with mentally challenged people for at least 25 years.

My stepfather was an alcoholic. I had had some things with him when I was younger. I don't remember all of it but I remember being in the bathtub with him and him doing some things. It must've looked like nothing was wrong, like he'd let me wash his hair, but then I also remember him doing other things, you know, that were very inappropriate. I never told my mother about that either, until later. They ended up getting divorced because he was an alcoholic. He hit my mother once and that was it, she threw him out and she changed the locks on the doors and she divorced him.

* * * * *

My mom was always working. About 5:30 she'd come home and she'd make dinner and I'd usually leave. There was a friend of mine who I met in first grade and we became real close and I would go to her house. Her mother was an alcoholic and a drug addict and her sisters were like partiers, you know, so there'd always be people over there drinking, partying. So I'd go over there and we would drink and do whatever, basically, whatever we wanted. I mean it was a very dysfunctional household. At the end, there was no hot water, no electricity, you know.

I got started with alcohol and cigarettes at like eight or nine. By the time I was 12, one of the sisters from that house became my best friend. She was like 17 and she had her own apartment and a drug-dealer boyfriend and I would go stay over there a lot. I remember being there during the week, going to school from there, being there all weekend. And those years—12 through like 14—I got into cocaine. I got into sex. I was putting myself into situations, you know, I had abuse. I had a couple times where men raped me.

[My friend's] boyfriend Javier was a drug dealer and I was totally in love with his brother and he was a real jerk but, anyway, I ended up getting pregnant. I had a miscarriage at like, I think I was 12, 13. I wasn't even sure if it was from his brother or from one of the guys on the footbridge. One night I was walking home late and there was a footbridge, a big bridge that you walk over and it goes from Main Street and these two guys like, I don't know, I think they were there drinking—we used to drink on the footbridge. There were these two guys there and, uh, you know, they asked me if I wanted a drink or whatever and I was like, "No, no, I'm going home" and that was it. You know, they just grabbed me and brought me under the footbridge. So, anyway, I didn't know if it [the pregnancy] was like one of theirs.

* * * * *

[After the miscarriage] I screwed up, ran away, didn't go to school, doing drugs, so they sent me over to my father. While I was living with my father, me and Javier started hanging out even more, and then he killed himself. I remember this girl called me and she's like Javier is gone

and I'm like, what do you mean? Where did he go? You know, and she's like, he's dead. I was devastated. I mean it was frickin' awful. I went to his funeral.

Then I started doing heroin. I was hanging around with my friends and their habits were getting bad and I was doing it sometimes. In the process of that, I met a dealer, Ricki, who's my daughter's father. He made a lot of money. He had a nice car. You know, he was real generous with his money. He was much older than me. He was 27 or 28. I moved in with him quick. I was 15, living with my father, got into a fight with my stepmother, grabbed all my stuff, and went and moved in with him in the projects. [My parents] were totally against [the relationship]. I lied for a while and made it seem like he was okay. I lied about the abuse. I lied about dealing drugs. They didn't know I had a dope habit. I mean I hid everything for years. I told 'em he had a job, this and that. They were totally against it, but I turned 16 so there was nothing they could do legally or anything else. I got hooked on heroin being with him.

I graduated from high school—I was heroin addicted and I was three months pregnant. I didn't care about school, I just wanted to get a D- just to pass so I can get out and that's what I did. I skipped a lot. I was a bad student because I was high. I smoked weed, I drank, you know, then I got caught out on dope. A lot of the times I'd go to school dope sick and the beginning signs of sickness are no energy. I mean you don't even want to walk. You don't want to write. You don't want to talk. Nobody knew. My friends from school didn't know—nobody knew! I just hid it. I mean I became an excellent liar. I could come up with a really good story like—look straight in the eye and just lie, you know. It was real easy for me.

* * * * *

Ricki was the meanest, most abusive person I have ever met. He was cruel, I mean crazy cruel—awful and I stayed with him for like three years. I had to be a wife, you know, cook and clean and sex every night. I got suicidal 'cuz of the abuse. Then after a few years, I got pregnant, and he abused me brutally when I was pregnant. One night I was like seven months pregnant, and he kicked me in my stomach and I remember my knees buckling and I just fell and the pain was so bad. I was bleeding, I couldn't walk, and the whole time he's telling me I'm faking it. I'm on the floor and I'm like help me, you know, and he didn't give a shit. He didn't care. And, finally, once I started bleeding, then he finally gave me the phone and I called my father. I went to the hospital, everything ended up being okay. I lied. I said that I was washing the floor and I tripped and fell. That's what I said, because he would also hit me where nobody could see. He hit me here on the back of my head so no one could see bruises, he'd pull my hair, drag me around by my hair a lot, he'd kick—ugh.

He took off—his grandmother was supposedly sick. I was eight months pregnant, had a dope habit for the most part he was supporting. He didn't use. He just sold drugs. I was getting state. I would blow all my money on dope, wouldn't pay my rent, would lie to my mother, say my check never came; she'd have to pay rent. So one night, it was the middle of a snowstorm, I was eight months pregnant, huge. I had no money. I was so sick. At that time I wasn't prostituting yet, so I couldn't get any money. There was no way to get to a store to return something. There was no money to steal. I'm sick, so five o'clock in the morning— at this point I hadn't talked to my parents in a little while 'cuz after all that happened, they were fed up, or they were sad—anyways, I ended up calling my stepmother's friend and saying I need help. Half an hour later, my father shows up. He knocks, he comes in, and I'm in the bed. There's puke, crap, throw-up, everything all over the floor, pee all over the bed. I mean when you're dope sick it's horrendous, especially being pregnant. He picked me up and he started crying and he carried me down the stairs and brought me to the hospital. That's when my mother found out I was a heroin addict. She didn't know. Everyone kept telling her, Bethany's using heroin. My mother didn't believe it.

At that point, I was still sniffing. I sniffed for years before I even started shootin' up. So, anyway, I went to the hospital. They put me on methadone. I stayed on methadone, had the baby, DCF got involved, had to go into treatment. Miraculously, she came out with no detox, no nothing. She came out fine, which is a miracle. My baby went with my mother. I went to [a drug treatment] institute, and stayed there for quite a while.

I was supposed to be gettin' myself together. I was supposed to get a job or do something, and I just ended up going back with [Ricki] and started usin' again and the abuse got bad again, got worse, and finally I left him for good.

* * * * *

After Ricki, I lived with Edgar, and he was very abusive also. Not as bad as Ricki but he was pretty abusive. He was a junky. That point was probably my worst time as far as being like on the street, being a street prostitute. The past few years, I was a prostitute but I wasn't on the street.

Like I had clients and I'm not saying it's any better but it's different. It's a different lifestyle [than] bein' on the street and also havin' a cocaine habit, as well as a heroin habit. I mean shootin' cocaine, it brought me so low [in my life]. So that was when I was with Edgar, in between Ricki and Alex. I was a prostitute on the street. He was like a pimp. I'd go and make money and he'd wait for me and I had to come back with the money. He'd go cop, and we'd get high and I'd go back out, make more money, and that was that. I'd give him half of everything.

* * * * *

So there was like two years in between Ricki and Alex. I was a stripper. I stripped and I did stag parties. Stripping wasn't as bad as I thought it would be. I wouldn't do it now. But back then it was a good way to make quick money. I mean a lot of money. Stripping at the bars, on a bad night you'd probably make about $95 in tips and then on a good night you could, you know, maybe $200. The hours sucked. I worked one in the afternoon till one o'clock in the morning. As my habit got bigger, I started prostituting at the stag parties. I could come home with, you know, 600 bucks for like two hours [at a] stag party. And you'd be amazed at the men that have these stag parties and like clean-cut guys that are gettin' married the next day. You know, wantin' to have sex or wantin' to have oral sex, you know, with a stripper. The good thing about that is you make a lot of money so [sigh], um, yeah.

I was stayin' with this guy [Mike]. His parents had died and left him 300 grand and he blew it on dope. He got hooked and he supported my habit for a couple years. We never did anything. We never had sex. We were just companions. [One night] I was trying to cop at the gas station and Alex was there; we went to middle school together. He asked me for a ride, so I brought him back to [Mike's] house. I was prostitutin' at that time and we ended up just hangin' out, and then we just started hangin' out more, and then we got together and like we've been together ever since. We went to Puerto Rico, you know, we had dope all the time. We brought like 30 bundles of dope with us on the plane to Puerto Rico, in plastic. This was before September 11, we did all those 30 bundles. Then we probably bought like another 50 bundles down there. I mean our habits were huge.

* * * * *

I got pregnant. The strange thing is that I wasn't gettin' my period anyway, because when I was on dope I went years without gettin' a period.

I was boostin' [shoplifting] at Wal-Mart. We had a real good scam to do it. I mean every day I'd go, me and Alex would go and we'd get two DVD players, 20 DVD movies, and an air conditioner, every day, but like a different Wal-Mart. Some days the same Wal-Mart, whatever. So I got busted and I went to the hospital because my detox was so bad. I didn't look pregnant, but they had a thing on my stomach and they're like, "Oh, there's the second heartbeat." And I was like, "What?" I was like five months pregnant and I didn't [know], but, I was a junky.

I wanted to put the baby up for adoption. Alex didn't want to. I continued to use, so eight months pregnant I got arrested again. I called my mother. We had a meeting with my mother and my mom's new husband, my father, and my stepmother. They said go into treatment right now, have the baby, and we'll take the baby—my father, because [my mother] got my daughter. They wanted me to sign over all my parental rights. They didn't want to take the baby while I got my shit together; they wanted to take the baby forever. I was like, "I can't do that." They're like, that's the deal. Either you give us the baby or we're not gonna help you. That's it. So I was like, all right, I'll think about it. I'll call you in a day. I never called them. They figured I'd have the baby and I'd take off and they'd end up gettin' the baby.

Well, I got here [to a program] on my own. I stayed, I had the baby. He was in the hospital for two months hooked on methadone. He's fine now. I was there every day. He's been here with me at this treatment facility ever since. It's for mothers with addiction that are trying to get their kids back or keep their children. I've been here for over six months.

TAMEKA: "I DON'T SIN, IT'S JUST THE FACT THAT I HAVE TO SURVIVE OUT HERE"

Tameka was a 17-year-old African American pregnant with her first child. Growing up with family violence and neglect, she developed survival strategies that left her feeling lonely and degraded. She attempted suicide numerous times, but with a new life growing inside her she found hope. Her narrative illustrates her wit, her intelligence, her determination, and the scars from a brutal childhood.

I was born in Connecticut and was raised in Detroit [with] my grandfather from three years old till 10. Then I came back [to Connecticut], and I went with my mother. She was always getting beaten on, I guess that's why she'd take it out on her kids. Every boyfriend she had beat her up. She would beat me. She would beat all her kids. Grab us by our hair—that's why I cut all my hair off—try to beat us half to death.

I got raped twice—by my uncle and by some guy that was just on the streets. [When I was] six years old, I was staying with my grandfather and his son was over there sleeping for the weekend. It so happens he got into the room that I was in and he said it was a mistake. He didn't know what he was doing. He just wanted to try something new on a baby and the next morning I was bleeding and stuff. I knew he did something to me that night. I couldn't get up. I was in shock and when my aunt found me I was like, you know, half dead, so they rushed me to the hospital and I told my grandfather what happened. He didn't believe me. To this day he don't believe me. He think that I fell off the bed or something.

I got raped when I was 12 out in the park. I was hanging with friends like around nine o'clock and we was chillin' and running around playing hide-and-go-seek. The next thing you know, I see a guy in a black mask and black clothes and I didn't know really what it was. I thought that my friends were just playing with me. When they found me on the rocks by the water, bleeding, couldn't talk, I just kept asking him to help me and I kept telling him, "Don't touch me, I'm scared!" He was holding me. I was real cold. He was like, "I'm not gonna do nothing to you. What's wrong with you?" My kidneys is messed up now, just messed up completely. They say it's not that bad now but in the future it could get bad.

I was scared of men for a minute, I really was, and I broke out of that because I know everybody doesn't hurt everybody but it's just some little chicks out there. So, that happened in my past but I'm livin' in the future.

*   *   *   *   *

I always try to ask God for forgiveness for all my sins, even though I don't sin, it's just the fact that I have to survive out here. Basically, I've been on my own ever since I was 15—on the streets, going to relatives, off and on, staying here and there or staying with friends, or I would find a boyfriend. I started staying with a friend and her mother like six, seven months, and then I run off and started going to the city [New York] every weekend getting money and that was all she wrote. Everybody started down-talking me. I'm like this for a reason. I can't just sit out here and be poor, just be like a little girl in the streets lost. I had to get money somewhere to survive so I got called all types of names.

I stripped. I didn't have sex with anybody. I didn't leave with nobody, ever. It was me and a cousin, we used to go up to the city or Bridgeport and make money every single day and I would never leave with nobody else. That's one thing my mom taught me—never have sex with somebody you don't know. That's one thing I could give myself respect because I was a stripper for two years and I never left with nobody.

I would come back with a pocketful of money and I'd just rent a room for like a week, me and my friends, and we would just smoke weed and I smoked so much. I was a alcoholic at one point, too. I drank to where I almost died. I drank like bottles of Bacardi, vodka, gin—anything I could get my hands on. I would drink it just to see if I would really pass, but I was so strong that God is like, you gonna make it. That's why He's not letting me go nowhere.

* * * * *

[My neighborhood is] not quiet at all. Drug dealers, I mean people shooting at each other every other day. If it ain't over a piece of weed, it's over somebody trying to take somebody's money. They be going crazy over here. Them hot days, oh my goodness. The girl down the street getting jumped and she got beat up again right here the same hour. She got beat up by two people—by three, actually. And the neighborhood, around here a lot of jakes [police] be over here on the bridge. Yeah, they be all over the place. Bounty hunters, the dogs. This ain't the neighborhood you want to live in. This is the hood. This neighborhood over here you gotta watch where you walk, watch your back every five minutes, make sure nobody poppin', shootin', doing this, that, and the forth.

The police around here are crazy. Sometime they harass you for nothing. Half of 'em drink and smoke on the job and then come out on the streets and harass people. They beat people up for no reason. And let it be [Billy], which is a white cop, and his brother, you might as just say you were a deathbed 'cuz they'll beat you till they see you bleed. They still got that racism in their blood. That's why they do what they do best to black people. They just think they're somebody 'cuz they got a badge and they got their rights to do whatever they want, kill people and get away with it. I ain't hear not one police officer shooting somebody and getting suspended or losing their job or going to jail. They don't give us no type of respect.

* * * * *

I wasn't always into boys. I was about money, just all about money because, where was I gonna stay? Where was I gonna eat the next day or all day? Where was I gonna do this, get clothes, get sneakers, get my hair done? I was all about money.

Once, I got hit by [a boyfriend]. He broke the right side of my face, bust my eardrum, kick me all in my ribs. My whole body was aching. Everything was bruised and my mother and my stepfather actually sat there and let him beat on me like that. He even dragged me down the stairs by my hair, put me in the car and child safety locks on the doors and the windows and [my family] didn't do nothing. They just let him pull off with me in the car. He locked me in that dirty hotel. He told me if I ever leave him he was gonna kill me 'cuz "he can't have me, nobody can have me." So right now he's in jail doing five to 10 years for beatin' on me and plus he got a lot of drug charges.

*　*　*　*　*

Kevin [her baby's father] lived right around the corner from me so he used to come by all the time and we finally got up like four months later, became boyfriend and girlfriend thing. I was 17 and he was 18 and we started as friends and the next thing you know it was like a sexual thing and we was too close. He nice to me, he sweet, kind. He like to talk, conversate. He be singing to me and stuff. We was real cool as friends and then we got into a deep relationship. Next thing you know, condom popped, then we like, we not going to use no more 'cuz he already knew the deal [laugh]. I'm too strong to not make babies.

Two months later, that's when it ended. Day after Thanksgiving we broke up. I found out I was pregnant like a month later and that's when I started going crazy. Crying. I knew I was pregnant because of the symptoms. I hadn't got my period, my breasts was growing. You know my attitude changed. I was like spazzing on anybody and anything. I was getting sick all the time.

First I wanted to kill it. Then I wanted to do something to myself for me being dumb like that to get pregnant by a man that don't even want to be bothered with me or my baby. I regret it but I don't regret my child and when I first got pregnant it was like, "Oook. Not you!" I always said I would never had no kids.

Kevin gets my symptoms for me. Yep, sick, throwing up, any smell bother him, perfume, anything bother him. Yep, and he did not like it 'cuz he tried to deny my baby at one time and it couldn't work. If my baby not yours, then who do you got pregnant 'cuz you got all the symptoms—all of 'em. He was like, "I don't want the baby. Forget you and the baby. Go get a abortion for all I care." His mother and father *put in his head that I was a ho and made him think that I was sleeping with other guys and she's gonna trap you like that other baby mother did.*

I was gonna take me and my baby out of this world. I did it twice when I was 16 and twice when I was 17. I was just collecting pills and taking 'em, and taking 'em and laying on the floor and my uncle came in and I was just shaking all across the floor and vibrating the whole floor and he called the ambulance and by the time I got there I was halfway dead. They kept me at the hospital in the psychiatric ward and they wanted to talk to me. They sent all kind of counselors to me to ask me why am I doing this and I told 'em because I'm tired of living alone. I'm tired of being alone and it's starting to get real ugly out here. It's kind of hard when you're not even 18 and you're on the streets.

I see him [Kevin] every day I go to school. He look at me, I look at him. And then I look at my stomach and I look back up. I will be all right, 'cuz I'm strong. I raised myself, so I could raise myself and my child by myself—you just make sure you there to sign my son birth certificate. I don't care what else you do. Just sign my son birth certificate.

* * * * *

I had to change my life around before somebody find me on the side of the street somewhere. I went from hanging in gangs, selling drugs, from stripping to where I'm at now. I done been through too much. I done try to escape from a rapist jumpin' out of cabs on a highway. I could make a movie based on me, upon this young girl that used to do what she had to do to survive. And ain't none of it worth it. I mean, it's money, it's fast money but that fast money not worth more than your life. There's better ways to make money—writing a book, playing with kids in a daycare, anything, you know, working at McDonald's. I don't care where but working is better than being on the streets.

I still struggle but it's not like it used to be. I sit out here on the porch some days and I just look at my past. I don't want no drama. I want a simple life where I could just go home with my child every day from work and school and just be in my house. That's why I feel me and my child is gonna make it. I'm gonna give God my heart, my soul, and my hands. I'm gonna let Him work with me and I'm just gonna pray every day; things comes to those who wait.

TAKING IT TO THE STREETS AND
LIVING TO TELL ABOUT IT

I can see a world where we all live
Safe and free from all oppression
No more rape or incest, or abuse
Women are not a possession
—"Break the Chain" by Tena Clark

Bethany's and Tameka's life stories reflect an extreme version of violence against women that is more commonplace than we want to believe. In the United States, it is estimated one in six women has been raped, and one in four has experienced physical abuse by a partner at some point in their lifetime.[1] In addition to the child sexual abuse discussed in the last chapter, other forms of interpersonal violence occurred at the hands of parents, partners, and strangers. Some saw their mothers viciously beaten by boyfriends and husbands, and, as with Tameka, their mothers turned around and beat their children. When these girls grew up, many of them partnered with men who abused them. The girls were beaten with belts, shoes, a cable wire, an electrical cord, a metal bat, a two-by-four, a broomstick, pans, fists, feet, knees, and hands; they used terms like "stomped," "kicked," "bashed," and "choked." Throughout are images of heads slammed into rocks and walls and women shoved down stairs, punched in pregnant bellies, dragged by their hair, locked in cars, trapped in hotel rooms and houses, and emotionally and psychologically tortured and tormented. In this chapter, we show how the story of early childbearing is embedded in interpersonal webs of violence and suffering, and maintain that understanding their young births requires that we examine them within these contexts.

EXAMINING VIOLENCE

In this chapter, we focus mostly on interpersonal violence, which includes violence between individuals in the home, on the streets, in schools, and in other public places. We conceptualize interpersonal violence as an expression of power and domination that occurs within a matrix of race, class, and gender hierarchies organized through institutions, laws, and public policies that both create and legitimatize power relationships.[2]

The organization of power and domination through gender is evident in the roles men have historically performed in the public sphere, particularly the most powerful economic and state leadership positions, but it is also evident in the private sphere, where they have assumed the roles of breadwinner, patriarch, and family disciplinarian. The gendered matrix of power organized through commerce, government, religion, family, and the media creates a cultural framework through which male power and domination are normalized and reproduced, that is, seen as part of *the natural order of social life.* The internalization of this cultural frame occurs as men and women perform their roles within their respective gendered locations in meaningful and intended ways. When women internalize these categories of perception, they participate in the organization and reproduction of masculine domination.[3]

Daily subjugation to interpersonal forms of power often generates irritation and frustration, if not anger and resistance. Interpersonal challenges to the "natural order" of gender relations create hostile situations that invoke male violence as a way of restoring the social order, or putting women in their place. As sociologist Gail Garfield describes, women navigate "the treacherous terrain between cultural and social expectations and their own self-defined needs, interests, and aspirations."[4] The potential for violence then exists "when agency collides with cultural and social constraints: when women's needs, interests, and aspirations are in conflict with cultural and social arrangements under which they live their lives."[5]

Dominant categories of perception are socially embedded and reinforced through stigma—for instance, stigmatizing people by where they live (in the "ghetto"), by what they do (early childbirth), or through cultural representations of women that are raced and classed (as in the "ho" or the "gold digger"). Words can be used to degrade, dismiss, and devalue women, thereby assaulting their integrity, as well as their emotional and psychological well-being. These words draw upon larger symbolic and cultural representations and meanings that are embedded in national and local hierarchies.

In this book, when we talk about national hierarchies, we are referring to the organization of power and domination by race, class, gender, and sexual orientation, within which perceptions and understandings of the social world are structured to legitimate a social order. The white racial frame discussed in chapter 2 or the three intersecting public narratives outlined in chapter 1 that demonize teen mothers are each a conceptual ordering of social categories that normalize and reproduce a national hierarchy of power and domination. At the local level, these hierarchies reflect power relations within concrete, specific social spaces (for example, the home, neighborhood, and school). Racial and economic segregation in Connecticut creates different local hierarchies and expressions of violence against women, as evident in the stories of Bethany and Tameka that begin this chapter as well as the stories that follow.

Gendered violence happens irrespective of class or racial privilege. In the small state of Connecticut, the Coalition for Domestic Violence provided services to over 54,000 victims of domestic violence in a 12-month period beginning in the summer of 2010 at 18 statewide sites, and members of all social classes and racial groups utilized these services.[6] While money, status, and prestige provide women with more resources to resist or negotiate male violence, intimate partner violence occurs in even the most privileged households, as many high-profile examples in Connecticut illustrate. In 2010, a Connecticut nightly television news anchor, Janet Peckinpaugh, disclosed her personal story of spousal abuse. Her husband beat her on the second day of her marriage, forbade her from seeing friends, stalked her to monitor her interactions with colleagues, and punished perceived improprieties by beating and then raping her.[7]

In 2009, Richard Shenkman, a former advertising executive, kidnapped his wife from a parking garage after she filed for a divorce, took her to their former home, handcuffed her to himself, threatened to kill her several times, and engaged in a standoff with police, before burning down the home. At his sentencing, he threatened to hire an assassin to kill his wife while he was in prison and looked forward to returning to court to be sentenced for his capital felony. On hearing this, Shenkman's attorney immediately rose from his seat and renewed his motion for a psychiatric evaluation. But was Shenkman insane, or was he exercising, in a rather extreme public manner, his gendered belief in his right to control his wife, even while locked away in prison?[8]

Even though gendered violence occurs across all class and racial groups, the social and economic marginalization of men can intensify masculine domination in the home and in heterosexual relationships. Joblessness, underemployment, police brutality, and other indignities in the public sphere can emasculate men and lead to a more compelling need to express masculinity within the constrained spaces where power and domination are still available.[9] Working-class and poor white males have historically experienced the emasculating effects of class injuries, white ethnic stigma, nativist rage, and exploitative wages. Class exploitation expressed through a racial caste system has reserved the greatest assault on masculinity for African American men, which has been organized historically through the institutional forms of slavery, Jim

Crow, and the urban ghetto, and now through hyperincarceration.[10] At times, these conditions have led to collective mobilization and effective political organizing, most evident in labor and civil rights struggles and perhaps best symbolized by Martin Luther King Jr.'s last campaign in 1968, when striking Memphis sanitation workers wore signs that read "I am a man."

These same emasculating conditions, however, when experienced as intractable can produce destructive forms of masculinity, irrespective of race. In the most extreme instances, swells of rage are misplaced as deeply felt injuries, and vulnerabilities convert loved ones, emotionally and subjectively, into "unworthy, immoral, or disobedient" others.[11] Victims become victimizers as households are disrupted by misplaced violence, and expressions of intimacy and vulnerability become intertwined in a destructive trajectory of verbal humiliations, physical violence, and contorted, self-preserving justifications. The insidious narratives of male dominance, integral to conventional expressions of manhood, get plowed into subplots of destructive masculinity and family instability.[12] As we examine these life stories scarred with interpersonal violence, it is important to remember that the home—often depicted as a safe space—is ironically the space where injured men feel most free to practice violence against women.

LIFE WORLDS OF CHAOS

Repeated incidents of family and partner violence were central in one-third (n = 37) of the life stories. These young mothers lived in what we refer to as life worlds of chaos. The chaos was continuous, extreme, and interwoven, thereby creating a "life world" and not simply an event. The masculine cocktail of alcohol and drugs, infidelities, and violence that injected insecurity, anxiety, and fear, if not terror, into the household often precipitated family disruption.[13] For nearly one-half of the mothers in this group, repeated domestic violence, drug and alcohol abuse, and physical child abuse were part of their childhoods (see table 3). The 37 mothers we focus on in this chapter distinguished themselves from the remaining 71 mothers on other indicators as well: they were more likely to have been sexually assaulted or abused, to exhibit serious behavioral problems, to have dropped out of school at some point, to have engaged regularly in illicit drug use as adolescents, to have been physically abused by a male partner, and to have experienced a mental illness.

TABLE 3   PERCENT OF MOTHERS WITH PROBLEMS IN HOUSEHOLD WHILE
GROWING UP

	Life Worlds of Chaos (n = 37)	Remaining Teen Mothers (n = 71)
Problems in family of origin		
Domestic violence	81%	22%
Illicit drug/alcohol abuse	92%	30%
Physical child abuse	70%	28%
All three family problems	53%	6%
Problems among teen mothers		
Sexually assaulted/abused	49%	14%
Serious behavioral problems	62%	24%
Ever dropped out of high school	73%	58%
Illicit drug use	44%	16%
Physically abused by partner	70%	27%
Mental illness	49%	23%

Violence in these families usually started early when parents had drug and alcohol addictions. Mothers and fathers were perpetrators of violence, especially mothers who were victims of violence themselves. Several girls left their homes at early ages to escape the volatility of family members: some moved in with other family members, some with friends, some with boyfriends, and some with their boyfriends' families. Escape often led them into the arms of abusive men, to early pregnancies, and in some cases into the sex business, as in the stories of Bethany and Tameka. And they were not exceptions. The following stories of Jackie and Kelly describe similar worlds of chaos.

Jackie was 18 years of age at the time of the interview, living in her hometown of New Britain, a small, dying industrial city. Born to a Puerto Rican father and a white mother, she described her father as an alcoholic, but he was the primary caretaker since her mother was often out "drinkin' and druggin'." Police were called frequently to their home for domestic violence, and on a few occasions they arrested her father, but her mother never pressed charges. Their fights were often about her father's infidelities.

Jackie started to hang out with an older crowd and began experimenting with drugs at age 13. By the time she was 15, she had been arrested three times (for drugs, truancy, and auto theft), and subsequently moved between juvenile lockup facilities and house arrest. At

14, Jackie's uncle attempted to rape her. Jackie escaped and obtained a restraining order, but not a conviction. At 15, she ran away to New York City with a friend and survived as a prostitute for four months: "we were staying with guys and, um, it was bad over there, very bad. These guys used to like pimp for us; we just sleep around with everybody and get money and just do drugs all day." When she returned to Connecticut, she "fell in love" with a man and they tried to get pregnant. Soon after moving in with him though, he became violent. Because of the physical abuse she witnessed growing up, Jackie had promised herself that she would never allow a man to abuse her, but "he used to beat the shit out of me everyday. Punch me in the face, pull my hair or rip my clothes." She stayed in the relationship for seven months, before "learning from my mother's mistakes" and "walking out."

As a self-described "out-of-control" runaway youth escaping a volatile household, Jackie was vulnerable to the sexual dominance and violence of men. Being a runaway is a structural situation that increased her risk for abuse. She was pimped by men and beaten by boyfriends. She tells us that she "fell in love" at the age of 16 and became pregnant at 17, not as an accident, but in a deliberate quest to "start over," a theme we will return to later in this chapter.

Kelly was a 20-year-old white mother at the time of the interview living in a crumbling midsized city that was once a prominent mill town. She grew up in a poorer area of the city that she colloquially defined as the "wrong side of the tracks." Despite horrendous spousal abuse, her parents remained married for 21 years. Her father worked third shift at a local factory for most of these years and regularly spent his free time in the bar. Kelly recalls that he would frequently come home drunk and beat her mother: "I used to wake to it all the time. I was scared because my mother was getting hurt. I thought that that was supposed to happen when I was little, you know, 'cause I really didn't know any different." Violence in the home caused "nervousness" and "anxiety attacks," and after one of the fights, at age 15, she attempted suicide. The following year she ran away from home. For the first six months, "I was going to friend, to friend, to friend, to friend. I was like in the streets for like six months, and then I found [Robert, her child's father,] and was with him for like two years. I don't know why but I did! [laugh]." At the time, she was 16 and he was 19.

Seeking solace and protection from her volatile home, however, quickly turned into a nightmare as Robert began to exercise male power and control over Kelly. She described:

I wasn't allowed outside. I had to stay in the house. I wasn't allowed to talk to my mother. He scared off all my friends and I wasn't like allowed to wear my clothes. I had to wear his clothes like when I was going outside. I had to wear a winter jacket in the summertime. I had to look down when I was outside. If I looked up I'd get smacked. Stupid things like that. It's just like why are you doing this to me? I stayed [with] him for like two years and I finally started to hit him back. It didn't help much but [shrug].

When we asked how often the physical abuse occurred, Kelly replied, "like every day, for no apparent reason at all. I'd like look the wrong way and he'd like smack the shit out of me!"

Kelly never called the police herself: "I was too afraid to tell anybody." But Robert was arrested when a stranger called the police after seeing them "fighting in the street." At that time, she was four months pregnant. After his arrest, Kelly left him. Escaping her volatile home at 16, Kelly returned home at 18, pregnant but relieved to finally extricate herself from the chaotic, violent life with the father of her child.

This pattern occurred in the life stories of white, brown, and black teen mothers living in both urban areas and small towns across the state. Violent childhood homes sent young girls looking for refuge, protection, and love, exposing and exacerbating their vulnerabilities in places where drug and alcohol use, sex, and sometimes petty forms of delinquency were folded into gendered patterns of power and dominance. Many of them returned to their families after a few years—bruised and pregnant.

VIOLENCE IN THE LIFE STORIES OF URBAN MOTHERS

Even though intimate partner violence happens across racial, ethnic, and socioeconomic groups, the sociospatial organization of vulnerability to violence does vary.[14] In our study, women living in areas of urban concentrated poverty had fewer resources and options to avoid or redress violent relationships; they sometimes had to negotiate violent circumstances in order to meet basic material needs; and they lived in neighborhoods where street violence was more prevalent and trust in the police or the courts for protection less customary.[15]

Listening to the life stories of mothers from cities in Connecticut was a reminder that the state harbors some of the greatest wealth and greatest poverty in the nation. Connecticut has led the nation in per capita income for more than 20 years[16] and, at the turn of the twenty-first century, housed the third largest proportion of millionaires and had the third lowest rate of poverty in the nation.[17] However, as we described in chapter 1, a different picture emerges in the urban areas. Child poverty in Hartford at the turn of the century was 41 percent, the second highest in the nation, and four times higher than the state average.[18] Further, nearly one-half of all blacks and Latinos in the state resided in the four largest and poorest cities.[19] Median family income in Hartford in 2000 was 38 percent of its 17-town regional average,[20] and while Hartford houses 24 percent of the region's children younger than six years, nearly 60 percent of all poor children in the region live in Hartford. Similar conditions exist in New Haven,[21] and roughly one-half of teen mothers in our sample living in life worlds of chaos resided in Hartford and New Haven.

We identified six common themes from the life stories of vulnerable mothers living in Connecticut's urban neighborhoods.[22] First, violence was interwoven into their struggle for daily financial survival, which was described as a lack of job opportunities, the inadequacy of state resources, and their dependence on men for material resources (often acquired from the illegal street economy). We saw this in the life story of Lilly, one of the young young mothers in the second chapter, who was beaten so badly by Rafael that she was admitted into the hospital for her injuries and he was sent to jail only to be bailed out by her mother. Lilly and her family depended on Rafael for his financial support. Second, their struggles to find intimacy and establish motherhood were compromised by violent partners, drug and alcohol abuse, infidelities, and, in some instances, polygamous lifestyles. Lilly and other mothers shared the fathers of their children with other women, with varying degrees of tolerance, resentment, and hostility.

Third, their childhood homes were usually disrupted by violence and drug and alcohol addiction, and, in the throes of addiction, parents abused and neglected their children. As a child, Alisha mistook her mother's crack pipe for a lightbulb; she was beaten with belts, bats, shoes, and hangers, and sexually molested by her stepfather. Fourth, street life, violent neighborhoods and schools, and, in several instances, street gangs were common in their stories as risky spaces that had to be negotiated.

Fifth, racial segregation and the accompanying territorial stigma were present in their stories in more subtle ways, as they imagined or fantasized about idyllic families and stable home lives and sought cultural respectability and personal dignity—often through motherhood. And finally, the lack of public safety in their neighborhoods was expressed by distrust in the police and their reliance on interpersonal violence for retaliatory justice and personal protection.

These six patterns were illustrated in the life story of Tameka at the beginning of this chapter—and we will return to her story shortly. Another example—and, sadly, these examples were not hard to find in this study—is the following life story of Cassandra, a Puerto Rican mother from Hartford who gave birth at 16. Cassandra was introduced in the prior chapter as a victim of child sexual abuse. We provide more of her life story here in an effort to see the intersection between individual lives and larger social forces of race, class, and gender.

Cassandra: "Everything Negative Comes from White People"

Cassandra grew up in one of the poorest neighborhoods in the state, with few institutional anchors or jobs, even though the golden dome of the state capitol was less than a mile away.[23] Except for a hazy memory of being sexually abused by her father (the Wonder Bread poking through the bag), she remembers little about him. Her aunt, however, told her that her father used to beat her mother regularly. The pattern was repeated by a stepfather and escalated until Cassandra's mother stabbed him with a knife. The incident led to state intervention: Cassandra's younger siblings were removed from the home and her mother was mandated to alcohol treatment.

At this point, Cassandra said that she became the equivalent of a domestic servant in the household, responsible for the cooking, the cleaning, doing the laundry, and waiting on one uncle who regularly smoked crack in the house. Cassandra finally left and moved in with her grandmother in a Puerto Rican neighborhood on the south side of the city. As Cassandra described: "I didn't have a childhood and I'm not even playing. I just let it be, like fuck it!"

Her new neighborhood was also very poor and at that time it was disputed space between two gangs, Los Sólidos and the Latin Kings. Cassandra carried a knife to school. She regularly engaged in fights with other girls: "I'm the type of person that I go to their face." Violence was an integral part of Cassandra's life and survival meant learning and engaging street culture. Cassandra described the entrenched drug trade in her neighborhood:

> Everybody sells drugs in this neighborhood. Everybody! They sell drugs everywhere, even close to *popos* [police]. We know *popos*, they tell us the narcs coming and we bounce [leave]. We know police that sell drugs and they police at the same time.

A violent street culture and a lawless drug trade dominated public spaces in Cassandra's south side neighborhood. She said, "At 13, everything starts." Her guardians attempted to intervene by appealing to the juvenile courts, and a judge placed her under house arrest when she was 16.

Economically depleted urban neighborhoods with vibrant street life pose difficult dilemmas for young women like Cassandra. Men dominate street life and the culture reflects this. The codes that govern street life, according to sociologist Elijah Anderson, encourage behavioral dispositions that emphasize masculine toughness and respect, which are reinforced through violence and the threat of violence.[24] In this hypermasculine setting, male status is acquired by successfully engaging in the hierarchy of illicit street trades and practices, through the public performance of violence, and through sexual conquest. In many ways, what Anderson describes is the exaggeration of conventional male practices that signify manhood—financial success and sexual prowess—or what Michael Kimmel and Michael Messner refer to as the mastery of the 2 Bs: the breadwinner and the bedroom.[25] In the context of disinvested urban areas, however, the organization of financial success has elevated physical violence as a means of status and respect and as a condition for access to street revenue. It is the exercise of hypermasculinity that secures men a place in the organization of street life and in the distribution of both material and cultural resources. And it is in this context of hypermasculinity that low-income urban girls like Cassandra come of age—girls who "have no childhood" and just "be, like fuck it!"

In her book *Between Good and Ghetto,* sociologist Nikki Jones extends the code of the streets to the lives of young black women. For Jones, black urban girls "embrace, challenge, reflect, and contradict normative expectations of femininity and Black respectability as they work the code [of the streets]."[26] As she explains, many girls, like Cassandra, engage in physical violence—often girl-on-girl violence—and adopt an identity, reinforced by the "ride-or-die bitch" image projected in the popular media and some music, that creates a "newly defiant image of Black femininity" in violent communities.[27] Inner-city girls, according to Jones, must negotiate the contradictory cultural messages as they walk the boundaries represented by defiant, street respectability and more normative, feminine respectability. In these settings, women may participate in violence or in the drug trade or become gang involved, but they must do so by managing gender differences and ideologies, as well as male domination on the streets.[28]

Cassandra provides an example of how women perform street agency that utilizes violence and other street skills to navigate their social circumstances from the lower rung of a gendered hierarchy of power and domination. At age 16, Cassandra became romantically involved with a 23-year-old member of Los Sólidos. The relationship was volatile, and Cassandra described how the codes of respect governing violence on the streets entered the domestic sphere and normalized intimate partner violence:

> Men got a right to hit women for some certain things and women got the right to hit men, that's as a rule. If she's disrespecting the man, slap her! If she disrespect him, oh, calling him a *cabrones*—like that's the biggest word—you slap her and you bounce. You don't disrespect a female, you don't let no female disrespect you. Women are crazy, women are cats, yo.

Cassandra's tough street identity did not spare her the injuries of gender oppression. She may have used drugs publicly, engaged in violence, and adopted the code of respect to mediate conflicts in both the public and the private spheres, but she was also expected to observe gendered distinctions in her relationship, which included tolerating her partner's infidelities and taking care of domestic chores and her boyfriend's needs. These lines became even more evident after the pregnancy.

Caught in a binary construction of femininity—between home and the streets, or between "good and ghetto," to use Jones's terms—Cassandra attempted to resolve culturally contradictory messages through motherhood. After she repeated ninth grade for the third time, she decided to become a mother at age 16 "to stop chillin' on the street." Cassandra was attempting to embrace what she saw as a valued and legitimate form of female respectability—being a mother. Her boyfriend, however, did not share her interest, which did not matter much to Cassandra. They had known each other for only a year and from the beginning Cassandra was clear about her motives. "I was like I want a kid, and he was like with who? I'm like with you, if you ready, if you ain't ready, then I'm gonna have it anyways, so it happened."[29] Neither Cassandra's grandmother nor her mother was supportive. In fact, her grandmother was outraged, criticizing her for becoming pregnant by an "*abandonao* and a Sólidos."[30]

The father denied paternity in the beginning, Cassandra said, and "when I was two months pregnant he was messin' with other girls. He got infected. He gave it to me and then I got it cured." Viewing the transfer of venereal disease as a blatant sign of disrespect, Cassandra adopted a confrontational pose, "So I was like yo, if anything happen to me or the baby, I'mma kill you." Choosing motherhood and, subsequently, domesticity as a way of leaving the streets, Cassandra normalized the demarcation between the public and the private gendered spheres, as the father of her baby claimed his male prerogatives: "He controlled me, always telling me stay home with the baby, when you go out, take the baby. So I changed because of him. I started being wifely with him." But being "wifely" also meant that the father was free to indulge himself in masculine street routines—he drank and used drugs regularly, slept with other women, and attempted to dominate Cassandra through physical violence and verbal humiliation, calling her names like "chickenhead" and "whore."

After exchanging stories with one of his former mistresses, Cassandra described his polygamous lifestyle: "I just realized that from his ex, he went out straight from me to her. It's from bed to bed, so it's like, even if you pregnant by him, he going to treat you the same way. He gonna still be fuckin' other bitches." Cassandra's exasperation with her boyfriend stemmed from her grudging realization that assuming domestic or "wifely" duties was not likely to alter the gendered dynamics that betrayed her. Cassandra's interest in having a child to leave the streets reflected her desire to live a more conventional lifestyle, imagined as motherhood, domesticity, and monogamy, but the social conditions in which she lived did not support such a conventional lifestyle.[31]

These were nonetheless the circumstances that women like Cassandra were attempting to negotiate. On the one hand, living in an impoverished neighborhood where a drug economy created both jobs and violence, Cassandra was more dependent on men, and especially on men who could work the underground economy. When asked if she thought that "a woman needs a man around," Cassandra responded that women in her circumstances need a man to be a provider:

> Yeah, it's really important because sometimes you need help with your kid like when there's no money and your kid needs Pampers and milk and it's hard for your grandmother [or] whoever to get it. The man always got it because the man will always be hustling. The man will always have some type of money there.

On the other hand, Cassandra also understood two things about the drug trade that are often misconstrued by popular media—that most drug dealers don't make much money and that the money is unreliable. She continued: "And when you hustle, you don't get a raise. You just get the same amount unless you know how to buy more and sell more, but you never gonna get that. The only people that will get that is the *bichotes* that got cars and motorcycles, all of it."

After Cassandra's boyfriend went to jail on a domestic violence charge that Cassandra described as "pushing my grandmother and my mother," she left him. Since his release, she has refused to allow him to see their son. She explained: "He look like he on crack or something. And I don't trust that type, that type is a low life, is nothing, nothing, nothing. If anything I'm looking for someone that's really gonna be there for my son. Other than that, then I just know how to be a daddy and mommy." She described one subsequent relationship that had filled her with false hope. She was living with a new boyfriend in her grandmother's house and saving for an apartment from income he earned at a formal job. While his regular paycheck may have removed them from reliance on the streets, he was apparently desired by other women as well who imagined family stability. He left Cassandra to live with another woman who was having his child. Feeling deep regret at the time of the interview, Cassandra distinguished herself from the other woman by invoking a gendered moral identity—or the "good and ghetto" theme. When he was with her, she emphasized, her boyfriend was "never late for work," while the other girl she described as nothing more than a "gold digger."

Cassandra was seeking an alternative life to the streets. While she knew the trials and tribulations that confront people in her neighborhood, she nonetheless wanted to stay in the neighborhood and live among "her people." "I like this neighborhood right here," she said, "yeah we got people selling drugs, whatever, but they still our peoples. It's like in the summer we have fun, everybody come out with they kids and all that." Moreover, she was aware that her struggle was related to racial domination. "Everything negative," she pointed out, "comes from white people." Police, for her, were an extension of that—they were corrupt and racist. Adopting her street pose, she said: "Stop acting because you got a blue outfit, people supposed to respect you. Stop acting like that because I really don't care—the badge is just nothing but plastic." She said that in her neighborhood calling the police was "stupid, really stupid!" Like many in her neighborhood, Cassandra relied on retaliatory or street justice to address violence. "You fuck with our family, you gonna fuck with us. You mess with our kids, oh, you definitely gonna mess with us and the other ones that are behind us."

These were the conditions that women like Cassandra were negotiating and in which teen births were occurring. Her experiences were similar to those of Tameka's story that opened the chapter.

Tameka: "Please Put Me in a White Home"

Cassandra and Tameka both grew up in racial minority neighborhoods in two of Connecticut's poorest cities. They both ran away from homes disrupted by poverty, violence, and drug abuse and entered a male-dominated street world shaped by social and economic marginality. Both Cassandra and Tameka were victims of sexual abuse; they were regularly beaten by mothers who were regularly beaten by boyfriends; and they were abused by their own partners. And both described the police in their neighborhoods as corrupt, mistrustful, violent, racist, and on the take.

Tameka's story is particularly illustrative of the symbolic violence that saturates the lives of people living in areas of relegated black poverty.[32] Angry with her parents for the abuse she had sustained, she blamed them for the chaos in her life using an internalized racial frame through which to make sense of it. Tameka fantasized about living in a family that she presumed would be the opposite of her own—a white family. She told state child protective staff, "If you ever do get me to a foster parent, please put me in a white home." Here she imagined that parents "go into the [bed]rooms and kiss and tuck 'em in good night" and "treat [children] with so much respect." Tameka continued, "Even with Puerto Ricans, I used to want to live [with them] 'cuz they got so much respect with each other." Her fantasies were shaped by the very discourse that demonized her community—she imagined escape from her nightmarish life, and her imagination took shape within a racial framework that posed all that is good as being nonblack.

Tameka's pregnancy also invoked symbolic violence. The father and his parents blamed her for the pregnancy. The father was, according to Tameka, having unprotected sex with another young woman at the time, but he and his parents ignored his sexual promiscuity and instead drew on gendered stereotypes to discredit Tameka. Attributing her street life to her character, they described her as "a ho" who was sleeping with other men, unworthy of their son, and just trying to trap him by blaming him for the pregnancy. In other words, they utilized a local social hierarchy that defined women who were street involved, promiscuous, and violent at the bottom of the hierarchy, as deserving of abuse and ridicule, and as "nasty" or as "ghetto chicks."[33] In short, the father of the child and his parents indulged in symbolic violence to discredit Tameka—to put her in her place—utilizing both larger racial and local gender hierarchies.

Both Cassandra and Tameka were 17 at the time of our interviews and both constructed narratives of survival. We have tried to understand their pregnancies within their life worlds of physical and symbolic violence against women, economic inequalities, racial hierarchies, and gender expectations that make motherhood a contentious domain of respectability. In the next section we contrast their narratives with their white counterparts.

VIOLENCE IN WHITE FAMILIES: SURVIVING IN SMALL TOWNS

While words like "the hood" or "ghetto" signify danger and violence and invoke the criminality of blackness, words like "the burbs" and "small town" signify whiteness, tranquility, and safety. The glare of the spotlight on urban violence, however, can blind us to violence that is occurring in white suburban and rural areas, and to similar expressions of destructive masculinity and gendered violence that exist in these areas as well.

As an aggregate, the white teen mothers in our study were distinguishable from black and brown mothers by having more economic and social resources, living in less economically distressed towns and neighborhoods, and experiencing more favorable interactions with institutional authorities. Despite these privileges, many of their stories were also laced with violence, drugs, and sexual abuse. In several cases, divorce or separation left white working-class households with limited resources; however, some families could rely on resources that had been accumulated by grandparents who had been gainfully employed during more prosperous years. The period of great American prosperity following World War II, combined with the strength of labor unions and governmental policies that facilitated college education and home ownership, left a generation of working-class families with homes, savings accounts, pensions, and life insurance policies for future generations to leverage.[34] Whites disproportionately benefited from these resources, and their life stories reflected it. After the economy was restructured in the 1970s and 1980s, however, conditions for resource accumulation among working-class families dwindled. In addition to using assets the prior generation had acquired to stabilize families, more women entered the workforce.

White families in our study experienced the economic and social consequences of deindustrialization that ripped apart white cities and towns like Torrington, Manchester, New Britain, New London, Willimantic, and Norwich. The stresses and strains of economic restructuring added to the struggles of working-class communities, and anger, violence, and drug and alcohol abuse reverberated within their homes. While violence on the streets was also evident, it was more often inside the white homes that women were being slapped, punched, raped, and otherwise brutalized.

As we saw, Kelly lay in bed at night and listened to her drunk father terrorize the household. Bethany's alcoholic stepfather molested her in the bathtub and assaulted her mother. Diane had an unemployed step-father who raped her mother and "smacked" her around; Jennifer had a father who physically and emotionally abused her and chased her with a knife; Kate's father molested her and her sisters; and Terese recalled that, during her father's spells of unemployment, his practices of corporal punishment crossed the line into cruelty, including beatings with a belt, hitting with objects like shoes, and, on one occasion, smash-ing her head into a wall. All are white mothers from small towns in Connecticut, where violence may be less public and less visible, but is no less destructive and consequential.

In their study of working-class families in two cities undergoing rapid deindustrialization in the 1970s and 1980s, Michelle Fine and Lois Weis found that while domestic violence was prevalent in the homes of white families, it was less publicly exposed than in black and Latino families, even to extended family members.[35] In our study, we noted deliberate lapses in the stories of several white mothers. This often became apparent when they started talking about a topic but then shut down, when they used a phrase like "slapped us around" but refused to elaborate, or when in the second interview things were revealed that contradicted the story they were telling in the first interview. Further inquiry sometimes led to a process of opening up conversation about rarely told incidents; just as often, however, it closed down conversation with a disclaimer of loss of memory. This happened enough that we coined the term "whitewashing" to describe those contradictory narratives where mothers presented their childhood and families as trouble free, but evidence suggested otherwise.[36]

One example was Terese, who in the first interview described a rather idyllic childhood with fond memories of riding dirt bikes and hiking on trails in the woods behind her house. She reported no substance abuse or domestic violence. She said both parents worked—her father in con-struction and her mother as a clerk at a local chain store—and described a predictable routine to her childhood days: her dad "left every morning at 6:00 and then returned at 5:00 and mom cooked dinner." In the second interview, when we asked about discipline routines, her idyllic childhood became more complicated. Then, Terese talked about the "the bad times" when her father was laid off and they were evicted from their home. In this context, she also mentioned that her dad was "abusive," but justified it by saying it was "all about discipline." She was emphatic, though, that she would not discipline like her father, whose style of corporal punishment, which we described earlier, included beating her with a belt and smashing her head against the wall. On one of these occasions he broke her nose, and her brother told the counselor at school, who "called the authorities who showed up at the door." The father was required to go to counseling for two years and after that "it was fine, nothing else happened," she said.

However, we learned later of several more instances where he hit her again and she said this was the reason she "ran away from home" when she was 17 years old. She ran to the apartment of her boyfriend, who was four years older. Initially, she said, "we were not sleeping together, we were just good friends," but after a few months "we got intimate with each other" and she got pregnant. She eventually moved back to her parent's home because the father of the baby went to jail on a weapon's charge. We also found out late in the second interview that the father of her baby was "an alcoholic, but has been clean for five months now." She said that the pregnancy was an accident and that she was "suing Depo-Provera."

The family's trauma (losing a job and a home), violence (corporal punishment), and alcohol abuse were not pivotal events that she used to narrate her life story—these were asides, things that probably would not have come out had we not done a second interview (and if the relationship with the father of the baby had not deteriorated between the first and second interview). Whitewashing suggests that there was even more violence in the life stories than was told to us. As with the conclusions we came to in the discussion of child sexual abuse stories, we think that stories of interpersonal partner and family violence were more likely underreported than overreported. While whitewashing may have tempered many of the life stories, it did not prevent some young mothers from betraying codes of silence, perhaps because violence was too central to their life worlds.

Laura: "My Heart Is Partly Sleeping Since This All Started"

When we met Laura, she was in a state of extreme anxiety, which permeated her interview. Dirty dishes accumulated on her kitchen table among overflowing ashtrays; toys cluttered the floor. She explained that she had lost 30 pounds since her fiancé had been arrested for murder a few months earlier. Her short auburn hair was pulled back in a headband, while she rested her five-foot, 105-pound frame on the sill of a partially opened window. She began the interview, "Now, you don't mind if I smoke cigarettes by the window, do ya? Especially if you're gonna have me talking about my life [laughs]."

Laura was 24 years old at the time of the interview. She considered her fiancé to be a surrogate father to her four-year-old daughter. Her fiancé had been in jail for 51 days at the time of our interview and was awaiting trial for his role in the abduction, gang rape, and murder of a young teenage girl. Several other men and women charged in the rape and murder were also Laura's friends. In the first interview, Laura lamented, "My heart is partly sleeping since this all started. The hardest part right now is not knowing. We don't know how long he's going to be in court. It's way too soon to tell how long he's gonna be in jail. I'm preparing myself for no less than five years." By the second interview she learned he had been sentenced to 25 years. Laura still maintained doubt about whether her fiancé participated in the rape and whether he remained at the scene when the murder actually occurred.

Laura and her fiancé had been together since she was one-month pregnant. "He held her," Laura recalled, pointing toward her daughter, "before I did, when she was born." His support for her daughter and her was a reason why she wanted to marry him. He made her feel "special":

> I've never been really fully made to feel special since my grandfather died and [my fiancé's] given me that feeling back and I know in my heart that I don't think anybody else is gonna be able to do that and I don't want to lose that. It's hard enough just being separated from him now.

Not all of her memories of their relationship, however, were as tender. Her fiancé was a heavy drug user and was violent, and she had thrown him out of the house a month and a half before his arrest. After the tape recorder was turned off, Laura revisited this topic and added that he usually hit her only after she had struck him a few times.

Laura traced her own delinquency back to age 13. Describing herself as "one of the troublemakers in town," Laura recalled, "my mother couldn't control me; 13 years old, coming home drunk, out till all hours of the night." At 13, she was placed in a residential home for juvenile delinquents and was raped that same year—what she described as "date rape." She bounced back and forth between living at home with her mother and living in residential treatment programs over the next four years.

Laura described herself as a heavy drinker and regular marijuana smoker. She boasted that her fiancé was not much of a drinker and that she could "drink him under the table. It's sad, because he's like twice my size and I can drink more than him or his brothers. It's not a good thing when a woman can drink a man under the table; they don't like that." Her drinking escalated when she turned 17, shortly after dropping out of high school. As she described in the last chapter, she quit school, moved out, and spent a lot of time drinking in bars underage: "I've always been able to make myself look older than I am."

Laura had a string of abusive relationships and miscarriages. The rape resulted in her first pregnancy at age 13, which ended in a miscarriage. Her second pregnancy was at age 15 with a boy who was legally her foster brother. As her boyfriend at the time, Laura begged her mother to adopt him after he was orphaned. The relationship turned volatile soon after the pregnancy: "It was a fairly abusive relationship, and he and I had gotten into an argument, and I got slammed into that wall and his shoulder was right in my stomach. I was only, like, maybe, a month-and-a-half, two months [pregnant]." The blow to her stomach apparently caused her second miscarriage. She was pregnant again at 17 and gave birth shortly after her eighteenth birthday, but her son died soon after the birth. She referred to him as her first child, which defined her as a teen mother. This relationship was also violent and resulted in Laura's first arrest for assault and disorderly conduct. The boyfriend, she claimed, did not get arrested. "The [prosecutor] was just a bitch. She's about the same size as me and she's jumping on my case for standing up for myself and he got off with jack shit!"

Laura was formally married to the next abusive partner, and was still legally married to him when we interviewed her because neither she nor her husband could afford a divorce. They married after three months of dating, and the marriage dissolved after a year and a half. "It was physically abusive," Laura explained, "emotionally and mentally abusive and I am thankful he left." He had three children with two different mothers, and at the time of the interview he was in jail in Georgia for failure to pay child support.

Shortly after her relationship with her husband ended, Laura became pregnant again at age 19, rekindling an old romance. The relationship was rocky and she said it "wasn't the right time in my life to be pregnant." After her last miscarriage, however, "because of the fact that I was told I most likely wasn't gonna have kids, I stayed pregnant." Although the relationship did not last, she considered her daughter "a miracle child." Laura did not think that the father's family liked her and said that the relationship ended because he would not stand up for her. She was three years older than he was:

> They didn't like the age difference, no matter how slight it was, and they didn't like me because of my tattoos, because I had had a child, they just didn't like me. They didn't even remotely give me a chance. They instantly judged me from my looks. [His family] started treating me like crap and he wouldn't stand up for me. I'm a high-risk pregnancy. I didn't need the added stress on top of what I already had, so I said you know what? You're not worth my time, so see ya later, bye.

By the time of the birth, Laura was in a relationship with her current fiancé (who was later incarcerated for murder).

Looking back, Laura lamented, "I had a habit of going through boy-friends like I changed socks." She offered an explanation, which seemed to be derived from her therapy: "I've had very low self-esteem and a lot of that stems from my mother and being picked on as a kid." She described her relationship with her mother as poor, claiming instead that she was "daddy's little girl," even though she had very little involve-ment with her father. Her parents divorced when she was four, mostly, she says, because her "father was a major druggie and alcoholic." Laura continued to see her father for a while after the divorce, but only through supervised visits because "he had threatened to kidnap me." The pri-mary father figure in Laura's life was her grandfather. After the divorce, they moved in with her grandparents, where they lived until her grand-father died when Laura was 15. A veteran of World War II, her grand-father had been a police officer and provided for his extended family through his pension. His death resulted in the family's financial demise: "When my grandfather died, his pension died and my grandmother couldn't afford the house anymore." Laura said that when he died her life "went into a total tailspin."

Laura eventually received some counseling for a life that included early family disruption, later financial instability, sexual, physical, and emotional abuse, early pregnancies, miscarriages and the death of a child, school dropout, alcohol and drug abuse, and the birth of her daughter. She claimed that her daughter was a turning point in her life. For instance, she had reduced her drinking considerably—"I think I've come a long way as far as that," she interjected. She imagined a more stable, monogamous life with her fiancé, who had assumed the father role toward her daughter. His lengthy sentence, however, had shattered her fantasy. Brokenhearted and still in search of a place of less chaos, she pulled out a body-sized pillow and squeezed it as she insisted, "I don't *need* a man! [her emphasis]. I don't feel any woman should need a man," she restated.

Laura's story is similar to Bethany's story that opened this chapter. Both are white, were 24 when we interviewed them, had families disrupted by early divorce, had their first child when they were 18, and had miscarriages before their first full-term pregnancies. Further, both were victims of sexual abuse and partner violence, had histories of drug and alcohol abuse, and told stories about how the birth of a child had changed their lives. Of course, there are differences as well. Bethany's story is dominated by heroin addiction. Moreover, she came from a family that had more education and financial resources than Laura's. Likewise, Bethany finished high school, despite her heroin addiction, something Laura was unable to do.

What is more interesting, however, is to compare the life stories of Bethany and Laura to Cassandra and Tameka. Here we can see the grooves of race and class. Both Bethany and Laura were able to take advantage of cumulative economic advantages, consistent with general historical differences in the experiences of the black and white working classes. Laura's mother was poor, especially after the divorce, but they had access to resources (for example, a family home) that Laura's grandfather had accumulated as a veteran and pensioned police officer. Bethany's mother earned her master's degree and began working as a social worker. Bethany attended a small, rural school, primarily white ("in my grade there was like one Hispanic and maybe not even one black," she said), and both parents had remarried and could offer homes for Bethany to live in when she was in crisis. Cassandra's and Tameka's families were more economically marginalized; neither had an intergenerational accumulation of resources to fall back on. Cassandra did move in with her grandmother, and while this may have provided some additional familial support, it did not provide economic support, nor did it move her away from concentrated neighborhood poverty.

Perhaps more striking are the numerous occasions that, according to Bethany, her drug addiction went unnoticed by institutional authorities. She graduated from high school, despite her heroin addiction and despite living in an extremely violent relationship. She stated that she was a poor student who skipped classes a lot. Moreover, she regularly went to school high or "dope sick" and was three months pregnant when she graduated. And yet, she insisted, "nobody knew" about any of this—not parents, friends, teachers, or school administrators. She explained this by saying that she was an "excellent liar." While this may be true, it was also likely that Bethany's white skin allowed her to pass unnoticed by institutional authorities. Whiteness helps wash deviant identities clean; it helps girls "pass" through school, airport security, and town streets while using and selling drugs.

There were also differences in how police were talked about. While none of these young mothers liked the police, we found Bethany's contact with the police to be surprisingly limited given her drug use, sex work, and shoplifting. The police arrested her only once. She was pregnant at the time and complained about their insensitivity toward her condition. "They were kind of jerks. I was pregnant and I was extremely sick, dope sick, and they just didn't care. I'm like, 'Listen. You need to take me to the hospital. I need methadone. I'm pregnant' and they didn't care. They're like, 'We don't have to do anything.' I mean the pains were unbearable."

Laura also did not like the police in her town. She asserted that the police have "their heads up their asses," adding that she did not "think very highly of the police in this town especially since my grandfather and all the old-timers are no longer on the force." Further she felt that "half the town's police are on the take." Laura had a historical view of the force because her grandfather had been an officer. She identified good and bad officers, described a changing culture on the force, and judged their performances based on how they had treated her and her friends.

Both Laura's and Bethany's descriptions and relationships with the police, however, were starkly different from Cassandra's and Tameka's, both of whom spoke from a different social location, which structured their perspectives and experiences with the police. Moreover, Cassandra's and Tameka's views of the police in their neighborhoods were strikingly similar to each other, even though they lived in different cities. To them, the police engaged in indiscriminate violence and abuse, and were often racist, corrupt, and untrustworthy—or, as Tameka said, they "got that racism in their blood." They both made cases for street justice because of the unreliability of the police in establishing public safety in their neighborhoods. Officers were not simply "jerks" or bad apples on the force, even though they could certainly tell stories about some being more violent and corrupt than others; for Cassandra and Tameka, the police were extensions of white power that had been given license to subdue and control their neighborhoods with impunity. They saw the police through a racial lens crafted within their neighborhoods and validated through sordid lived experience.

Last, because of the territorial stigma associated with the urban ghetto, Laura and Bethany escaped some of the humiliations that Cassandra and Tameka had to endure. Cassandra's street activities and her involvement with the Los Sólidos were, in part, a survival strategy—a way of navigating a violent neighborhood and school—and with it she risked being labeled an unredeemable "ghetto chick." From the perspective of those living in safe, economically stable, white suburbs, Cassandra can be skewered in public opinion for her participation in violence, her rejection of school, and her early pregnancy. Even within local social hierarchies, she was chastised by her mother and grandmother for getting pregnant by an irresponsible gang member, and she was continually put "in her place" by the father of her child who referred to her as a "chickenhead" and a "whore" as he sought sexual indulgences elsewhere. The hierarchies of race and gender intersected to disparage Cassandra as she struggled to navigate her social circumstances and the assertions of moral culpability.

Tameka faced a similar stigma as well as discourses of gendered humiliation. She turned to stripping in clubs as a survival mechanism, and attempted to squeeze out dignity by insisting that she stripped but did not have sex with her customers. She battled swells of rage and despair in her life, but pulled herself back from the edge of self-destruction on numerous occasions. "They said black women don't make it too often," she asserted. "They start smoking that stuff and I never got to that point. I always just talk to myself in the mirror or I'll write or I'll just take my anger out on working, drinking, smoking weed and that's it." When she became pregnant, however, the father and his parents could still invoke the weapon of gendered humiliation embedded in a local social hierarchy and distance themselves by defining her as a "ho" and a "nasty" girl trying to trap their son.

Contrast these experiences with Bethany. As a heroin addict, Bethany had internalized the identity of a "junkie." She used the self-reference regularly throughout her life story. To survive, she too negotiated a gendered world to make money, maintain relationships, and manage her drug habit, mainly, through prostitution and stripping. Sex work for Bethany, however, led to her becoming a high-priced prostitute—to having a coterie of clients who paid good money for both drugs and sex. This gave her more distance from public scrutiny and scorn, and from the more derogatory identity of the "street whore." Similarly, she used her body to make money in strip clubs, but soon transitioned into stripping and sex work at stag parties, where, again, the money was better and the practice privatized in a way that diminished the stigma. Moreover, at one point in her life, she lived comfortably with a white man who she said had spent his substantial inheritance on his and her drug addictions. As his companion, she was a beneficiary of accumulated intergenerational wealth. Of course, Bethany was still navigating a male-dominated world, in which her survival strategies were based on the indulgences of male fantasy and female objectification, but her white skin and her access to more privatized middle-class networks enabled her to mitigate the harsher forms of stigma and humiliation that Cassandra and Tameka confronted. Instead, Bethany more singularly battled the stigma of "the junkie," without the additional baggage of ghetto caricature.

Laura, though, could not sidestep the insults and humiliations as gracefully as Bethany. Class injury was more apparent in her story. The family of her child's father rejected her because of her tattoos and lifestyle. They treated her like "crap," invoking local social hierarchies more common in white working-class neighborhoods that symbolically degrade hard-living white residents as "trailer trash." But moving from a local to a more national discourse, Laura gains status from her white skin by avoiding the stigma and the media spotlight more commonly focused on "ghetto teen moms" or "violent ghetto chicks."

Differences notwithstanding, there were similarities that all of these women confronted irrespective of racial identities and geographical stigma. Their gender identities exposed them to violence, sexual vulnerability, and varying forms of male domination. Moreover, within these contexts, young women—white, black, and brown—adopted early motherhood as a self-affirming strategy.[37] Motherhood fulfilled a universal human destiny to reproduce, a cultural script for life fulfillment promised to women, and a strategy for "starting over" for young women from distressed childhoods.

STARTING OVER AND TEEN MOTHERHOOD

Starting over was a prevailing theme among the women in this chapter and in many instances lent meaning to their pregnancies, births, and motherhood. These young women were attempting to break free of oppressive lives—abusive homes, violent men, neglectful parents, drug and alcohol addiction, and dangerous streets. The desire to start anew is powerful, particularly among individuals with histories of trauma and psychological burden, as starting over signifies hope and the reorganization of self within life streams. But life streams are about far more than individual desire and decision-making. Starting over requires more than hope, more than resiliency, more than individual will; it requires the types of social, psychological, geographical, and economic resources and supports that are necessary to establish individual, familial, neighborhood, and regional stability.

Often, starting over was articulated in very conventional terms. These young women wanted to be mothers, to have faithful partners, to live in safe homes and quiet neighborhoods, and to have jobs.[38] And none of this seemed entirely out of reach—being a mother was not rocket science, there were "good men" out there, they had their eyes on neighborhoods with "less drama," and they were not unfamiliar with work. Further, they were often pragmatic. Motherhood was something they had always imagined and, to a greater or lesser extent, had been prepared to embody. While they desired love and kindness in their romantic relationships, they were also prepared to live alone and raise children by themselves, if necessary, since, as they all said, no woman *needs* a man. Many already knew how to live in less desirable neighborhoods or in crowded households if more suitable housing was not yet within their reaches. And despite their young age, most of the mothers had work histories, and while the low-wage jobs did not provide much security, they did provide hope of a ladder to something better.

Jackie's starting-over story illustrates this hope. We referred to Jackie's life story earlier in this chapter as an example of a teen whose escape from an abusive home exacerbated her vulnerabilities to violence and mistreatment by men. Heavy drug use, delinquent activities, juvenile lockup, and house arrest characterized her life between 13 and 15 years of age. At 15, she spent four months in New York City doing drugs and living with predatory older men who pushed her into prostitution to sustain the household's income and drug habits. After returning to Connecticut, she started a relationship with a violently controlling man, who beat her regularly for seven months, until she was finally able to extract herself from his destructive clutches. At 16, she met Alejandro, a Puerto Rican man who was eight years older than her with a similar street history, and she said, "we instantly clicked."

A victim of severe physical abuse from his father, Alejandro never progressed beyond the third grade in school. He raised himself on the streets. A large muscular man, Alejandro was gentle and soft-spoken (we also interviewed Alejandro). Their similar pasts became the Velcro for a relationship of mutual empathy and new direction. They conceived and Jackie delivered twins at age 17, something she said she had wanted to do since she was 13 years of age. At the time of the interview, the twins were seven months old and Jackie and Alejandro had been together for nearly two years. Each expressed a deep sense of empathy for the other as they enacted their mutual dream of starting over. Alejandro received SSI (Supplemental Security Income) for a disability attributed to the physical abuse he sustained as a child, while Jackie worked at a fast-food restaurant. They lived in an impoverished, noisy neighborhood, where Alejandro assumed child care activities during the day and patrolled the borders of the household at night. Alejandro was, in Jackie's view, an involved father: he attended all of her doctor appointments, selected names for the twins, and shopped with her in preparation for the birth of their sons. She described him as "a very good father" whom she trusted "more than anybody else." Their daily lives were dominated by the drama of two infants, for whom Jackie expressed her hopes that they "don't go to jail, get a good job, have a family, and be with one girl, that's it."

Again, we remind readers of the young ages of the mothers at the time of the interview and make it clear that we are not making an assessment about whether or not their lives did change or will change, only that they hoped they would.[39] This "hope for change" was often an incentive for carrying the pregnancy to term and becoming mothers. However, re-creating one's life amid histories of violence and chaos is difficult without community economic investments, family supports, viable psychological services, and neighborhood efficacy in managing collective problems. "Starting over" was an attempt to reorganize their lives and transform themselves. It was rooted in a context of violence and poverty as well as national and local hierarchies that created dehumanizing circumstances for many of these young women; it was in this context that they sought the valued identity of motherhood to overcome the emotional trauma associated with colliding forms of violence.[40]

CONCLUSION

Gendered violence occurs across all racial, ethnic, and class groups as the exercise of male power and dominance that enacts, restores, and reproduces a gender hierarchy. Intimate partner violence is one of the ways in which this happens, and it occurs in the most privileged and in the most disadvantaged households. But vulnerability to violence and the availability of resources to contest or negotiate violent circumstances do indeed vary by social location within the matrix of racial, ethnic, class, and gender characteristics that largely define access to power, resources, opportunities, and social networks. In this chapter, we explored the contexts of interpersonal violence that one-third of the mothers in our study described.

Young mothers residing in the poorest urban neighborhoods of Connecticut told stories about violence in their families of origin, as well as in their neighborhoods, schools, and relationships. Violence disrupted their homes at early ages and then reverberated through their lives as they negotiated conditions in which resource deprivation, institutional neglect, and territorial stigma shaped their communities, families, and relationships. Their own strategies to secure income included drug dealing, sex work, and theft, but more often, they relied upon men who dominated these street trades. Surviving violence often led women to engage in violence, in their romantic relationships as well as in the streets. But survival itself always meant negotiating male dominance, particularly in their relationships, where varying combinations of alcohol and drug abuse, infidelities, and partner violence were woven through the exercise of male prerogative. Women's own participation in street trades, in violence, and in relationships with street-involved men left them vulnerable not only to physical violence but also to symbolic violence, where they were relegated to the bottom of national and local social hierarchies and where they were stigmatized.

Violence was also occurring in white suburban and rural communities and homes as well. Less visible and less public, violence particularly permeated the life stories of white mothers residing in towns and small cities that had been economically scarred by deindustrialization. Violence disrupted homes, violated young girls, and infected romantic relationships. Drug and alcohol abuse infused their stories along with rape and male terror. Some of these mothers, however, had family resources to rely on, often accumulated in prior generations. This provided more options for escaping or addressing violence and for getting counseling. Relationships with police in their communities were less alienating and contentious, allowing for more community-mediated forms of public safety. Finally, young white mothers escaped the harshest epithets of social stigma, which were reserved for black and brown urban youth, although class injuries were at times apparent.

Homes that were disrupted by violence in cities and towns across Connecticut pushed several of the adolescents in our study out of their homes and into circumstances of uncertainty, and in some cases danger, with few emotional or financial resources to deal with them. Leaving abusive homes often enhanced their vulnerabilities to violence and exploitation. Some mothers sought protection in relationships with men, who turned out to exhibit classic battering characteristics of control and dominance in the relationships, eventually leading to early pregnancies. Others moved in with friends and immersed themselves in adolescent alcohol and drug use, delinquent criminal activities, and sexual activity. Still, others moved in with their boyfriend's family, often in crowded housing conditions, which created new, and often difficult, obstacles to navigate. Later, some of these young women returned to their home of origin—the very homes they had escaped—disappointed, dejected, and pregnant, while others began a rapid transition to adulthood, living on their own as single mothers.

Very often, their pregnancy stories conveyed a desire to "start over"—whether it was to escape violent homes, leave the streets, sober up, or just transition out of adolescence. These young women were looking for a new direction, a way out, and many did so by laying claim to conventional desires to become mothers. Starting over was an especially powerful aspiration when it was shared by a romantic partner who was also looking for a way out of a labyrinth of dead-end streets. But creating new directions, motivated by conventional desires, is difficult for several reasons. First, the violence and chaos of one's past are reorganized within emotional relationships in one's present. This may provide for deep insight and empathy in the relationship, but it may also reproduce self-protective, volatile forms of relating. Second, aspirations need to be supported by reality. In working-class and poor communities, where economic and social support has dwindled over the past 40 years, establishing a stable family has become extremely challenging. In some of the stories, when an intense desire to start over was shared, but failed, the results were emotionally explosive and volatile. In other stories, where a shared capacity for empathy and accumulated resilience occurred, the relationship appeared to have the prospects for surviving, against the odds.

For many of the mothers in our study, starting over was not just about having a child and forming a stable, monogamous relationship; it was about straightening out their own lives, getting a job, going back to school, and trying to find a place in a precarious workforce for low-income workers. Education is, of course, central to finding a place in the workforce, especially in an economy in which school dropouts have fared poorly. It is this relationship between school failure and early childbirth that we take up in the next chapter.

CHAPTER 5

Education

MONIQUE: "MY HOME SITUATION TOOK A KILL ON
ME WHEN I GOT TO HIGH SCHOOL"

Monique, an African American mother of a one-year-old girl, was 18
when we interviewed her. Monique grew up in a black urban housing
project but attended a white suburban elementary school. Her transition into high school was derailed by family instability, violence, juvenile detention, and inadequate school services. She did not get pregnant
until after she dropped out of school.

*What I remember most about my childhood is my mom dying. I was
seven. She had to have open-heart surgery when she was like 13. That's
why she had me and my sister. And then when she was 22 she had her
second one [operation]. She died from that one. My mom, even though
she was a drug addict, she always took care of us. That's the main point
I remember about my mom, she made sure we were fed, she made sure
we were clean, I mean, she made sure that, you know, we were fine.*

*The person that kept my family together really was my grandma.
When she died everything went really apart. She passed away right after
my mom passed away. My aunt is my legal guardian. I love her to death
but [laugh] me and her always clashed. We always had arguments. I
always ran away. I always did something, you know, to make her upset
or she did something to make me upset. It's like mainly me and my sister*

were competing against her son to get affection and love. When she was mad at somebody else, she used to take it out on me and my sister. One time we had a argument that we left the washcloth in the shower on the rail, which was not me or my sister—it was her son—but I got a beating [with] an extension cord.

*   *   *   *   *

Third grade until like eighth I went to school in Suburban Elementary. When I got to high school, that's when everything went downhill. I went to Suburban High. It was a large high school, mainly white. To other people it was small but it was large to me. I was having problems in my home with my aunt so I didn't know how to deal with it so I just stopped going to school. I stopped in like January, ninth grade. I was afraid to talk to the teachers 'cuz I didn't want nobody know nothing like I was dumb or anything. I was very smart but I just kept everything in. If you would show me and sit down with me and, you know, explain things to me then I was actually a student. If you didn't show nothing to me or you didn't try to make any effort for me, I wouldn't make no effort for you. The teachers didn't really care. Maybe a small percentage really sat down with you and asked you, "Do you understand this?" [They] mainly just had you write down notes, do your homework, and that was it.

The problem I really had was my test scores. I didn't really study. I mean I always studied at the last minute. It's just that my family, it was like my home situation took a kill on me when I got to high school. Seventh—eighth grade was fine. I passed. As long as I passed with Bs and Cs, then I was fine, as long as I passed and say I was going to high school, I was fine.

Then me and my aunt had gotten into an altercation—I pulled a knife out on her and she called the police on me—so she had put me in the system 'cuz I was an out-of-control teen. They arrested me. I ran away, moved in with my father. I stayed there until I had to go to court and they put me in detention, and then from there I went to my placement, a group home, for about eight months. I went to school there and I was doing excellent. I was a straight-A student at my placement. I was a good student. It worked for me 'cuz I liked the small setting.

After I left there I went back home and they enrolled me into City High. They put me as a ninth grader but I had tenth grade classes and stuff like that. That's the part that really got me upset and I didn't understand. I went to City High for a week and then after that I just left. I wanted to go into an alternative high school like where this is a small setting. I had been in my placement for like eight months so I was used to being in a small setting. Then, when I got to City High, I was like ugh, I can't deal with this, so I just made it seem like I was going to school and I used to go to my cousin's house. And then my mom—my aunt, I call her my mother—found out and she didn't like that so she talked to my [social] worker and then I talked to a guidance counselor and that's when I wanted to go to Job Corps.

I finished at Job Corps within three months. That's when I found out I was pregnant with my daughter. I got my CNA license because they found out I was pregnant so they told me I had to choose between my GED and my trade and they told me, well, it's better for you to get your trade 'cuz it was gonna take me a long time to get my GED there.

* * * * *

When I found out I was pregnant her father was happy but I was kind of upset because I was trying to get everything situated so, you know, my aunt could be proud of me and stuff like that. Then I came out pregnant and I had my counselor at Job Corps tell my aunt because I was scared to tell her. She was like, well, there's nothing I could do and that was it. That's all she said to me. She kicked me out.

Deshan is older than me—he's about to be 25, I'm 18. He was there at Job Corps, he went there to get a trade—he has his high school diploma. We were together like a year before and we still have a relationship. It's like back and forth. He's not from here. He's from Guyana. He always take care of his daughter, Shaki, that's no matter what. He's very protective over her. I gotta let him know where she's going; I have to ask him, you know, if she can go or stuff like that. He acts totally different now compared to the way he was before. She can't get enough of him. He can't get enough of her. He's over here every day. Every day until she sleeps.

He mainly buys her clothes and her diapers and stuff like that. When she needs her shoes and all that stuff, he buys. I don't look for finance from him. It's mainly that Shaki know who he is and feel comfortable around him so that's mainly I ask for is just his attention and time for her. That's all I ask 'cuz I don't want her growing up saying that nobody loves me and I didn't get any attention and that's not true about that little girl. She get a whole bunch attention. I hope just that she'll have a better life than I did and she won't go through the things that I had to gone through. I don't regret my baby, but right now she should not be here.

TITA: "I WAS THE PERSON THAT DIDN'T BELONG AT THE SCHOOL"

Tita, a Puerto Rican mother with a one-year-old daughter, was 20 when we interviewed her. She was born in Hartford but moved to and from Puerto Rico several times. The interview was conducted in Spanish and English. Tita never completed tenth grade. Her education was disrupted by frequent moves often precipitated by violence in the home. Constantly starting over in new schools, she fell behind and eventually stopped going. She was out of school for almost two years before she became pregnant. She decided to carry the pregnancy to term as yet another attempt at starting over.

I was five months old when [my mother] took me to Puerto Rico. She got married and bought a house and me and my two sisters lived there for about four years. We moved back here 'cause she was having trouble with her relationship, and then she got back with him and we went back to Puerto Rico. We were there until I was about eight.

I had a sad childhood 'cause [my stepfather] was umm abusive toward her. One night we woke up because we heard all this crying and screaming and we saw him dragging my mom by her hair outside and he just slammed her head in the rocks real hard, just kept on slamming her and he'd see us crying. After he got tired or he got weak, he just stopped and he looked at us and he walked away and just left her there. I was in shock. I didn't know what to do. She was bleeding everywhere. We went down the hill to some neighbor's house and told what happened and the neighbors just went crazy over my stepfather and started fighting and they kicked him out. That was when we left. I was about eight.

* * * * *

When we moved back here we got our own place. That was the good part of our family, when we settled down. My mother, she was real nice to us at that time 'cause she was by herself. And we got along great. We had our own house, that was nice, without all the noise and stuff, and she worked at a grocery store at night, and on weekends she would go out to the clubs. She had a problem with boyfriends. I think she wanted someone to give her attention.

When I was 13 we moved to New Jersey. My mother was reading a newspaper and she found an ad for a man who was looking to get a relationship, but the catch was that he was from Peru and he needed someone to get married with so he can get his green card. She didn't know that until she visited him. They agreed that he would give her two thousand [dollars]. He didn't give her that much but she ended up marrying him and she fell in love with him; she really did love him. She moved in with him in New Jersey. We had no choice but to follow.

That's when my life just flipped because we left a house, a home that we had that we felt so, you know, like comfortable as a family. It was hard to get used to a new place. That year, I was just crazy. I couldn't take the pressure of going to a new school, meeting new friends.

It was mostly white people and that was different for me 'cause, I mean, living in Hartford most of the population is not white at all. I felt like I was the problem, like I was the outer person, everyone was normal but I was the Puerto Rican one that they would think "oh she's like a gang member" or something. I was the person that didn't belong at the school. I just didn't feel like I fit in. I think it's because, you know, not just because there was a lot of white people, but I didn't think people wanted to be my friend because I lived on the other side. They lived in nice houses, and I lived in a little apartment with my little tight family. They had their own dress code, expensive, like everyone knew how to dress nice and I was the outer one.

In the whole school I was the third one, let's say Hispanic, 'cause they were like Colombian, the other one [was] half Puerto Rican. I felt like if I would blend in with them it would work out. I tried being friends with one of them, the Colombian lady, and she was just totally different. She was real wild, she wanted to be with a lot of boys. At 13 she was already having sex, I was like whoa I haven't even kissed a boy yet. I was introduced to the cheerleaders by her, and I tried being a cheerleader and it was fun but they would like influence me to do things that I didn't want to do, like tell my mom I'm going to cheerleader practice and going somewhere else, to a boy's house.

* * * * *

And then one night, everything went wrong. I remember my sister was going crazy crying and like my mom was on the phone screaming and I got nervous. I'm like, what happened? She's like, "Well, Virginia's coming over." Virginia's my older sister, and I'm like, "Why, what happened? She went to jail or something?" Then my mom sat down she's like, she couldn't talk, she's stuttering, she's like, "Yeah umm, she has AIDS," my sister, my older sister, and when she told me aaaahhh, it hurt. In the past two years I've had three uncles and I've had two friends that died of drugs and HIV, so in two years I lost five people between drugs and HIV.

After that I wanted to leave New Jersey. My mom never paid attention to me, she was stressed because she felt like my sister blamed her. At that time my cousin moved to New Jersey and she got her own place, and she was my buddy. We went out, we did everything together, she was much older than me, she have two kids and a husband. I learned a lot from her. I learned a lot about sex. What not to do, how to do it, when not to do it, what guys want, what they needed. So I hung out with them a lot and then I met one of her husband's friends and he was a much older guy, he was 26, I was at that time 13. I remember it was in December, it was snowing and I, I liked him, I kind of felt like I needed a man in my life, like I needed a father figure. And that's when I did it, I lost my virginity with him. I was supposed to go to cheerleading and that's when I stopped going, when I met this boy. I just totally didn't care 'cause I felt like he loved me.

I wanted to get attention for my mom, I just wanted her to see that you know, I wanted attention. She found me with that boy in the car and she dragged me out and she told me I would end up like my sister and we were arguing and she punched me in my face and she said, "You see, that's what happens to girls who lose their virginity, they become whores." That's when I turned around and I was like [sigh] and I just picked up the phone and I call 911 and I said, "She just hit me," and the cops showed up and it was all this commotion. They didn't do much. My mom was crying, she was like, "I think I just hit her 'cause she was out with boys."

After that, [my mother] decided that if I want to leave, I [could] live with my cousin in Hartford. My mother was happy with [her Peruvian husband], she didn't want to come. She used to come visit us when she's not working and one day she went back and all her stuff were gone. He sold her bedroom set, her radio, her clothes, everything in the apartment, and disappeared, just walked away from her life forever. Maybe that's what he intended to do from the beginning, get the green card and just leave. He left her with nothing, she only had just a couple of clothes, that's it, everything she owned was in the apartment and he sold it. So she came up here.

* * * * *

We moved when I was 14. I was going to City High and I got into the bad crowd, let's just say, the crowd that would go to school just to strut their new clothes. It's not a school; it's a fashion school. The prettiest *people are there; you cannot be ugly and be at that school. My freshman year was great 'cause it wasn't so hard. That's when I had my best friend in the world, which I adore, and we just did everything together. We worked that whole summer and we saved all our money and then we bought a whole bunch of clothes for the beginning of school.*

My second year it became harder and harder 'cause I wouldn't pay attention, you know, so I'm lost. My teachers would not do their job; just talk, talk, talk but they wouldn't really look at you. I would just sit there at times and daydream or just do my makeup and they wouldn't care. They didn't care, they would just go on with their day, just read and write. They do pay attention to chewing gum, but [putting on] makeup was fine, I could stay putting it on all day, they didn't care. The one I liked, my science teacher, I liked him because he let me skip. He was great, he said, "Okay, if you're not coming today, just let me know." I used to be like, "I'm not showing up, I'm leaving now," and he was okay, bye, go. I'm like okay, bye. And we'd just walk out, me and my best friend.

Halfway through the year we decided "let's not go to school; let's just do something else." We didn't want to wake up early, that's what I think that was, and we had to walk to school and we didn't want to walk. We had high heels, we had little thin coats, we wanted to look cute. We just kept skipping. My principal had a lot of talks with me about skipping classes. He said, "You can't be skipping or you're going to get suspended." I got suspended a couple of times. I would stay [home] and my mother would scream at me and tell me I have to do something with myself. She would just lecture me a lot. So sometimes I'd pretend I'm going to go school when I'm suspended and I'd go to somebody else's house, like I wouldn't tell her about it.

After while I decided I'm not going back, I'm just going to drop out. I felt older. I felt like I didn't belong there. My mom was like, "Well, whatever, do whatever." She couldn't do anything about it. Like she cared but she didn't know how to handle me. Do whatever you want! Okay. I got a job at [a department store]. I was 15. I felt like high school wasn't me. I felt like I was grown up already, like, what do I wanna go to school for? I could still get a job, I know people that got good jobs that don't have a high school diploma. That was my thinking back then. I felt old, I felt like I was already 20. And now I feel like I'm 30.

* * * * *

I missed my period so I took a pregnancy test. I wasn't sure if I wanted to have the baby because I was so use to being by myself and not caring so much. At that time I was dating two guys and I wasn't sure who it was. I had told the one guy, James, that I was really involved with, and he told me, "Oh, you gotta have an abortion because, you know, I mean I can't raise a kid right now." He was about 20 I think at the time, and I was 18.

Then I told Marcus, that's actually the baby's father, and he was okay with it. At first he told me to think about it, "If that's what you really want, you know, but maybe you should get an abortion because you're not really prepared, you need to have money," you know, 'cause he already had a child, he had a daughter. He was 20.

I went and asked my sister for advice and again someone else told me to get an abortion. She said, "You can't have a kid, you're not prepared, you're not ready, you will never change." So I thought about it and then I told my mom. She wasn't really a religious person but she said, "Well you better have it 'cause people that have abortions go to hell." I'm like, uh, okay, so I had the baby. I felt like she knew best.

No one would ever think that I would ever have a baby, like they never thought I would ever even think about it twice, just have an abortion. So everyone was surprised, like "whoa, I can't believe it, you gonna have a baby, you?" Yeah that's me. So I was kind of scared 'cause I wasn't the baby type. I was not the babysitter, you know how the youngest one is always the babysitter, I wasn't the babysitter.

I stopped calling Marcus and we just drifted apart. He stopped calling me 'cause he was trying to avoid, you know, being a father. He had his daughter when he was 17, so he was like kind of scared. He wasn't into having kids, it wasn't his thing. James, we were friends, but then I just felt like I shouldn't be involved 'cause he wanted to go to the clubs, to have drinks, smoke you know. So I wasn't. I wanted to have a baby, I didn't wanna drink, I didn't wanna smoke, I wanted to change everything. So I stopped, I told him we can hang out but we can't drink and smoke. He kind of felt weird about it, then he would just stop calling me. So I was like well I don't need him, he's too much of a party person; I didn't wanna be involved with that.

* * * * *

I met Clarence through my sister. We used to hang out at her house and he kind of liked it that I was pregnant. I don't know why but he used to tell me all the time, "You look beautiful, you're beautiful pregnant, you look better pregnant than skinny the way you were. You looked like you were anorexic." My mom didn't really accept him because my mom wasn't sure if he really loved me and she didn't want me to get all stressed; I'm pregnant and he leaves me, you know. No one really had a lot of faith in him. They didn't think he was up to it but he really was. He was patient with me because I didn't know what I wanted for myself and he actually brought this whole idea to me like, well, you should go to school. So that's when I started going to my GED classes and he would take me in the morning and I would catch the bus back home.

When I was pregnant he would go with me to the visits in the hospital. He enjoyed it actually more than I did, I didn't enjoy being pregnant really. He did, he read the books, he went to the hospital, he asked the questions to the nurse and I'm just sitting there like I can't wait to get out. The nurses loved him, he loved every second of it. When he first heard the heartbeat he cried, I didn't. I was like okay just a noise. And he was the only one that heard the baby kick. Everybody else is there for hours and the baby wouldn't move but she always moved for him. But at times he overprotect me like when it was snowing and I was pregnant, and I had to go to work and he would get out of work early just to walk with me down the stairs and take me in the car. I was like, I'm not handicapped.

Before we got together, he was doing his whole bunch of girlfriends thing, got him cars, got him clothes; and I was doing the same, I had two guys, one was my friend I hanged out with, and one was my lover and got me clothes and took me out. I think we were meant to be, in a way that we both wanted a change. [Clarence] just told me, "I really wanna change and I have the opportunity with you 'cause I know you're the type that will change." We both had a chance to change and just by meeting each other we both influenced each other to get an apartment, work, and at the same time we had the baby; you know, you gotta change.

DROPPING OUT OF SCHOOL AND INTO MOTHERHOOD

National statistics paint a grim picture of high school achievement for adolescent mothers. Depending on whether school completion is measured as a high school diploma or an equivalency credential such as a General Education Development (GED) certificate, estimates are that 20 to 40 percent of adolescent mothers do not complete high school, at least twice the national average.[1] Moreover, when college enrollment is considered, teen mothers fall even further behind women who delay childbearing.[2] These low rates of graduation, however, are not that different from the graduation rates for low-income students in general. Students from poor families, living in impoverished communities and attending inadequately funded schools, have higher rates of school dropout than the general population.[3] Because this describes the backgrounds of many teen mothers, especially racial minorities living in impoverished urban areas, it can be difficult, but all the more important, to separate the effects of economic and social disadvantages from the effects of early childbirth.

As noted in the previous chapters, racial minorities in Connecticut reside disproportionately in cities with high child poverty rates, such as Hartford, New Britain, Bridgeport, New Haven, and Waterbury. The racial and economic disparities in the state are manifest in school performance. Statewide, in 2008, only about one-third of black and Hispanic sixth graders were scoring at or above grade level on Connecticut Mastery Tests, compared to three-quarters of whites.[4] Similarly, urban school dropout rates are considerably higher—for instance, in 2002, when we began the interviews, nearly three times more students dropped out in the Bridgeport district (32 percent) than statewide (11 percent).[5]

In this chapter we want to move beyond the distraction (and myth) that teen births cause school dropout and focus on the precursors to school failure for mothers like Monique and Tita who dropped out of school before they were pregnant.

One of the patterns we found in their life stories is that having a baby did not greatly alter the young mothers' school trajectories: those mothers who were doing well in school generally stayed in school; those who did not complete high school either had dropped out before pregnancy or were already disengaged from school when they became pregnant. This chapter showcases the stories of teen mothers who dropped out before they were pregnant to examine the process of school failure. Shifting our attention from teen motherhood to school failure forces us to confront the larger problems of family and neighborhood poverty, violence against women, underfunded and overburdened schools, and racial and class marginalization.

DISENTANGLING THE EFFECTS OF EARLY CHILDBIRTH FROM THE EFFECTS OF DISADVANTAGE

In one unique study, Joseph Hotz and his colleagues attempted to answer this question: *"What would be the adolescent mother's (behavioral) outcomes if she were to delay her childbearing until she was older but nothing else changed in the wider social context?*"[6] Using data from the National Longitudinal Study of Youth, they tried to "exploit a natural experiment" by comparing educational outcomes of teens who became pregnant and carried the child to term with teens who became pregnant and had a miscarriage (who, on average, delayed having a child by three to four years). While this study had limitations, they found that when controlling for conditions of disadvantage associated with socioeconomic status and family background, delaying childbirth did not significantly improve graduation rates. While only 46 percent of the teen mothers had a high school diploma, only 56 percent of the comparison group who delayed childbirth had a diploma.[7] Moreover, when they included GED certification as a form of high school completion, those who had a teen birth were slightly more likely to complete school than those who delayed childbearing.[8]

While it may be politically expedient to blame school failure on early childbirth, Kristin Luker asserts, "the assumption that early pregnancy and childbearing *cause* many students to drop out of school is wrong."[9] Many scholars theorize that the causal direction should be reversed, and they point to empirical studies that suggest the high rate of school failure among teen mothers is more of a consequence of social and economic disadvantages than early childbirth.[10] And yet, the correlation between teen births and school dropout continues to be identified as one of the key reasons early childbirth is considered a social problem.[11] This focus on early childbirth as a cause of school dropout is a distraction because it pulls our gaze away from social and economic inequality. To use academic language, early childbirth is often used as an independent variable causing school dropout when it is more of an intervening dependent variable resulting from poverty, family instability, and underfunded and inadequate schools.

Moreover, teen mothers are not a monolithic group—some drop out before pregnancy, some after pregnancy, some never drop out, and some drop out and then return to school after (and because) they have a baby. If we want to understand the relationship between early childbirth and school achievement, we need to acknowledge the varying trajectories and ask why some teen mothers complete school and others do not. Failing to do so reinforces stereotypes of school dropouts. Not all students drop out because they cannot do the coursework. Some leave because school interferes with adult responsibilities. Without plans for attending college, they may leave school their senior year to begin working or to start a family and get a GED certificate or their diploma

TABLE 4   EDUCATIONAL STATUS AT TIME OF INTERVIEW

	Number	Mean Age at Time of Interview	Age Range
Dropped out of high school	68		
Not enrolled in any school or program	33	19.3	15–24
Enrolled in GED or diploma program	27	18.4	14–22
Received GED or diploma	8	20.0	19–21
Did not drop out of high school	40		
Enrolled in school (includes one middle school enrollment)	23	16.4	14–20
Received high school diploma (includes six with some college)	17	20.2	18–25
Total	108		

through night school. Students who leave high school in their junior or senior year with sufficient basic skills are different from students like Monique and Tita who were not academically prepared to do high school work and, subsequently, did not make the transition into high school.

In our study, of the 68 mothers who had dropped out of school, one-half of the mothers had received a GED certificate or were enrolled in a diploma or certificate program (see table 4). We again remind readers of the young age of the mothers at the time of the interviews. Those who dropped out may yet return to school and those in school may still drop out.[12] We also should recognize the difference between a GED certificate and a diploma.[13] While a GED certificate can help students get credentialed, these programs often do not do a good job of educating students, and can be more of a badge of "moral" achievement than an indicator of educational competence.[14]

One way that we try to separate the effects of early childbirth from the effects of social and economic disadvantages is to examine the life stories of those teen mothers who dropped out of school *before* they became pregnant. Most studies that link teen births to school failure are based on simple correlations, and yet, as sociologist Howard Becker argues, "all causes do not operate at the same time, and we need a model which takes into account the fact that patterns of behavior *develop* in orderly sequence."[15] One of the values of the life story is that we can examine the sequencing of behavior, and, by doing so, we can see the problems they had before they became teen mothers.

DROPOUT: A MISNOMER

The term "dropout" is a misnomer because it implies a sudden departure (or drop) from school. Most of the young mothers in this chapter bounced, tripped, and slid out of school.[16] Dropping out was a process, not a one-time event. Students left school and came back and left again; they were held back a grade because of absences, tried to catch up, became discouraged, and stopped attending; they changed schools and tried again in a different state or country. Alienated and disengaged, they developed a new set of friends outside of school and gradually spent more time hanging out at the park, in the mall, on the street, or at home watching television and smoking marijuana. They started working full time, "playing house" with their older boyfriends, or babysitting their cousin's children. Sometimes parents, school officials, and the courts intervened by placing them in alternative schools, juvenile detention centers, reform schools, rehabilitation centers, psychiatric hospitals, or Job Corps. When the reluctance to attend school persisted and alternative options dwindled, parents and school officials would extract promises from the young dropout that she would enroll in summer school or night school or a GED program—or maybe even return to high school in the fall and start afresh. Then other things got in the way—a boyfriend went to jail, a parent returned from jail, a sister became pregnant, a father or mother lost a job, or the young girl herself became pregnant—and she put off returning. An already unpleasant experience became even more unpleasant when classrooms, buildings, and school policies were not designed to meet the needs of pregnant and mothering students—for example, desks that did not accommodate rounding bellies, locked bathrooms two flights of stairs away from the classroom, and inconveniently timed exams.[17] Late-term discomfort and a needy infant provided temporary excuses for not going to classes. Later, child care, medical problems, and financial needs interfered with school schedules. Consequently, girls who were suspended for fighting, marginalized within schools, or failing classes stopped attending as the physical grind of pregnancy slid into the permanent problem of child care.

School disengagement went hand in hand with early childbirth. Studies have found that adolescents disengaged from school are more at risk of becoming adolescent mothers, and once they become young mothers they become even more disengaged. Having poor grades and being weakly integrated academically and socially increase the likelihood of risky sexual behavior and pregnancy; conversely, school attachment and success increase the likelihood of a teenager using contraception and not becoming pregnant.[18]

While we focus this chapter on mothers who dropped out before pregnancy, it was not always so clear cut who actually belonged in this group. Many mothers were still technically enrolled in school when they became pregnant, but they were attending sporadically, getting into fights, missing exams, and failing to complete assignments. They already had one foot out of the school door, and their disengagement from school made them similar to those who had already dropped out.

We eventually developed a metric that defined a dropout as a student who stopped going to school for at least four weeks for reasons other than illness or pregnancy and did not engage in home schooling while she was out of the classroom.[19] Using this definition, 38 mothers dropped out before pregnancy, 30 after pregnancy, and 40 never dropped out.[20]

If we compare those who dropped out before pregnancy to those who never dropped out, those who stayed in school were more integrated in school, more often in regular or Advanced Placement classes, and more often had parents who graduated from high school.[21] In contrast, those who dropped out before pregnancy were not well integrated in school—they did not play sports in high school (though some did play sports in grade school), did not belong to school clubs, and were not involved in extracurricular activities.[22] Eight of the 11 girls in special education classes dropped out before they were pregnant.[23] In addition, those who dropped out before pregnancy had more troubled family histories, including domestic violence and child abuse, and more reported that they had abused drugs and alcohol, had a history of mental illness, and had been placed in juvenile detention (see table 5). In their families, at least one parent (and in many cases both) was absent from their everyday lives because of illness, death, long work hours, divorce, alcoholism (and recovery), incarceration, or migration.[24]

As we saw in previous chapters, while there was variation within racial and ethnic groups, white teens, on the whole, lived in less disadvantaged economic and social conditions compared to Puerto Rican and African American mothers. One primary distinction was that whites

TABLE 5 COMPARISON OF MOTHERS WHO DROPPED OUT BEFORE THE
PREGNANCY, DROPPED OUT AFTER THE PREGNANCY, AND NEVER DROPPED OUT

	Before Pregnancy (n = 38)	After Pregnancy (n = 30)	Never Dropped Out (n = 40)
Family history of domestic violence	23 (61%)	13 (44%)	11 (28%)
History of partner abuse	25 (64%)	12 (40%)	11 (28%)
History of substance abuse	17 (46%)	5 (17%)	5 (13%)
History of mental illness	15 (40%)	10 (33%)	9 (23%)
Victim of child sexual abuse	12 (32%)	5 (17%)	11 (28%)
Placed in juvenile detention	14 (37%)	7 (23%)	6 (15%)

generally did not live in urban poverty, so even if they were from low-income households, the white mothers often attended better-funded schools. Much of this is related to the sociospatial organization of race and ethnicity in Connecticut, where blacks and Latinos are more likely to live in urban areas and whites in small towns. Dropout rates reflected these patterns, where about one-half of mothers in our study living in towns dropped out of school, compared to nearly three-quarters of mothers residing in urban areas.[25]

We also found that blacks and Puerto Ricans were more often placed in special education and vocational tracks, and that no Puerto Rican was ever in an Advanced Placement course. Four of the five mothers in Advanced Placement courses stayed in school.[26] In contrast, five out of six students in bilingual programs dropped out after pregnancy.[27]

In our sample, more Puerto Rican mothers dropped out (70 percent) than African American or white mothers (both at 61 percent); when white mothers did drop out, it was usually before they got pregnant.[28] Although many of our mothers were still young at the time of the interview, and we are therefore unsure if they later returned to school, other studies have found that whites and blacks who drop out are more likely than Hispanics to return.[29]

One important factor is *when* they drop out, because even if students do not graduate, studies have found that every year a student stays in school reduces the chances of becoming dependent on state assistance later in life.[30] Numerous studies have identified the transition to high school—between eighth and ninth grade—as a crucial period for students. Those who fail to make the transition usually have academic and behavioral problems, and it is the accumulation of problems over time that leads to them dropping out.[31] We turn now to mothers like Monique and Tita who dropped out early, unable to make the transition into high school.

THE EARLY DROPOUTS: "THE HARDER I TRIED THE LESS GRADE I GOT"

Many students who do not make the transition to high school start falling behind in elementary school. In Hartford, for example, only 15 percent of third graders were reading at grade level in 2006, which means 85 percent of students were already behind in the first quarter of their school careers.[32] The girls in our study who dropped out before completing tenth grade could not read, write, or do math at the levels required for high school course work. No one factor explained their failure, but we heard three patterns in their life stories that help us understand school failure: gender violence and residential dislocation; unresponsive schools that pushed out failing students; and racial marginalization in white suburban schools.[33]

Gender Violence and Residential Dislocation: "I Was in So Many Different Places"

A childhood of moving around created problems because of the basic fact that "it's difficult for you to start again in another school," as Glorimar said.[34] Many of the students who dropped out early had a history of repeated residential moves. Two types of moves that were particularly disruptive were those precipitated by violence (domestic violence and child sexual abuse) and those that crossed language borders (in particular, the *va y ven* or circular migration found in Puerto Rican families).

While studies find that divorce and separation have detrimental effects on children's school performance, it is often the conflict that precedes the breakup of the family that creates the problem, and repetitive partner violence is exceptionally destructive.[35] In our study, of the 38 women who dropped out before they were pregnant, 23 had a history of domestic violence in their childhood homes, twice the number of those who never dropped out.[36]

Domestic violence disrupted school attachment when it led to frequent and sudden residential moves. For example, Violet told us that her father was "aggressive, you would probably describe him as a big ape."

She described her mother as "mentally unstable. Just depressive, mostly, and every time she'd leave my father, 'cause my father would beat her and cheat on her and stuff like that, so every time that she'd leave my father and get back with him, she'd be so depressed that she'd just stay in her room." To escape the physical abuse, her mother would move to another city, state, or country. Moving around, Violet found herself in new schools, and she described a history of having problems getting along with other female students: "The girls were like really jealous, so I'd always run into problems with their boyfriends looking at me, or things like that."

When her parents reconciled, the violence eventually started up again. One night, things escalated and Violet called the police because "he was trying to kill her at the time. They came; he went to jail. My mom lied for him in court and he got out and found out it was me who called the cops and then he started threatening to kill me and stuff like that." She continued, "That's one of the reasons why I moved out." After she moved out, she "quit school because I had to get a job." She was 16 years old when she left home and in the middle of tenth grade when she dropped out. She got pregnant five months later. When we interviewed her, she was 18 years old and trying to complete a GED program, but she said it "was going slow, because I been out of school for two years."

Child sexual abuse (CSA) and substance abuse also destabilized homes, leading to frequent moves and new schools. We discussed the effects of CSA on school performance in chapter 3, but here we want to identify its link to residential mobility. LaRonda was sexually abused when she was five years old, held back in kindergarten, and then put into the foster care system when she was six years old because her father was in jail and her mother abused drugs. She lived in several foster homes (and was raped in several of those homes, which prompted the move to a new foster home); she changed schools with each move. Talking about her childhood, LaRonda said, "I was in so many different places, it's like the way they teach is different from another place and it was too hard to catch up with whatever they were trying to do. So I just stopped going." She fell behind in school and was placed in classes "for slow people." After attending four different high schools, she finally quit. She was 17 at the time and had only completed ninth grade. It would be another two years before she became pregnant.

In addition to gender violence, circular migration also contributed to school failure. In many cases, as evident in Tita's story that opened this chapter, violence and *va y ven* went hand in hand. When Tita and her mother returned to Connecticut after her stepfather's brutal attack on her mother, Tita was eight years old. She was held back that year because, as she said, "I was in the middle of coming back and forth from Puerto Rico so I would miss a lot of stuff." Studies have found that for Latino students, low rates of school completion are related to frequent residential moves.[37] Moves across language borders complicate school readjustment, especially when English Language Learners (ELL) are not provided with adequate language services.[38] Given the unique relationship between the United States and Puerto Rico, circular migration has led scholars like Edna Acosta-Belén and Carlos Santiago to refer to Puerto Rico as a "commuter nation." Studies have found that almost two-thirds of Puerto Ricans who come to the mainland have done so at some point before.[39] For Puerto Ricans, it is not simply residential mobility that explains the high rates of school failure, but circular migration, inadequate programs for ELL students, and high rates of poverty.[40] In 2007, for instance, 29 percent of Puerto Rican children residing in Connecticut lived below the poverty line.[41]

In our study, of the 36 Puerto Ricans, 19 of them were born on the island. Many others, including Tita, were born on the mainland and traveled back and forth to the island during their adolescence. It was typically the search for jobs and health care that precipitated the moves, but in some instances, it was the escape from domestic violence. For example, Glorimar moved from Puerto Rico to Connecticut when she was eight years old and returned to the island for several months when she was 11 and again at the age of 14 because she was having problems with schools and home life in Hartford. Her stepfather "beat" her mother, who became suicidal and spent time in a residential institute. In eighth grade, Glorimar was held back because of 16 suspensions for fighting with other girls. Rather than repeat eighth grade a third time, and to avoid problems in court for "running away from my house, not respecting my mother," she went to Puerto Rico. She was a self-defined "bad child." Despite the efforts of her father, who was a teacher, she did not do any better in Puerto Rico and soon wanted to leave: "I had told [my father] that as soon as I get back here I would start school." When she returned to Connecticut, she tried to complete a GED program but the course was "too difficult." Her poor English language skills, exacerbated by circular migration, made school difficult; the chaos in her home and her own wild street life sealed the deal. She never finished eighth grade. She was out of school and 16 years old when she got pregnant.

In sum, frequent residential mobility disrupted their educational trajectories. When this move traversed language borders, or when it was precipitated by violent men (and the mother and children departed abruptly in the middle of the school year), moving took a toll on school performance. The violence and changes in residence and schools preceded the school failure, which preceded the pregnancy.

Unresponsive Schools: "You Should Drop Out"

Dropping out of school is not just about chaotic families, child abuse, and juvenile delinquency; it is also about institutional failure.[42] It is about teachers who have too many classes with too many students, counselors who are overworked and undertrained, administrators who are unfriendly and distant, and policies that are unbending and exclusionary. Large high schools unable to meet the needs of students who have cognitive or learning disorders, emotional trauma, unstable family life, or ELL needs often lose students in the transition from middle school into high school.[43] In our study we found that many students with family problems held on during middle school when classes were smaller, course work easier, and teachers more attentive, but they got lost in the scuffle of the high school hallways, the impersonal settings, and, especially, the increased educational expectations.[44] In crowded classrooms, the quiet student doing poorly was overlooked and slipped away while the loud-mouthed sassy fighter was kicked out. Some of those suspended never returned, rejecting the institution that rejected them.[45]

Shelley described her problems transitioning into high school: "As I got older, it just all started to go downhill. [High school] was bigger and more classes. It seemed harder. The teachers are too preoccupied 'cuz they got like these five, six classes a day and 20 to 25 students in a class each. They don't have time to reach out. They're too overworked. I really didn't like it too much." Shelley did better when she was in a smaller class, as did several of the other mothers. Erica, who was often "distracted by a lot of things," said she was able to "concentrate better when it's a smaller class." Jackie also said she did better when she was placed in a special education class because moving from classroom to classroom "makes me crazy, [being] in one class all day actually made me do better."

Programs that provide comprehensive interventions can help students stay in school, but these programs require resources and service a small number of students.[46] Unfortunately, small classes with adequate teacher attention are not common in urban public high schools, except for students in Advanced Placement courses.[47] Scholar-activist Laura McCargar found that students in Connecticut high schools who had problems were often counseled into alternative programs and adult education programs that grouped special education, bilingual classes, and remedial classes together and staffed the polymorphic class with unqualified personnel.[48] These alternative programs often became dumping grounds, not learning environments, for students with problems.

Many of the girls who had problems transitioning into high school had cognitive disabilities or ELL needs or both. Several mothers talked about having language needs misidentified as learning disabilities, and circular migration made Puerto Ricans susceptible to this misclassification.[49] Janisa, for example, was born in Cleveland but at six months her family moved to Puerto Rico. After her parents divorced, she moved with her mother and brothers to New Jersey. Her mother remarried, but within four years her stepfather, to whom Janisa was very attached, died of lung cancer. "I was holding his hand when he died," she told us. She was 10 years old. After his death, they moved to Connecticut, and when she was 12, her older brother, who was "like a father," died in a car accident. "He always told me, 'You go to school.'" After he died, she became depressed and spent long periods of time alone in her room. A year later the family moved back to Puerto Rico, where Janisa struggled in school because she did not speak Spanish well. When she returned from Puerto Rico, she was forced to repeat eighth grade and then was placed in a vocational track "because of absences." She went to school in the morning and worked in a convalescent home in the afternoon, "washing clothes, folding clothes."[50] The morning classes were no more stimulating than folding sheets in the afternoon. "It was a low-level class for kids that couldn't read or write," she said, and the teachers told them simply to "copy off the books." She became frustrated. "I didn't want to be here, so I stopped going to school for awhile. But then they brought my mom to court." Janisa was forced back into school. She tried to get placed in the "regular class" but was unsuccessful, so she stopped attending when she was 16 years old. She did not become pregnant until she was 19.

Large, bureaucratized schools develop procedures and policies to manage large numbers of students. Policies designed around the norms of the majority often do not accommodate the needs of children from different backgrounds. At times, these policies can be educationally unproductive, if not absurd, as was the case for Janisa. Another example was Kelly, who first stopped going to school in the spring of her sophomore year. When she reenrolled the following fall, they listed her as a junior and created a schedule that included both sophomore and junior classes simultaneously. "I would go to tenth grade English after eleventh grade English," but "couldn't do it. It was just too hard for me." Her grades slipped and "the vice principal was like, 'You should drop out.'" She did. Two years later she was pregnant.

Sandy also got the message to leave school. She had special needs related to both language and cognitive abilities. She was born in Connecticut and lived in an insular Puerto Rican neighborhood in a high-poverty, urban area. Sandy's father was in jail most of her life and her mother was an alcoholic who would "smack her" as a form of discipline. When she was in first grade, her mother had a serious accident driving while intoxicated. Because Sandy and her siblings were in the car at the time, the state's child protective services placed them in foster care for a month and then they went to live with their grandmother (who was also an alcoholic) for a year while their mother was "in a program." Sandy was held back a grade in school that year. In middle school she received passing grades with attentive teachers in small classrooms that focused on her needs. When she was placed in a larger classroom, however, she fell behind. As she explained:

> My freshman year I was in special ed, there was like 10 students in one class. When I asked the teacher for help she would come and explain to me, you know, what I have to do, and give me an idea how to. There was a teacher and a teacher's helper. And then my sophomore year they changed me to regular classes, you know, they have like 20-something students in a class, and that's when I was having all the problems. And they put me with different teachers and I was telling them I didn't understand because they was switching me from Spanish to English, and my writing is not good at all and they were expecting me to do all these essays and stuff.

She was already failing her courses when she had to miss classes for several weeks because she was sick.

When Sandy returned to school, she said her biology teacher "used to laugh at me and say little comments, oh like, 'So, why don't you just go look for a job,' and stuff like that, and I'm like, you know what, I ain't got time to deal with you, you know, I just wouldn't go to his class no more." She got the message from her teacher that she was not expected to finish school, but she also picked up that same message from institutional authorities who would not place her in skill-appropriate classes. She tried to tell them: "I spoke to the principal and I told him I'm not doing good in those classes. Then at the end of the year when I was already failing he decided to change my classes. So, I was like I'm not, I'm not gonna go now, I'm already failing so what's the use." She dropped out and one year later became pregnant; she was 17. When we interviewed her, her child was four months old and she had not returned to school, or even attempted a GED course. She said she wanted to get pregnant and even though the 21-year-old father of the baby was "scared, at first. I'm like you know it was gonna happen sometime, we were already living together in our own apartment." They got married before the child was born.

In Tita's school narrative she also tells us that she received the message from teachers that they were not interested in her educational achievement as she sat in classes and daydreamed and put on makeup, and that she liked her science teacher who "let me skip."[51] And while the principal told her she needed to stop skipping, he punished her for missing class by suspending her from school—a practice that ironically has the same effect as skipping classes.

Like Sandy and Tita, the teen mothers who dropped out of school early were all having problems in elementary school, and by the time they entered high school they had fallen behind academically. They felt lost in the classroom, overwhelmed by the course work, and shuffled aside by administrators. McCargar found that school districts in Connecticut used the practice of pushing students out to "circumvent reporting, responsibility and accountability for student discipline and achievement measures."[52] School districts with large concentrations of racial minority students had high rates of suspension, a practice that explicitly removed students from the classroom. In Bridgeport and Hartford, one in three students was suspended at least once in the 2005–2006 school year and in some middle schools 60 percent of students were suspended.[53] In general, studies have found that suspensions increase the prospects for grade retention, and students repeating a grade are more likely to drop out or be counseled out of school and, subsequently, to become teen mothers.[54]

In the life stories, we heard how grade retention weakened ties to peer groups and lowered self-esteem. Allie said, "I stayed back in eighth grade and that made me feel bad 'cuz all my friends graduated to like high school and like I had to stay back and I felt really dumb." When Lauren had to repeat high school, she "didn't have any friends 'cause they were all new kids [laughs]," and repeating a grade made her "feel like an idiot." Allie and Lauren both dropped out before they were pregnant. Danielle, whose story we told in the chapter on the youngest mothers, had not officially dropped out until after she had a child, but she had been suspended from middle school at least four times for fighting. The last time her principal suspended her one week for fighting, Danielle laughed and told him, "I wasn't coming back anymore." And she didn't. At the age of 20, she still had not earned a GED certificate.

Almost one-half (n = 13) of the mothers who dropped out before pregnancy had repeated a grade, and four had been suspended at least once for either fighting or truancy. Of course, school officials searching for affordable strategies to maintain order in the school, while providing whatever resources they may have to obedient students identified as educationally promising, may find school suspensions an expedient practice. But do they recognize these practices as contributing to the pathways to early motherhood?

Race Marginalization: "Not to Be Racist, but People Down There They're Prejudiced"

In 1989, Milo Sheff, a fourth-grader, and 17 other students filed a lawsuit against the State of Connecticut for violation of its equal education statute. The plaintiffs argued that as a consequence of racial segregation, concentrated poverty, and overburdened schools in Hartford, children were being deprived of their right to an equal education.[55] It took three years for the case to be heard and six and a half years before they lost their case. After the decision was delivered by Judge Harry Hammer in 1995, Governor John Rowland stated triumphantly, "The state did not force whatever balance or imbalance exists. . . . It's a natural occurrence. It's a result of human nature, people's decisions to live where they want to live."[56]

The decision, however, was overturned the following year by the state supreme court. Chief Justice Ellen Peters wrote: "Students in Hartford suffer daily from the devastating effects that racial and ethnic isolation, as well as poverty, have had on their education."[57] The court's decision confirmed that Hartford public schools were racially, ethnically, and economically isolated, and mandated that the state meet its obligation to provide all Connecticut's public school children with a substantially equal educational opportunity.[58] The arguments in this case provided compelling evidence of the inadequacy of the public schools in Hartford, which could have been easily applied to other racially segregated urban areas and school districts in Connecticut, such as Waterbury, New Haven, and Bridgeport. The court's mandate that the state develop and implement a remedy led to more years of legislative debate, court motions, hearings, and a second settlement. Falling considerably short of the goals initially set in 2003, the state, in a revised effort in 2008, promised to construct more magnet and charter schools in the region and to more aggressively encourage and support placement of urban children in suburban schools.[59] Given residential segregation, this meant more black and brown children in white schools.

While several studies have documented the positive effects of moving students to better-resourced schools, including early outcomes from the Hartford project,[60] other studies have focused on the hostile environments and misplaced racial assumptions that students encounter which lead to experiences of marginalization.[61] Moving urban minority students into resource-rich suburban schools is not an educational panacea, and, as we saw in several life stories, it can contribute to school dropout. While this strategy is important to desegregation objectives, it poses significant challenges, especially if students are academically underprepared and if support is not available to help them navigate racial dynamics. There were several instances of racial marginalization (often intersecting with class marginalization) in our study.

Monique, whose story appeared at the beginning of this chapter, participated in the Open Choice program (that enrolled urban students in suburban schools). She described her elementary school years in positive terms, but had trouble when she transitioned into the high school (although her story is mostly about problems she had in her home that interfered with school). When she talked about her years in the suburban school, however, she mentioned no friends or teachers. When asked what the students were like, she answered, "they were all white," and when asked to describe what it was like in school, she instead told us the story about running away and getting into a fight with her aunt. These narrative ellipses and evasions suggest that she was not well integrated in her suburban school.

Several other black and Puerto Rican mothers attended white suburban schools. For instance, when Yajaira was in fourth grade, her family moved from an urban school of mostly blacks and Latinos to a suburban white school district. During middle school, Yajaira maintained average grades, worked on the yearbook, and played basketball: "Sixth and seventh grade was hard but I was able to manage it. Then eighth grade is like when it started getting more work and more projects and that's when I fell behind." She repeated eighth grade but she "skipped all the time and then started not wanting to go to school" because she could not do the work: "I tried my hardest and it seemed like the harder I tried, the less grade I got."

Yajaira attributes some of her school problems to the expectations that the suburban teachers had of Puerto Rican students: "The reason why it wasn't working out was 'cuz, not to be racist, but people down there they're prejudiced and stuff like that. They used to talk about Puerto Ricans, they wouldn't treat us the same as other kids, like [as] if we didn't have no education or whatever." She also became severely depressed.[62] She said she had difficulty "just getting up, having to take a shower, get dressed, be at school, and it's just tiring for me. I was really depressed and I tried to hurt myself." After this call for help, she received therapy and medication to manage the depression, and her family moved back to the urban school district because they "noticed that being [at the suburban school] wasn't gonna help me. It was just making it worse for me." She liked the urban school, but she had to repeat ninth grade, which made her two years older than her classmates. She said she started "hanging with the wrong people" and began skipping school again. She dropped out having never completed ninth grade. A year later she became pregnant. She was 17 years old. The pregnancy was unintended and she considered having an abortion until her grandmother said she regretted her own abortion. Yajaira is still with the father of the baby, her family is supportive, and the child counteracts her depression: "What makes me feel good about myself is that I have a son that he looks at me and smiles."

In Tita's story that opened this chapter, we also heard that she felt isolated by her class and ethnic identity: "I felt like I was the problem, like I was the outer person. Everyone was normal but I was the Puerto Rican." Tita's experience was shared by Rose, who has a racially diverse heritage (Puerto Rican, African American, Irish, and Cherokee) and attended a rural white school, where, as she described, the students were "snobs, like the whole school, they're rich white people and they don't like Spanish or black people, you know. If you don't play sports then you're not going to make it in that school. Like they're just rude. I hate that." Adrianna, who is Puerto Rican, also lived and went to school in a small white town, where she and her friends—two black and one racially mixed—were known as the "posse" and in the school cafeteria "always sat at a table by ourselves." All four members of the posse dropped out of school.

* * * * *

For students who dropped out early, no one factor explained why they dropped out; instead, poverty, violent men, overburdened and underfunded schools, unstable families, cognitive disorders and delinquent behavior, and racial and class marginalization occurred in varying combinations and resulted in the failure to transition into high school. What is common in almost every one of their stories is that they were not prepared to do the work expected of them in high school. Their lack of readiness, we surmise, was related to frequently moving and changing schools, moving across language borders, violence in the home that interrupted their schooling, fighting in schools that led to suspensions or juvenile detention, and the lack of school programs to address their emotional, cognitive, and language needs. Schools are better prepared for students who do not have problems. Along with current, well-funded initiatives to increase the school-readiness of children, similar efforts might be considered to improve the *student-readiness* of schools.

The enduring disadvantages of those girls who did not make the transition into high school will stem, most likely, from their lack of skills. It was not simply that they did not have a diploma, but more importantly, they did not have the academic skills expected of high school graduates. At the time of the interview, they were still young (their mean age was under 20), but none of these early dropouts had returned to school to get their diploma, and those who had tried to complete a GED program failed (although two did get Job Corps training). We fully expect that these women will not find decent paying jobs and will most likely use state assistance more than their peers who have the skills to complete high school. Their low-paying jobs and welfare supplements will not, however, be a result of having had a child when they were teenagers. Clearly, their babies will make them eligible for some entitlements, but their lack of self-sufficiency will be related to school failure. Having a child was something that came after they dropped out; it was something that gave them joy, counteracted depression, gave them a reason to change unproductive behaviors (drug and alcohol abuse), and provided a purpose for living.

LATER DROPOUTS: GROWING OUT OF SCHOOL

Seven other mothers in our study dropped out in their junior or senior years—also before they were pregnant—but they *did* have the skills to graduate. These mothers were similar, in many ways, to the mothers in our study who never dropped out. They did not have childhoods crippled by violence and abuse or disrupted by constant moving; they did not have cognitive or language problems; and they did not report feeling like they were marginalized in high school because of their race or class.

Of these seven teen mothers, five were white, one was African American, and one was Jamaican. None of them complained that the schoolwork was too hard, the classrooms too large, or the teachers inattentive. Poor grades among this group stemmed from school truancy or alcohol and drug use, not cognitive disorders or language needs. They usually left high school because it interfered with working. They believed their career goals (for example, to attend cosmetology school or get an associate's degree in accounting) could be achieved by getting their GED certificate or high school diploma through adult education. At the time of the interview, two were enrolled in night school and five had completed their secondary schooling (through night school or a GED program); one graduate was enrolled in a community college.

The two black mothers were living in urban areas but not in poor neighborhoods, and the five white mothers were living in towns and rural areas. The white mothers are a part of a national trend in rural areas, where, in 2010, teen birth rates surpassed rates in urban areas (a reversal from the 1990s).[63] As the following stories illustrate, they were engaged in adult routines and responsibilities (for example, working and taking care of children) before they dropped out of school, and before they became pregnant.

Caitlyn's father left the family when she was eight years old. Her mother, who owned a small business and later was a manager of a department store, worked long hours and was often not home. Caitlyn said she was a cheerleader in her freshman year, the same year she started "being bad or getting badder. I smoked cigarettes and that's against the cheerleading rules so I just quit [cheerleading]. I [became] a bad student. F, D, C student. I hated school. I always skipped. I used to smoke weed. I'm not gonna lie. I used to. I don't do it no more." In many ways, Caitlyn's pattern of deviant behavior—smoking marijuana and skipping school—resembled those life stories described earlier in the chapter. One important difference, however, was that Caitlyn did not experience the trauma of domestic violence in her childhood home or child sexual abuse, nor did she move or change schools, and she never had to repeat a grade. So when she started skipping classes, she had a solid foundation of nine steady years of relatively successful schooling. Moreover, her delinquency and rebellion may have led her toward school dropout, but they did not lead to state surveillance (no probation officers or social workers) or juvenile detention.

When her mother found Caitlyn skipping school, she grounded her, and this became one more reason to rebel. Caitlyn said she "ran away" from home: "I didn't feel like going to school because I thought I could do whatever I wanted, so I dropped out. I was living with my friend's sister and she has four kids and I watched those kids from 9:30 in the morning to probably about 10:30 at night. They were mine all day long." She was a junior when she stopped going to school. After dropping out, she met her boyfriend and within five months she became pregnant. Her boyfriend convinced her to return to night school. She quickly earned enough credits to be placed in the twelfth grade, and at the time of the interview she was attending night school, close to earning her diploma, and planned on becoming a dental assistant. She was also once again living with her mother.

Caitlyn's life story was anchored in conflicts with her mother. The divorce was a prominent part of her life-story interview and, although she did not blame her mother for the divorce, she linked the effects of the divorce to her mother's long work hours. Her mother's absence led Caitlyn to contest her authority—"she can't tell me what to do"—and this attitude spilled over into breaking laws (drug use), challenging school authorities, and violating school policy (truancy). Caitlyn was in battle with adults—her mother and school officials had lost their legitimacy as authorities in her eyes. Caitlyn established her own adult identity by moving out and assuming responsibility for the primary care of four young children. She had already defined herself as an adult when she became pregnant, but having a child helped her establish an adult identity in relation to others—for example, she reestablished a relationship with her mother on adult terms, a relationship she defined in positive terms. She also returned to school.

Like Caitlyn, Julie also fought against the structures of confining adolescence and asserted her independence from adults. She said she had problems with the principal, her mother, and other teachers because "I don't like people telling me what I have to do. I know what I have to do, and I want to do what I want to do, not what they want me to do." It was the same with homework: "I never did my homework 'cause I wanted to have my own life. I knew I could do the work in Public High, and I knew I could have gotten good grades, I just didn't want to." She started being truant: "I would make my mom think I was going to school like I'd get on the bus and everything but I would have my friend pick me up right before school started and I just wouldn't go at all." Julie stopped showing her report card to her mother, intercepted letters from the school, and erased messages that school officials left on the family answering machine to hide her truancy. When a school administrator asked her why she was not in school, she responded with cocky defiance, "Because I didn't want to be here," and then told us, "The detentions added up to in-school suspension for three weeks straight for all the days that I missed and that's when I just stopped going." She moved in with her boyfriend and five other adults, and three months later she became pregnant. Just before she delivered, Julie moved back home with her mother, and a few months later enrolled in night school to get her diploma with plans to go to college.

The third illustration is Liz, who did not have a contentious relationship with her parents, but she was engaged in adult routines when she was an adolescent. She started working at age 13 to help pay the family bills. She grew up in a rural town surrounded by a large extended family (she has 30 cousins living in the area). Her grandfather owned several houses in the neighborhood that his children inherited. Her neighborhood was all white (the town was 93 percent white) and mostly working class. Several people from her neighborhood were serving in the military and her current boyfriend (who is not the father of the baby) was in the army. Both of her parents dropped out of high school, although her father did have his GED certificate. Growing up she seldom saw him because "he was always the one working." He worked in a variety of manufacturing industries. Her parents divorced when she was 18 years old; she reported no violence, substance abuse, or infidelity in her family. The only problem they had growing up was "money. It was always money because my dad was always in and out of jobs and I remember turning 13 and I was babysitting and I was the one putting the food on the table and I was the one helping pay for the bills."[64]

When Liz was 16 she moved in with her same-age boyfriend and his parents. Her own parents tried to stop her; her father even "smacked" her. "They didn't like that. Didn't like it at all. Called the cops on me. Tried to have me arrested for moving out and I was like, 'Guys, can't do this. I'm 16. I can do what I want as long as I have a roof over my head.' I was too smart. I knew all the laws."

Once she moved in with her boyfriend, Liz started staying home from school, complaining she was sick. Then she thought she was pregnant: "So I didn't go to school. I ended up just dropping out." If she stayed home from school sick when she lived with her own parents, she was required to stay in her bedroom "with no phone and no TV and go to bed at 8:00. Sucked! Sucked." But when she moved out, her parents "didn't have any say in it. They were upset about it, but they both dropped out of school too so they weren't going to preach at me about something they already did, so. They got over it [laugh]."

When Liz found out she was not pregnant, however, she did not go back to school. Her boyfriend's parents, with whom she was living, said, "If you're going to drop out of school, then you got to get a job. So I ended up getting a job." Within a few months she and her boyfriend moved into their "own place," which was the house next door. They took care of three children in exchange for room and board: "All you had to do was stay home and get her kids off to school every day." They stayed there for a year and then moved back in with his parents. Shortly after that, she became pregnant. She had been with the father of the baby for over two years by this time and the pregnancy was not a surprise; his parents "were expecting it a long time ago." To her own parents she said, "I'm 18 and, you know, make my own decisions, so they were all right with it." Liz claimed her adult status vis-à-vis her parents—they can't tell her what do; she knows the law. The baby gave her adult status by formalizing her adult responsibilities—she no longer took care of someone else's children; she had her own.

Three years after the birth of her daughter, Liz completed the GED exam, she said, because "I need it for a job. Can't get a job anywhere these days without a GED, a high school diploma, something." But she did have jobs; in fact, she had worked steadily since she was 13 years old. Work provided an alternative to school. Work (not just motherhood) became her route to adulthood. This was a common pattern we saw in the narratives of the teen moms who dropped out late in high school. They were already engaged in adult routines before they dropped out and before they became pregnant.

MOTHERHOOD AND ADULTHOOD

In the twenty-first century, sociologists have pointed out that the period of adolescence has been extended for some segments of the population, as more 20- and 21-year-olds legally, emotionally, and psychosocially fit under the rubric of not-yet-fully-adults. They are not self-sufficient economically or emotionally, and are often still living at home. This extended transition holds truer for middle-class adolescents who have more income and education and consequently more opportunities and resources to extend their transition to adulthood.[65] Unfortunately for teen mothers, this lengthened transition to adulthood for the middle class accentuates the deviance of their early childbirth.

It is not uncommon to think that early motherhood is an *alternative route* to adulthood.[66] Whereas middle-class women achieve the markers of adulthood in career, education, and material wealth, women with limited opportunities gain adult status by becoming mothers. School experiences are central to this process. For young women who drop out of school, particularly those who leave early in their educational careers, a funneling effect occurs—as other routes to adulthood fall away, motherhood is perceived as the *main*, if not the only, route to adult status.

In this chapter, we identified two routes to early motherhood. Those who dropped out *early* embraced motherhood because the school route was no longer perceived as viable or meaningful, and it was their disengagement from school that made motherhood more desirable. These mothers chose motherhood as much as motherhood chose them. In contrast, those who dropped out *later* were already adopting adult routines. While they had the skills to graduate, they chose to complete their educations in night schools or GED programs. They were already performing adult roles such as working full time, living on their own, or caring for other children; they had crossed the adolescent-adult border and left school as adults.[67] For them, motherhood was a validation of their adult identity.

Those who dropped out before pregnancy (whether early or late in high school) were twice as likely to say they intended the pregnancy.[68] It was not motherhood, however, that constricted their adolescence: for the early dropouts, it was school failure (and failing schools); for the later dropouts, it was the adoption of adult responsibilities at a young age. For both groups, however, having a child followed dropping out of school, and for both groups, having a child led others to treat them as adults.[69]

CONCLUSION: THE BABY DIDN'T DO IT

The common public assertion that teen births cause school failure is an oversimplified and empirically erroneous explanation that likewise suggests an oversimplified and erroneous solution. If we could only postpone births among adolescents, the prevailing belief contends, we could reduce poverty, increase educational achievement, and create ladders for young girls to move up and out of poverty. This assertion becomes a rallying cry for scores of well-intended policy-makers, human service providers, researchers, and members of the public, but our life-story discussions suggest that these constructions are narrow and often misleading. Just as teen births do not create poverty, teen births do not create school failure.

Students doing well in school generally stay in school even after they are pregnant and become mothers—especially with adequate child care and the educational equality provided under Title IX.[70] Over one-third of the young mothers in our sample were still in school when they became pregnant and they stayed in school after their babies were born. Access to daycare and accommodating school policies were critical to their success.

The public misconception about early childbirth—that early births cause school dropout, unemployment, and welfare dependence—concludes with the popular parlance that, by having a baby early, they are "repeating the cycle" of poverty. Viewing teen births and high school dropout from this perspective makes young mothers morally culpable for their own poverty and life trajectories and ignores the clustering of problems that precede the birth. It also ignores the fact that for teenagers who are not poor or educationally unskilled, having a baby usually does not derail their school trajectories.

School failure for those who dropped out early clustered with family instability, neighborhood poverty, domestic violence, frequent moves and circular migration, cognitive disorders, child abuse, underfunded and overwhelmed schools, and misdiagnosed or poorly addressed ELL needs. The public preoccupation with and condemnation of teen motherhood distract us from addressing these broader and deeper social forces that lead to school failure and pave the way for early motherhood. We believe that the answer to the question "why did 152 girls in Hartford under age 18 have babies in 2006?" could be found in the answer to the larger question "why were only 48 percent of black students and 36 percent of Hispanic students in the Hartford school district proficient in reading at their grade level (compared to 80 percent of white students in the district) in 2008?" Connecticut has the widest achievement gap in the country, and this gap reflects social class differences and racialized residential patterns.[71] The distraction of teen births prohibits us from having a serious, focused conversation on the ravages of racial apartheid and social class inequality. Without comprehensive and sustained efforts to address the latter, we are unlikely to make much further progress on the former.

Moreover, for students from impoverished neighborhoods with learning disabilities and special needs, school represents an arena of struggle and failure if they are not provided with well-funded programs, small classes, and special instruction. Families and school districts with more wealth are better able to meet the needs of students with learning disabilities. Affluent school districts in Connecticut, such as Greenwich and Westport, are able to pay for programs to help "slow learners" or "special needs" students, and when the state or school district will not pay, wealthy parents spend their own money on tutors and private evaluations or send their children to private schools.[72] In contrast, special education programs in Hartford (one of lowest performing school districts in the country) lag well behind its wealthy neighbors. Further, poor and working-class parents are less likely to have the human, social, and economic capital needed to get their children into special courses, tutoring, or private evaluations that would designate their children as entitled to special services.[73]

Without intervention early in their educational careers, students with special needs fall further behind with each passing year, and many drop out during the transition into high school and later drop into early motherhood. Twenty years ago, Margaret Simms pointed to the need for improving education (as opposed to promoting abstinence programs) as a policy for addressing adolescent motherhood.[74] Before we turn to our final chapter, which discusses contraception and comprehensive sex education, we want to concur with Simms: one of the best teen pregnancy prevention programs is a good educational system.

CHAPTER 6

Contraception and Abortion

PAMELA: "COLLEGE, COLLEGE, COLLEGE"

Wearing sweat pants, her long brown hair with blonde highlights pulled back into a ponytail, Pamela, a second-generation Latina, looked like one of our college students. In her life story, she mentioned college 29 times. Her father was a lawyer with a degree from an Ivy League university; her mother attended college but did not have a degree. Pamela was in her first year at a state university at the time of the interview, living at home in an affluent (white) community. Her parents paid her tuition and cell phone bills; her grandmother gave her a car. Tommy, the father of her child, came from an Irish working-class background.

I grew up in Easton, played soccer, was in the drum corps, and always had a lot of friends. Then we moved here and then I got into an accident, so I couldn't do sports anymore. They told me I wasn't gonna be able to walk ever, and then my therapist had me walking in seven months. This was freshman year in high school. I had physical therapy five times a week. It was pretty inconvenient, like I remember once I was at a birthday party at a lake and it started raining and I was in a wheelchair and nobody had anywhere to put me. So it was just always a big inconvenience, but I learned to deal with it. And then I went through a few surgeries and that was like a lot of pressure on everyone. It got better 'cuz I can walk now but I still can't run. I still can't play any sports and stuff.

I had plastic surgery, like reconstructive surgery on a few of the scars, but for three years I didn't even wear shorts and I didn't let anyone see my scars so that was like a big deal to me. I've been with my boyfriend for two years now and that was always like a big issue too, letting anyone close to me, like I was always hesitant about telling people like explaining the scars, they're pretty gruesome so I never really wanted anyone to see them.

* * * * *

[My mom] is a people person. She is really loving and caring, like always. It's a good relationship. [My dad] is very serious. He doesn't have a sense of humor. He's not a people person. He's loving to me and to my mother and to my brother and to my son, his grandson, but that's it. I don't even know how to describe him. He says like what needs to be said and that's it—we don't speak very much, like if we're in the car together it's usually silent. We just don't have much to talk about 'cuz we're at such different levels. He's really educated, obviously, like he went to Princeton. He's always been smart. He's into music, so when I was in the drum corps and when I could play soccer, he's really into soccer, it was a lot easier 'cuz we had like some stuff in common, but now there's not really much to talk about.

* * * * *

I was a pretty good student—Bs and Cs. I never failed any classes. I was good at math so I always took like extra math courses. [My parents] always cared about grades. Like if I got a bad grade, I wasn't necessarily punished for it but I would hear it. Like college is expected so they knew that if I didn't do good in school, then I wouldn't get into a college I wanted to go to. So college was definitely expected. That was the big deal. Like high school wasn't the issue; it's getting into the college I wanted to go to.

There's not very much like diversity in the students [at Public High School], mainly just white and not much of anything else there. The friends that I had grown up with in Easton weren't white—they were black, Asian, anything else—so like a lot of people didn't like that and if they saw me with them, like if I were to go to a football game with my other friends, it would just be a big mess. That's just how the whole town was basically. Like if I were at the mall and I was with a black person, the whole school knew about it the next day, so it was just a big mess.

Nothing was ever said like to a black person or to an Asian person but they would say it to me. So it was just always like fighting, like verbal fighting not like physical. I think it was mostly my sophomore year. My freshman year I was in a wheelchair so like, what am I gonna do to you? But like my sophomore year a lot of my friends ended up dating senior boys and the junior girls they just didn't like that.

* * * * *

I used to date this one kid who used to like beat the crap out of me. I started dating him actually when I was in a wheelchair. We were really close and my family was close with his, but like one day he's like, "Look at this," and pulled out a gun and put it to my head. It wasn't loaded, it was just joking around and I'm like, holy crap. And then he hit me a few times, like harder than it should've been, and then one day I was like, "Get out of my car! I don't want anything to do with you and get out of my life."

I talked to my mom—I didn't really talk to her, I was like, "He hit me," and she's like, "Well, maybe you should go back and apologize." And I'm like, "Apologize? He just slapped me across the face," and we were in the middle of a restaurant too, it was just so embarrassing. She knew because when she picked me up I was bright red with like scratch marks and stuff but, um, I never really talked to her about it. My dad didn't know. He would've killed him.

Right after that, I started dating Mark, and I was with him for a good two years. He never laid a hand on me and then one night he got so frustrated he slapped me and I just got out of his car and then left. I stayed with him for a little while longer. He never touched me again but then the day before we broke up I was at his house and he just started like wailing on me.

I know that they shouldn't have hit me but like it doesn't seem like it had a very big effect on me. I don't think it hurt me in any way. I don't look at them and like, "I hate you," only because I don't think it really had anything to do with me. I think it was just their problems. If they're gonna do that to their significant others for the rest of their life, that's their problem, not mine. Like they have nothing to do with me. I don't ever think maybe it was my fault. It's nothing like that. There's obviously something wrong with them. There's nothing wrong with me.

The night Mark and I broke up, Tommy and I ended up just hanging out—I wasn't friends with Tommy, I was friends with his older brother. And then like the next night I went there to hang out again and like

Tommy showed up again. And like it was weird, like, I never even actually told my parents about Tommy so when I told them I was pregnant, they were like [laugh]—I think a few times they knew that I was going over to his house but they had no idea that it was like anything like that. I got pregnant right away.

Nobody ever expected me to get pregnant by him. We didn't get along at all and when I did see him in school, we were like really secret. We'd have to go into a hallway to kiss good-bye and we didn't really let anyone see us together. I still had a lot of friends that were guys and I kissed them and stuff, like I was a teenager, you know what I mean?

*   *   *   *   *

When I first found out I was pregnant, I was already three months pregnant. For a while I didn't even have a clue 'cuz my period was so irregular, but I was always sick. I'd wake up in the morning and like I'd throw up and then go right to school. My biggest problem was, how am I gonna tell my parents? I took a pregnancy test and I threw the pregnancy test out but I kept the receipt 'cuz I'm an idiot [laugh]. And I put the receipt in my back pocket and my mom did my laundry that night so it didn't even like give me time to like contemplate on how I was gonna tell her and it was like that night and she was like, "So, what were the results?" I'm like, "Can we talk about it in the morning?" And she came up and she was like, "You need to talk to me now." It was actually like a relief, like I didn't keep anything from her for that long. She knew the day I knew so.

She was like, "Tommy, huh?" I'm like, "Yeah." And then, she was mad. She's like, "I'm gonna kill him!" Da-da-da-da-da-da-dah! My mom came downstairs and told my dad. She's like, "Your daughter's pregnant." And he's like, "It's not my problem." And that was it and I called Tommy and I'm like, "My mom's freaking out but my dad doesn't care." My dad came up an hour later ripping pissed. He's like, "Are you stupid?!" It was like a big mess and then like the next day they took me to the doctor's, like you need a blood test right now, like they didn't waste any time. And then it took like three to four days for the blood test to get back. My dad's like, "Don't tell anyone because the results might come back negative." And I'm like, "Dad, the results are positive. I'm pregnant." And like he still didn't want to believe it. He waited until that phone call came in and said your daughter's pregnant. My dad was hoping for like the benefit of the doubt for that test to be wrong.

I was really uncomfortable being pregnant around Tommy 'cuz we weren't close—we had only been together for a few months. Tommy and I didn't plan it but we obviously weren't being careful so as soon as I told him he was like, "Okay. I'll have to get a better job." Everyone always jokes around about his family, like if you ever need a baby, go to Tommy's family, they're really fertile. His dad has 11 grandkids in a matter of four years—they just pop out babies like nothing in that family 'cuz it's all girls.

* * * * *

I went to my doctor and he was like you have three options. "You keep the baby, you give it up for adoption, or you get an abortion. Those are the only three options, pick one of them," and I'm like, "I'm keeping the baby." I don't think I would've been able to have a baby and give it up for adoption and then abortion never even occurred to me. My family is really against abortions.

So when my parents found out they were like, "Uh, you're getting an abortion." I'm like, "No! You did not just say that." They're like, "Yeah. You're getting an abortion. You're 16 years old. There's no way you're having this kid." They were pushing for a good month and even sent me to a gynecologist and he's like, "If you think of any other options you want to choose, I can send you to another doctor," 'cuz he doesn't perform abortions himself. So like my parents had talked to him already about having the abortion 'cuz they're like, "You're not having this kid." So it was just weird 'cuz they were always so against it and then when it came to their daughter they're all for it. But throughout the whole pregnancy I was like, I'm gonna have the baby and there's nothing they can do about it now. I couldn't give it up and then it was too late for an abortion so even if I wanted to I couldn't have done it.

My mom became comfortable with it before my dad did. My dad and I didn't speak very much and everything came down to me being pregnant, it was always the center of every argument that we had. So one night I was like, "I wish I never got pregnant." And I told Tommy, "I shouldn't have gotten pregnant. I should've got the abortion." But that was just once and then after that I was excited and we were ready to get all the baby's stuff.

* * * * *

It was difficult [being pregnant and in school] only 'cuz like most of my teachers were helpful, but some of 'em kind of like saw a pregnant person and thought, like, that I couldn't handle whatever was coming up. I was out of school for my six weeks and it was right during finals. I had my son December 21 and we had off the following week for our Christmas break. The week after that you took your midterms and my tutors brought my tests here. My teacher wanted me to go there and I was like, "I just had a kid. I can't even walk and you want me to go to school to take a final?" Some teachers just weren't cooperative but others were fine.

It was my senior year, luckily, so I was friends with everyone in my grade and everyone, everyone helped. Like I would have to take like my prenatal vitamins when I ate lunch. That was the only time I could take 'em 'cuz when I wasn't sick I was throwing up and when I wasn't throwing up I was sleeping. So the only time I could take 'em was at lunchtime so everyone was like, "Pamela, you have to take your vitamins!" They all thought it was like cute and stuff like that. No one was rude to me— none of the students—it was just a few of the teachers that maybe like didn't think I'd be able to handle what I had in store for me, I guess.

I became pretty close with my English teacher in my senior year 'cuz she's really involved in women's rights and stuff like that. So if my boyfriend and I were having a problem or if my parents and I were having a problem, she would always talk to me. She was always there for me. And I was close to my guidance counselor, who was also my brother's guidance counselor, so our family had already known him and I would talk to him—like not as much about being pregnant, just about what I need to do while I'm out on my six weeks leave, and what I need to do to make sure I get into college and all that stuff.

* * * * *

In Tommy's family, no one ever went to college, like a high school diploma is satisfactory. The way I look at it is everyone has a high school diploma and everyone even has like a bachelor's degree and now that's not even enough anymore. If you want to be successful, then you gotta go get at least your master's. That's definitely a big thing with my parents.

I wanted to go to Duke but I can't really because I have Brandon and I wouldn't want to take Brandon away from Tommy and I know he wouldn't like move with me. He just doesn't have enough money to do that anyway. I went up to Philadelphia to visit some schools there, and I put my application in. That was actually spring break in April of the year I was pregnant and I didn't know I was pregnant yet. I was sick the whole vacation and the doctors told me I had gotten food poisoning 'cuz they didn't think that I was pregnant.

My dad's gotta be disappointed, only 'cuz like my brother went to Southern [Connecticut State University] and my dad was always like, "I don't want you to go to a school like Southern. I want you to go to a better school." And like he always says stuff like that and like now I'm at a worse school—not worse than Southern but it's like the same. We pulled up to one of the buildings one day, he's like, "Well, it's not Princeton but I guess it'll do."

I had planned to go away to college so I'm sure it would've been different but like I don't mind now. I just try to get out of school as soon as I can. I definitely want Brandon to go to college. I always like tell Tommy, "He's gonna go to Harvard or Yale," and Tommy's like, "Are you paying?"

HAYLEE: "MY FATHER WANTED ME TO HAVE AN ABORTION"

When we interviewed Haylee, a biracial mother of 17-month-old twins, the house was immaculate with well-kept plants, numerous baby photos on the wall, and a chocolate cake on the table. She became pregnant at the age of 15, shortly after her parents divorced. She was 18 when we interviewed her, living at home with her mother and her twins, and enrolled in college. The father of her twins, Stephen, was an active parent and they were still a couple.

I grew up all over while my father was overseas in the Marines. He's a correction officer now and he's gonna retire in a couple years. When I began the second grade I came here. [I remember] playing outside at the basketball court and the pool with a big slide. My dad used to play with me a lot, he's like a big kid. I remember playing Nintendo with him and playing with my friends outside. The summertime was the funnest.

[My mother's] cool—down to earth but she's cautious, meaning like she won't let my brother skateboard in the road. She's a good mother. She's definitely a good mother. She was home a lot. She's used to having my father support her so she didn't need a job. She said she met my father and they fell in love and so she put college off and never ended up going.

The divorce was hard. I was 13. I had no idea. I didn't even know that there was anything wrong, except they were arguing a lot more and sometimes he wouldn't be around at night. I guess they had been having problems [but] it was behind closed doors. I was worried but I never knew that they were gonna actually separate. That was really devastating for me. I remember I was crying and asking them if they would be willing to try to work things out. My mother always was willing to go to counseling but he wasn't.

I didn't really know, until my mother told me, that there were other women that he was seeing. There was never any kind of violence and my dad has a very calm temper. She kept giving him another chance every time because she loved him and she had a really hard time with it. I remember one night he was going somewhere and she ran after the car crying and that was really hard. My mother went into a deep depression and she wasn't eating. That was a really tough time.

* * * * *

School was easy. I made high honors in freshman year and then sophomore year I made honors, so I was getting As and Bs, um, more Cs in math but I brought 'em up to Bs if I could. My mother always wanted to make sure that I was doing my homework and getting good grades. I never really got in trouble or anything. I got along with all of [my teachers]. I went and saw my biology teacher the other week and she was real excited because I sent her a Christmas card with the babies' pictures and stuff like that. And my English teacher I grew close to, she was really nice and I think she really appreciated my work. It wasn't always A work but I tried my best so I got closer to her. When the babies were like six or seven months old, I brought them in to see her and I was like, "Well, I want to get my associate's degree," and she said, "At least your associate's degree!" She said I should go further, so she encouraged me a lot so that was cool.

In my sophomore year I found out I was pregnant. Before I was pregnant I used to have a lot of fun at school. When I was pregnant everybody looked at me funny, and when I started getting big, some people would come and like touch my belly which is kind of weird 'cuz I didn't really know them that well. But people would come up to me like, "You're pregnant, you're pregnant?" I'm like, "What the hell does it look like?" I remember I was walking out of my Spanish class and this girl was talking about me. She was like, "Well, one is bad enough but she's having two!" That kind of hurt, because I had known her since elementary school. Things like that were hard. So when I was pregnant, I was a lot more cut off and I didn't have as many friends at all.

I didn't go to the Teen Parent Program until I had already had the kids because the daycare there was free and it's right in the school. For like three months I was out of school because the [paperwork] for the daycare took like a month to fill out and then I think I didn't send their birth certificates and then all of a sudden they wanted it so it took a long time for that. I was gonna go [to Teen Parent Program] for my junior and senior year but it took me less than half the time to finish. When I went to the Teen Parent Program, you can't have electives; I took two years of Honors Spanish in high school in freshman and sophomore year and I made the Spanish National Honor Society. But they don't have elective classes over at the Teen Parent Program so I couldn't take a Spanish class.

My [sophomore] English class was tough. It was a CP class [college preparatory] and the teacher was really strict, so a lot of people dropped that class. I stuck it out and I think I got a B+ and I'm usually an A student in English, but she had some hard stuff but that was good because it taught me a lot about English. In the Teen Parent Program there wasn't much English at all. Not at all. They had like grammar packets—you had to do underline and circle stuff like prepositional phrases and just a whole bunch of crazy stuff—but the English in my sophomore year, she made us do like a research paper, and you had to do citations and things like that and it was like a five-page research paper, and I think that is what prepped me for like college.

[In the high school] you could hang around with your friends in the hallways and stuff but over at the Teen Parent Program you were like in this one room with all your books all day and you could go get your lunch and come back to the room. And now they changed it. You can't even go get your lunch anymore—you order your lunch and then the teachers go get all the lunches and bring them back to the room. So we really didn't get out much. We went out for like a walk around the hall after everybody left and that was it. That was boring, I mean, I got my work done. I definitely did that quick, but high school was a lot more fun because between classes when the halls were all crowded it was exciting and I'd just see my friends and stuff.

I knew the vice principal and I asked her if I could go to the Senior Prom and she said probably not because the Teen Parent Program was not part of the school. I called my guidance counselor and she said she doesn't know if I could go. So when I went down there for one of my transition to college classes, I saw the principal and he said I could definitely go.

* * * * *

I met Stephen at a Halloween party that my aunt has every year; my cousin brought him. When he walked in the room I just had this big *crush on him [laugh]. I thought he was really cute and I liked him a lot. He started asking me questions like my age and stuff like that and then we just started from there. He's a year older than me. He asked me out and then he asked my dad if he could go out with me. And then we got close really fast. I actually kind of pursued him so it was my decision. Maybe it wasn't the best decision because I was really young but I met him in October and I was pregnant by January.*

We wanted to spend like every minute of every day together and it was fun. It's funny looking back on it because I remember I used to cry when I had to leave. He used to call my house all the time and my mother used to get annoyed 'cuz he would call and then I would say call me back later 'cuz I'm busy and he would call like two minutes later and ask if I was still busy [laugh]. It was fun.

I would say it was a deep infatuation. I don't think I was in love with him before I had gotten pregnant, but I wanted to be with him all the time. He was the only one that I wanted to be with and we were always like hand in hand or hugging each other or whatever so it was good. I think we got too involved too fast but we learned, I mean, even now we still learn more about each other because we've only been together for two years so we still learn more about each other every day, which is neat because it keeps the relationship interesting.

* * * * *

I knew in the back of my mind that I might be pregnant but I wasn't really facing up to it. Then when I found out, I was like almost devastated because I felt like I wasn't ready for it. I didn't know how to change a diaper even. I didn't really know anything about it so. I was really scared. I don't want to say that in a negative way but I was just terrified. I was a little girl. I didn't really know anything.

I told my mom that I thought I might be pregnant and then she told my father and my father was the one who brought me to the doctor and then we just got home and I was sobbing and crying to my mother.

I considered abortion and I look back at that and I feel terrible that I considered it but I did. I was hoping that something would lead me in the right direction. I prayed about it and when I actually went to an abortion clinic it was sad, it was hard because they had protestors outside. I was very confused. I went to the abortion clinic and they did a sonogram and I had prayed that something would enforce me to make the right decision. The sonogram indicated that they were twins so my father just said, "Let's leave," and we left. I was crying.

My father wanted me to have an abortion. He was scared that I wouldn't be able to go to college and pursue a career. Um, several people on his side of the family felt that I should have an abortion, most of them thought that I couldn't handle it. They encouraged me to have an abortion because I wouldn't be able to go out to the clubs or whatever and even some people on my mother's side told me that abortion might be the best idea for me because I was so young. My aunt has three kids and I figured that she would encourage me to have them but she told me that I should take adoption and abortion into consideration.

My grandmother, I think, has had an abortion but I think she's really against it. I remember calling my grandmother up and when I said they were twins and I didn't have the abortion she started crying. She was really happy. My mother didn't agree with the abortion at all, but she said it was my decision and she said she cried every night and she prayed that I would keep the baby but she didn't know that it was twins. When she found it was twins, they threw like a party for her at work and stuff and she was really happy so that was good and then my feelings changed about it.

Stephen was always happy that I was pregnant. He enjoyed it. I think he might have broken up with me if I would've had the abortion. He used to cry, oh like for over an hour he would cry on my belly. He would like apologize to my stomach. He was, "I'm so sorry!" Because I was gonna have an abortion and I was thinking about that and he just kept telling me, please have this baby, please have the baby. And so when I told him it was twins he was really excited.

He was so happy that I was pregnant, he always wanted to take pictures. He took pictures of me when I was sleeping and took pictures of my belly and sometimes he's even like, "Oh, I wish you still had that belly so I could feel the baby kick." He was really into that. He liked it a lot more than I did. He said that he wished he could go through it. I was like, "No, I don't think you want to go through that!" [laugh].

*   *   *   *   *

Stephen did really bad in school. He dropped out his last semester of his senior year and went to Adult Ed and dropped out and he never finished. He is working at an appliance center and he repairs refrigerators. They're really good to him over there and he likes what he makes now. I don't think he would make it elsewhere because he doesn't have his diploma or anything. He knows how to read but he has trouble writing and like sometimes he'll call because he has to fill out the form to fix the refrigerator and like what's wrong with it or whatever and sometimes he'll ask me how to spell something real easy. It doesn't bother me because I love him. He told me he had Attention Deficit Disorder and he had a lot of trouble in school. He got kicked out of school a lot and he's straightened himself out a lot. I think he's matured a lot and I think a lot of people think that too. So he's a very good person.

We're in a different stage of our relationship now, where we've been together a little while, so it's not as exciting as the first time we saw each other but we still have a good relationship. Sometimes I feel, not lonely, but like, "dang, I wish I could go back there just for one day when we could never separate for anything." I plan on marrying him. We were thinking about this summer. He has a lot of money saved up.

*   *   *   *   *

This whole college thing is stressing me out. I mean, people will help you if you ask them a little but only to a certain extent so you have to do most of it yourself. I had to figure out my own schedule. I had to figure out when I had time to work around my schedule at night and my mom's gonna help me with babysitting. My grandparents paid for a printer for me. Stephen helped me with the money and my dad babysat a couple times. Financially, I've been coming to some problems but people have been helping me. I have a great support system.

WHEN "GOOD GIRLS" GET PREGNANT

I was the least likely person to get pregnant to tell you the truth. All the other kids in school, they're like, "Oh my, you! Goody, goody two shoes, having a baby?" Yeah, the least likely person in the entire school. I was 15, grade 10. I was scared out of my mind. I was depressed almost all the time and not happy at all. Joey was really scared and worried just like I was. We discussed abortion and all but it didn't quite go there. We didn't tell anybody until I was five months along. I was worried that my mom was going to ring my neck. They took it okay. There was no furniture being thrown. I stayed out of school six weeks postpartum so when I went back I was a little bit behind but I did eventually catch up. They gave me more time than they would have given someone else. Joey plans on going into the Navy. He wants me to go to college, with Danny going into child care. My mom doesn't want me to marry Joey at all. [My dad] thinks we're too young too. He wants me to wait until after college.

—Roxanne, 15-year-old white mother

Many women have at some point in their sexual lives put themselves at risk for an unwanted pregnancy by not using contraception and consequently know that sinking feeling associated with a late period. Every time they go to the bathroom, they check for blood. Some deny the pregnancy like Haylee, who said, "I knew in the back of my mind that I might be pregnant but I wasn't really facing up to it." Others, like Roxanne, know they are pregnant but keep it hidden.

According to a 2002 national survey, roughly one-third of all births in the prior five years were unintended, but over three-quarters of births to women under age 20 were unintended.[1] Many women terminate unintended pregnancies, especially teenagers; roughly one in four teen pregnancies ends in induced abortion.[2] For others, however, the pregnancy is carried to term and over the course of nine months the "trouble" becomes a child.

In this chapter we look at unintended pregnancies and early childbearing and ask, why not use contraception or have an abortion? We focus on the mothers in our study who were middle teens (ages 15 to 17), and who, like Roxanne, were "good girls" perceived as not likely to get pregnant. As Gail said, "The ones from church were like, 'I never would have thought that *you* would have a kid.'" The mothers in this chapter came from "good families" and were unencumbered by child sexual abuse, extreme gender violence, and concentrated poverty. Not surprisingly, without these life strains, they did well in school; and when they got pregnant, they stayed in school.

In 2008, adolescents who gave birth between 15 and 17 years of age accounted for a little less than one-third (135, 664) of all teen births nationally (but they represent over one-half of the mothers in our study).[3] This age group is different from the young young mothers who fit the "kids having kids" profile, and the older teens who are already in transition to early adulthood. We might even say that this 15 to 17 age group best represents "adolescent" mothers—between childhood and adulthood. Their rights and entitlements are more restricted than those of older teen mothers (even more so after the 1996 Welfare Reform Act and through the last two decades of incremental abortion restrictions). Clear differences between these age groups appear in the data on pregnancy, birth, and abortion rates. For example, in 2006, the birth rate for 15- to 17-year-olds was three times lower than that for the oldest teens and 36 times higher than that for the youngest teens. (See figure 6.)

Most middle teenagers are not having sex. In 2006, almost three-quarters of adolescents between 15 and 17 had *never* had sexual intercourse, and less than one in 10 were having sex on a regular basis.[4] One of the reasons that most 15- to 17-year-old girls are still virgins is because

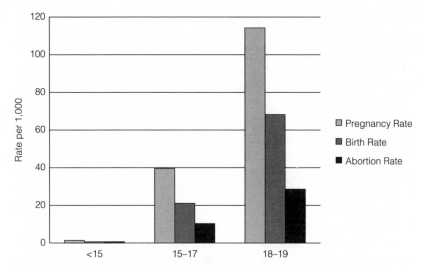

FIGURE 6. Pregnancy, Birth, and Abortion Rates by Age Group, 2008. Source for Pregnancy and Abortion Rates: Ventura et al. 2012, table 2. Source for Birth Rates: Martin et al. 2012, table 8.

they do not want to get pregnant.[5] Nonetheless, among teens who have sex, this is the age when sexual intercourse is most likely to be initiated—more than one-half experienced sexual intercourse before the age of 17.[6] For most teens in this age group, the pregnancy is an "accident" or a "mistake," terms we heard frequently in the narratives of the "good girls."

The mothers in this chapter were different from most of the mothers discussed in the previous chapters that focused on contextual problems such as child sexual abuse, gendered violence, and poverty. In this final chapter, we focus on the teen mothers who did not have these problems—roughly one-fifth of the sample.[7] With a few exceptions, the adolescents' households were economically stable. The mothers were not sexually abused, and other violence in their lives was minimal. The girls in this chapter were not failing school. Many were National Honor Society inductees taking Advanced Placement classes and headed to college. Their families were not beleaguered by death, illness, substance abuse, incarceration, or mental health problems. Their "normalcy" (the absence of disadvantages) presents a different face of adolescent mothers. In everyday terms—the language of the dominant culture—these adolescent mothers were "good girls" from "good families."

Lina came from a close-knit Chilean family and the father of her baby, Rizol, was raised in an extended Vietnamese family. Both immigrant families were economically stable. Lina's mother had been a dentist in Chile, her father worked for a state agency in Connecticut, her brother was a senior at the University of New Hampshire, and Lina planned on going to college for business. When we interviewed her, she was working 20 hours a week as an assistant at one of the large insurance companies in Hartford. She worked a retail job on the weekends and was finishing high school. She gave birth during her senior year and only missed six weeks of school. Lina and Rizol had been dating just a few months when she became pregnant. She confirmed she was pregnant at two months, and then kept it a secret for another two months, afraid of how her family would react. As Lina and Rizol expected, their parents were "horrified."

Lina and other "good girls" from "good families" did not suffer from what Elaine Kaplan has termed a poverty of relationships—disconnections or estrangement from family, teachers, and men—that leads girls to look for love and attention from men.[8] Their mothers and fathers or stepfathers had a strong positive presence in their life stories (a contrast to many stories in the earlier chapters where an aunt was the primary caregiver or the grandmother was the "rock" of the household). They spoke about their parents fondly, even when they had divorced. Their parents were ever present in their lives: they disciplined them, nurtured them, encouraged them, materially provided for them, and were involved in their schooling. It was heartbreaking telling their parents they were pregnant (and many of their parents found out their daughters were sexually active at the same time they found out they were pregnant). Parents were shocked, saddened, and embarrassed by their daughters' pregnancies, and some suggested that they have an abortion.

Gail grew up in a stable two-parent home in a small white ("I think there's one black family") town that she described as quiet ("we tip cows for fun [laughs]"). The property prices in the area were high because of its proximity to New York City. She described her town as a good place to raise children because "houses here have lots of land, plus we have a lake and beaches on the lake." Her mother worked in retail and was home with her children after school. Her father was "a steady worker" and "a bible scholar." They went to church every Sunday. When she found out she was pregnant at age 17, she "just started crying." Her first thought was, "my dad's gonna kill me." She told her mother while they were in the car and her mother "swerved off the road and pulled over and we both started crying, I mean, it broke her heart." The small and exclusive character of her town accentuated her swollen belly. She said, "I couldn't hide my pregnancy because everyone knew."

One way these mothers managed the stigma of the early pregnancy was to tell us that the father of the baby was their first and only sexual partner—a disavowal of promiscuity. The fathers of their babies were also similar in age, and when the mothers tell their stories, it is easy to hear the innocence of romance and the ignorance of reproduction. For example, Victoria was 16 when she met Victor in early August while working at a summer school program and by September she was pregnant.

> So that day I was outside. He was looking at me and looking. I mean he got annoying. I couldn't stand him and then he gave me his phone number. I called him and that's how we started talking. We used to go to parks, talk. We did a lot of that stuff but that's how I got pregnant.

Her narrative skips from talking in the park to being pregnant in a few words. Victor was not an older man with the smooth I-love-you line, but a boy younger than Virginia and her first and only partner.

We are mindful that in an effort to show how this group of "good girls" is different, we may inadvertently reinforce stereotypes of the "other" young mothers as "bad girls" from "bad families." We need to point out that the majority of the mothers in the previous chapters were not promiscuous either; many of the fathers of their children were similar in age and most of the pregnancies were not intended. We feel it is important, however, to train our eyes on these young mothers who did not experience major tragedies or disadvantages. Looking at their life stories, we even questioned why they were participating in a home-visitation program designed for vulnerable parents. What put them at risk for bad parenting? The program was voluntary, and when these particular mothers were invited to participate they met three of the criteria on the vulnerability index—they were young, unwed, and had not yet finished high school.

These mid-adolescents from families without major traumas (roughly one-fifth of the 108 mothers we interviewed, but one-half of the 57 mothers who gave birth between 15 and 17) were not sexually abused, did not drop out of high school before pregnancy, did not grow up in violent households or extreme poverty (though several lived in low-income households), and did not have mental health or substance abuse problems. None of them intended to become pregnant. They said that if they could do things over, they would have waited to finish school and get married before they had a child. Given this, what we try to understand in this chapter is why they did not use contraception and why they did not have an abortion. These questions are of particular interest because their young motherhood represented what Erving Goffman would call a spoiled identity.[9] They were shamed and ashamed; their bulging bellies were stigmata.

"HA, HA, YOU PREGNANT. LOOK AT YOU. YOU ARE A DUMB ASS."

While we refer to the teen mothers in this chapter as "good girls," their behavior often straddled "the good" and "the bad." We are also aware that families cannot be neatly divided into mutually exclusive good/bad categories, which poorly represent the complexity of the social world. What then is the benefit or harm of using such evocative labels as "good" and "bad"? First, the distinction helps point out variation among teen mothers. Too often social scientists mistake categories for the actual behavior of people. When a stereotype or ideal type overshadows in-group diversity, the monolithic group gets a one-size-fits-all explanation that influences public policies. Given the varying routes to teenage motherhood discussed in this book, it should be evident that different life trajectories call out for different policies or foci. In this chapter, the pregnancies raise questions about birth control and abortion. Why do they have unintended pregnancies and why do they carry them to term? The answers to these questions differ for the teens in this chapter compared to those in previous chapters who were victimized by child sexual abuse, who were escaping violent homes, or who became pregnant after they had dropped out of school.

The second reason for using the normatively redolent "good girl" and "good family" terms is to illustrate how teen mothers have been demonized in our society. Most people in this country think that it is wrong for teens to have children, especially if they are not married and have not completed high school.[10] We spend millions of dollars on research and programs trying to prevent these pregnancies, and when teen pregnancy or birth rates go down or teen sexual behavior declines, we call this a "good trend."[11] Defining young, out-of-wedlock childbirth as wrong carries over to identifying the young mother as bad. Using the term "good girl" helps to disconnect the girl from the behavior of having a baby. Having a baby does not make her a delinquent, or even a deviant, although it does carry a stigma.[12]

A recent example of the public shaming of teen mothers is New York Mayor Bloomberg's campaign that plastered posters around the city shaming teen mothers. While Planned Parenthood of New York came out against this campaign because it further stigmatized young mothers,

Sarah Brown, the CEO of The National Campaign to Prevent Teen and Unplanned Pregnancy, said in a radio interview that she thought the Bloomberg campaign was "edgy," and even though it may "offend" people and make them feel "disrespected," it was done for the purpose of preventing negative outcomes and therefore she supported it.[13] This persistent stigmatization of teen mothers reaffirmed our decision to use the term "good girl" in an effort to counterbalance the negative framing of teen mothers.

We also use this term to undo the racialization of the good girl/bad girl dichotomy, where the good are white and the bad are black and brown. In our study, the "good girls" were from a variety of racial and ethnic backgrounds—they were black, white, biracial, West Indian, Asian, Puerto Rican, and from other Latino groups.

"Good girl" is also a self-referential term. Many young women in this chapter described themselves as "good girls" or, as Lark said, not the "the black sheep" of the family. Words like "shame" and "embarrassed" occurred often in their narratives, and the pregnancy story almost always included crying and disbelief because this was not the life trajectory they imagined. Teenagers like Hayley and Pamela expected to go to college, and pregnancy complicated those plans. Unlike the mothers living in life worlds of chaos, the baby did not represent a chance to start over, nor was it a chance to make a bad situation better; instead, it represented the risk of swerving off the road to the middle class.

Their stories also provide a counterbalance to the public narrative that teen mothers drop out of school. The mothers in this chapter did not drop out: most were headed to postsecondary schooling, and some were already attending a four-year college. They were *not* using motherhood as their route to adulthood. And yet, while they had middle-class ambitions, they were still socially located as women, and this created ambivalence around the pregnancy (which led some to consider abortion).[14] In many cases, the tension was resolved by straddling two worlds—the gendered familiar world of motherhood and the middle-class promise of college. They adopted a determination, albeit fraught with personal angst and uncertainty, to have children without sacrificing college or class stability. The family also grappled with the disruption and worked toward reorganization, both culturally and materially, because the stigma of being an unwed adolescent mother extended to them as well.[15]

Chery, a Jamaican mother, was "scared" to be pregnant at the age of 16. "I wanted to finish high school, you know, go away to New York and go to school. During the pregnancy I was very depressed. I didn't want to go to church. I was like very ashamed of myself, you know." She was afraid to tell her mother, so a friend from church broke the news. "She came to the house and took her outside and she told my mom that I was pregnant and she came back in crying" and said she was "disappointed, very disappointed."

Zina, pregnant at 15, said her Trinidadian mother was "angry." When she first told her, "It kind of felt like the world just stopped turning for a moment." Her mother had immigrated to the United States and was working double shifts at a restaurant to provide a better life for her children. Her mother turned to the Pentecostal church to deal with her anger.[16] Zina said, "It was a difficult time period for her and they were very supportive of my mother, they helped her through my whole pregnancy and they were there for her." The church also helped Zina by giving her a baby shower because, as she said, "my mother was like I really can't have a baby shower for you. It's, it's, uh, just like she wished that I would've been older and married and she said it was just something that she couldn't see herself doing, she just couldn't do it."

Zina worked hard to fight the stigma of being a young mother. She was an honors student and she would not let the pregnancy derail her—as much to "show them" as for herself.

> I keep my grades up, you know, and my teachers they commend me for that. A lot of girls they say, "oh, I'm gonna finish school," but they don't actually do it. It's like your teachers are proud of you because you beat the odds and you held on. 'Cuz a lot, even teachers, they expect you just gonna give up, so it's like you always want to prove people wrong. That's how I feel, like I always want to show people that I'm better than that.

She continued to attend classes even when she did not want to. "I had morning sickness, I was sick for the first five and a half months and I still got up and went to school, and like I'd throw up in school and everything." She was out of school for only six weeks after she delivered.

At the time of the interview, her child was almost one year old and Zina still felt that she "did something wrong." When asked about her dreams for her child's future, she hoped that "history doesn't repeat itself. You know, I wouldn't want this for her and I just want her to finish school and accomplish all her goals." She went on to say:

> I was always like the type—school—you know, accomplish all, achieve all my goals. Like I knew what I wanted and that was really what I was striving for. If I could turn back the hands of time, I know I wouldn't be a parent right now. A lot of people look down on you when they hear, "oh, you're a teenage mom" and stuff like that, like you shouldn't be having a child.

Zina and other young mothers were dealing not only with physical sickness in their efforts to continue school, they also had to manage the stigma of being a young mother.

Wanda also expressed the sting of the stigma. She said, "every time my sisters and my brothers would come by they would make fun of me, [saying,] 'Ha, ha, you pregnant. Look at you. You are a dumb ass.'"[17] In addition to the social-psychological stress of embarrassment, the stigma can lead to denial and hiding behavior that can limit prenatal care and have detrimental effects on the fetus.[18] Valeria, a black mother who became pregnant at 15, hid her pregnancy for six months: "I was kind of in denial. I was scared [and] mad because I wanted to finish high school." And when the pregnancy began to show, the denial turned into shame: "I didn't want to go out, I just wanted to stay in the house."

Lark's story is similar, but her denial turned into being shamed. Her story also reminds us that for younger teens their menstrual cycle is often too irregular to suspect pregnancy, so "denial" may be too strong of a word—maybe "unsuspecting" is more appropriate. Lark explains:

> When I first came out pregnant that was real scary. Her father was my first boyfriend, the one who took my virginity. That was my first everything. I met him in middle school. We used to go to school together and we just started talking and we started going out and one thing led to another. We was together like a year and a half and then I came out pregnant. I had went to go get my Pap smear done. [The doctor] asked me when was my last period, and I was like January and she was like, January? She was like, well, "Let's take a pregnancy test," and we took a pregnancy test and it came out positive and that's when I was like, "Oh!" She's like, "You're about to be a mom." I'm like, "Uh-uh, you're lying." I made her take like three pregnancy tests to really believe that I was pregnant. "I ain't pregnant." She's like, "Yes you are." I'm like, "No I ain't." I was real in denial about it. I always had an irregular period; it was a normal thing to me. I thought I didn't get it because it was just one of them months.

Like many of the girls in this chapter, Lark's boyfriend was a same-age schoolmate and her first sexual partner, and her parents found out that she was no longer a virgin at the same time that they learned she was pregnant.

> I had to break the news to [my mother] that I lost my virginity and that I was pregnant at the same time. She took it really hard. My mother told my father and then my father told everybody else. They couldn't believe it 'cuz I was, I don't know. Everybody spoiled me like the little baby of the house, so they would never think that I would be the one to come out pregnant. They would always think it was my cousin Daisy to do it. Daisy's like the fast one of the

family. You know what I'm saying? So everybody would picture that she would come out pregnant. And it wasn't her. It was me. So my cousin's like the black sheep of the family but I just took her place. Everything changed. Everything went downhill when I came out pregnant. I became the black sheep of the family.

Lark expresses her feelings of dejection at having to live under the cloud of the stigma. She was not only shamed but she felt ashamed.

Lark and the other mothers in this chapter agreed with the dominant narrative that defines the "right" life-course trajectory—complete school, get a job, get married, and have children "in that order."[19] They felt what they did was "wrong," which is a little different than thinking of early childbirth as simply bad timing. Damaris, who became a single mother at 17, was a well-rounded student who performed well in the classroom and in sports (she ran the sprint hurdles and threw the discus). The father of her child was on the football team. Damaris found out she was pregnant during track season when she went to see a doctor because she thought she had "the flu or something." She argued with the doctor, who told her, "You're pregnant. You have to stop track." Damaris bargained with her: "'How about I go for a couple more weeks?' I had a meet coming up so I went and did my meet and then I told my track coach I couldn't run no more. He got mad at me 'cuz I didn't tell him why." At the end of the interview, when we asked Damaris what her hopes and dreams were for her daughter, she echoed the view of the majority of people in the country: "Finish school, go to college, meet a nice guy, marry, have two kids, and then put them through school. She can't have kids until after she graduates and gets married."

In their stories, these young mothers acknowledged early childbirth as deviant. They tried to manage the good girl/bad girl contradiction internally (self-recrimination accompanied by a conviction to work even harder) and externally by managing their social status in public: in schools (proving teachers wrong), with families (avoiding parents' scrutiny), and at church (not attending). The tension had a moral and practical dimension.

Today, sexual activity outside of marriage is normative within committed relationships, especially for adults, but it is still somewhat deviant for adolescents in the United States. The "good girl" can have sex without too much damage to her identity under certain conditions—for example, when it is within a monogamous relationship. Kate Sutherland argues that "the virgin-whore dichotomy has flattened out into a continuum: rather than attempting to keep the virgin side of the dichotomy, girls expend considerable energy to attain a safe ground between virgin and whore. Distinctions are drawn between good and bad based upon which sexual acts are engaged in, at what ages, between which partners, and in what circumstances."[20] The girls in this chapter were on moral safe ground (in committed relationships, with same-age boyfriends, and with good prepregnancy reputations), but not on contraceptive safe ground.

WHY NOT USE BIRTH CONTROL?

The swollen belly on a young girl without a wedding ring is no longer the scarlet letter for sexual indecency; it is instead the flunking grade for not using contraception. As Constance Nathanson described 20 years ago: "The new 'good girl' may be 'sexually active' but she takes her pills by the book."[21] Today, respectability is not as much about being a virgin as it is about not getting pregnant and not getting a sexually transmitted disease; girls are respected for practicing safe sex.[22] The pregnancies of the mothers in this chapter, defined as "accidents," were a result of adolescent hubris ("it won't happen to me"), ignorance ("I can't get pregnant the first time"), and naivety ("we did it before and nothing happened"). Practicing safe sex, however, requires more than overcoming hubris, ignorance, and naivety; it also requires that girls negotiate contraception within relationships that are shaped by systemic gender inequality.

The number of 15- to 17-year-olds who become pregnant in the United States has been declining for the last two decades.[23] Some researchers attribute this change to a decline in sex, but this depends on how sex is measured. The term "sexual experience" refers to ever having vaginal intercourse, and the term "sexually active" refers to having had sexual intercourse in a specifically defined time period; the latter is considered to be a better measure for risk of pregnancy.[24] For females age 15 to 17, sexual experience has decreased from 37 percent in 1988 to 28 percent in 2006, with most of the decline occurring in the 1990s; but sexual activity has remained more constant, with roughly 20 percent reporting sexual activity.[25] In short, the number of virgins increased slightly since the late 1990s but sexual activity has remained about the same.

Contraception, of course, plays a central role in pregnancy rates. Frank Furstenberg and others argue that changes in contraception—frequency of use, correct use, access to and better forms of hormonal methods—explain the decline in pregnancy rates.[26] Even proponents of abstinence models agree that abstinence explains, at best, only one-fourth of the decline in pregnancy rates, while better contraceptive use explains the bulk of the change.[27] Joyce Abma and her colleagues have found: "Since 1995, more than 96% of sexually experienced female teenagers had ever used a contraceptive method" and the vast majority used contraception on their first experience with sex.[28]

Condoms were the most commonly used form of contraception for teens during the 1990s; their use increased in this decade in response to the AIDS epidemic and HIV prevention education.[29] Condoms remain the most common form of contraception today, especially for females the first time they have sex.[30] The use of birth control pills decreased slightly in the 1990s but was offset by an increase in the use of new hormonal methods and emergency contraception.[31] Since 2002, however, there has been a slight decline in all hormonal methods and an increase in less reliable forms of contraception, such as withdrawal or periodic abstinence (the rhythm method).[32]

Although the majority of teenagers use contraception, one in five females report using no contraception the first time they had sex; and studies find that those who do not use contraception the first time have a high probability of becoming teen mothers.[33] Social scientists have identified a variety of factors that are associated with contraceptive use. First, contraceptive use is more likely if the teen has an open relationship with her parents, if she lives with both biological parents, and if at least one of her parents has a college degree.[34] Second, the younger the girl, the less likely she is to use contraception, because of both barriers to access and more spontaneous sex.[35] Third, contraceptive use is associated with self-esteem, peer sexual behavior, school integration, drug and alcohol use, and age of sexual initiation.[36] Fourth, middle-class girls with educational and career trajectories are more likely to use contraceptives.[37] Fifth, studies have identified differences by race and Hispanic origin: Hispanic women are least likely to use contraception, and white females slightly more likely than black females; black and Hispanic teens are more likely to use injectable contraceptives, and whites more likely to use emergency contraception.[38] Finally, the barriers to contraception for poor women are not likely to be financial. Title X funds subsidize contraception, making it accessible to many teenagers through local clinics, and wealthier and more liberal states like Connecticut have numerous clinics.[39] None of the mothers in our study mentioned availability or affordability as barriers to contraception.

While these research studies show important patterns, they do not explain processes; they do not show us how contraception is negotiated and shaped by social contexts—both the context of personal relationships (the local) and the context of larger cultural meanings (the symbolic). It is in these contexts that gender inequality becomes salient.

Contraception and Relationships: Negotiating Condom Use in a Patriarchal Society

Constance Nathanson writes that the "decision to use contraception is seldom made with the intention of preventing pregnancy *in the abstract* . . . young women make these decisions in the context of *particular relationships*."[40] For instance, when women are not in monogamous relationships, they are more likely to use condoms; when they are in committed relationships, condom use drops and oral contraception increases; and when relationships end, they are less likely to use any contraception, which, not surprisingly, leads to unintended pregnancies—"transitional babies"—conceived between relationships or on the rebound from a breakup.[41] We heard Iris narrate her pregnancy story as an accidental birth that "happened" after breaking up with Tim.

> I didn't start having sex until I met Tim—well, the summer before I met Tim, and it was only once, and then with Tim—and then after we broke up that's when I got pregnant 'cuz I missed him. It sounds very weird but I was hurting and Joe made me feel special for a short period of time.

We understand why women would quit using more invasive hormonal forms of birth control when they exit a relationship, but why not use a condom?[42] In this section we show how the negotiation of contraception, and condom use in particular, is embedded in a power disparity that gets played out in the bedroom, the backseat, the family den, and the park.

Birth control pills, injectable hormonal methods, IUDs, the ring, a diaphragm, emergency contraception (or morning-after pill), and abortion involve parents, doctors, and policy-makers.[43] These methods do not, however, require the consent of the partner. In contrast, condoms (and withdrawal) require the cooperation of the male partner. If a female wants her partner to use a condom (and studies show that most females prefer that their partners wear a condom), she needs his consent.[44] She has to negotiate contraception with him, and this is easier to do if she has a language and framework for these discussions.

It would be easier to have these interpersonal discussions if there were also national discussions about how to contracept and why it is important. Unfortunately, in the United States, we have no national dialogue on contraception because most Americans do not think teens should be having sex.[45] In the national discourse, teen sex is "risky behavior" driven by "hormones" with negative consequences (unwanted pregnancies, diseases, and spoiled reputations for girls).[46] A narrative that defines sex as something to be avoided or postponed until adulthood does not lend itself to conversations about how to negotiate contraception.

Amy Schalet, in her comparative analysis of US and Dutch attitudes toward adolescent sexuality, argues that American parents do not expect their children to have sex until they are adults—and indicators of adulthood include finishing high school, getting a job, and having their own residence. She contends that this attitude, summarized in the title of her book, *Not under My Roof,* derives from the US understanding of individualism, which requires independence—being *apart* from the family and not dependent on the family or the state—and influences parenting strategies. American children can be sexually liberated only after they move out of their parents' homes. Until then, their parents engage in strict oversight of their sexual behavior, and this tends to limit conversations about sex and contraception.[47] The absence of conversation does not mean that American teens are not having sex, but it does make it less likely that they will use contraception.[48]

Contraception requires prethought and discussion *before* bodies get hot with hormones or heads swim with alcohol and girls end up spontaneously pregnant. As mentioned earlier, the years 15 to 17 are prime for sexual initiation, and education works best before the onset of activity. Several of the young mothers blamed their parents for not having "the talk."[49] Gail, a 16-year-old mother pregnant by her 16-year-old boyfriend (her first and only partner, she told us) whom she had been dating for two months, said, "It would have been better if they talked to me more about sex." Wanda, who gave birth at 16, said, "No one ever talked to me about sex or anything. Not my mother, not nobody." Most of the girls in this chapter needed education before they were 14, or 15 at the latest, if the education was to precede sexual initiation.

The silence that characterizes parenting at home extends into the schools. A recent study found that 20 percent of students never had any sex education in school, and of those who did, only one-quarter had it before age 15.[50] Public schools in Connecticut are not required by federal or state law to teach sex education; instead, local school boards make the decision.[51] At New Britain High School (NBHS), located in a city with a teen pregnancy rate two and a half times the state rate, students were required to complete a one-half credit course. Moreover, social workers and health care workers, including a nurse practitioner at the Community Health Clinic located in NBHS, were barred from discussing contraceptives. Instead, the clinic was only allowed to test for pregnancy and STIs. In the 2009–2010 school year, they did 140 pregnancy tests and had the second highest number of girls testing positive for chlamydia in the state; they also had 42 pregnancies.[52] That same year, the school board voted against the distribution of contraception at the school clinic.[53]

If parents think schools are teaching their children, and schools think parents are teaching their children, and their mouths are both gagged, one for political and the other for cultural reasons, then youth rely more on the media and their peers for education—entering the realm of myths, misunderstandings, and magical thinking.[54] A 2009 national study found that inaccurate and insufficient information led women to mistrust birth control pills, fearing cancer, infection, weight gain, and mood swings.[55] Inflating the problems while underestimating its benefits, girls are more likely to resign themselves to fateful thinking: "it doesn't matter whether you use birth control or not, when it's time to get pregnant it will happen."[56] Through ignorance, myths are passed along: you can't get pregnant the first time you have sex; you can't get pregnant standing up; you can't get pregnant when you go off the pill. For example, Lorinda stopped taking the pill, she said, "'cause my chest was getting too big. I didn't get pregnant right after I stopped taking the pills. Months passed by and then I ended up getting pregnant." For younger girls the lack of information is exacerbated by irregular menstrual cycles, so that they are uncertain about the "safe" days or less fertile days when using periodic abstinence. In this bed of misinformation, young girls get pregnant.

While we support comprehensive sex education, we also agree with Kristin Luker's argument presented in *When Sex Goes to School* that the sex education–abstinence debate is a distraction—a political football in our two-party electoral system that can be used by single-issue candidates to distinguish themselves from their opponents. Like abortion, it can be a deal maker or breaker for an electorate that has strong feelings on these issues. Luker argues that the higher US teen birth rate (compared to other advanced industrialized countries) is not related to how much or what kind of sex education is in schools.[57] She points out that teenagers in the United States have sex as frequently as Europeans; they initiate sexual activity around the same age, and yet their rates of births, abortions, and sexually transmitted diseases are much higher.[58] The lower European rates are not, she argues, because they have better sex education but because they have less social and economic inequality.[59] Moreover, the debates about sex education in the United States are not actually about pregnancies, she maintains, but about "deeply felt ideas about gender, and women's roles in particular."[60] The debate on sex education—with the focus on *sex*—diverts attention away from discussions that focus on *gender*.

We advocate for a more comprehensive discussion around entrenched gendered beliefs and disparate gender expectations—for example, the belief that boys have hormones and girls crave relationships, or that men have sex and women have babies. Deborah Tolman argues in *Dilemmas of Desire* that we don't have a language for talking about the positive aspects of sexual desire; we instead talk about teen sex as a disposition in boys that has to be controlled and as a hidden dimension of girls.[61] Listening to teen girls talk about desire, she heard that desire is dangerous: desire could give them "a bad reputation"; it made them vulnerable in physical, social, and relationship realms; and it led to risks of pregnancy and disease.[62] Acting on desires can bring troubles, so girls attempt to "control themselves when they feel desire."[63] One of the ways they cover their desire is by talking about sex as spontaneous, or adopting the "it just happened" narrative.

"It Just Happened"

In the life stories, the adolescent mothers moved quickly from the start of a relationship to having a baby, and sex was an ellipsis. The mothers told us they "came up" or "just got" pregnant. Their pregnancies were things that happened *to* them. In Lark's story told earlier, her boyfriend "took" her virginity. Roxanne described how she met Joey and "ended up" pregnant.

> We first met each other in high school. I was a freshman. Joey is 26 days older than me. We had the same home room and saw each other every day. He is really, really funny and cute. We had the same mutual friend and so I went to lunch and he called me over 'cause he was sitting with her and she told me to sit down so I sat down next to him and she said do you like him and I said yes and he said do you like her and he said yeah. She said okay you two are going out now. Like he was too shy to ask me out, I was too shy to ask him out. We were seeing each other for a few months. And then after I turned 15 that's when we started getting sexually active and all, or I should say, more. And that's when Danny [her baby] came round.

In her narrative, she talks in more detail about how she met Joey in the lunchroom than she does about the pregnancy.

It could be that the interview format silenced their discussions of sex and desire. When teen mothers discuss their pregnancy with adults (researchers, journalists, parents, school officials), they are probably aware of the residual danger of being sexually active or having sexual desire—that it is not quite acceptable for young girls to admit to wanting sex, to having casual sex, or to claiming a sexual persona. Saying "it just happened" may be a way of managing their impression as a "good girl" by implying the sex was "spontaneous."[64]

In the life-story interviews, we can see both teen mothers and interviewers reading from the same cultural script that permits teen girls to claim relationships but not their sexuality.[65] In our prompts, we used the language of "relationships" in the concrete—for example, when did you meet Joey? how old were you? where did you meet? The teen mothers answered by talking about what year they were in school and about parties, cafeterias, and classrooms where they met. As Wanda described:

> I met Jimmy at a carnival. I was like, "Oh my god, he's cute." And he smiling and I'm smiling at him. And I said, "Could I have your number?" Then we just talked. We was friends for like four months. Best friends. Do everything together. I never been with no other guy but him. I was a quiet girl. I didn't know nothing. And he just kept coming to the house. And my family liked him. And then we started looking at each other different. And then, you know, I just got pregnant.

It is hard to know how to interpret the phrase "I just got pregnant," which disconnected the pregnancy from sexual intercourse. It could be impression management during the interview; it could be the taboo topic of sexual desire that makes both narrator and interviewer uncomfortable talking about sex; or it could be that sex was a blur and they passively assented rather than actively consented. Perhaps there really were no desires or discussions about contraception to include in their stories.[66] Tolman gives an example of what she calls a typical "good girl" story—it happened quickly, she was drunk, and she didn't enjoy it. She doesn't say "No" because she can't say "Yes" because she hasn't acknowledged her own desire.[67]

In the whirlwind of romance, the sex "just happened." While spontaneity helps girls deal with the gendered tension of denying and desiring sex, it also puts them at risk of getting pregnant.[68] Hiding thoughts of sexual desire, when she gets caught up in intimacy and her body surrenders to undeclared desire, the body is blamed while the girl is shamed.

Is it fair? Girls receive competing and contradictory messages: Don't have sex, but if you do, contracept.[69] Don't be a prude but don't be a slut.[70] Be desired but don't desire.[71] The persistent double standards around sexual behavior that influence boys' and girls' reputations differently muddle the message even more unfairly. While the whore-Madonna continuum that Kate Sutherland describes is somewhat of an improvement over the stark binaries in the pre–sexual revolution era, girls are still trying to negotiate a respectable sexual identity in the right place on the continuum given their age, family, neighborhood, and peers.[72] Boys are expected to desire sex and girls to deny sex, so when boys carry condoms they are considered thoughtful and respectful; when 16-year-old girls carry condoms, they risk being seen as promiscuous or labeled as sluts. This double standard creates a power difference that makes it harder for girls to negotiate and use condoms because one way of managing the "promiscuity-label" is to not carry condoms.[73]

The inequality is extended to the dating game. When boys' sexual desires are seen as "natural" and girls' as repressed, girls' bodies become objectified and bartered for male attention. Bridget, a heavy-set white mother, pregnant at 16, said she was "in love" with her boyfriend, whom she had been "dating off and on" for two years. The "off" part was when he was dating someone else. As she explained:

> I was a freshman and he was a sophomore. I was scared to death about getting lost in the school 'cause it's so big to me. I was in a Catholic school before that and the high school was 10 times bigger so I was just terrified of being lost. And then he was in one of my classes and we start calling on the phone and we just had a relationship on and off for that year. I heard about him with girls, like him flirting, but I was too quiet and shy to really mention it to him. So he'd break up with me and then, I guess, go do his thing with a girl and come back and I always went back with him. But then I guess he found interest in somebody else, like a *good girl*, like, supposedly, like, you know, um, this girl was a virgin and a church girl. So, he kind of turned on me, went to her, but he only used me, I guess, for sex. As soon as he called I went over there and then he was looking for sex.

Bridget did not describe herself as a person in a position of power in this relationship, and it is difficult to negotiate contraception from a position of weakness. Bridget lived in a moral world of right and wrong with terms like "virgin" and "church girl." In this world, Bridget surrendered her good girl status for male sexual attention.

Women seek attention from men to affirm their self-worth, and this makes them vulnerable to men who exploit the sex-for-attention swap.[74]

When women's ability to attract men is linked to their sexual identity, women with less desirable appearances have less power. Girls like Luanne, who defined herself as ugly because she had African features, or heavy-set Bridget were vulnerable to male predation because of racist and sexist definitions of beauty. We also think issues of attractiveness were apparent in Pamela's story at the beginning of this chapter. She explains how a car accident put her in a wheelchair her freshman year—at a new school, in a new town—and how the scars were so "gruesome" she would not wear shorts. The premium placed on attractiveness and male attention puts girls with stigmatized body types at a disadvantage.

In our gendered heterosexual society, a boyfriend gives a girl status. In many narratives, girls listed a string of boyfriends (not sexual partners) and at times overlapping boyfriends, as if to verify their self-worth. For example, Iris, whom we mentioned earlier in the chapter, became pregnant with Joe ("who made me feel special") on the rebound from her boyfriend Tim. She recalled:

> I was with Joe for a little while and then his best friend wanted to go out with me and then while I was with him I found out I was pregnant and he broke up with me and then one of the other friends went out with me for a little bit and then I had another boyfriend who knew that I was pregnant and I was in the hospital for a little bit for toxemia and he got bored and then I called [Tim] and we started hanging out again and three months later we were back together so.

When having a boyfriend is a capstone of adolescent self-worth, a girl's power is circumscribed and her ability to negotiate contraception compromised. Deborah Rhode and Annette Lawson argue that understanding the negotiation of sex requires an understanding of the culture and context: "Saying no in a society that links masculinity with virility and femininity with sexual attractiveness carries a cost."[75] A girl's self-esteem informs her ability to negotiate contraception and her *self*-esteem is formed in a social mixing bowl of gender inequality.[76]

The distracting discourse of adolescent motherhood that defines sex as risky behavior closes off more important conversations about sexual desire and power. It is when the mind knows the body's desires that the body is best able to act on them and is best able to not be acted upon. The "it just happened" narrative may be a cover story that hides desire not just from the listener (interviewer, counselor, parent) but also from themselves. If girls are more aware of their sexual desires, they can make distinctions about what they do and do not desire.[77] When girls cannot identify sexual desire in their own bodies and are subsequently guided by cultural scripts that tell them that boys "need to have sex," they are more likely to disassociate from their bodies and to have sex when they do not want to.[78] This is a salient precursor to teen pregnancy because a young woman is less likely to use contraception if she did not intend or want to have sexual intercourse. To reduce the number of unintended teen pregnancies, we need to understand the power differences that lead girls to assent to sex when they are either ambivalent or against it.[79]

In short, the threat to reputation and the silence of desire create barriers to initiating discussion about contraception; consequently, this places women in a state of dependency and diminishes their power in relation to men.[80] Sex can jeopardize the "good girl" status and the required hiddenness of the behavior creates shame and disempowers women, making them less likely to contracept.[81] To reclaim power, women have to first claim their sexual desires. To negotiate power, they need more equal footing. And to challenge power, we need to critically examine and reorganize gendered sex relations and disabuse young women of discourses of blame and shame.

ABORTION: GETTING BEYOND THE MORAL RESPONSIBILITY NARRATIVE

Telling the story of their pregnancies as an "accident," the mothers also talked about taking responsibility for the consequences of their "mistake." This created a moral narrative that sustained their status as "good girls." It also represents a historical shift in terms of what is meant by "taking responsibility." In the mid-twentieth century, taking responsibility meant marriage to the father or surrender to adoption. In the 1950s, over 90 percent of unmarried adolescents chose (or were forced) to surrender their children to adoption; by the late 1980s, however, only 5 percent of unmarried teens chose adoption.[82]

In the 108 life-story interviews, only one mother seriously considered adoption (she had chosen an adoptive family but changed her mind after she gave birth) and three others said they had thought about it, but did not take action. Adoption was not unfamiliar to some of the mothers—they knew aunts who had adopted, cousins who were adopted, and friends and family members who had surrendered a child for adoption, and some of the teen mothers themselves were formally (or informally) adopted by families and friends. And yet, some of these same mothers said that adoption would have been harder for them than abortion, because, as Sara described, "it's like me wondering, you know, someone else has my kid, wonder how he is doing, and what I could have done if I stayed with him." Others rejected adoption because they viewed it as irresponsible. Rosa said adoption is "fine if you are in a predicament. But I am not a lazy person. I got off my butt to do what I had to do."[83]

Why not abortion? Again the responsibility narrative predominated. Many of the mothers defined abortion as immoral, selfish, and unfair to the child.[84] In Luanne's life story at the beginning of chapter 2, she told us that her father wanted her to have an abortion but that she did not "believe" in abortion because even though the pregnancy was a "mistake," "it wasn't the baby's fault." This narrative repositioned her identity as a "good girl." She made a mistake; it was not the baby's fault, and she made a "choice" to carry the pregnancy to term and keep the child. She was acting responsibly.

Zina, the young Trinidadian mother we spoke about earlier who was ashamed of being pregnant, was an honor student and played flute in a prestigious conservatory. When she thought she was pregnant, her sister took her to Planned Parenthood. She derived a moral identity in opposition to the clinic.

> My best friend had bought me a home pregnancy test. It came out positive and I was like, "I can't be pregnant. This thing is probably wrong." So my older sister took me to Planned Parenthood 'cuz they do like free pregnancy tests and other stuff like that. And they were like, "You're pregnant," and like the first thing the lady told me that did the pregnancy test was, "Well, um, you can have an abortion." That was like the first thing she said to me. That was the first thing she basically—like she kind of put emphasis on it like that, like that was more or less something she wanted but I, honestly, I didn't know what I wanted to do 'cuz I was kind of still in shock and I was like I'm pregnant and I wanted to tell my mother, and I, I really didn't know what I was gonna do at all. Well, they gave me all the information, the doctor at Planned Parenthood. She gave me all the information about abortion clinics and like the price ranges, and so I had called up an abortion clinic and I made an appointment and everything, but like part of me knew I wasn't gonna go through with it. In my heart I didn't want that. I was scared, I really didn't know what to do but I just, I didn't see it as an option.

We were not in the clinic with Zina and do not know what the clinician said. Nonetheless, when Zina tells her story, she is able to place herself on the side of the angels by constructing a devil—an aggressive Planned Parenthood staff member pushing for abortion.

We heard that abortion was "not an option" many times. Some, like Luanne, framed it as a moral responsibility that would make amends for errant behavior; other mothers used religious doctrine to frame their choice (Tita's mother told her she would go to hell); and still others said, nondescriptly, they don't "believe in abortion."[85] Like the "it just happened" discourse around sexual intercourse, the "I just don't believe in abortion" discourse simplified a complex issue. Moreover, it was told to us after the fact—after they had their children. Digging deeper into their narratives, however, we found more ambivalence and conflict than the cover story suggested.

In our study, one-third of the mothers (n = 37) either considered abortion or had it suggested to them (with no significant differences by race or ethnicity). Three white and four black teen mothers had already had abortions before they delivered their first child. Nine of the 23 mothers that we defined as "good girls" for this chapter mentioned that they or someone else explored the possibility of abortion for them. As stated earlier, these mothers defined their pregnancies as shameful accidents. They were young and often did not have strong relationships with the baby's father at the time of the pregnancy. They did not see their pregnancies as expressions of love or commitment. They were doing well in school. They fit the national profile of the teen girl likely to have an abortion. And yet they did not. It was not because they did not have access or could not afford the abortion, and it was not because they wanted to have a child; so why is it that they did not have an abortion?

Abortion Decisions in Real Time

Before abortion-law reform in the 1960s, there was an estimated one abortion (most illegal) for every three to four births in the United States.[86] After the *Roe v. Wade* decision in 1973, abortions more than doubled by the end of the decade.[87] Beginning in the late 1970s, prolife advocates helped pass legislation designed to restrict public funding and reduce abortions. These restrictions raised the cost of abortion for poor women (most insurance policies cover abortion, so the withdrawal of government funding is more of a hardship for poor women), created preabortion waiting periods and laws barring information about abortions in government-funded programs, decreased the number of places where abortions are performed (moving them out of hospitals and into clinics, which are easier for antiabortion activists to target), stripped away teenagers' privacy (by requiring parental consent), and created cultural and moral barriers with campaigns like The Silent Scream designed to dramatize fetal development and persuade women that they were "killing babies" when they had an abortion.[88] The adolescents in our study were not impervious to this antiabortion discourse and some had unpleasant experiences; for instance, recall how Haley told us that going into the clinic "was hard because they had protestors outside."

Following this conservative push, abortion rates stabilized in the 1980s, but have been declining since 1989.[89] The decline in teen abortions is related to the decline in pregnancies as well as the overall decline in the percent of pregnancies ending in abortions (see table 6). This decline in the percent of pregnancies ending in abortion was steepest for white teens, but the percent has always been the lowest for Hispanic teens.[90]

Some predictors of abortion are marital status, income, and education—unmarried women from economically stable backgrounds with high levels of educational achievement are more likely to have abortions (regardless of race). Studies have found that teenagers who have abortions tend to have higher academic achievements and aspirations, less traditional views of gender roles, and a greater sense of control over their lives.[91]

A first trimester abortion is a quick, low-risk, and quite common medical procedure—which is not to say it is easy.[92] Today, one-third of women in the United States have had abortions by their mid-40s.[93] Connecticut reports more abortions than most other states: almost one-half of all pregnant teens 15 to 17 have abortions, compared to less than one-third nationally, and fewer than 15 percent in Kentucky, Arkansas, and Utah.[94] Connecticut teens 15 to 17 have similar pregnancy rates as teens in the rest of the country, but are more likely to have an abortion than a live birth.[95] To understand why the women in our study did not abort—especially the "good girls" in this chapter—we looked for reasons other than accessibility.[96] We found that religion and the opinions of family members and boyfriends were influential.[97]

For some, abortion was not something they ever considered, particularly Roman Catholics. For example, when Bridget, a Roman Catholic, found out she was pregnant, she said, "I was shocked that I was only 16, but I certainly didn't believe in abortion [sigh], you know?" Gail also came from a Roman Catholic family, describing her father as a "bible scholar" close to the teachings of the Church. When she first found out she was pregnant, she said, "My mom's like, 'Oh, she does have options' and stuff like that. My dad's like, 'No, she doesn't.' It's not like they imposed anything. I made up my mind that I was gonna have a baby 'cuz I'm totally against abortion."

TABLE 6 PERCENTAGE OF PREGNANCIES ENDING IN ABORTION BY AGE, RACE, AND HISPANIC ORIGIN, 1990 AND 2004

	All	Non-Hispanic White				Non-Hispanic Black				Hispanic			
	15–19	15–19	<15	15–17	18–19	15–19	<15	15–17	18–19	15–19	<15	15–17	18–19
1990	35%	38%	56%	40%	36%	36%	44%	34%	38%	23%	26%	22%	25%
2004	27%	25%	46%	28%	24%	37%	50%	38%	37%	20%	31%	19%	21%
% change	-23%	-34%	-18%	-30%	-33%	3%	14%	12%	-3%	-13%	19%	-14%	-16%

SOURCE: Ventura et al. 2008, table 3.

Others considered having an abortion, but the decision was not easy and the time was short. As Pamela said in her narrative, she was debating whether or not to have an abortion, going back and forth "and then it was too late for an abortion." Most teenagers who have an abortion do so within weeks of finding out they are pregnant.[98] The urgency is exacerbated by the young age of the mother, who is more likely to misread (or ignore) the signs of pregnancy and not find out until she is well into the first or even the second trimester. Wanda, for example, did not find out she was pregnant until she was six months along. She discussed having a late-term abortion with Jimmy, the father of the baby.

> And at first I was like I think I'm gonna take it out because I'm too young. And then he was like, "Don't kill my baby." And then I was like, "Okay." And then he really thought and he said, "Yeah, okay, you should take it out." And I said, "No, I already made up my mind." So we kept changing minds. You can still take it out at six months. They gave me a paper. They said, "If you really, really want to and you really don't want it, and you really feel like it's the right choice." They gave me a number in New York.

This back and forth took place over a few weeks. In her narrative, the pronoun for the fetus changed as their decision changed. When they considered terminating the pregnancy, the fetus was an "it" ("take it out"), but when deciding against abortion, the fetus was a human ("don't kill my baby"). We heard this shift in other narratives as well.

When teens "come up" pregnant and have to make a quick decision about whether to "take it out," they are often doing so without full deliberation or sufficient information.[99] If families or schools refuse to have an open discussion about abortion, then having access to abortion clinics may not be enough, especially if teens have misconceptions or lack a clear understanding of the risks.

Terminating a pregnancy is a momentous decision with important consequences. And yet, like the narratives of sex abuse and sexual desire, their narratives here were at times opaque, short, and shallow (as they are in the larger culture as well). Marcelina's family, for example, was middle-income. Her mother, the primary caretaker, had a college education and worked in the military. Marcelina was headed for college when she became pregnant at age 17. She had been dating the father of the baby, Tom, who was a few years older, for over two years. Like the others, she was "shocked" when she found out she was pregnant.

> I didn't know what to do. I'm young! He's young! We didn't know what to do. I think he wanted to get an abortion first and then like I didn't. Like, they

gave me this paper to think about abortion, um, it was like, you know, some depression because some girls when they abort their babies and stuff and just, I don't know. I asked Tom, what do you think, you know, do you want to keep it? He was like, um, I guess, you know, it's here. You know, some girls can't get pregnant so I guess, you know.

The ambivalence and hesitation were evident in her speech.[100] She worried about psychological consequences and inferred she should be grateful she was fertile, while Tom made a shoulder-shrug decision, "Well, it's here."

Other mothers had thicker narratives. Marisol, a mother at age 15, and Chino had been together for almost two and a half years when she became pregnant. She had an older sister willing to provide her with contraception, but she did not go to her because she worried her mother would find out she was "not a virgin." Chino was a senior in high school, played on the football team, worked steadily at a fast-food franchise, and was intending to go to college. Marisol had a supportive, stable family and she was well integrated in school. Chino was her first and only sexual partner. On finding out she was pregnant (her older sister told Chino to buy Marisol a pregnancy test), Marisol said she was "scared."

> I didn't really think I was going to have her because I was young and I knew I had a whole bunch of things to finish before having any children. But then I couldn't picture myself having an abortion, getting rid of what's mine, what's my own child, my own flesh and blood. I think I would have kept living to regret that. Well [the counselor at school] told me that nobody could tell me what I had to do, that it was my decision. That this was my child and I'm the mother. And he told me, "If you do have an abortion, it's going to practically be as if you were never pregnant because your baby's not going to be there. But you were pregnant and just because you got it done it's never going to change that fact." And he said some people live to regret it and people that he does know still regret that from years ago. But that even if I had the baby, things would be difficult, but it doesn't mean I can't accomplish what I always wanted to accomplish. That I can still go for my goals. And I just pretty much spoke to him and told him how I felt and how scared I was and he told me he would be there for me and I can talk to him about anything and he just basically told me how life would really be. But he didn't make it look bad because life isn't bad unless you make it. So after a while I made an appointment for an abortion.
>
> Chino found out the same day when I took the test. When I told him, uh, his head dropped, his head went down and he put his hands over [his] face and he was nervous, he didn't know what to say. He told me he'd support me with whatever decision I wanted to. When I told him I'm going to have an abortion, he just looked at me like, "Are you crazy?" Like he didn't want to

do it. And then he said, "Well if you're not ready, I'm not going to force you into, you know, being ready if you're not." And he, um, told me whatever my decision was he'd be there for me. No matter what. That this was his child too and if I had her, he'd take care of her, and if I didn't he'd still take care of me. And before my appointment, we got attached to the stomach. He would always lay on my stomach or rub it and it's like he was getting real close to it, and I started feeling a little comfortable with it. And that's why I couldn't do it because we got so close that we both, he even told me, "I don't think I can let you do it anymore because that, that's our baby, that's my baby too and you getting rid of it is like me getting rid of it because it's both of our child." So the day that I had to go [for the abortion], I called and canceled. I just couldn't do it.

The pregnancy became a stomach and then became a child, her baby, his baby, and she canceled the abortion. In her narrative we hear the underlying message of her school counselor telling Marisol that abortion is something she will regret and that having a baby did not need to disrupt her life goals. Her counselor also talked about the fetus as "her baby" (at least she reported this) and invoked her identity as a mother. Her counselor and her boyfriend both said that it was her choice, but the looks of dismay and the discussion of regret sent another message. Marisol did not make her choice in a vacuum but in the context of a relationship and in a local culture—as represented by her counselor, her boyfriend, and her Roman Catholicism.

Multiple Voices and Fragmented Choices

The mothers in this chapter fit the profile of teens more likely to have abortions, yet they did not. In the narratives of those contemplating abortion, one parent pushed or supported the decision to abort while another parent or grandparent discouraged it. Luanne, Pamela, Haylee, and others named friends, family members, and partners who were both for and against abortion. David Harding theorizes that multiple messages can weaken the dominant script.[101] Multiple voices reflected varying social locations: some from migration and intergenerational mobility, and others from mixed-income neighborhoods where there was less agreement that an early pregnancy would disrupt educational and career trajectories.

The two life stories that opened this chapter provide good examples: Haylee's father and other voices on the paternal side pitted having a child against having a career. Her father wanted her to have an abortion because "he was scared that I wouldn't be able to go to college and pursue a career." Her mother and grandmother, however, were strongly opposed to Haylee having an abortion. For Pamela, the mixed message came from parents who were against abortion until their daughter got pregnant.

In Chery's story, she was for abortion and everyone else was against it. Chery was college-bound and doing well in school when she became pregnant her junior year. When she first found out, she could not go back to church or tell her mother. With these feelings of shame and a mind-set of going to college (out of state), she said, "I was gonna abort my daughter." She made an appointment at a clinic, keeping it a secret from her mother. The day before the abortion was scheduled, a friend of her mother's from her church came over.

> She had a dream that I was gonna, you know, something, you see somebody dying, but not an abortion. So she came to the house and she told my mom that I was pregnant and she took her outside and talked to her and she came back in crying and I was like, oh, God! My mom had asked me before but I told her no 'cuz I hate to see my mom cry.

Chery's boyfriend, the father of the baby, "didn't believe in abortion. He wanted me to have her." The combination of the religious community, the desires of the father, and the portending dream made her cancel her appointment at the clinic. The religious community supported her by giving her a baby shower and helping with child care.

Along with the family, the father of the baby can have a strong voice in the choir.[102] Lark said, "I never wanted kids. It was like, 'No, I don't want it. I want to take it out.' Then, he [the father of the baby] was like, 'No, don't take it out.'" Lorinda had a similar story. She had been taking birth control pills and then stopped because she didn't like what they were doing to her body. When she found out she was pregnant, she was "shocked" and, crying, said, "I didn't want it. I didn't want the baby." The conflict is evident in the use of both "it" and "baby." The interviewer asked: "So why didn't you have an abortion?"

> 'Cause he wanted the baby and he wanted me to have his baby. And then I thought about it and I wanted it, but then I didn't. I didn't have a job and I liked to go out and I liked to go to parties and stuff and I liked to be out with my friends. But I felt that he had a right. He didn't want nobody to kill his baby even if I didn't want it; he said that he'd keep the baby here. He said it was his child and he wanted the baby.

The language shifts here as well: when abortion is considered as a negative thing, the language is "killing," but when it is considered in more neutral discourse, they refer to "taking it out." Moreover, his words, "nobody to kill his baby," animate the fetus, while her words, "I didn't want it," do not.

An adolescent has to make a decision with meaningful consequences—whether or not to bear a child—in a matter of a few weeks. The decision is not always so clear when there are multiple voices. This unresolved conflict can create lingering tensions. For example, at a later point in her life story, Pamela said she regretted her decision to not abort.

Just as it is important to have the discussion about contraception *before* teens surrender to hormonal-libidinal pleasure or the gendered pressure to have sexual intercourse, it is important to have discussions about abortion *before* an unintended pregnancy occurs, especially in households with less cultural congruence and more contradictory messages embedded in their structural location and local culture. And yet, as Pamela's story indicates, a discussion in the abstract can change when the issue becomes concrete and personal. This makes it all the more imperative to have discussed choices in advance.

The lack of discussion about abortion limits reproductive freedom—it limits women's thoughtful consideration about if, when, and under what circumstances they would consider an abortion until it is too late. Having a thoughtful conversation is difficult, however, in a society in which the issue is so polarized. Instead, abortion gets folded into a moral discourse and gets legislated, mostly by men. Once again, we feel that this closes off an arena of thoughtful, empathetic consideration for the pregnant teenager. There is a range of emotions, influences, consequences, and memories that are involved in this process that cannot be easily reduced to "taking responsibility." Suffice to say, we need rational, public discussion of abortion and adoption, just as we do of sexual desire and contraception, that allows for tension and contradiction, as well as the realization that these decisions are never easily resolved, not now, nor over their lifetimes.

CONCLUSION

The adolescent mothers presented in this chapter did not grow up in homes corroded with violence or disrupted by substance abuse. They were doing well in school and the pregnancy was unintended and unwelcome. Most of them lived in economically stable households, although a few were lower income; they all had strong, supportive, caring families, whether headed by two parents or not. Addressing teen births among this demographic group draws our attention to somewhat different issues and dynamics than those addressed in earlier chapters. When we strip away the violence, the poverty, the racial isolation, and the overt exploitation, we draw back a curtain on the roughly one in five teen mothers who are "the girl next door." It is in the more normal life (one not filled with trauma) that we are able to examine some of the less visible ways that gender inequality exists within our culture. We catch a glimpse of modern-day patriarchy in the gendered negotiation of sex and contraception.

In the United States, the discourse on adolescent sexuality frames it as risky behavior to be averted rather than a normal developmental process that is to be explored, understood, negotiated, managed, and, dare we say, enjoyed. The narrative of risk makes it difficult to talk about sexuality, especially among girls as young as 15. Gender scholars have focused on the double standards indicative of gender inequality and sexuality, but some of the silence regarding contraception is related to our national discourse (or lack thereof) or comes from contradictions within it (don't have sex, but if you do, use contraception). Teen sexuality is framed as a site of conflict and drama where girls have to control boys' hormones while they simultaneously deny their own.

Many of the young women in this chapter conceived during a stage of life in which they were attempting to manage sexual desire and gender identity. Pregnancy set off a new stream of negotiations that invoked gender and class identities and yet another decision that rarely anyone had talked to them about—and that decision had an expiration date. In moments of indecision, if not familial panic, they were often consumed with mixed messages regarding their pregnancy outcomes and future aspirations. They chose both—to be mothers without sacrificing education (even though they may have compromised their choice of which college to attend)—and their families reorganized to support these decisions. This chapter is a reminder that teen mothers are not a monolithic group and that trajectories vary, but that all life stories are located within social contexts that are shaped by broader political-economic and cultural forces, and are lived through social and personal relations running along the fault lines of social class, gender, race, and ethnicity.

Getting beyond the Distraction

Teen mothers are a diverse group—so diverse that they challenge the taxonomic impulses of social scientists. They include 13-year-old adolescents and 19-year-old adults; girls with an accumulation of disadvantage (who see their pregnancies as hope for new directions) and girls with less economic or social disadvantage (who choose to carry the unintended pregnancy to term without altering their current directions); girls who are victims of male predation and girls in sophomoric romantic relationships. For most, the unintended pregnancy causes shame and parental dissatisfaction, while a small number walk out of the bathroom waving the pregnancy tester to their families. Their educational tracts are as varied: some drop out of school before they are pregnant, some return to get their credentials after they have a child, some never drop out of high school, and some continue on to college. Many talk about how they have to "grow up" after they have a child, while others have "grown up" long before they were pregnant, moving through adolescence at a fast pace and assuming adult responsibilities at an early age.

Not only are teen mothers not a monolithic group, they are also decreasing in size. In the past 20 years, teen pregnancy, abortion, and birth rates have fallen precipitously for all racial and ethnic groups. Teens are managing their sexuality better, using contraception more effectively, and having fewer babies than at any time in US history—half as many as in 1991.[1] So, why have we written a book about teen mothers? We haven't. We have written a book about child sexual abuse, gendered violence, structural violence in neighborhoods and institutions, racial and class inequality in education, and gender inequality in sexual relations. We are writing about these problems because they were prominent in the young mothers' stories.

For many of the mothers in our study, their struggles were associated with poverty, racism, poor neighborhoods, and inadequate schools. For some, experiences of child sexual abuse, domestic violence, parental abuse or neglect, substance abuse, or unstable relationships with the fathers of their children added to their troubles. For others, the difficulty of negotiating sex and contraception in a male-dominated society created problems.

Focusing on the backstory to teen pregnancy and birth, we show the contexts within which these teens became young mothers. We illustrate the complexity of their lives and, in too many cases, the suffering. These contexts, complexities, and sufferings are presented to restore the integrity of their decisions to become mothers at early ages and to challenge the stigmatizing constructions of teen mothers. We argued in the first chapter that the demonization of teen mothers was rooted in the intersection of three public narratives—the underclass narrative, the politics of blame and gain, and the neoliberal narrative. We have attempted to challenge this construction of teen mothers, to humanize them through their stories and their voices, and to identify the more salient problems in their lives that should be addressed if we are concerned about their lives, the lives of their children, and the justness of our society.

Even though mothers are not a monolithic group, most of the mothers in our study were from more disadvantaged households, as they are nationally. In other words, young girls who become teen mothers generally have childhoods that offer fewer opportunities and more roadblocks when compared to the larger population. We maintain that the higher rate of teen births in the United States compared to other industrialized countries is because we have bigger and deeper pockets of disadvantaged communities.[2] With fewer opportunities available, the value of motherhood is elevated and having a child is less likely to interfere with some other life plan.[3] Opportunities are shaped by our material and social environments as well as by our perceptions of these environments. What we perceive as possible life routes influences our decisions; and gender shapes perceptions. Motherhood is an identity of respect and confers status. There are other ways to achieve status, but when these other veins are blocked more blood flows into motherhood. Many of these mothers said they always wanted a child, and while this was not the perfect time or the right father, they did not perceive the child as altering their trajectories. It might be more difficult to manage conditions of poverty while raising a child; but then, it might also be more meaningful.

Some young women in our study were from more economically and emotionally stable families, allowing us to examine more explicitly issues of gender inequality in their lives. Our national and parochial discomfort with sex makes it ripe for political polarization, exploitation, and scapegoating—narratives of gain, blame, and shame. The burdens of cultural and political partisanship have fallen hard on teen girls, who are negotiating their sexuality in circumstances infused with misinformation and contradictory messages. We advocate for a public conversation that begins with the following premises: that sex is pleasurable and therefore desired by both men and women; that the exploration of sexual pleasure is a lifelong practice; and that sex can be a form of violence and we as a society need to protect children from child sexual abuse, predation, and rape. Cultural inhibitions about sex—and in some cases our insistence on silence—enhance the anxiety, confusion, and isolation that teens feel about sex and increase the likelihood for early pregnancies and sexual exploitation. We need to pry open this conversation in national fora, in local communities, and around kitchen tables.

Listening to the mothers, we might conclude that their children were not problems for them. Very often they told us that children gave them focus, purpose, and determination, especially those who had experienced the death of family members and friends, as well as abuse and trauma in their childhoods, all before the age of 12.[4] These mothers imagined better futures for their children: they would graduate from high school, their sons would grow up to treat women respectfully, their daughters would not be dependent on men, and, in general, their children would "not make the same mistakes" they had made. These mothers were young, however; they were new mothers full of hopes and dreams—and their futures are something about which we can only speculate.

Nonetheless.

We worry. We worry about the scars of child sexual abuse, about the deplorable housing conditions in which some of them lived, about unresolved issues with their parents and family members, about violent and socially marginalized fathers, about the schools their children will attend, and about public indifference toward their suffering. We may understand their decisions to be mothers, but we worry about them.

After listening to their stories, we were grateful that the state had invested in a home-visitation program (from which we drew our study participants). As first-time mothers, they developed relationships with culturally compatible home visitors, whom the teen mothers described as "baby experts," advocates, and "friends"—people they could learn from, rely on, and confide in.[5] Home-visitation programs help in two general ways: home visitors focus on the needs of children and provide emotional support to mothers. Early home visitation is part of broader initiatives in many states to address the needs of children born to low-income mothers, including early educational efforts and school-readiness programs, subsidized facility day care, and identification of and early intervention for developmental delays. Funds for these programs vary considerably across states, as do the quality of the programs.[6] These are important investments in children that need to be supported and strengthened, and they address several of the problems we identified in this book that are likely to affect mothers who are survivors of traumatic childhoods. Structural problems, however, cannot be resolved with individual solutions, and state interventions need to be supported by broader strategies that require bolder politics.

Structural changes require social movements. We draw some hope from recent global protests against gendered violence that call attention to persistent inequality in nations, schools, and homes. As we bring this book to a close, the headlines remind us of this violence: the gang rape and murder of 23-year-old Jyoti Singh Pandey that took place on a public bus in India, and similarly, the gang rape and murder of 17-year-old Anene Booysen in South Africa; the murder of Oscar Pistorius's girlfriend Reeva Steenkamp only weeks before she was to deliver a public talk about her own experiences as a victim of domestic violence (the Olympian Pistorius was convicted of culpable homicide); and the attempted murder of the 15-year-old Malala Yousafzai, a Pakistani who spoke out for the right of girls to be educated.

Closer to home, high-profile incidents of violence against women include the rape case in Steubenville, Ohio, that was propelled by a graphic video posted to social media networks of teen boys verbally and sexually abusing a 16-year-old girl who was inebriated and unconscious (as they claim on the video "deader than a doorknob") and carried around to parties by two football players as a sexual play toy.[7] At the same time, a Pentagon report generated public discussion about widespread, if not normalized, sexual abuse in the US military. The report estimated that 26,000 women and men were sexually assaulted in the armed forces in 2011, an increase of 37 percent from the previous year.[8] The report followed the award-winning documentary, *The Invisible War*, which explicitly exposed the institutional nature of sexual assault in the military and the resulting trauma for many of its victims interviewed in the film.[9]

We are encouraged by such reports and documentaries that expose the hidden hand of patriarchy and that contribute to national and international conversations and movements to address violence against women. On V-day, February 14, 2013, the Billion Women Rising movement danced across the globe, with videos showing young and old women of all colors and nationalities dancing in the streets and raising their voices to condemn violence against women in every patriarchal pantry of the world. These international and national incidents are fueling movements to address violence against women, which are raising awareness and demanding action to challenge the culture of gender inequality, where male entitlement to women's bodies, as well as power and domination through violence, is woven into social histories that affect intimate relationships, institutional behavior, and public policy. We wait to see if domestic events and reactions will lead to a groundswell of indignation in the United States that might lend even more momentum to the incipient movement we are witnessing across the globe. And that is a reason for hope that extends to the mothers in this book.

Many of the young mothers in our study are daily survivors of the brutal effects of these gendered dynamics manifest in corners of the world where their voices and their stories reach little beyond their immediate social milieus; and they are less likely to be heard if we remain solely focused on their pregnant bellies. The dominating narratives around teen motherhood distract us from more vital parts of their suffering. These parts of their life stories get buried in a media and scholarly stampede to illuminate the presumed crisis in teen births and to construct more barriers to contraception and to safe and legal abortions. Leading the media stampede are derisive voices that humiliate and degrade women—whether it is calling them "sluts" or "prostitutes" (Rush Limbaugh), debating the vagaries of "legitimate rape" (former Congressman Todd Akin), or asserting that a conception that results from rape is "God's will" (Indiana Senate candidate Richard Mourdock). We need to connect these mothers' lives to the international and national movements that are challenging patriarchy and violence against women in order to reframe their struggles, to give them more control over their bodies, and to have any hope in reorganizing the social contexts in which their early births are inextricably related.

We push for a similar public discourse around poverty, and particularly urban poverty, where conditions for the black and brown poor in many cities have reached crisis proportions. In 2011, almost half of all children in Hartford were living in poverty, and most of those children were black and Latino.[10] The relegation of the black and brown poor to concentrated urban communities and the heartless public indifference toward these social spaces leave residents and advocates alike in alternating states of anger and despair. We are reminded of Paul Farmer's assertion that we need to spend less time focusing on the pathologies of the poor, including the preoccupation with teen motherhood outside of marriage, and more time on the pathologies of power.[11] The lives of young women like Cassandra, Tita, Deidre, Ivalesse, and Tameka require it. However, in tackling issues of poverty and its related problems, we are less sanguine.

In 2010, Hartford's local National Public Radio host, John Dankowsky, interviewed Mary on his show *Where We Live*.[12] At one point during the exchange, Dankowsky declared, "We're not going to solve the poverty problem in America," which he said with an uncomfortable laugh. He then followed by saying, "but if we do a better job of solving the poverty problem in America, you're suggesting we [would also] do a very good job of reducing teen pregnancy?" Dankowsky considered the conundrum, and then asked Mary what could be done in lieu of eliminating poverty in the United States. The thoughtful Dankowsky exposed a common assumption in the United States that, like Margaret Thatcher's famous dictum about the triumph of capitalism at the end of the Cold War, "There Is No Alternative" (TINA)—poverty is a part of the American landscape, or more appropriately, it is part of American capitalism. So then, tell us what we can do, he asked, *given this reality.*

What we can do, we have done. We have continued to reduce the teen birth rate despite intractable poverty. For this, we can thank mostly parents, grandparents, community leaders, teachers, medical doctors, nurses, clinicians, and nonprofit organizers who have inspired, cajoled, consoled, and supported adolescents facing otherwise grim futures. But as we have seen, these are difficult challenges, especially for adolescents who have few other avenues to adulthood that provide a modicum of respect and purpose.

As with global and domestic uprising around violence against women, the women in our study and others like them need a groundswell of indignation exposing and addressing the urban and rural conditions of restricted opportunities, economic obsolescence, and public indifference. Rather than focusing on a so-called epidemic of teen motherhood, we believe we should focus on an epidemic of inequality, or on a political and economic system that generates obscene wealth and abhorrent destitution. The United States may be the richest country on earth, but as Frank Furstenburg points out, it "leads all advanced industrialized countries in economic inequality, child and family poverty, and family instability."[13] Reducing inequality, poverty, and family instability would decrease the teen birth rate and fortify the efforts made by families and community institutions in low-income areas to help children stay in school, develop their potential, and cultivate self-respect through their work, families, communities, and citizen participation. It would increase opportunities, inspire imagination, and give women more freedom and control over their lives.

Further, decreasing inequality would please most Americans. Gallup polls taken since 1985 show that the majority of Americans support the redistribution of income and wealth.[14] Reducing inequality needs to begin with a movement to challenge the deeply held assumption that "there is no alternative." When nearly six in 10 Americans believe we should redistribute income and wealth, we might consider leveraging these beliefs to bring social change.

We also advocate for income and social support for low-income, childbearing mothers. While we have focused on the backstory of teen childbearing in this book, it is clear from the life stories that the conditions that many of these children are being born into are inadequate to meet the hopes and determination of the mothers to provide better lives for them. And this is under the best of circumstances. Comparatively, Connecticut does a much better job of providing support than most other states, largely because of the wealth of the state as well as statewide advocacy organizations that have a strong presence at the state capitol. Support for home visitation, early education, subsidized day care, subsidized wages (State Earned Income Tax Credit), and a higher minimum wage (which was $8.25 per hour in 2013) provides the basis for healthier families and children in the state.[15] However, even wealthy states like Connecticut cannot address the larger income and social inequities that exist, nor have they made much, if any, progress in addressing the conditions of racial apartheid in the state. Connecticut cities, as we have seen, are in desperate straits, and being born into many neighborhoods in Hartford, New Haven, and Bridgeport—the three largest cities—produces deep disadvantages that accumulate over a lifetime. Rebuilding our cities will require large federal investments in jobs, housing, neighborhoods, and education, all of which seem challenging, given the organization and nature of intertwining economic and political power today.

It is not only cities, however, that are in need of federal support; many small towns in Connecticut are also struggling financially and have related problems that are growing. There are policies that the federal government could adopt that would help families and children in both urban and rural areas, including an increased minimum wage, a full employment policy that would require the creation of government jobs, paid maternity and paternity leave, a family wage subsidy, universally funded day care, early education, and health care.[16] Any progress on these fronts will require immense political struggle, but they would also provide an economic stimulus to overcome the failed policies of austerity politics.

More importantly, these policies would catch up to and be more appropriate for larger cultural changes. Like it or not, people are marrying less before childbearing, divorcing and remarrying more, and cohabiting before marriage more, and this is occurring across all social groups. There is a silver lining in these trends—namely, that we are adapting the institution of the family to the pursuit of individual happiness. We no longer feel the need to remain in unhappy and, in some cases, unhealthy relationships. Women are, as a whole, achieving more economic independence and more autonomy in pursuing their own desires and charting their own lives. This is, of course, much easier among higher-income groups, which underscores the need for public policies that support similar trends among lower-income groups. Marriage is an easier choice when there is more income, but it is also an easier and more satisfying choice when there is more autonomy in making those choices. Autonomy requires more than individual determination; it requires economic and social resources to create a foundation to more fully exercise independence.

As painful as it was to listen to some of the life stories, we were moved by the determination and profound hope that most mothers articulated concerning their children and their futures. Moreover, many were already making changes in their lives to make their visions a reality. In some of their stories we heard moments of political resistance. They resisted internalizing social injustices and fought for better lives for themselves and their children. More often, we heard plans based on personal resilience. They were determined to find the right man, the right training program, the right apartment, and the right job so they could get ahead.

But as sociologists, we know that they cannot do it alone, that their lives rest at the crossroads of twenty-first-century economic decline in the United States, in which the discourses of blame and stigmatization are likely to grow even sharper and louder. For them—and for us—we need to consider strategies that address their lives on all three levels: the larger structural level through which power and domination are organized; the smaller, more immediate level, where parenting occurs; and the level in between—the schools and workplaces—where we can chart more effective public policies to support families and children.

Listening to Life Stories

I learned to listen with patience and care and never to
interrupt even when people were having great difficulty in
explaining themselves, for during such halting and imprecise
moments . . . people are often very revealing—what they
hesitate to talk about can tell much about them. Their pauses,
their evasions, their sudden shifts in subject matter are likely
indicators of what embarrasses them, or irritates them, or
what they regard as too private or imprudent to be disclosed
to another person at that particular time.

—Gay Talese, "The Origins of a Nonfiction Writer"[1]

The life-story method is an exercise in listening. Everyone has stories to
tell, and they tell them at different times to different people for different
purposes. People volunteer stories to a new love interest; they are forced
to tell a story to a child protective service officer; they have stories
drawn out by therapists; and they sell their life stories to researchers for
$50. They construct a life story from their memories, frame it within
their worldviews, weave together disparate threads, and prepare it for a
particular audience. The life story is a reconstruction of the past; it is
not "the life" but a re-presentation of a life. In our study, these representations come from women participating in a home-visitation
program designed to assist vulnerable first-time mothers.

The mothers spoke to us within a program context that most likely
had a bearing on their storied constructions. We repeatedly assured them
that their identities would remain confidential, particularly in our interactions with program personnel and with representatives of child welfare
and other state agencies, as well as in public talks and publications. We
repeatedly told them that we were not working for the state or the home-

visitation program, but instead that we were researchers interested in understanding their lives. Some appeared to trust us more than others.

Trust was an extension of their belief (or disbelief) in our ability to hear their stories. Did they view us as representing the dominant public opinion that it was wrong to have a child at such a young age? If they saw us sitting in judgment, would they tell stories of justification or view the interview setting as a place for moral redemption? Aware of these concerns, we worked to gain their trust, examine our own biases, and reflect on our role in the construction of these life narratives.

We used several strategies to minimize distrust. First, we did not contact the young mothers directly, but worked through their home visitors, a person they typically did trust. Tim had evaluated the program for five years prior to our study and had developed relationships with many of the home visitors, who were hired to be culturally appropriate service providers. Moreover, this study was initiated as an effort to reorganize program policies and practices by acquiring a more thorough understanding of the mothers' biographies and daily struggles, and to see how program practices affected their lives. Home visitors worked as cultural brokers between program leaders and families, and program leaders' desires for "best practices" in the field sometimes conflicted with the home visitors' understandings of the needs and daily lives of families. So our study was potentially validating of the home visitors' experiences—it held out the prospect for program change based upon a more indigenous view of *their* mothers and children. In this sense, they became allies in the study with an interest in exposing us to the complexities of their jobs and the challenges posed by their families. The home visitors explained the project to the participants and put us in contact with interested mothers. This allowed mothers who were uncomfortable to self-select out of the project. It was only after we received the mothers' assent from their home visitors that we contacted the mothers to schedule the interviews.

Second, while we had an interview schedule, the interviewers were trained to collect stories rather than answers. Given that many of the teen mothers had previous experience with social workers and other agents of the state, we wanted to distance ourselves from any interview where they felt compulsion or coercion to answer questions. When we reviewed the consent form at the beginning of the interview, we emphasized their right to stop the interview at any time or to decline to answer any questions. We used plain language and communicated to them that they had power to direct the interview. Some young mothers exercised this right and told the researcher that they "didn't feel comfortable talking about" some topic, or that they "did not want to discuss" something. Some of them, however, returned to the topic later in the interview or in the second interview. Mary interviewed one woman who said that she was raped but then went on to say she did not want to talk about it. This was during the first interview. At the second interview, the mother asked if they could sit outside because she wanted to smoke, and out on the front porch in January, bundled in down parkas, the young mother smoked and described the rape. Mary smoked and listened.

Third, we tried to match interviewers by gender, race, ethnicity, and language, decreasing the social and cultural distance between the interviewer and the participant as much as possible. We used Spanish-speaking interviewers for mothers who preferred to speak Spanish, which allowed mothers to move comfortably between English and Spanish to express themselves. Over the course of the study, there were six female interviewers—two whites (one was Mary), two Puerto Ricans, and two African Americans. While matched by race, ethnicity, and gender, the interviewers, for the most part, did not share the teen mothers' experiences of school failure, early childbirth, child sexual abuse, or domestic violence. In this important way the interviewers and teen mothers were not matched, which required that we reflect on how we were hearing stories so very different from our own.

This reflexive practice raised important questions about how we were understanding and interpreting their stories. Weekly meetings provided the time and space to examine our own biographies and predispositions in an effort to better "hear" and "see" the mothers with whom we were spending three to four hours engaged in intensive conversation. Mary took lengthy notes of these meetings that she later typed up to analyze the process of doing life-story interviews.

THE INTERVIEW PROCESS

We interviewed 171 mothers (and 47 of their partners) from 15 statewide program sites and, from this sample, 108 of the mothers (63 percent) were under 20 when they delivered their first child (63 percent of statewide program participants were also in this age group).[2] Together, Mary and Tim developed the interview schedule, conducted some of the interviews (Mary with mothers, Tim with fathers), trained and supervised the other interviewers, and managed the interpretive work with the research team—especially the processes of reflexivity, representation, and legitimation.

We conducted the life-story interviews in 2002 and 2003. Each person was interviewed twice, with each interview lasting one to two hours. Mothers and their partners were each paid 50 dollars at the completion of the second interview. They were interviewed separately. Most interviews took place in a private place in the participants' homes. We initially tried a neutral location such as a hospital, but participation increased when we went to their homes. In a few cases, the home was unsuitable (for example, it was too noisy or the participant did not feel comfortable speaking with a parent or partner present), so the interviewer took the participant to a local restaurant.

After each session, the interviewers recorded their observations, including descriptions of the house or apartment, the physical appearance of the teen mother (or father) and others present (the child, grandmother, or partner), and comments about the interview itself (for example, interviewers' assessments of whether the participants were forthcoming, reluctant, hostile, or tired). From the interviewers' comments we learned about the immaculate, stylishly decorated low-rent apartment, the cluttered, noisy duplex where they ate homemade egg rolls during the interview, the apartment with the pet ferret, and the basement apartment with large dogs that walked in circles around the interview space.

The interview schedule had sections on family background, school, relationships, pregnancy, parenting, work, resources, and experiences with state welfare services and law enforcement officers, as well as home visitors. Each section began with a "grand tour" question (for example, what was it like when you were growing up?) followed by numerous prompts (for example, what do you remember most about your childhood?). The questions were used as starting points to initiate conversations and elicit storytelling. We encouraged the young parents to narrate their lives on their terms, allowing the order of the topics to emerge with the flow of the conversation. We may have started with their childhood only to have them turn quickly to school or boyfriends; as listeners, we followed their leads.

In between the two sessions, interviewers reviewed notes and developed strategies for addressing parts of their lives overlooked, stories that seemed incomplete, or topics the mothers avoided. In the second session, we tried to flesh out unfinished stories, resolve contradictory information, and introduce topics we did not ask about (or they stepped over) in the first session. Sometimes they talked more freely during the second session about events they were unwilling to discuss in the first; sometimes they seemed open in the first session but reticent in the second.

We sought complexity over uniformity. The complexity was layered in the contexts through which their stories were being told: where the interviews occurred; who was present; what the relationship was between the mother and home visitor and how this affected her feelings toward us; where her child was during the interview and whether he or she was safe; how practiced she was at telling her story; what her current feelings were toward family members and intimate partners; and how she viewed the interviewer and her motives. We knew that we were not getting *the* story, but *a* story that was conditioned by numerous invisible factors that required reflexivity on our part and an acknowledgment that our understanding of the encounter and her life would be incomplete.[3]

While the interviewers were in the field, we held weekly meetings to discuss problems, refine our grand tour questions and probes, and reassess our purpose for doing the research. These meetings helped us to remain flexible and incorporate emergent ideas. For example, we initially had no probe about religious community but quickly recognized the importance of these communities in providing support for the new mother, informing attitudes regarding abortion, and, in some cases, stigmatizing the unwed young mother.

These weekly meetings also represented our earliest stage of analysis and allowed us to incorporate reflexive strategies of inquiry and understanding. We reflected on our role as interviewers in relation to what we were learning (and perhaps not learning). We discussed our own self-presentations and performances, and encouraged self-critiques and mutual critiques. We discussed the quality of the interviews and the varying abilities and willingness of mothers to articulate their life stories, which raised issues around emotional maturity, language, and cognitive abilities.

We also used these meetings to reinforce our code of ethics and guidelines. While our consent form protected the rights of the respondents, we also paid attention to the more subtle consequences of the interviews. For example, by asking women to talk about violence and trauma in their lives, we were opening wounds; when we finished and said goodbye, were we leaving them more emotionally vulnerable than before we came? We tried not to exploit their vulnerabilities and tragedies. For example, if a young mother mentioned she was raped, we expressed concern and asked her permission to continue (for example, "would you mind if I asked you a few questions about it?"). We talked about humanist interviewing practices: if a young mother started crying, how should we comfort her? Should we proceed with our questions? Was it okay to cry with her? We emphasized our belief that people come before data. We assured our interviewers that they could cry and encouraged them to show compassion because, in our scholarly minds, empathy does not invalidate data.[4] We nonetheless constantly reminded interviewers that we were not mental health providers and, therefore, not trained to provide professional assistance. When a mother appeared to be emotionally distressed, interviewers suggested that they talk to their home visitors and provided phone numbers of agencies where they could get professional help (for example, domestic violence hotlines). In sum, interviewers worked to be empathic listeners without posing as therapists.

The weekly meetings also helped us to be reflexive about how we were hearing the stories and what we were seeing in the houses, and this gave rise to an examination of our own values and prejudgments. In the beginning, we noticed the tendency for our discussions to focus on the disturbing stories. At one meeting, it almost seemed as if interviewers were competing with one another to see who could describe the most disorganized and unsanitary house or apartment. Finally, Mary interrupted and asked, "are all the houses dirty?" One interviewer replied, "No, most of the ones I've been in are not." We then agreed to devote as much attention to our observations of orderliness in homes, lives, and communities as we did to disorder, and as much attention to normalcy as to dysfunction; we did not want to slip into a mind-set that was drawn to the outrageous and overlooked the commonplace. In our analysis of the data, we were aware of this tendency toward stories of disorder and were conscious of how it influenced our representations of the mothers in the narratives.

During the weekly meetings, we also learned that several interviewers thought mothers were "making up stories" because they seemed too horrendous to be real. One interviewer thought the mothers were trying to "shock her" or get a "reaction" from her. We first had a discussion about our own backgrounds (most of us did not grow up with traumatic childhoods) to understand why we might doubt their stories, and then we discussed why they may have exaggerated or fabricated. Good interviewing involved being able to hear the parts of the story that "did not add up," to search for the holes and misleading statements and then probe for consistency. When we found persistent inconsistency, we needed to ask why they were telling stories this way.[5]

We also considered how the listener shaped the story they told by examining our own moral judgments. For example, Mary does not believe drug use is morally wrong and so heard these stories more pragmatically, but she did realize she was making judgments about women who stayed with violent men. Because her moral order structured her listening, she found herself probing women more about their abusive relations than she did about their drug use. In contrast, another interviewer treated any 16-year-old who drank beer as an alcoholic and anyone who popped her child on the Pampers as a child abuser. During these weekly meetings, we tried to put our biographies, presuppositions, and prejudices on the table so we could see how we, as listeners and interpreters, influenced what was said and what was heard. Often, it was easier to identify another person's biases than our own, so there was a calling-out process whereby interviewers questioned and probed one another. In sum, in order to understand our involvement in the life-story construction, we had to listen to ourselves listening to stories.

THE ANALYSIS OF LIFE-STORY NARRATIVES: INTERPRETATION AND STORYTELLING

The life story is unique in that it is told in the person's own words (which separates it from a case study, an ethnography, or a biography where someone else is telling another person's story).[6] This method is also different from open-ended or semistructured interviews in that the purpose is to elicit a story rather than to get answers; the narrator is encouraged to talk about what she thinks is important—telling the listener what to hear instead of answering the researcher's questions. So then, how did we analyze these stories?

First, interview tapes were transcribed and, if necessary, translated (nine of the 108 interviews were in Spanish). After the transcription, each interviewer listened to the tape while reading the transcription to correct mistakes and fill in parts the transcriber could not hear or understand. This was particularly important for interviews that were in English and Spanish. We then developed 60 codes (about half of them emerged from the coding process) and organized the coded text using QSR Nud*ist software, version N6.[7] The codes ranged from concrete topics (for example, occupation and schooling) to more abstract concepts (for example, social support and school integration). Mary, Tim, and the project manager coded the transcripts independently and then met as a group to discuss the coding. As we began coding, we realized that even "concrete" topics could be ambiguous. Topics like occupation and education became open to discussion as we debated whether job training should be coded as the former or latter (we coded it as both).

The coding of the transcripts, however, fragmented the life story, as each narrative became divided up into "nodes" in the QSR program and belied the value of the life story, which is to show the trajectory of the biography within a social context. The value of the life story is the "story" or the plot.[8] Without the full narratives of their lives, we lost the meaningful connections they described between events in their lives: she was sexually abused *and then* she became promiscuous and started having sex with older men; she dropped out of school *after* being suspended for fighting *and then* she became pregnant and decided to carry the pregnancy to term. In our construction (or analysis) we looked for the pivotal events, what sociologist Norman Denzin calls the major and minor epiphanies that shape the trajectory of a life story, to help us understand how they became teen mothers.[9]

To find the plot, Mary, Tim, and a research assistant *reread* all of the transcripts and wrote a comprehensive summary of each. These summaries provided an overview of the life story in general, along with summaries of each section of the life story (for example, family background, education, relationships). They included our interpretations of the life stories, but they also contained long passages from the interviews themselves; and these long passages eventually became the life stories told in the mothers' words that appear at the beginning of each chapter. Our summaries explored the events told and how they were told, the quality of the interview and the interaction between the interviewer and narrator, and an interpretation of the worldviews embedded within the stories.[10] We paid attention to voice: did she use active or passive grammar constructions, "I" and "me" or "he" and "they" statements? Two mothers could identify similar events in their lives (for example, dropping out of school), but their understanding of the event and its significance for their life trajectories could be very different—one feeling empowered with a narrative of action, another feeling helpless with a narrative of passivity.[11] This listening method "embraces" the relational nature of "interpretive work" and pays attention to the giggles and pauses—which were written into the transcripts—and the ways that a voice changes.[12]

Creating narrative summaries of the life stories moved us from description to analysis. Finding the plot required interpretation—and as sociologists, our interpretation was informed by our understanding of how larger social forces affect individual lives. We did not just read and summarize; we interpreted the life stories using a critical paradigm that examined inequality and power at the intersections of gender, race, and class, where we searched for agency and resistance.[13]

When we paid attention to how they told the story, and not just to the content of the story, we started hearing the silences and developed interpretive suspicions about what they were not telling us. We could see, for instance, several of the white families "whitewashing" their lives as they constructed white picket fences around dysfunctional families. We heard the closeting of sexual abuse and noticed the absence of sexual desire. We heard bravado and the puffing up of the chest, which did not necessarily correspond to the outcomes of the stories they told, or even to their behavioral descriptions in the stories themselves. Silence, missing explanations, and contradictions appeared along the seams of their stories. But we also paid attention to the part of their life stories that they most wanted to tell us—most apparent in the longer paragraphs in the transcripts. And then, as storytellers ourselves, we condensed the story, looking for what Studs Terkel called "the gold in the ore."[14]

Their narratives often looped and the young mothers repeated themselves and used filler phrases (for example, "so" and "like") that created a rhythm in their oral speech. Writing their stories from oral narrative, we kept in some of these filler phrases and false starts so that the reader could "hear" the women talking. But we also spliced together sentences—sometimes from pages apart—so that the story flowed more readably. We did not misrepresent the substance of their narratives, but as story tailors, we admittedly sewed together snippets to construct coherent stories with hidden stitches and invisible glue.

Our representations of the mother are intended to engage readers about broader issues concerning the matrices of domination that troubled the mothers' lives. There is tension and, sometimes, disparate intentions between their stories and our interpretations. This is the nature of our interpretive craft, and it is in these spaces that the quest for validity exists and uncertainty prevails—or where we learn to live with what Wanda Pillow calls "a reflexivity of discomfort."[15]

In the end our written interpretations of their lives are fusions of their stories, the sociological imagination that their stories inspired in us, and the word-count constraints of the publishing industry. Our sociological imagination led us to tell the backstory, to write about the pivotal life moments that occurred before their pregnancies and how these personal moments were shaped by larger structural conditions. It is through this interpretive process that we remain indebted to the legacy and craftsmanship of C. Wright Mills.[16]

Tables

TABLE 7   CHARACTERISTICS OF THE SAMPLE (n = 108)

	No.	%
Race and ethnicity		
(European American) White	36	33%
Puerto Rican	36	33%
(African American) Black	18	17%
Other Latina	3	3%
Multiracial	11	10%
Asian and West Indian	4	4%
Age of mother at first birth		
13–14	7	6%
15–16	31	29%
17	26	24%
18–19	44	41%
Age of mother at time of interview		
13–14	2	2%
15–16	18	17%
17	15	14%
18–19	32	30%
20–25	41	38%

Age of child at time of interview

0–12 months (includes 4 prenatal)	60	56%
13–24 months	19	18%
25–67 months	29	27%

Type of residential municipality

Urban 100,000	44	41%
City 50,000–100,000	33	31%
Town < 50,000	31	29%

Problems

Victim of child abuse*	49	45%
Victim of child sexual abuse**	28	26%
Domestic violence in family of origin	47	44%
Victim of partner abuse	48	44%
Past or present mental illness	34	32%
Has been arrested before	28	26%

Educational level at time of interview

Currently enrolled in school (includes middle school, high school, GED program, or night school)	33	31%
Less than high school (not enrolled in any school or program)	50	46%
Completed high school (diploma or GED)	19	18%
Some college	6	6%
Ever dropped out of high school	68	63%
Dropped out before pregnancy	38	35%
In school while pregnant	78	72%
In school after had baby	63	58%
Married or partner w/father of the baby	58	54%
Father of baby lives with mother	31	29%
Child lives with parents and grandparents	68	63%

Live in household receiving assistance+

WIC	90	83%
Food stamps	50	46%
TANF	52	48%
Housing	32	30%

* Child abuse includes sexual abuse.
** Sexual abuse refers to rape, molestation, and statutory rape.
+ Currently receiving assistance excludes those who received in the past and those who applied but do not yet receive. Child abuse includes sexual abuse.

TABLE 8   AGE OF MOTHER AT TIME OF BIRTH FOR
TEEN BIRTHS IN CONNECTICUT, 1998–2010

	<15	<18	<20
1998	71	1,373	3,621
2000	66	1,144	3,350
2002	49	1,031	2,946
2004	40	957	2,909
2006	34	948	2,905
2008	26	872	2,817
2010	20	642	2,294

NOTE: All numbers given in the table are cumulative.
SOURCE: Connecticut Registration Report, 1998–2010, table 4.

TABLE 9   NUMBER AND RATE OF BIRTHS FOR TEENS AGE 10 TO 14 BY RACE AND
HISPANIC ORIGIN, 1990–2010

	All Races	Non-Hispanic White	Non-Hispanic Black	Hispanic
2010	4,497 (0.4)	968 (0.2)	1,573 (1.0)	1,811 (0.8)
2005	6,722 (0.6)	1,331 (0.2)	2,697 (1.6)	2,466 (1.3)
2000	8,519 (0.9)	1,840 (0.3)	3,736 (2.4)	2,638 (1.7)
1995	12,242 (1.3)	2,711 (0.4)	5,822 (4.2)	3,187 (2.6)
1990	11,657 (1.4)	2,602 (0.5)	6,204 (5.0)	2,346 (2.4)

SOURCES: Menacker et al. 2005, table 1; Martin et al. 2007, tables 2, 6; Martin et al. 2012,
tables 2, 6, 8.

Notes

INTRODUCTION

1. While racial, ethnic, and age descriptions are accurately reported, names and other identifying information have been changed to ensure confidentiality.

2. We use the terms "Hispanic," "Latino," and "brown" interchangeably. Typically, we use "Hispanic" when referencing government data, "Latino" (or "Latina") when referencing studies or groups who self-reference as "Latinos," and "brown" when we want to emphasize the racial significance of the identity.

3. www.thenationalcampaign.org/latino/default.aspx.

4. See Mac Donald 2006.

5. Gordon 1990, 393.

6. See Fine et al. 2000 and Pillow 2003 for excellent discussions about the problems of representation when studying disadvantaged populations, the need for reflexivity, and an awareness of the ethical responsibilities of researchers when they re-present their stories.

7. Black, Erdmans, and Dickinson 2004.

8. Gee 1985, 11.

9. Bertaux and Kohli 1984, 215.

10. Denzin refers to events that leave a mark on a person's life as "the epiphany" in the story, which can take the form of a "major epiphany" that influences all aspects of a person's life (for example, having a child) or a "minor epiphany" that represents an important moment in a person's life or relationship (1989, 70–72). See Elder, Gimbel, and Ivie 1991 and Starr 1994 for a discussion of turning points.

CHAPTER 1. THE DISTRACTION

1. Brown 2008.

2. Martin et al. 2010, 5, table A.

3. Between 1990 and 2004, for teens 15 to 19, the percent of pregnancies that ended in induced abortion dropped from 35.5 percent to 27 percent (Ventura et al. 2008, table 3), and by 2008 it had dropped to 25.5 percent (Ventura, Curtin, and Abma 2012, table 3).

4. Between 1990 and 2008, pregnancy rates dropped 49 percent (from 77 to 39.5) for teens 15 to 17, and 32 percent (from 168 to 114) for teens 18 to 19 (Ventura, Curtin, and Abma 2012, 3).

5. United Nations, *Demographic Yearbook*, 2006, table 11. Data in the text is for 2006. The rate for the United Kingdom in 2004 was 26.7 per 1000 teens 15 to 19, much higher than surrounding countries; for example, in Italy the rate was 7.0 that year (United Nations, *Demographic Yearbook*, 2006), but still lower than the US rate of 41.1 (Martin et al. 2009, 42, table 8). In England, teen mothers are "demonized as agents of social disruption" much the same way they are in the United States (McDermott and Graham 2005, 59).

6. Gordon 1990, 455; Singh, Darroch, and Frost 2001.

7. Santorum 1996, S8076.

8. Ventura 2009, figure 4. Gordon argues that in the 1960s "both scholarly and popular writing identified teenage *marriage* as the problem" (1990, 449). In the early 1960s, 59.3 percent of all teen births conceived out of wedlock were born in wedlock; by the 1990s it was only 15.5 percent (Bachu 1999, 5).

9. Furstenberg 2007, 14. See also Phoenix 1993, 89. In 1970, half of all births to unmarried women were to teenagers, this dropped to 23 percent in 2007 (Ventura 2009, figure 5). Between 1990 and 2008, the birth rate for unmarried teens 15 to 19 declined 41 percent for blacks, 10 percent for non-Hispanic whites, and rose four percent for Hispanics (Martin et al. 2010, table 16).

10. The recent increase in nonmarital childbearing is for women 20 years of age and older. Even though teen mothers have a smaller share of the unwed birth pie, they are more likely to be unmarried. In 2007, 93 percent of teens 15 to 17 who gave birth were unmarried compared to 60 percent of births to women 20 to 24 (Ventura 2009, 3). The share of births to unmarried women who are teens continues to decline. In 2013, their portion of the pie was only 15 percent (based on preliminary data, www.cdc.gov/nchs/data/nvsr/nvsr63 /nvsr63_02.pdf).

11. Ventura 2009, 5.

12. While marriage is declining among all groups, 64 percent of college graduates were married in 2008 compared to only 48 percent of those with high school or less (Pew Research Center Publications 2010).

13. Pew Research Center Publications 2010. The other choices were "a good thing" (4 percent) and 24 percent said the trending increase made "no difference" for society.

14. *In Touch Weekly*, November 1, 2010.

15. An editorial in *Glamour* magazine's online edition, "Let's Stop the New Teenage Mom Craze," claims that "we have started to glamorize teen pregnancy," and, according to Sarah Brown, CEO for The National Campaign to

Prevent Teen and Unplanned Pregnancy, "Some teens mistakenly think that being a young, single mom is cool" (Glamor.com, October 2009). The CEO and Senior Researcher of The National Campaign also wrote in an editorial for the *Journal of Adolescent Health* that "teen childbearing is often portrayed as fully acceptable if not actually glamorous (think *Juno* and Jamie Lynn Spears)" (Brown and Suellentrop 2009, 2).

16. Lauren Dolgen (2011) said she created the show *16 and Pregnant* to tell the "honest, unpleasant truth about teen pregnancy," and she has partnered with The National Campaign to create a website that provides information about how to prevent teen pregnancy. Rather than glamorizing this trend, this show presents teen mothers having to manage a spoiled identity amid this negative characterization of teen childbirth (Smith, Powell, and Erdmans 2013).

17. A 2010 national survey conducted by The National Campaign found that among teens 12 to 19 who watched the show *16 and Pregnant*, 82 percent reported that the show helped them understand the "challenges" of pregnancy and motherhood, while only 17 percent said the show "glamorizes" teen pregnancy. Among adults who watched the show, the majority believes the program depicts the challenges of early parenthood (56 percent), but 41 percent thought it "glamorizes" these pregnancies (Albert 2010, 33). See the working paper of Kearney and Levine (2014) that claims that watching the show lowered teen births by 5.7 percent. Their study was picked up by the *New York Times* and heartily endorsed by The National Campaign CEO Sarah Brown. www.nytimes.com/2014/01/13/business/media.

18. See Solomon-Fears (2011) for an overview of these programs and expenditures including the Personal Responsibility Education Program (PREP), which was funded for five years (2010–2014), and the Title V Abstinence Education Block Grant to states (funding expired in 2009 but was restored and funded for 2010–2014). The projected goals for reducing teen pregnancy set by the Center for Disease Control (CDC) extends to 2015 as part of the Teen Pregnancy Prevention Initiative (TPPI). www.cdc.gov/teenpregnancy/PreventTeenPreg.htm. The CDC has nine Participating Community and State Based Initiatives and five national organizations receiving funding as a part of the prevention campaign. www.cdc.gov/TeenPregnancy/State-Community-Orgs.htm. It has also partnered with the Office of Adolescent Health, which has funded 31 evidence-based programs to prevent teen pregnancy. www.hhs.gov/ash/oah/oah-initiatives/tpp/programs.html.

19. Albert 2010, 21.

20. Furstenberg 2007, 1. For information on The National Day to Prevent Teen Pregnancy (May 1), see www.thenationalcampaign.org.

21. Reed 1991, 20.

22. Williams 1994, 549.

23. Gordon 1990, 133–136. See also Linda Gordon's work on the orphan trains in early 1900s that documents how white indigent women were forced to surrender their children to adoption (1999, 3–20).

24. Neubeck and Cazenave 2001.

25. Gans 1995.

26. Gans 1995.

27. Gans 1995, 32.

28. See Black 2009, 215–217.

29. For good critiques of the underclass concept and the research industry it inspired, see Gans 1995 and Katz 1989.

30. Jencks was not, however, an advocate of the term "underclass." In fact, he did not believe the term could be empirically distinguished from the more commonly used term "lower class," and he thought that the term lumped together a range of behaviors that were historically distinct and empirically unrelated. His use of the term "reproductive underclass" was an attempt to show, first, that it was not related to other behaviors, like joblessness, and, second, that it was empirically misleading since the rates of teen births were falling during the time that the term was gaining public currency (Jencks 1991).

31. These funding organizations included not only conservative foundations but also more liberal political groups like the Rockefeller Foundation that funded the Social Science Research Council's large underclass research agenda (Gans 1995, 51).

32. Gordon 1990, 450.

33. Mead 1986.

34. Katz 1989; Quadagno 1994; Neubeck and Cazenave 2001.

35. Moynihan 1965, quoted in Quadagno 1994, 124.

36. Neubeck and Cazenave 2001.

37. Neubeck and Cazenave 2001. This language is taken from Patricia Hill Collins (2000) who argues that controlling images of racial stereotypes reproduce racial, class, and gender oppression. See also Gordon (1990, 452) for how the Moynihan report racialized the discourse on teenage pregnancy.

38. Pillow 2004.

39. Gordon 1990, 390.

40. Gilder 1981; Murray 1984; Mead 1986; Omi 1991.

41. Nathanson 1991; Luker 1996; Ehrlich 2006.

42. For a discussion of AFLA and the conservative reproductive policies of the 1980s, see Rhode 1993–1994, 652–8, and Weinstein 1998.

43. Edsall and Edsall 1991.

44. Edsall and Edsall 1991, 177.

45. Pillow 2004.

46. The increase in the welfare rolls and out-of-wedlock births provided additional leverage for this narrative (Edsall and Edsall 1991).

47. This narrative was also evident in England. Prime Minister Margaret Thatcher defined young single mothers as a "threat to the welfare state" (Walkerdine, Lucey, and Melody 2001, 189), while Tony Blair later referred to England's higher teen birth rate relative to European countries as a "shameful record" (reported in Lawlor and Shaw 2002, 553).

48. www.nomoremoney.org/history.html.

49. www.nomoremoney.org/history.html. The third funding stream for abstinence-only education came through the Community-Based Abstinence Education program, established in October 2000. The Bush administration spent $176 million annually on abstinence-only programs. www.nytimes.com/2007/12/06/washington/06birth.html.

50. Sawhill 2002; Kristof 2005; Stein 2007.

51. Peet 2009. It is ironic that Richard Nixon, whose presidency in many respects represented the final hurrah for Keynesianism, would quip in 1971, "I am now a Keynesian" (Reich 2010, 44).

52. The ideas of economists like Friedrich von Hayek, Milton Friedman, and others rejected Keynesian New Deal measures by philosophically endorsing the traditions of classical liberalism and neoclassical economics. The economic crises in the 1970s created the conditions for the reorganization of the state and capitalism, as corporate interests were solidified through political action committees, funding organizations, think tanks, and the media. See Ferguson and Rogers 1986 and Piven and Cloward 1985.

53. O'Connor 2010.

54. Luker 1996; Weinstein 1998.

55. Between 1960 and the early 1970s, Aid to Families with Dependent Children (AFDC) rolls quadrupled, while Food Stamps, Medicaid, Medicare, job training, and housing subsidies were enacted (Piven and Cloward 1985, 14–15).

56. Pillow 2004.

57. Oliveri writes: "Whatever the data actually reveal, the *perception* of teen pregnancy on the part of the legislators and the public became the more important motivating factor in the welfare reform debate" (2000, 469–470).

58. Sylvester and Reich 2002.

59. Phoenix 1993, 81.

60. Dash 1989.

61. Nathanson 1991; Phoenix 1993; Luker 1996.

62. For example, in 2006 the German birth rate was 10.1 for every 1000 births for teens 15 to 19 and in Sweden it was 5.9 (United Nations, *Demographic Yearbook,* 2006, table 11), while the US rate for non-Hispanic whites was 26.6 (Martin et al. 2009, 44, table 8). Gordon alerted us to this comparison two decades ago (1990, 456).

63. In 2008, there were 437,518 births to women under age 20 that were classified by race and Hispanic origin: 38.8 percent were non-Hispanic white, 33.7 percent were Hispanic, 24.4 percent were non-Hispanic black, and 3.2 percent were non-Hispanic races other than black or white (Martin et al. 2012, table 6).

64. Martin et al. 2003, table 9. Most studies on Hispanic teen births are based on Mexicans and Mexican Americans (Afable-Munsuz and Brindis 2006). The term "Hispanic" becomes a proxy for "Mexican" because nationally they account for two-thirds of the Hispanic group, which has the highest fertility rate across age groups (one-third higher than the general population). And yet there are significant differences: in 2005, the Mexican birth rate for teens 15 to 19 was 87.5, but the Puerto Rican rate was only 59.2 (Martin et al. 2012, table 8). Recently we have seen a narrowing of these differences. By 2009, the rates were 62.9 for Mexicans and 50.8 for Puerto Ricans (the distance narrows even more by 2011 but the data are based on population estimates that may later be revised) (Martin et al. 2013, 32).

65. The Hispanic rate was 77, the black rate 43, and the non-Hispanic white rate 11. www.guttmacher.org/pubs/ustptrends.pdf.

66. Martin et al. 2012, table 8. These represent data from 2009.

67. Acosta-Belén and Santiago 2006; Kasinitz et al. 2008.

68. Edwards 1992; Brewster 1994; Luker 1996; Furstenberg 2007.

69. Dash 1989, 11, italics in original.

70. Dash 1989, 15, italics in original. Coles (1997) also spoke with low-income girls who wanted to get pregnant. Anderson (1990) argues that some girls intentionally get pregnant to trap a man into a relationship.

71. Gordon 1990, 450.

72. Debates swirled around the supposed "pact" but evidence suggests otherwise: most of the girls who were pregnant did not know one another; some who supposedly intended the pregnancies had abortions; and the number of births that year was not out of the norm for this high school located in a city with high rates of unemployment and a depressed economy. See the documentary "The Gloucester 18," produced by John Michael Williams (2010).

73. Luker 1996, 151–154; Buckingham and Derby 1997; Fischer et al. 1999; Rubin and East 1999; Abma et al. 2004. Unmarried teens who intend the pregnancy are more likely to be poor (Luker 1996, 153; Henshaw 1998), older (Abma et al. 2004), school dropouts (Rubin and East 1999), or victims of abuse (Rainey, Stevens-Simon, and Kaplan 1995).

74. In the 2006–2008 National Survey of Family Growth (NSFG), 19 percent of unmarried teens 18 to 19 said they would be pleased if they became pregnant, while only 9 percent of teens 15 to 17 said they would be pleased (Abma, Martinez, and Copen 2010, table 21).

75. Kaplan 1996, 432–439. See also Mollborn and Jacobs 2012. Burton (1990) argues that neighborhood effects lead to different attitudes toward and support of early childbearing. Here we recognize that life-story interviews are not the best method for understanding culture. Dash found that it took ethnographic engagement in the community for young girls to confess their intended pregnancies. Without immersion into the daily lives of these women, we are reluctant to advance more definitive cultural explanations. For a discussion of strategies for conducting cultural analyses of the poor, see Lamont and Small 2008.

76. Edin and Kefalas found in their study of unwed mothers (who were not all teen mothers) that the majority of births outside of marriage were "neither planned nor unplanned but somewhere in between" (2005, 37). In their study, four of 10 said the birth was accidental; in our study of only teen mothers, six of 10 said it was accidental.

77. Trent and Crowder 1997, 532.

78. Luker 1996, 170.

79. See Geronimus 1992, 1997, 2003; see also Burton 1990.

80. Reed 1999, 192.

81. SEC 101 of the H.R. 3734 Personal Responsibility and Work Opportunity Reconciliation Act of 1996.

82. Fagan 2001, 35.

83. www.dlc.org/ndol_ci5085.html?kaid = 139&subid = 277&contentid = 250715.

84. Maynard and Hoffman (2008) estimate that the public costs of teenage childbearing to taxpayers are $7.3 billion annually, based on the lower produc-

tivity of teen mothers, fathers, and their children (which results in lower income and consumption taxes), more medical care for children paid by public monies, foster care costs, and money to build and maintain prisons. See also Hoffman 2006 and Wolfe and Rivers 2008. Other researchers, however, have challenged these estimates; the most salient argument is that these taxpayer costs are related to poverty and racial disadvantage, not early childbirth (Gordon 1990; Rhode and Lawson 1993; Luker 1996; Weinstein 1998; Furstenberg 2007; George, Harden, and Lee 2008).

85. Hearing Before the Subcommittee on Human Resources of the Committee on Ways and Means, House of Representatives, 107th, First Session, November 15, 2001.

86. In this "neo-Moynihan" construction of the problem, Nathanson argues, the use of phrases like "accelerated role transitions" suggests there is a right and wrong time to have children, and unmarried teen moms are not doing it right (1991, 157). Geronimus agrees that the social construction of the problem is a result of the values of the dominant group being imposed on the values of the minority group. Teen pregnancy, she argues, "is more political tool than valid construct" (2003, 887).

87. Krugman 2009; Hacker and Peterson 2010; Reich 2010.

88. Isaacs, Sawhill, and Haskins 2008. Contrary to popular opinion, the United States does not fare well on mobility measures compared to other peer countries. For instance, Germany is 1.5 times more mobile, our neighbor Canada is nearly 2.5 times more mobile, while Denmark is 3 times more mobile. Only the United Kingdom is slightly less mobile than the United States. See also Foster 2006 and Sawhill and Morton 2007.

89. This draws on Foucault's concept of power and knowledge as a form of hegemonic power through which the appropriate timing norms and situations for when to procreate get accepted as natural and ordinary and lead to self-policing as a means of controlling who should reproduce (Foucault 1980). See Gordon 1990 for a US history of eugenics, sterilization, and birth control.

90. See, for example, comments made by the CEO of The National Campaign (Brown and Suellentrop 2009, 2).

91. Erdmans 2004, chapter 5.

92. Studies examining the academic and behavioral outcomes of children born to teen mothers include Chase-Landsdale, Brooks-Gunn, and Paikoff 1991; Corcoran 1998; Moore and Sugland 1999; Levine, Pollack, and Comfort 2001; Lipper 2003; Dahinten, Shapka, and Williams 2007; Manlove et al. 2008; Haveman, Wolfe, and Peterson 2008. Studies examining the physical outcomes (low birth rate and infant mortality) include Taborn 1990; Moore and Snyder 1991; East and Felice 1996; Manlove et al. 2008. The relationship between early birth and incarceration rates is shown in Grogger 2008 and Scher and Hoffman 2008.

93. National Longitudinal Study of Youth (NLSY) data show lower educational achievement and earnings (Hotz, McElroy, and Sanders 2008, 55–57). Numerous studies show correlations with low income (Hogan and Kitagawa 1985; Furstenberg, Brooks-Gunn, and Morgan 1987; Duncan and Hoffman 1991; Lundberg and Plotnick 1990; Haveman and Wolfe 1995; Corcoran,

Franklin, and Bennett 2000; Hogan, Sun, and Cornwell 2000; Bickel et al. 1997; Blake and Bentov 2001; Lanctot and Smith 2001; Singh, Darroch, and Frost 2001; Clark et al. 2003; Furstenberg 2007; SmithBattle 2007).

94. Geronimus 1997, 405.

95. Furstenberg 2007, 162. See also Burton 1990; Gordon 1990; Geronimus 1987, 1992, 1997, 2003; Merritt 1996; Phoenix 1993, 79–86; Rhode and Lawson 1993; and Weinstein 1998, who argue that the negative consequences of teen births have been overstated.

96. Furstenberg 2007, 20. He argues: "I think it is not rash to conclude that teenage parenting, as such, does not produce the powerful negative effects on children that most commentators predicted years ago and that most of the public still assumes to be almost inevitable" (2007, 69). Saul Hoffman, a well-respected scholar in this field, agrees that earlier research may have overestimated the costs, but he also believes that early births exacerbate the problems of poverty (1998, 243).

97. Geronimus and Korenman (1992) compared sisters in the same family. Hotz, McElroy, and Sanders compared teen mothers to their peers who were pregnant but had miscarriages and found that teens who gave birth did not suffer in terms of education or income. They argue "the failure to account for selection bias vastly overstates the negative consequences of adolescent childbearing" (2008, 73). For other discussion about the importance of controlling for preconditions, see Butler 1992; Corcoran and Kunz 1997; Bissell 2000; and Hoffman and Maynard 2008.

98. Hotz, McElroy, and Sanders (2008) found that girls who had early births earned more, married men with higher incomes, and used welfare support less frequently. Sometimes the child becomes a motivator for the mother to complete school, move away from violent relations, and become self-sufficient (Geronimus and Korenman 1992; Leadbeater and Way 2001; Furstenberg 2007).

99. Wasserman et al. 1990; Coles 1997; Luker 1996; Erdmans 2012a.

100. Upchurch and McCarthy 1990; Hotz, McElroy, and Sanders 2008. Furstenberg (2007) found that in the first five years after birth it looked as if young mothers paid a cost in terms of education, but as their children got older some mothers returned to school.

101. Chen, Boyce, and Matthews 2002; Burton and Whitfield 2006; Kishiyama et al. 2008; Pachter and Coll 2009.

102. Geronimus, Korenman, and Hillemeier 1994; Furstenberg 2007; Haveman, Wolfe, and Peterson 2008. Manlove and her colleagues found that the best predictor of a child's academic achievement was the mother's education, not the timing of first birth, and they conclude that "improving mother's educational and social circumstances would contribute to better outcomes for children" (2008, 196).

103. Furstenberg now agrees that the "advantage of waiting to have children is not nearly as great as is widely believed" (2007, 39–40).

104. Luker notes that social class and educational inequality are greater in the United States than in Sweden or France (2006, 215). See Luhby 2011 for similar comparisons using World Bank Data. See Pickett, Mookherjee, and Wilkinson (2005) on the links between teenage pregnancy and social inequality

both globally and within the United States. Kawachi and Kennedy link inequality to numerous health indicators and note that the United States has more inequality than most industrialized nations (2002, 25–27).

105. Studies assessing the consequences of early childbirth are more accurate when the participants are at least 30 years old at the time of the interview (Hotz, McElroy, and Sanders 2008).

106. Gordon 1990, 457.

107. Geronimus 1997.

108. Geronimus 2003, 885.

109. Geronimus 1996. See also Burton and Whitfield 2006 for a discussion of cumulative disadvantage.

110. Burton 1990.

111. Garey 1999.

112. Sidel 2006, 26, 28. In the 1965 Moynihan report, the rise in female-headed families was presumed to be the demise of the dominant father figure in the black family. This belief is still current, as evidenced in a *Washington Post* article quoting the president of the National Fatherhood Initiative as saying, "Growing up without a father is like being in a car with a drunk driver" (cited in Sidel 2006, 22). In patriarchal expectations manifest in social policy, the father has been largely seen as the source of child support payments. Only recently have our policies begun to support a broader version of father involvement (Johnson, Levine, and Doolittle 1999; Hamer 2001; Waller 2002). Patriarchy can also be seen in chastity laws and statutory rape laws that form what legal scholar Kate Sutherland refers to as "a backdrop to negotiations about sex and sexual expression among teenagers, and also between teenagers, parents, school officials and various other actors" (2002–2003, 313).

113. Wacquant 2001.

114. For a report of this evaluation see Black, Erdmans, and Dickinson 2004.

115. In Connecticut, in 2002, at the time we began this study, 41 percent of births to mothers under age 20 were to Hispanic mothers, 32 percent to non-Hispanic white mothers, and 23 percent to non-Hispanic black mothers (Connecticut Registration Report 2002, table 4). In that same year, in Connecticut, 58 percent of all Hispanic births were Puerto Rican, 12 percent were Mexican, and 25 percent Central and South American (Martin et al. 2003, table 12).

116. As measured by per capita income. Source: US Department of Commerce, Bureau of Economic Analysis. Released March 2010. Table prepared by Bureau of Business and Economic Research, University of New Mexico. http://bber.unm.edu/econ/us-pci.htm.

117. Ali 2007.

118. Connecticut Registration Report 2005, table 4.

119. The Center for Population Research at the University of Connecticut even suggests that Connecticut is better referred to as five Connecticuts, given its vast social and economic inequality (Levy, Rodriguez, and Villemez 2004). It is also important to remember when we examine income data that Connecticut has a high cost of living and poverty rates are not adjusted accordingly. Consider, for instance, that an updated self-sufficiency standard issued by the Connecticut Office of Workforce Competitiveness in 2005 showed that a single

adult with two children would need to earn $44,141 a year to "get by" in a lower-cost city like Hartford, and $61,181 in a more expensive city like Stamford. Given these figures, we might consider the federal poverty standard for this same family in 2005 at $16,243 to be irrelevant.

120. Levy, Rodriguez, and Villemez 2004. Racial disparities across a number of indicators reflect these geographical distributions of privilege and burden. In 2005, around one in three of Connecticut's black (31 percent) and Latino (33 percent) children under age six lived below the poverty line, compared to one in 20 white children (5 percent) (US Census Bureau, American Community Survey, 2005, http://factfinder.census.gov). Furthermore, the average net worth for white households in Connecticut in 2002 was $153,900, securing college educations, home ownership, inheritance, and general future security to white children throughout the state. In comparison, the average net assets for nonwhite households in the state were $5,446, less than 5 percent of white wealth (Hall and Geballe 2006, 3). See also Hall 2005, 9. One of the most striking racial disparities is incarceration rates, where, in 2005, Connecticut had the greatest white-Hispanic disparity (1:6.6) in incarceration rates in the nation, and the fourth highest white-black disparity (1:12) (Mauer and King 2007).

121. They were seen as at risk for abusing their children; however, program leaders and home visitors generally preferred to think of these families as at risk for poor parenting and in need of support and advocacy, rather than as likely to abuse or neglect their children.

122. Program eligibility required that mothers meet two or three criteria, depending on their weighted severity.

123. Only one in five mothers expressed positive feelings or sentiments toward their biological father. One-third said they had no current relationship with their biological father (and this percent excludes 10 mothers whose fathers had died), and another one-quarter said they had a poor relationship. Moreover, roughly one-quarter could not name their fathers' occupations (and this does not include those who identified their fathers as disabled, unemployed, or incarcerated), and one-third did not know their father's highest level of education. For those who did know, 23 percent had some postsecondary education.

124. See Phoenix 1993, 89, for a discussion of how defining a problem as a "black problem" is based on essentialist arguments that black and white girls have different cultures, in particular, that there is a "black cultural pattern."

125. For an excellent analysis of this interconnectedness, see Belenky et al. 1986 [1997]. See Hareven and Masaoka 1988 for a discussion of how the age of the interviewee influences the memory and evaluation of life events.

CHAPTER 2. YOUNG YOUNG MOTHERS

1. In 2002, only 48 percent of mothers under age 15 received prenatal care in the first trimester compared to 79 percent of mothers age 19, and 13.5 percent of children were born with a low birth weight compared to 8.9 percent (Martin et al. 2003, tables 33 and 45).

2. See table 8 in appendix B.

3. From 2003 to 2008 the rate remained steady at 0.6 births for teens 10 to 14, and then it dropped to 0.5 in 2009 (Martin et al 2012, table 8).

4. Hamilton and Ventura 2012, 2.

5. In our sample, the percent under age 15 when they gave birth is more than three times the national or state levels, a reminder that we recruited mothers from a vulnerable population.

6. Of the 16 mothers, five reported domestic violence and four reported child abuse and neglect. Of the remaining 92 teens, 46 percent reported domestic violence and 52 percent reported child abuse and neglect.

7. This thesis places the cause of teen pregnancy on men and includes narratives where father abandonment and child sexual abuse lead girls to partner with older men or to be in unhealthy relationships with men (Luttrell 2003, 33). For examples of these narratives, see Lerman 1997 or Lipper 2003, 35. The predatory male theory has a long history in legislation that regulates the sexual activity of young women (Cocca 2004).

8. According to the General Social Survey, between 1986 and 1998, two-thirds of respondents believed premarital sex between teens 14 to 16 was "always wrong"; an additional one-sixth thought it was "almost always wrong" (Cocca 2004, 30–32).

9. In the National Survey of Family Growth (NSFG) 2006–2008, 10.8 percent of females said they had sex before age 15 (Abma, Martinez, and Copen 2010, table 7) compared to a reported 18.6 percent in 1995 (Abma et al. 2004, table 3).

10. Alan Guttmacher Institute 1994, 9; Kaufmann et al. 1998; Hacker et al. 2000; Manlove et al. 2000.

11. Moore, Nord, and Peterson 1989; Alan Guttmacher Institute 1994, figure 17; Elo, King, and Furstenberg 1999, 79–80.

12. Moore, Nord, and Peterson 1989; Males and Chew 1996; Urban Institute 1997; Elo, King, and Furstenberg 1999, 79–80; Leitenberg and Saltzman 2000, 211.

13. Girls from impoverished communities are more likely to be sexually active (Kowaleski-Jones and Mott 1998) and initiate sex at an earlier age (Brewster 1994; Kirby 2002), a pattern found in the United States, Canada, Great Britain, and Sweden (Darroch, Frost, and Singh 2001; Alan Guttmacher Institute 2002). Factors correlated with lower risk for early onset include higher family socioeconomic status and college aspirations (Koon-Magnin, Kreager, and Ruback 2010, 210).

14. Miller 2002; Kirby 2002; Abma, Martinez, and Copen 2010.

15. Kowaleski-Jones and Mott 1998; Blinn-Pike 1999; Trad 1999; Hacker et al. 2000; Lanctot and Smith 2001; Little and Rankin 2001; Kirby 2002.

16. These emergent patterns came from prompts such as "what was it like in your home when you were growing up?" and "how were you disciplined when you were growing up?"

17. See hooks 1993 for a discussion of strict parenting practices used to offset the stereotype of African American mothers as poor parents. See also Jarrett 1995, 1997. Furstenberg and colleagues argue that parents in disadvantaged neighborhoods are often good parents who are overvigilant and restrict children's

activities to protect them from dangers (2000 [1999], 20). Studies have also found Latino parents in the United States often strictly control their daughter's activity outside the home (Garcia 2012, 1–3, 88).

18. Katz 1986; Gordon 1990, 1999.

19. Garcia 2012, 15. Garcia describes sex education classes that constructed the Latina teen as "always at heightened risk for pregnancy" (2009, 531). The identification of Latinas as at risk for teen pregnancy led to a joint program between the Center for Latino Adolescent and Family Health and The National Campaign to Prevent Teen and Unplanned Pregnancy that designed a handbook for Latino parents and community health workers (Guilamo-Ramos, Lee and Jaccard 2012).

20. On cultural adaptations to urban poverty, see Kasinitz et al. 2008.

21. Mac Donald 2006. See also Rumbaut 2005 for a discussion of high rates of teen birth among Mexican and Puerto Ricans: he concludes that even after considering a variety of other factors, Mexican ethnicity was a strong predictor of early births (2005, 1082).

22. According to the 2000 Census, nearly 70 percent of the neighborhood was Hispanic. Information taken from *One City, One Plan.* 2010. City of Hartford, Hartford, CT, 15–6, http://planning.hartford.gov/oneplan/Chapters /15-Demographics Adopted.pdf.

23. Stack 1974; Burton 1990. In one study of 43 pregnant Puerto Rican teenagers, Ortiz and Nuttell (1987) found that teens who did not abort had more family support.

24. In Black's ethnography of a Puerto Rican family, one father said, on finding out his 15-year-old daughter was pregnant, "Family is always there. . . . Family is there to pick you up when you fuck up. That's what family's for" (2009, 344). He was not happy she became pregnant; in fact, he defined it as "fucking up," but he would support her.

25. Basu 2009. See also Perales 1999 for a discussion of how cultural stereotypes have been misinterpreted by courts and media as representing norms, including the stereotype that early births are normalized in Mexican culture.

26. Mac Donald 2006. Since her publication, data on birth rates have been revised based on 2010 census population estimates: in 2003, for teens 15 to 19, the Mexican birth rate was 88.8, the black rate was 63.7, and the white rate was 27.4 (Martin et al. 2012, table 8).

27. Feagin 2006, 25–28.

28. The Hispanic teen birth rate for teens 15 to 19 peaked in 1991 at 104.6, and has declined precipitously to a low of 49.6 in 2011; for Hispanic teens 10 to 14, it dropped from 1.4 to 0.4 (Martin et al. 2013, table 8). The release of the 2011 Hispanic rate made headline news, with the report noting that not only had the US birth rate fallen to a record low, *the decline was greatest among immigrants* (Livingston and Cohn 2012).

29. Martin et al. 2012, table 8. In the text, we use the age group 15 to 19 because data for Cuban teens 10 to 14 are not available. Also, Mac Donald (2006) uses the age group 15 to 19 for her data.

30. Ventura et al. 2008, table 3. Most of the Latinas that Garcia interviewed said abortion was not an option; however, she noted a 2007 national survey

that found second-generation Latinas/os more accepting of abortion than those of the first generation (2012, 88–90).

31. Data on Connecticut births are from the annual Connecticut Registration Report, for the years 1998 through 2006, table 4. See also Gottlieb 2004, B7. In Connecticut, Hispanics are primarily Puerto Rican. In 2000, Puerto Ricans made up 61 percent of the state's Hispanic population (Census 2000 Summary File 1 [SF 1] 100-percent data).

32. Connecticut Registration Report, 2008, table 4.

33. In this case, "black" does not refer to non-Hispanic (Martin et al. 2006, tables 2, II). The population number is an estimate based on 2000 census data.

34. Martin et al. 2012, table 8.

35. Canny, Hall, and Geballe 2002.

36. According to this report the 2000 statewide poverty rate for African American children was 25 percent, for Latino children 31 percent, and for white children 4 percent (State of Connecticut 2005, 11).

37. Connecticut Registration Report, 2004, table 4.

38. Connecticut Registration Report, years 1998 to 2006, table 4.

39. Oberman 2000, 800.

40. Statutory rape laws date back to chastity laws designed to protect the chastity of young women. The earliest laws made it illegal to have intercourse, with or without consent, with any girl before the age of 10. For an excellent history of these laws, see Cocca 2004 and Ehrlich 2006. The age of consent was gradually raised during the late nineteenth century, and feminist reforms in the 1970s opened the laws to apply to any minor.

41. In 2012, the age of consent was 16 in 33 states. www.ageofconsent.us.

42. Number of states with age-span provisions at 2 years (5), 3 years (12), 4 years (14), 5 years (8), and 6 years (4). Age-span provisions were adopted by 21 states in the 1970s, nine states in 1980s, and 13 states in 1990s (Cocca 2004, 36–38). Koon-Magnin, Kreager, and Ruback (2010) argue for an age span of five years as most reasonable.

43. Connecticut's age span of two years was challenged in 2007 (Malone 2007). In May 2008, the Connecticut legislature passed a bill to extend the age span to three years.

44. In our study, we separated statutory rape from child sexual abuse (CSA) using state statutes. In Connecticut, at the time of the study, if the girl was under the age of 13 and the partner was a guardian or family member this violation was defined as CSA, which carried a harsher sentence. If the girl was between 13 and 16 and in a sexual relationship with someone she defined as her boyfriend who was at least two years older than her and who was not a guardian or family member, it was defined as statutory rape.

45. Oberman 2000, 808. Numerous studies provide a history of statutory rape laws and the changes that occurred when statutory rape was linked to teen pregnancy and used as an attempt to reduce out-of-wedlock teen births (Oberman 1994; Donovan 1996; Oliveri 2000; Cocca 2004; Beck and Boys 2012).

46. P.L. 104–193, section 906 (b)(1). This legislation specified that states "conduct a program, designed to reach State and local law enforcement officers,

the education system, and relevant counseling services, that provides education and training on the problem of statutory rape"(Cocca 2004, 101–102).

47. States that raised the age of consent or increased penalties included Florida, Georgia, Delaware, Washington, and California; states that enforced existing laws included Louisiana, Virginia, and California; and states that had public awareness campaigns including billboards and radio advertisements warning about the law included New York, California, and Connecticut (Oliveri 2000, 475–476).

48. Cocca 2004, 60. Fornification laws existed in 17 states and while they apply to everyone who is not married, the court in Idaho targeted teenagers (Brooke 1996). After 1996, 10 states "revised statutory rape laws to target sexual activity resulting in teen pregnancy" (Cocca 2004, 93).

49. Florida created MAMA (Make Adult Males Accountable) requiring mandatory reporting when a teen under age 16 was impregnated by a man 21 years or older; Delaware placed police in high schools to identify girls' older partners; and Tennessee required that health care providers become mandated reporters (Cocca 2004, 105–106).

50. Cocca 2004, 106.

51. Ohlemacher 1997, A3.

52. Donovan 1996; Oliveri 2000, 468; Cocca 2004, 93–107. Not all prosecutors, however, interpreted the law this way. In one study, service providers reported that deterring teen pregnancy was not generally the reason for prosecuting adult males (Elstein and Davis 1997, 24).

53. Lieberman 1996, S8419.

54. Quoted in Levin-Epstein 1997, 4–5. From Congressional Record, s.12700. September 6, 1995, italics added.

55. The "Findings" (P.L. 104–193, Section 101, 1996) precede the legislation and provide the rationale for overhauling the welfare system. Section 101.6 named nonmarital teen pregnancy as a problem, using data showing an increase in teenage pregnancies from 1976 to 1991. Not surprisingly, it did not mention that the pregnancy rate had been in decline for five years when this bill was written.

56. Clayton 1996, H5738; Santorum 1996, S8077.

57. P.L. 104–193, Section 101.7.

58. Cocca 2004, 106.

59. Section 101.7(A), 7(B), 7(C).

60. Lindberg et al. 1997; Elo, King, and Furstenberg 1999; Leitenberg and Saltzman 2000. The AGI report was "cited by virtually every article on the topic across the political spectrum as well as by public officials" (Cocca 2004, 96).

61. Lindberg et al. 1997; Urban Institute 1997.

62. Elo, King, and Furstenberg 1999, 78. They found that young girls were more likely to have sex compared to an earlier cohort, but less likely to have older partners (1999, 79).

63. Congress continues to cite the AGI report "without the caveats of the Urban Institute" (Cocca 2004, 99). See, for instance, a Congressional Research Service Report by Carmen Solomon-Fears (2011).

64. Cited in Oliveri 2000, 505. Males and Chew (1996), using California data, found that most children born to "school-age" mothers (those younger

than 18) were fathered by "adult" men who they defined as over 18. The youngest mothers (10 to 14) were more likely to have a larger age gap with the fathers, but the teens 10 to 14 represented only 3.3 percent of their sample.

65. See Becker 1963, chapter 8, for a discussion of moral entrepreneurs. California Governor Pete Wilson was one of the leading moral entrepreneurs of the 1990s (Donovan 1996).

66. Cocca 2004, 102. See also Oliveri 2000, 474, and Erhlich 2006, 158. In some ways this reframing was welcomed as a counternarrative to claims such as those made by Dash (1989) and Anderson (1999) that girls were intentionally getting pregnant and victimizing young men by tricking them into fatherhood.

67. Oliveri 2000, 477.

68. Gottlieb 2004.

69. Becker is again useful in a discussion of moral entrepreneurs and the way that their moral crusades can lead to a selective enforcement of rules (1963, chapter 7). The enforcement of statutory rape laws tended to come down on the backs of those with the least power to protect themselves, those already labeled as deviants. Oliveri argues that when the law is used to go after "deadbeat dads" or welfare users "the door is open for arbitrary and discriminatory enforcement" (2000, 503).

70. The 1980s crack cocaine campaign extended the arm of the state into hospitals, where presumably black women were producing a new generation of crack babies, and it reopened debates on the viability of a fetus (Beckett 1995; Cherry 2007; Fentiman 2009; Lynch 2012).

71. Elstein and Davis 1997, 24; Oliveri 2000.

72. Ten states (including Connecticut) that revised laws have mandatory reporting by health care providers or state welfare workers (Cocca 2004, 124). However, one study found that service providers are reluctant to report the relationships to authorities for several reasons, including the "chilling effect" it will have on the relations with their client as well as their mistrust of the criminal justice system (Elstein and Davis 1997, 10).

73. One prosecutor said he applies statutory rape laws "to stop the baby machine" (Oliveri 2000, 504).

74. Urban Institute 1997.

75. Cocca 2004, 126. The vast majority of those prosecuted are men. Women tend to be prosecuted only when there is a large age or status difference, for example, between a teacher and student (Sutherland 2002–2003, 319).

76. Class, race, and behavior (for example, substance use) influence the perceived "goodness" of victims and perpetrators (Delgado, 1996, 87; Sutherland 2002–2003, 317–318, 326).

77. In California, in 1999, 58 percent of those prosecuted were teenagers (Sutherland 2002–2003, 316). See also Koon-Magnin, Kreager, and Ruback 2010, 208.

78. Landry and Forrest found that less than 20 percent of children born to teen mothers had partners more than five years older (1995, 161, table 2). See also Males and Chew 1996. Older teen mothers are likely to have partners in their 20s, but middle and young teens are likely to partner with other teens (Elo, King, and Furstenberg, 1999).

79. Landry and Forrest 1995; Lindberg et al. 1997; Elo, King, and Furstenberg 1999.

80. An American Bar Association study using interviews with 48 service providers reported that many parents and community members supported those relationships between young females and older males, and found that, while some were exploitative, most of them were not (Elstein and Davis 1997). Oliveri found that clients who want to prosecute usually do so because of some other issue (lack of child support, domestic violence), meaning they do not use these laws to protect them from predatory men but to get financial assistance or stop abuse (2000, 502). She argues against the strong enforcement of the laws because, if prosecuted, the father will not have contact with the child and the mother can lose the resources he may have been providing (2000, 497).

81. Alan Guttmacher Institute 1994. Based on 1987 data, of teens who experienced sexual intercourse before age 14, 25 percent reported only voluntary intercourse, 13 percent reported having both voluntary and involuntary intercourse, and 61 percent had experienced only involuntary intercourse (1994, figure 17). See also Moore et al. 1995; Elo, King, and Furstenberg 1999, 81; Leitenberg and Saltzman 2000, 207.

82. For findings regarding unhealthy relations with older men and negative consequences, see Elstein and Davis 1997; the Urban Institute 1997; Elo, King, and Furstenberg 1999, 79; Leitenberg and Saltzman (2000, 209–211). Garcia found younger girls with partners more than two years older felt less able to ask their partners to use condoms (2012, 187n33). See Koon-Magnin, Kreager, and Ruback 2010 on the relationship between educational context, partner age, and sexual risk.

83. Butler and Burton 1990; Boyer and Fine 1992; Musick 1993; Hamby, Finkelhor, and Turner 2012.

84. Oberman 2000, 800.

85. Sutherland 2002–2003, 332. See Oberman 1994, 2000 for a thorough discussion of consent.

86. Drobac 2013, 4. She distinguishes consent from acquiescence (stemming from unequal power relations) and assent (which is approval), arguing that for children, consent "is more like assent or acquiescence" (2013, 9).

87. See Oliveri 2000, 483. One of the most widely viewed illustrations of this variance can be seen on the reality television show *16 and Pregnant*. For example, in season 1, the level of emotional maturity varied greatly between Caitlyn and Whitney as well as between Tyler and Josh.

88. Cocca 2004. In *Lawrence et al. v. TX*, 2003, the opinion of the court was to protect an individual's right against the intrusion of the state in consensual sexual relations.

89. Elstein and Davis 1997, 21–22.

90. Elstein and Davis 1997, 25.

91. Oberman 1994, 35, 37.

92. Elstein and Davis 1997, 22–25. This can be a severe punishment for an 18-year old who was having sexual relations with his 15-year-old girlfriend. In the most absurd cases, it can result in the father of the child, now classified as a

sexual offender, being unable to attend activities at his child's school (Beck and Boys 2012, 4–5).

93. In 2005, Genarlow Wilson, an African American, was given a 10-year prison sentence for aggravated child molestation for having oral sex with a white 15-year-old classmate. After appealing, his sentence was reduced, but the conviction was not overturned. After two years, he was released. During the appeals process, Jimmy Carter wrote to Georgia Attorney General Thurbert Baker: "The racial dimension of the case is likewise hard to ignore and perhaps unfortunately has had an impact on the final outcome of the case." http://campaigndiaries.com/2009/04/02/two-unexpected-twists-in-southern-governors-races/. See Sutherland 2002–2003, 322–326, for a fuller discussion of selective prosecution and enforcement of age of consent laws. Lindberg et al. (1997) and Elo, King, and Furstenberg (1999, 76) found age differences were similar across race.

94. Oliveri 2000, 488. Latina women are also singled out with "cultural essentialism" theories that define them as "full-bodied and oversexed" (Sutherland 2002–2003, 324–325). See also Garcia 2009. Perales shows how Mexican girls can be unprotected by state and family guardians when cultural essentialism arguments are used in courts and the media to normalize relationships between young adolescent girls and older men (1999, 81).

95. Bumiller 2008, 8.

96. Cocca 2004, 124; Elstein and Davis 1997, 22; Oliveri 2000, 484. Girls can be prosecuted for "aiding and abetting the offender" or held in contempt of court for not testifying (Sutherland 2002–2003, 317).

97. When the state is empowered to act independently of the victim's wishes, some important consequences can follow: (1) animosity and distrust can develop between the family and the mandated reporter; (2) an irreparable separation can occur between the mother and the father of the baby; (3) defining a teenager as a "sex offender" can have long-lasting effects on his ability to be a provider for his child; and (4) the pregnant teen has a disincentive to get early health care if she fears that her boyfriend will be charged with statutory rape (Elstein and Davis 1997).

98. Sutherland 2002–2003, 332–333. In this book we are focusing on heterosexual relations because of the interest in the pregnancy. For a discussion of statutory rape laws in same-sex relations, see Sutherland 2002–2003, 326–328.

99. Cocca 2004, 127.

100. Cocca 2004, 61. See also Drobac 2013, 6, and Sutherland 2002–2003, 318. Oberman argues that rape victims are often under age 18 and the perpetrator is likely to be an acquaintance, and if these perpetrators are getting charged with statutory rape rather than rape, "they are getting off easy" (2000, 822). See her reference to the *State v. Hamme* 1998 decisions (2000, 818).

101. He was not charged with either rape or statutory rape. Celina did get pregnant by him at age 15 but she aborted the pregnancy. Her story is another example of the problem of age categories. She was not technically a "young young" mother because she delivered her first child at age 17; but her life story helps us understand the complexity of consent and predation with young teens.

See Tita's story in chapter 5—she was sexually initiated at age 13 with a 26-year-old partner, but did not have her first child until she was 19.

102. Oberman 2000, 813.

103. Oberman 1994, 15–18.

104. Kimmel 2008; Lefkowitz 1997.

105. Most recently, a US Justice Department investigation found that "corrections officers have raped, beaten and harassed women" inside the Julia Tutwiler Prison for Women in Alabama for the last 18 years, an institutional transgression as more than one-third "of the employees have had sex with prisoners, which is sometimes the only currency for basics like toilet paper and tampons." www.nytimes.com/2014/03/02/us/troubles-at-womens-prison-test-alabama.html?_r=0.

106. Abma, Driscoll, and Moore 1998, 107.

107. The one boy arrested had climbed through the bedroom window of a 10-year-old girl and it was determined that her "terror led her to acquiesce" (Oberman 1994, 54).

108. Oberman 1994, 54. The boys in the Spur Posse made a distinction between "good girls" of whom they said, "you give them the all night thing, you please them and romance them" and the "whores you just nut and you leave" (1994, 17). Still, whether perceived as "good girls" or "whores," they were all considered their property to have. See Cocca 2004 for a discussion of the case of a 20-year-old man who was HIV positive and who had sex with 47 young women. He said he persuaded girls—most of them homeless, runaway teens—to have sex with him by "my ways of talking with girls," telling them he loved them and listening to them talk about their problems (2004, 59).

109. Albert 2010, 29–30.

110. Oberman 1996; Elstein and Davis 2007. There is the extreme case of "running a train" on a young girl (serial rape) that gets defined in the community as "training" or "getting influenced into screwing" (Bourgois 1998, 341). This is a form of male domination that is expressed as entitlement to women's (and girls') bodies for male sexual pleasure, which is a manifestation of patriarchy. Similar behavior has been documented in intensely male-dominated organizations, such as fraternities and the military. See also Sanday 1990; Franklin 2004; Miller 2008.

111. Oberman 1996, 41.

112. Oberman 2000, 824. She is building on arguments developed by Catherine McKinnon in the 1980s. See also Oberman 1994 for discussion of the dilemma of consensual sex in a patriarchal culture.

113. See Orenstein 1995, 51–66, and Pipher 1998 for discussions of how self-esteem is shaped by gender inequality.

114. Gilligan 1982; Pipher 1998; Debold et al. 1999.

115. Oberman 1994, 66.

116. Elo, King, and Furstenberg (1999) argue that it can be economically rational for poor young women to have children with older men who are more likely to have a job, a car, and other resources. But the story of younger women being with older men because they have resources cuts across class lines. One example that played out on the front pages of the *Hartford Courant* in 2008 and 2009 was the case of the former CEO of United Technologies, George

David (age 64), who allegedly cheated, lied, and emotionally tormented Marie Douglas-David (age 37) for several years before she exposed his behavior in divorce proceedings.

117. Leitenberg and Saltzman 2000. Studies show that statutory rape laws have limited influence on adolescent sexual behavior (Koon-Magnin, Kreager, and Ruback 2010, 211).

118. More studies need to be conducted to understand how neighborhood conditions and household economies influence parenting strategies. Good examples include Furstenberg et al. 2000 [1999] and Lareau 2003.

119. See Harding 2007.

120. Cocca writes that the case of a much older man and a very young girl in an obviously exploitative situation "is the type of case that many perhaps assume represents the universe of statutory rape, and builds support for enforcement of the laws" (2004, 57).

121. Clayton 1996, H5737–8.

122. Delgado 1996, 87.

123. Cited in Donovan 1996, 34.

124. Cited in Donovan 1996, 34.

CHAPTER 3. CHILD SEXUAL ABUSE

1. A big-timer in criminal operations, usually referring to a drug dealer.

2. The title of this section is from a short story of the same name written by Fred Pfeil, published in *What They Tell You To Forget* (Pushcart Press, 1996). For an earlier and shorter version of this chapter, see Erdmans and Black 2008.

3. Altimari 2008.

4. As a consequence, we proceed with humility and caution, and with a determination to directly address any misattributions of our work.

5. See Wacquant 2009. This issue is also addressed in its complexity in Russell Banks's 2011 novel *Lost Memory of Skin*.

6. For stories in the *Hartford Courant,* see Hunt 2008 and Waldman 2008. Another Connecticut case of a serial pedophile hidden by his occupational status was probation officer Richard Straub, who, in 1999, was convicted on more than 200 sexual assault charges and is serving a 15-year prison sentence (Altimari 2008).

7. Of course, there are other institutions to consider, including the military, college fraternities, and sports. The Jerry Sandusky case at Penn State University, which shocked the sports world and sullied the reputation of football icon Joe Paterno, is another reminder that sex abuse is not a poverty issue.

8. Elliot and Briere 1995. See also Nancy Whittier 2009 for an excellent historical description of the politics of child sexual abuse.

9. Finkelhor 1994, 45.

10. Finkelhor, Jones, and Shattuck 2010. The number of substantiated cases has fallen considerably and consistently since 1992, when 149,800 cases were substantiated. Similar trends have been found among all child maltreatment, even though incidents of child sexual abuse have decreased more over the past two decades (61 percent) compared to child physical abuse (55 percent) and

child neglect (10 percent) (Finkelhor, Jones, and Shattuck 2010). It is not clear, however, to what extent the decline is attributable to true decreases in incidents or to changing standards, norms, policies, and procedures within state agencies (Jones, Finkelhor, and Kopiec 2001).

11. The discrepancy between official rates of child sexual abuse and general population surveys suggests that less than 10 percent of all abuse is reported to authorities. In one study, 39 percent of the victims told about the abuse for the first time when they took the survey (Musick 1993, 93). Tolman (2002) also found that some young women in her study talked about their sexual abuse for the first time during the interview.

12. Polit, White, and Morton 1990; Finkelhor and Dzuiba-Leatherman 1994; Kaplan 1997; Putnam and Trickett 1997; Dunlap, Golub, and Johnson 2003. Peters, Wyatt, and Finkelhor (1986, 54) argue that while most victims will not report the abuse to child protective agencies, they will report the abuse to researchers when they are asked.

13. Douglas and Finkelhor 2005. Examples of noncontact abuse include public exposure of genitals, forced viewing of pornography, or, as in Deidre's life story, having her grandfather watch her bathe.

14. Putnam 2003. See Finkelhor 1994, 15–59, for a discussion of variations in estimating incidence and prevalence. In his summary of 19 adult retrospective studies, the range of reported child sexual abuse for women was between 2 percent to 62 percent, and for men 3 percent to 31 percent, the wide range influenced in part by varying definitions of sexual abuse. A stringent measure included only rape, whereas a broader (and more common) measure was to ask whether or not "someone touched you in places you did not want to be touched or did something sexually to you they shouldn't have done," including noncontact abuse. See Nagy, DiClemente, and Adcock 1995 and Chandy, Blum, and Resnick 1996 for a discussion of measurements, characteristics of the sample (for example, age, region, class, response rates), and methods used to collect data (for example, number and type of questions asked). A thorough discussion of the problems with and variations in the reporting on child sex abuse is found in Peters, Wyatt, and Finkelhor 1986.

15. Putnam 2003.

16. Douglas and Finkelhor 2005.

17. In 2008, African American, American Indian or Alaska Native children, and multiracial children had the highest incidence rates at 17, 14, and 14 per 1,000 children from the same racial and ethnic groups, respectively. The rates for Hispanic, White, and Asian children were 10, 9, and 2, respectively. Looking at the numbers, nearly one-half of the reported victims were white (45 percent) and a little less than one-quarter were African American (22 percent) and Hispanic (21 percent) (US Department of Health and Human Services 2008).

18. Putnam 2003, 270.

19. Douglas and Finkelhor 2005.

20. Gershensen et al. 1989; Boyer and Fineman 1992; Musick 1993; Stevens-Simon and McAnarney 1994; Stevens-Simon and Reichert 1994; Nagy, DiClemente, and Adcock 1995; Chandy, Blum, and Resnick 1996; Fergusson, Horwood, and Lynskey 1997; Kenney, Reinholtz, and Angelini 1997; Roosa et al.

1997; Stock et al. 1997; Elders and Albert 1998; Raj, Silverman, and Amaro 2000; Miller 2002; Brown et al. 2004; Roberts et al. 2004; Saewyc, Magee, and Pettingell 2004. For narrative accounts of adolescent mothers who were sexually abused as children, see Dash 1989, chapter 4; Kaplan 1997, 35, 220; Lipper 2003, stories of Liz and Sheri; Lerman 1997, chapter 3. For two key meta-analyses of studies, see Blinn-Pike et al. 2002 and Noll, Shenk, and Putnam 2009. For studies examining social class, sexual abuse, and teen pregnancy, see Fiscella et al. 1998 and Butler and Burton 1990. For studies examining the sexual abuse of boys and teenage pregnancy, see Luster and Small 1994; Pierre et al. 1998; Raj, Silverman, and Amaro 2000; Saewyc, Magee, and Pettingell 2004; McGuffey 2005, 2008.

21. The only exception to this is the case of Keisha. We included her in our count of statutory rape because that is how she defined it, but she fit the criteria of child sexual abuse because she was 12 years old when she was repeatedly raped by her aunt's boyfriend, who was her temporary guardian.

22. Anderson and Jack (1991) make a similar point. Gershenson et al. (1989) argue that discussions of coercive sexual experiences can be therapeutic for victims if interviewers are well trained. In our study, we held weekly meetings during the data collection phase, and as these child sex abuse stories were emerging we discussed ethical ways of listening and asking follow-up questions. We also stressed that they were interviewers, not therapists. We instructed them to carry contact information for service providers, and to encourage the mothers to talk with their home visitor about their past abuse. We also mentioned the prevalence of child sexual abuse in the final report to the agency with the suggestion that home visitors be sensitive to the potential for this violence in the mothers' histories.

23. Russell and Van de Ven 1976, 110–111, quoted in Whittier 2009, 29.

24. Studies finding links between sexual abuse and depression, suicide, mental illness, and eating disorders include Young 1992; Nagy, DiClemente, and Adcock 1995; Chandy, Blum, and Resnick 1996; Stock et al. 1997; Raj, Silverman, and Amaro 2000; Hagan and Foster 2001; Peleikis, Mykletun, and Dahl 2004; Roberts et al. 2004; Romano, Zoccolillo, and Paquette 2006. See also studies from the Adverse Childhood Experiences (ACES) project (Felitti et al. 1998; Felitti and Anda 2009; Anda et al. 2010; Brown et al. 2010).

25. Butler and Burton 1990; Boyer and Fine 1992; Downs 1993; Musick 1993, 98–99; Chandy, Blum, and Resnick 1996.

26. This last line is a play on the title of the novel *She's Come Undone* by Wally Lamb, which is about child sexual abuse. In his story, the abuse is turned inward and manifested as obesity.

27. Finkelhor 1986, 1994; Kaplan 1997; Douglas and Finkelhor 2005.

28. Finkelhor and Brown 1986, 180. This article provides a good early review of the literature. See also Musick 1993 and Kirby 2002. The effects of the abuse are influenced by the severity, the length of time, the use of force, the relationship with the perpetrator, and the age at onset of abuse (Friedrich, Urquiza, and Beilke 1984; Finkelhor 1986; Wyatt 1988; Downs 1993; Musick 1993, 85–105; Mullen et al. 1994; Putnam and Trickett 1997).

29. Studies have found relationships between sexual abuse and earlier and riskier sexual behavior. Early first coitus and younger age at first pregnancy were found in the research of Wyatt 1988; Polit, White, and Morton 1990;

Nagy, DiClemente, and Adcock 1995; Fergusson, Horwood, and Lynskey 1997; Roosa et al. 1997; Stock et al. 1997; Fiscella et al. 1998; Mason, Zimmerman, and Evans 1998; Noll, Trickett, and Putnam 2000; Raj, Silverman, and Amaro 2000; Lipper 2003; Brown et al. 2004. Studies finding links between sexual abuse and prostitution include Widom and Kuhns 1996 and Dunlap, Golub, and Johnson 2003. Sexually acting out is more often noted when the perpetrator was the father (Putnam and Trickett 1997).

30. Musick 1993, 96.

31. Studies have found relations between child sexual abuse and nightmares, phobias, somatic complaints, dissociation, aggression, and delinquency (Downs 1993; Mullen et al. 1994; Brown et al. 2004); depression (and suicide), mental illness, and eating disorders (see note 24); and substance abuse (Stevens-Simon and McAnarney 1994; Nagy, DiClemente, and Adcock 1995; Stock et al. 1997). Studies have also found that children born to adolescent parents with a prior history of physical and sexual abuse were more at risk of low birth weight because these mothers were more likely to have abused drugs (Stevens-Simon and McAnarney 1994).

32. Studies have found that CSA victims are at increased risk for sexual and physical violence in later relations (Briere and Runtz 1987; Boyer and Fine 1992; Wolfe et al. 1998). Some studies found that abused teenagers had older partners more often than nonabused teenagers (Boyer and Fine 1992; Rainey, Stevens-Simon, and Kaplan 1995), but another study did not (Harner 2005).

33. Finkelhor 1986; Butler and Burton 1990; Musick 1993, 74–77, 94–102.

34. Musick 1993, 92. See also Wallach 1997.

35. Musick 1993, 95–96.

36. Not all of the life stories could be categorized into one of these four motifs. See Erdmans 2012b.

37. See Erikson 1968 and Downs 1993 for a discussion of adolescence in general.

38. See Moore, Nord, and Peterson 1989 and Polit, White, and Norton 1990.

39. Ronai writes that "child sex abuse survivors can be both active and reactive in their ability to control the definitions and conditions contributing to their self-identities" (1995, 418).

40. Musick 1993; Finkelhor and Dzuiba-Leatherman 1994; Ronai 1995; Douglas and Finkelhor 2005.

41. Dash writes that one school counselor said, "more girls suffered assaults than were willing to seek help . . . they didn't tell. There was something wrong with you if it were known you were a victim of a sexual attack. You'd been spoiled" (1989, 52).

42. Dunlap, Golub, and Johnson 2003.

43. Fontes 1993; Dunlap, Golub, and Johnson 2003; McGuffey 2005. In general, girls are less likely to be believed if they are seen as promiscuous, something that often happens after sexual abuse has occurred. Girls who report the abuse months, or even years, after the incident occurred, and after they have developed delinquent behaviors, defiant attitudes, and sexualized personas, are often dismissed by parents and other adult authorities. Lipper writes: "high-risk self-destructive behaviors ruin a girl's credibility" (2003, 335).

44. Victims are less likely to be believed if the parents or guardians feel complicit or responsible for not protecting the child or if the offender is the family provider (Dash 1989, 52; Chandy, Blum, and Resnick 1996; Dunlap, Golub, and Johnson 2003). Further, the mother may feel responsible for the abuse, especially incest, because of gendered expectations that the ideal mother should be with her children at all times (Breckenridge and Baldry 1997; McGuffey 2005). However, "the available research challenges the assumptions that the majority of mothers are covert conspirators in the abuse" (Breckenridge and Baldry 1997, 68–70). If they have a network of support outside the home or neighborhood, then it is easier to report the abuse and get help. But if mothers are isolated, they have few ties to begin with and may not want to sever them. Moreover, if the male is someone who provides support for the family—a father, stepfather, boyfriend, uncle—the mother may be reluctant or fearful to believe that the hand that feeds them also abuses her daughter (Dash 1989, 52; Dunlap, Golub, and Johnson 2003; Chandy, Blum, and Resnick 1996).

45. Tolman 2002; Romano, Zoccolillo, and Paquette 2006.

46. Quoted in Campbell 2008, D4. Convicting the perpetrator helps the healing process (Musick 1993). Organizations like Sexual Assault Nurse Examiners (SANE) and Sexual Assault Forensic Examiners (SAFE) provide medical care for victims and help collect evidence to make court convictions (Campbell 2008, D1).

47. Schmidt 1995; Fine and Weis 1999.

48. See Dunlap, Golub, and Johnson 2003.

49. Comas-Díaz 1995.

50. Whittier 2009.

51. Ronai 1995, 406.

52. We are also aware that the media can turn discussion into voyeurism and potentially revictimize. See Letters to the Editor in the *New York Times Magazine,* February 10, 2013, 8.

53. Mills 1959.

54. Finkelhor reports that in one study, only 42 percent of the substantiated cases were prosecuted (1994, 45). See also Dash 1989 and Kaplan 1997, 34.

55. Whittier 2009.

56. Musick 1993, 72. Others who advocate for the importance of counseling include Finkelhor 1986; Polit, White, and Morton 1990; Downs 1993; Chandy, Blum, and Resnick 1996; Stock et al. 1997; Wallach 1997; Romano, Zoccolillo and Paquette 2006. Fiscella et al. (1998) found that victims who receive counseling were less likely to have adolescent pregnancies.

57. Otterman 2013.

58. Whittier 2009, 192.

59. It is these larger beliefs in male supremacy encoded in patriarchal families that set the stage for incestuous relations (Ronai 1995, 406).

CHAPTER 4. VIOLENCE AGAINST WOMEN

1. Rape data are from the 2004 National Crime Victimization Survey and data on intimate partner violence are taken from the 2000 Domestic Violence

against Women Survey. www.ncadv.org/files/DomesticViolenceFactSheet(Natio nal).pdf. These are underestimates since they include only reported cases.

2. As Bourgois and Schonberg explain, "violence operates along a continuum that spans structural, symbolic, everyday, and intimate dimensions" (2009, 16). See also Bourgois 2001 and Scheper-Hughes and Bourgois 2004.

3. Bourdieu and Wacquant 2004; Wacquant 2008.

4. Garfield 2005, 25.

5. Garfield 2005, 245. Randall Collins (2008) provides an important caveat to our argument. He points out that the organization and exercise of power and domination do not usually result in interpersonal violence, but that mediating situational characteristics must occur that produce acts of violence. His micro-sociological theory of violence focuses on physical and emotional entrainment and evolving situational circumstances that produce violence as a means of resolving fear and tension. We agree that interpersonal violence is a rare occurrence, and is therefore not a *likely* outcome of poverty or emasculation, or even of contested power dynamics in intimate partner relationships. Further, we acknowledge that our discussion of violence focuses on mothers in our study who have experienced violence and therefore omits the mothers who lived in similar circumstances but were not victims of violence—the problem, using Collins's terms, of oversampling on the dependent variable. Nonetheless, like Garfield and others whom we cite in this chapter, we argue that the organization of power and domination and the perceptions that legitimate and reproduce national and local hierarchies of power and domination structure power relationships on an interpersonal level, and that the negotiation of these power relations creates circumstances in which physical violence occurs, even if it is a rare outcome. Collins himself does not deny that these larger social forces, or "background conditions," affect the violent encounter, but argues instead that these explanations have been overstated. His approach in his book is to "push as far as possible with a situational approach" and then eventually "to work backward and incorporate some background conditions" (2008, 21).

6. *Domestic Violence Fact Sheet: A Connecticut Perspective*, East Hartford: Connecticut Coalition Against Domestic Violence, www.ctcadv.org/Portals/0/Uploads/Documents/FACT-SHT%202010%20-2011%20for%20email%20%20.pdf.

7. Peckinpaugh 2010. A year earlier, Alice Morin, an executive assistant at a local television station, was shot and killed in her suburban home by her husband shortly before their divorce was to become final (Owens and Dempsey 2009).

8. Owens 2012.

9. Fine and Weis 1999.

10. Wacquant 2000, 2002; Alexander 2010.

11. Bourgois 2009, 37.

12. hooks 1995.

13. Menjívar (2011) also describes violence, infidelities, and drinking as expressions of masculinity in Guatemala that normalize everyday violence. See also Guttman 1996.

14. Tolman 2002.

15. See also Miller 2008 and Dunlap, Golub, and Johnson 2003.

16. US Department of Commerce, Bureau of Economic Analysis. Released March 2010. Table prepared by Bureau of Business and Economic Research, University of New Mexico. http://bber.unm.edu/econ/us-pci.htm.

17. U.S. Census Bureau, www.census.gov, February 27, 2008. www.netstate. com/states/tables/state_millionaires.htm. Source for poverty: US Census Bureau, Census 2000 Summary File 3, Matrices P53, P77, P82, P87, P90, PCT47, and PCT52. http://factfinder.census.gov/servlet/GCTTable?_bm = y&-geo_id = 01000US&-_box_head_nbr = GCT-P14&-ds_name = DEC_2000_SF3_U&-format = US-9.

18. Canny and Hall 2003, 1. By 2011, the state child poverty rate was 15 percent, but in Hartford, New Haven, Bridgeport, Waterbury, and New Britain the rates were 48 percent, 41 percent, 40 percent, 35 percent, and 36 percent, respectively (Connecticut Voices for Children 2012, 5).

19. This is based on 2000 census data reported in Levy, Rodriguez, and Villemez 2004, 1.

20. These data are taken from 2000 US Census data compiled as Census CD (released by Geolytics in New Brunswick, NJ).

21. New Haven's 2000 median household income was a little less than one-half of that of its 21-town region and, while New Haven is home to 22 percent of the region's young children, 62 percent of the region's poor young children live within its city boundaries (Hughes et al. 2008).

22. The violence they describe, however, is not a description of poor neighborhoods in these cities, but it does reflect the lives of *vulnerable* mothers living in poor households located in poor urban neighborhoods in Connecticut. Poor urban neighborhoods are complex social spaces, and the experiences of some do not represent the experiences of all residents. We are looking through the lens of the life stories of a few poor racial-minority girls living in neglected, urban neighborhoods.

23. For a description of this neighborhood and its isolation, see Eaton 2007.

24. Anderson 1999. See also Bourgois 1995; Sykes 1997; Contreras 2013.

25. Kimmel and Messner 2012.

26. Jones 2010, 11.

27. Jones 2010, 78.

28. Sykes 1997; Miller 2008; Contreras 2013.

29. See Edin and Kefalas 2005 for a discussion on short-lived relationships prior to and after pregnancies and births.

30. Mollborn and Jacobs (2012) argue that there is less economic and social support and less approval for adolescent mothering in low-income urban communities than have been reported in earlier studies.

31. See also Edin and Kefalis 2005.

32. Symbolic violence describes the cultural mechanisms through which oppressive conditions are viewed as the natural order of things, generating a sociospatial or territorial stigma and an associated sense of indignity in which individuals are held morally culpable for their own social locations. Wacquant (2008) and Bourgois and Schonberg (2009) provide particularly good discussions of this.

33. Jones 2010.

34. Pollin and Luce 1998; Krugman 2009.

35. Fine and Weis 1999.

36. For a fuller discussion of this narrative, see Erdmans 2012b. Of interest were the times that one of the white interviewers did not question the contradictions. We surmise that the interviewer herself was operating within a white racial frame that was less likely to see dysfunction in white families. Kelley (2000) talks about the "wrong family frame" as a discourse of teen pregnancies, and these whitewashing narratives could be seen as a way to manage this frame. See Schmidt 1995 for a discussion of hiding narratives of trauma as related to sexual abuse.

37. See Burton 1990; Hagan and Wheaton 1993; Fernandez-Kelly 1994.

38. See Edin and Kefalis 2005 for an elaboration of this point. Fernandez-Kelly argues that there are "few milestones in poor neighborhoods that people can call upon to separate stages in their life-cycles." Having a baby distinguishes them. It is "about the articulation of meaning, not solely the consequence of careless behavior" (1994, 104).

39. A true assessment of whether the baby changed their life would require interviews with them when they were at least 30 years old (Hotz, McElroy, and Sanders 2008; Furstenburg 2007).

40. See Hagan and Wheaton 1993.

CHAPTER 5. EDUCATION

1. Numerous studies look at the relation between early childbirth and school dropout, leading to this wide range of estimates (Upchurch and McCarthy 1990; Luker 1996; Manlove 1998; Gest, Mahoney, and Cairns 1999; Kelly 2000; Yampolskaya, Brown, and Greenbaum 2002; Beutel 2000; Luttrell 2003). Nationally in 1999, 11.2 percent of youth between the ages of 16 and 24 were high school dropouts: non-Hispanic whites were least likely to drop out (7.3 percent), followed by non-Hispanic blacks (12.6 percent) and Hispanics (28.6 percent) (Kaufman et. al. 2000, iii). See also National Institute of Child Health and Human Development 1998. Even though teen mothers are more likely to complete high school than they were 40 years ago, graduation rates have increased for all teenagers, so young mothers are still relatively disadvantaged.

2. Hofferth, Reid, and Mott 2001. Controlling for disadvantage, they found that age at first birth was not a statistically significant predictor for high school completion (measured as a diploma and not as a GED certificate), but it was significant for having completed some college (2001, 264–266).

3. Wilson 1987; Weis, Farrar, and Petrie 1989; Danziger and Farber 1990; Crane 1991; Mayer 1991; Duncan et al. 1998; Lewis, Ross, and Mirowsky 1999; Seccombe 2000; Bettie 2003; Harding 2003. Longitudinal studies show the disastrous educational effects of persistent poverty (Haveman, Wolfe, and Spaulding 1991; Axinn, Duncan, and Thornton 1997; Smith, Brooks-Gunn, and Klebanov 1997; Conger, Conger, and Elder 1997; Haveman, Wolfe, and Wilson 1997; Pagani, Boulerice, and Tremblay 1997). Entwisle and Alexander coined the term "summer setback" to understand why "children in poverty do well in

the winter but suffer losses in summer" (1992, 82). Forste and Tienda (1992) found that poverty had a more salient effect on graduation rates for Hispanics teens than black or white teens; however, Fine argues that income matters more than race or ethnicity, pointing to one finding that in the lowest income quartile, whites dropped out more than blacks or Hispanics (1991, 22).

4. CT State Department of Education, 2008, www.cmtreports.com /CMTCode/Report.aspx.

5. The cumulative dropout rate in Connecticut for the Class of 2002 was 10.8 percent, and for the individual school districts: Bridgeport 31.9 percent, New London 30.8 percent, Hartford 28.7 percent, and New Britain 28.6 percent (Lohman 2004).

6. Hotz, McElroy, and Sanders 2008, 53, italics in original.

7. Hotz, McElroy, and Sanders 2008, 61–64.

8. Teen birth was defined as having had a child before the age of 18. Educational attainment was measured at the age of 30. School completion (diploma or GED) was 68 percent for teen mothers compared to 64 percent if they delayed childbearing (Hotz, McElroy, and Sanders 2008, 68).

9. Luker 1996,123–124, italics in original.

10. Furstenberg, Brooks-Gunn, and Morgan 1987; Butler 1992; Geronimus and Korenman 1992; Records 1993; Bickel et al. 1997; Bissell 2000; Geronimus 2003; Furstenberg 2007; Hotz, McElroy, and Sanders 2008. While Rumbaut uses survey data to claim that early childbearing among the children of immigrants (especially Mexicans and Puerto Ricans) "derails" education trajectories, he admits that "the temporary order" of the effect of early childbearing "on educational attainment cannot be clearly established" (2005, 1077).

11. In response to New York City's ad campaign in March 2013 that was seen by many as publicly shaming teen mothers, Sarah Brown, the CEO of The National Campaign to Prevent Teen and Unplanned Pregnancy, said in a radio interview that she was in favor of the ads because "they are true." In particular she noted the negative relationship between adolescent childbirth and high school completion ("Teen Pregnancy Ads: Shame Campaign?" March 20, 2013, National Public Radio, *Tell Me More,* host Michael Martin).

12. Furstenberg found that when measured in the early years after the birth, teen mothers did fall behind their peers on educational attainment, but that 30 years after having a child, only one-fifth of the mothers did not have a high school diploma or GED certificate (2007, 38).

13. The GED certificate does not have the same value as a diploma (Horowitz 1995; Hofferth, Reid, and Mott 2001).

14. Horowitz's evaluation of a GED program for young mothers led her to define the certificate as a "moral indicator" and to challenge the idea that a GED certificate was a "ticket into a 'good job'" (1995, 109). See also Black 2009 for a similar discussion of the lack of educational value in GED programs for poor minority men.

15. Becker 1963, 23, italics in original.

16. Kelly (2000) also notes the term "drop out" is ambiguous because it implies that students leave and never return to school, and yet many do. It also implies that exiting from school is a matter of choice, even though many schools

push students out. See McCargar 2011 for an analysis of how students are pushed out of schools in Connecticut.

17. See Erdmans 2012a for more details on how these barriers represent violations of Title IX.

18. See Kirby 2002 for an overview of the research. Studies have found that problems in school precede pregnancy (Wasserman et al. 1990; Coles 1997; Yampolskaya, Brown, and Greenbaum 2002), that teen births exacerbate already existing school problems (Marini 1984; Allen et al. 1997; Corcoran 1998; Beutel 2000), and that high levels of school engagement were associated with postponing pregnancy (Manlove 1998; Fertility of American Women 2003).

19. If she left high school and later enrolled in night school or GED classes, we defined her as a dropout. If she was on bed rest in her ninth month and received home schooling and returned to school soon after her child was born, we did not define her as dropping out. The important distinction was whether there was a substantial break or disengagement from the school. For a discussion of the various and problematic definitions of "dropout," see Weis, Farrar, and Petrie 1989 and Neild and Balfanz 2006.

20. This distribution is similar to what other studies have found. Manlove (1998) found that 28 percent of adolescent mothers dropped out before pregnancy and 30 percent after pregnancy. Luker estimated that one-quarter to one-third of mothers dropped out before they were pregnant (1996, 120–124). Fergusson and Woodward (2000) found that nearly two-thirds of young mothers had dropped out for some period of time before they became pregnant.

21. We made the assessment of "being integrated" by looking at grades, truancy, the extent to which they had friends who attended the same school, whether they played sports or participated in school clubs, and overall whether they enjoyed going to school. Four of the five mothers who were in Advanced Placement classes never dropped out of school; 70 percent of those who never dropped out were in regular classes as compared to only 55 percent of those who dropped out before pregnancy. For those who never dropped out, 73 percent had a mother who completed high school (diploma or GED) compared to only 42 percent who dropped out before pregnancy. Studies have found mothers' education to be a significant predictor of school achievement (Haveman and Wolfe 1995; Peters and Mullis 1997; Lewis, Ross, and Mirowsky 1999; Teachman et al. 1997).

22. Studies have found school-related factors correlated with lower risk of teen pregnancy and birth to include playing sports (Miller et al. 1999; Sabo et al. 1999; Bearman and Brückner 2001; Eitle and Eitle 2002) and being involved in school clubs (Moore, Nord, and Peterson 1989).

23. Only one student with a cognitive impairment completed high school, and this mother was 19 when she became pregnant, had been in special education classes throughout her schooling, and after she became pregnant completed her education at an alternative school for pregnant students. See Prater 1992 for a case study of "slow learners" and adolescent mothers.

24. Scholars have argued that dropping out is related to absent parents and a lack of supervision (Danziger and Farber 1990; Astone and McLanahan 1991; Haveman, Wolfe, and Wilson 1997; Brown et al. 2004; Bridgeland, DiIulio, and Morison 2006).

25. SmithBattle also found that the teen mothers who dropped out before pregnancy lived in a "very poor, segregated city known for its inferior school system," while the nine who were still in school "lived in more prosperous areas" (2007, 413).

26. While most of the mothers in our study said they hoped to finish high school, the fact that only five students had taken Advanced Placement classes suggests that few saw high school as preparation for college. It is easier to leave school when the payoffs for finishing school diminish. In her study of teen mothers, Fernandez-Kelly also found "skepticism about the rewards of education" (1994, 102).

27. The mean age of first birth was lower for Spanish speakers (16.7) than for non-Spanish speakers (17.0). Teen mothers born in Puerto Rico dropped out at the same rate as those who were born on the mainland (67 percent vs. 63 percent), but were less likely to drop out before they were pregnant (19 percent versus 41 percent).

28. For white mothers in our study, nearly one-half of them left school before pregnancy, compared to less than one-third of Puerto Rican mothers and one-quarter of African American mothers. Puerto Rican and African American mothers were more likely to leave after pregnancy.

29. National data show that Hispanic teen mothers are much less likely to have graduated from high school compared to non-Hispanic black and white mothers (Martin et al. 2003, 60–61). Manlove (1998) found that high levels of school engagement were associated with postponing pregnancy for all racial and ethnic groups (see also Beutel 2000); however, the relationship between dropping out and early pregnancy was highest for Latinas and lowest for black mothers. Luker documents that black teen mothers are more likely to graduate than white teen mothers (1996, 121), and other studies confirm that blacks are more likely than whites to be in school when they are pregnant and after they have a child (Stevenson, Maton, and Teti 1998; see also Haveman, Wolfe, and Wilson 1997, 429). Forste and Tienda (1992) found that blacks were more likely to get pregnant than whites and Hispanics, yet their graduation rates were similar to whites and significantly higher than Hispanics. They assert that the "experience of a teen birth had less of a deleterious effect for blacks than it did for whites," and that becoming a teen mother was "the most significant factor determining school outcomes for Hispanics" (1992, 25).

30. McIntosh et al. 2008, 244.

31. Hertzog and Morgan 1999; Mizelle and Irvin 2000; Newman et al. 2000; Neild and Balfanz 2006; McIntosh et al. 2008.

32. Simpson 2007.

33. Other scholars agree that no one factor explains school failure (Gleason and Dynarski 2002); instead, they see a "matrix of disadvantage" (Mullen et al. 1994), whereby dropping out is the culmination of a long-term process (Astone and McLanahan 1991; Alexander, Entwisle, and Horsey 1997) that begins in elementary school (Pagani, Boulerice, and Tremblay 1997; Bridgeland, DiIulio, and Morison 2006) and is embedded in class and racial/ethnic inequality (Fine 1991; Lareau 2003; McIntosh et al. 2008; Black 2009).

34. Numerous studies have found a relation between residential mobility, school transience, and school performance (Haveman, Wolfe, and Spaulding

1991; Haveman and Wolfe 1995; Alexander, Entwisle, and Horsey 1997; Moore, Nord, and Peterson 1998; Franke, Isken, and Parra 2003).

35. Kelly 1998; Sun 2001.

36. All four black mothers who dropped out before pregnancy told us that they experienced domestic violence in their homes, as did seven of the 11 Puerto Rican mothers, and nine of the 17 white mothers.

37. Tapia 2004; Ream 2005; Stearns and Glennie 2006; Gandara and Contreras 2009, 70.

38. Garcia 2001. Gandara and Contreras argue that when students are placed in inadequate bilingual courses their overall educational progress suffers, and this contributes to high rates of school dropout (2009, 122–123).

39. Acosta-Belén and Santiago 2006, 3. See also Rivera-Batiz and Santiago 1994 and Torre, Vecchini, and Burgos 1994.

40. Nieto 1992; Flores-Gonzales 2002; Black 2009; Gandara and Contreras 2009. One in four Puerto Ricans in the United States (mainland) was living below the poverty level in 2000 (Acosta-Belén and Santiago 2006, 131). According to the report *English Language Learners, School Year 2009–10*, in Connecticut 73 percent of the ELL were Spanish speakers, and only 53.4 percent of the ELL students graduated compared to 80.6 percent of the non-ELL students. Moreover, three-quarters of the ELL were eligible for free or reduced lunches. http://sdeportal.ct.gov/Cedar/Files/Pdf/Reports/db_ell_report_11_2010.pdf.

41. The State of America's Children 2008, 24. www.childrensdefense.org /child-research-data-publications/data/state-of-americas-children-2008-report .pdf.

42. Fine argues that the real problem is that schools are "structured in ways that do not accommodate students experiencing family problems" (1991, 77). Of course, strong intact families, especially when there is a tight family-school dynamic, decrease the risk of school dropout and teenage pregnancy (Astone and McLanahan 1991; Manlove 1998), but the question is, how do schools manage the education of children when there is not a tight family-school dynamic?

43. For a comparison of middle schools and high schools, see Bickel et al. 1997; Hertzog and Morgan 1999; Mizelle and Irvin 2000. Bridgeland, DiIulio, and Morison (2006) refer to the problem of a "one size fits all" school that needs to be revised. One response to this has been to create smaller, separate ninth grade schools as bridges between middle and high school. Fine found that ELL and bilingual classes helped to build safe, comfortable places in the school where the students took care of one another, encouraged one another, and created a "shared sense of inclusion and cooperation" (1991, 55). Fine and Zane (1989) recommend that large high schools be divided into smaller units that promote more familiarity, solidarity, and community-building.

44. In one study, 45 percent of the dropouts said they were poorly prepared for high school, 32 percent had repeated a grade, and 35 percent said that "failing" in school was the reason for dropping out (Bridgeland, DiIulio, and Morison 2006). Fine and Zane (1989) found that the demands of family responsibilities, which fall disproportionately on the shoulders of adolescent females (and are exacerbated by poverty), become overwhelming when they collide with the increased demand and decreased familiarity of large public high schools.

45. See Rios 2011 for a discussion of how delinquency is a form of resistance to negative labeling in school. Fallis and Opotow argue that cutting classes becomes the grounds for moral exclusion and a form of structural violence when students are blamed for institutional failures (2003, 112). We should note, however, that our understanding of these problems is based on the young mothers' testimonies. We did not interview teachers or administrators, and so we only have the views of our study participants—but we did see patterns across several of the life stories.

46. One school in New Britain, for example, working with chronically truant students, has an intervention team that includes educators, social service providers, police, probation officers, and Connecticut Department of Social Service workers. After 11 years, it has a success rate of 98 percent. However, in a school district with 11,000 students, this program provides services to only 40 students a year (Burgard 2007).

47. In Connecticut, the median public school student-teacher ratio for high school for the 1999–2000 school year was approximately 13:1, while the ratio for private schools was 3:1 (National Center for Educational Statistics, nces.ed.gov/pubs2001/overview/table06.asp).

48. McCargar 2011. Her report on schools in Connecticut documents how students were counseled out of school, without due process, and placed in alternative schools and adult education programs. She found that nearly one-third of students in adult education programs in Connecticut were teenagers within the legal age limit of high school. Unlike the comprehensive intervention identified in note 47, adult education programs are often less rigorous and less expensive. In 2009, the average per pupil expenditure for students in regular schools, K–12, was $13,607, compared to $1,602 per student in adult education programs (2011, 5–6).

49. This also happened to a native-born white mother who spent her adolescence in a Scandinavian country because of her father's work. While she spoke English at home, her reading and writing skills were not strong. In Connecticut she lived in a small, mostly white town, and there was no ELL program in the school. She had some problems in school (low grades and fighting with other girls) and was classified as "slow" (even though, she said, she received good grades in math and science). She was placed in special education courses, where she "felt like a dummy." Discouraged and stigmatized, she started skipping classes and spending time with her older boyfriend, who had his own apartment. She dropped out in tenth grade.

50. Oakes discusses the limitations of vocational school experiences, noting that they often serve to prepare minority students for low-paying jobs. She agrees with other scholars who find "the underlying function of vocational education has been to segregate poor and minority students into occupational training programs in order to preserve the academic curriculum for middle- and upper-class students" (2005, 153).

51. See Bettie (2003), who also noticed, in her ethnography of a public high school in California that teachers would say nothing to the Latina students who were sharing baby pictures in class, which Bettie interpreted as evidence of the teachers' low academic expectations for them (chapter 3).

52. McCargar 2011, 4. Suspensions are only one of the exclusionary school policies designed to push out students with problems rather than provide sufficient counseling, additional mentoring, or special needs education. See also Farrar and Hampel 1989; Fine 1991; Kelly 2000; Bridgeland, DiIulio, and Morison 2006.

53. These school districts have the highest suspension rates in the state (Frahm and Kaufman 2007). Carter (2005) found black and Latina students in the Yonkers Public School System were suspended at disproportionately higher rates than white students in the 1990s after an attempt at desegregation using a magnet school system (2005, xi). Zero-tolerance policies passed in the wake of high-profile events of school violence are also a part of the structure that pushes students out of schools (Mongan and Walker 2012). Administrators assessing the effects of these programs have found they cause more harm than good (American Psychological Association Zero-Tolerance Task Force 2008). The National Association of School Psychologists issued a communiqué critical of these policies, which are in practice disproportionately more punitive for minority students, students with disabilities, and students in urban schools (www. nasponline.org/publications/cq/mocq375zerotolerance.aspx). See also a policy statement by the American Academy of Pediatrics that calls for a review of suspension and expulsion practices in the wake of "zero-tolerance" because of the adverse effect these policies have on student retention (http://pediatrics.aappublications.org/content/131/3/e1000).

54. Studies have found that students retained a grade have an increased chance of dropping out (Fine 1991, 71; Bridgeland, DiIulio, and Morison 2006) and getting pregnant (Manlove 1998; Moore, Nord, and Peterson 1998; Clark et al. 2003, 112).

55. For an excellent discussion of this case, see Eaton 2007, parts 3 and 4.

56. Eaton 2007, 162.

57. Eaton 2007, 177.

58. *Sheff v. O'Neill* 1996.

59. Dougherty, 2012.

60. Students in regional magnet schools and the Open Choice (suburban school enrollments) program outperformed students in regular Hartford schools on the Connecticut Mastery Test, with a few schools performing above the state averages in some tested areas (Megan 2012).

61. See Wells and Crain 1997 for a discussion of how institutional racism becomes internalized and then manifest in ideologies and strategies regarding school choice. They found that African Americans had been "faced with hostile responses to their entry into white schools" (16), and thereby resisted integration and embraced a separatist ideology. They also identified a group they dubbed "white is right" who had an assimilationist policy and "tried hard to cross the color line. . . only to be treated less than equal by whites" (17). Black students who had bad experiences in white suburban schools and ended up returning to the city schools said that they were pushed out by disciplinary policies that they felt reflected racial bias, that they found white students unfriendly and did not feel comfortable in the suburban environment, and that the academic coursework was more difficult than in the city schools (223–225). Prudence Carter, who studied the desegregation attempts in the Yonkers school

system, argues that student engagement in school is shaped by "noncognitive factors such as 'fitting into school' or feelings of inclusiveness . . . [and] students' perceptions of fitting in are linked to their ideologies of themselves as racial, ethnic, cultural, and gendered beings" (2005, 11). The revised initiative in Hartford acknowledged that more academic and social support was necessary to enhance the success of these programs.

62. Linares et al. (1991) found that depressive symptoms preceded dropping out and teen pregnancy.

63. Ng and Kaye 2013. Carr and Kefalas's study of a rural community in Iowa found that marriage and childbirth were likely to occur close together and three years earlier, typically around the age of 21, among women who did not leave the area to attend a four-year college (2009, 73–76). They conclude that single-motherhood and poverty were on the rise in rural areas and resembled earlier trends associated with distressed urban areas. See a recent report by The National Campaign that examines teen birth rates in rural counties, showing that while they declined between 1990 and 2010, the decline was slower than in suburban and urban areas (http://thenationalcampaign.org/resource/science-says-47).

64. In their study of dropouts, Bridgeland, DiIulio, and Morison found that one-third of the students dropped out because they had to get a job to make money, and 22 percent said they had to care for a family member (2006, iii). See Debold et al. (1999, 185). Fine (1991) also found family responsibility was a common reason for dropping out of school.

65. See Waters et al. 2011. The *twixter* generation, or the new "adultolescent" stage of life (students on the six-year college plan, postcollege students moving home with parents), more aptly describes middle-class families. In an edited volume, Richard Settersten Jr. found that while many middle-class young adults are postponing marriage and childbirth until they are "ready," others are entering these stages "before they are ready" (2011, 173). With this growing age gap in fertility timing norms, early childbearing for low-income populations makes them more susceptible to being branded irresponsible. For these populations, however, when the traditional markers of adulthood are harder to achieve (schooling, employment, economic self-sufficiency), having a child early becomes one of the few markers available.

66. Bettie found that for girls who did not look forward to college as their route to adulthood, "motherhood and the responsibility that comes with it can be employed to gain respect, marking adult status" (2003, 69). Anderson writes that for inner-city, low-income teens, motherhood "becomes a rite of passage to adulthood" (1991, 383). See also Luker 1996, 120–124; Bickel et al. 1997; Edin and Kefalas 2005.

67. Fernandez-Kelly writes, "motherhood represents the extension of responsibilities assumed at an early age and expresses a specific relationship with the labor market" (1994, 104).

68. Only six mothers (15 percent) who never dropped out of school said that they intended the pregnancy, and four of them were older than 17 when they became pregnant. Rubin and East (1999) found that adolescent mothers who intended a pregnancy were more likely to have dropped out of school before they were pregnant.

69. Horowitz found that teen mothers wanted respect and enjoyed the more equal status they had with their own mothers who would "include them in adult activities and supervise them less" (1995, 154).

70. See Erdmans (2012a) for a discussion of the importance of Title IX legislation for pregnant and mothering students as well as violations of the mandates. Others also found that teen mothers most likely to finish high school were still attending when they became pregnant (Leadbeater 1996). Upchurch and McCarthy (1990) found that women who were still enrolled in school when they had a child were just as likely to graduate as women who did not have children. See also Danziger and Farber 1990 and Bridgeland, DiIulio, and Morison 2006.

71. http://www.cga.ct.gov/coc/achievement_gap.htm.

72. Brown 2008.

73. See Lareau 2003.

74. Simms argues for a battle on three educational fronts: those students at risk of dropping out; those who just became young parents; and the children of the young parents (1993, 248–251). Rhode also advocates for better school programs and reducing dropout rates as an important prong in any policy designed to prevent pregnancies and lower teen births (1993, 323). And Plotnick suggests that "interventions to improve adolescents' school experiences could have large indirect benefits in terms of reducing premarital childbearing" (1992, 810).

CHAPTER 6. CONTRACEPTION AND ABORTION

1. Abma et al. 2004, table 25. In 2002, only 12 percent of births to mothers under 18 were intended, 29 percent of births to those 18 to 19 years old, and 76 percent to those 25 to 44 years old (2004, table 25). Finer (2010) calculates the rate of unintended pregnancies as 40 per 1000 women between the ages of 15 and 17, but 147 per 1,000 *sexually active* women ages 15 to 17. Abortions are also a measure of unintendedness (Finer and Henshaw 2006).

2. In 2000, 29 percent of pregnancies to females 15 to 19 ended in abortion (Guttmacher Institute 2006, table 3.2). By 2008, this figure dropped to 25.5 percent—with little variation between teens 15 to 17 (26.5 percent) and those 18 and 19 (25 percent) (Ventura, Curtin, and Abma 2012, table 3). Teens are the most likely to end pregnancies in abortion; only 23.6 percent of women 20 to 24 ended their pregnancies in abortion in 2008, and the percent is lower for all other age groups, with women 35 to 39 having the fewest pregnancies ending in abortion (12.9 percent) though the percent increases to 18.3 for women over 40 (2012, table 3). All references are to induced abortions (as opposed to fetal losses).

3. Martin et al. 2010, table 2.

4. In the National Survey of Family Growth (NSFG) 2006–2008, among 15- to 17-year-olds, 72 percent of females (and 71 percent of males) reported they had never had sex (Abma, Martinez, and Copen 2010, tables 9 and 10). In addition, 18 percent of females (and 19 percent of males) had had sexual intercourse in the three months prior to the survey (table 3), while only 6 percent of females

were having sexual intercourse on a regular basis (4 times or more in the month prior) (table 5).

5. Abma, Martinez, and Copen 2010. Among 15- to 17-year-old virgins, 38 percent said they had not had sex for moral or religious reasons, and 22 percent said they did not want to get pregnant (table 18). In addition, 61 percent of females age 15 to 17 said they would be "very upset" if they became pregnant, and 29 percent said they would be "a little upset." Interestingly, only 53 percent of males that age would be "very upset" and 32 percent "a little upset" (table 21).

6. The 2009 National Survey of Sexual Health and Behavior (NSSHB) of 14- to 17-year-old adolescents found the steepest increase in sexual experience for females between the ages of 15 and 16 (12 percent to 32 percent) (Fortenberry et al. 2010, 307–311). In the 2006–2008 NSFG, among females who reported they had ever had sex, 26 percent said they had their first sexual experience before age 15, while 46 percent had their first experience between ages 15 and 16, and 28 percent between ages 17 and 19 (Abma, Martinez, and Copen 2010, table 7). In another national survey of 1,800 unmarried men and women age 18 through 29, roughly one-half of females who had ever had sex said they initiated it before they were 17 (Kaye, Suellentrop, and Sloup 2009, 20).

7. Given that we sampled from a disadvantaged population of mothers, 20 percent is probably an underrepresentation. A point we want to stress in this chapter, however, is that even though teen mothers are more likely to have been sexually abused as children (chapter 3), to experience higher rates of school failure (chapter 5), and to be poor or very poor (80 percent according to Luker 1996, 39)—a sizeable number are not socially or economically disadvantaged.

8. Kaplan 1997.

9. Goffman 1963.

10. Albert 2010, 15.

11. Abma, Martinez, and Copen 2010, 10.

12. Kaplan outlined the community norms: "if a girl did not steal, was not truant from school, and did not have a baby before marriage, she was a good girl. Bad girls were deviants—people who, in the eyes of society, have 'engaged in some kind of collective denial of the social order,' as Erving Goffman put it" (1997, 12). Walkerdine, Lucey, and Melody use the term "good girls" in reference to daughters "always trying to please, particularly their fathers," but they always bracket the term in quotation marks (2001, 200–201).

13. "Teen Pregnancy Ads: Shame Campaign?" March 20, 2013, National Public Radio, Tell Me More, host Michael Martin.

14. See Walkerdine, Lucey, and Melody 2001 for a discussion of the psychosocial effects of pregnancy outcomes for upwardly mobile, working-class girls in Britain.

15. See Goffman 1963, 28, for a discussion of how an individual's stigma is shared by the family.

16. Kaplan also found that mothers felt the stigma of their daughters' pregnancies and were angry and resentful toward their daughters (1996, 429).

17. Other scholars found that that teen mothers know that they are violating social norms which require that they manage the stigma of being a deviant (Horowitz 1995; Lipper 2003, 324–325; Luttrell 2003, 21).

18. Taborn 1990; Zabin and Hirsch 1992; Lipper, 2003, 277.

19. As Dr. Patrick Fagan (1999) of the Heritage Foundation put it.

20. Sutherland 2002–2003, 334–335.

21. Nathanson 1991, 170. Attitudes on premarital sex have flipped: in 1969, 68 percent of people thought it wrong but only 32 percent in 2009 (Pew Research Center Publications 2010, 4).

22. Garcia 2012, chapter 3.

23. According to NSFG data, for teens 15 to 17, the pregnancy rate was 37.2 in 1988 and dropped to 27.7 in 2006–2008 (Abma, Martinez, and Copen 2010, table 1). The most significant decline was between 1990 and 2004, when pregnancy rates for all teens 15 to 17 declined 45 percent (48 percent for black and white teens, and 21 percent for Hispanics) (Ventura et al. 2008, 4–5).

24. Furstenberg 2007, 95; Abma, Martinez, and Copen 2010, 11.

25. Data on sexual experience are from the NSFG (Abma, Martinez, and Copen 2010, table 1). For teens age 15 to 17, the decline between 1995 and 2002 was steeper for Hispanic females (49 percent to 25 percent) than whites (36 percent to 30 percent) and blacks (49 percent to 41 percent) (Abma et al. 2004, table 1, Supplement). According to the Youth Risk Behavior Survey (YRBS) of students in grades 9 to 12, sexual experience increased sharply in the 1970s and more gradually in the 1980s; however, between 1991 and 1997, sexual experience declined from 54 percent to 48 percent and has stayed just under 50 percent since then (Furstenberg 2007, 95). In the 2009 YRBS in Connecticut, roughly one-quarter of ninth graders were sexually experienced and two-thirds of seniors (Merritt 2010). Data for sexual activity from the NSFG are that 22 percent of females age 15 to 17 reported they had sexual intercourse in the three months prior to the 2002 survey (Abma et al. 2004, figure 3), and 18.3 percent prior to the 2006–2008 survey (Abma, Martinez, and Copen 2010, table 3). Using YRBS data, Santelli et al. report that sexual activity (during the prior three months) did not change significantly between 1991 and 2007, except for a decline among black students (2009, 29).

26. See Furstenberg 2007; Santelli et al. 2006, 2009; Abma, Martinez, and Copen 2010. Scholars have found that when contraceptive use is restricted, pregnancy rates are higher (Lundberg and Plotnick 1990).

27. Darroch and Singh 1999, 8; Alan Guttmacher Institute 2002. Furstenberg (2007, 93–96) is skeptical that abstinence programs contributed to any of the decline given that the steepest decline in sexual activity was in the early 1990s before most abstinence-only programs were introduced, and Bearman and Brückner (2001) found that those who make virginity pledges and then break the pledge are less likely to use contraception the first time they have sex.

28. Abma, Martinez, and Copen 2010, 14. In the 2006–2008 NSFG, 79 percent of females 15 to 19 and 87 percent of men reported that they used contraception the first time they had vaginal intercourse (table 14). YRBS data show that contraceptive use increased the most for ninth graders, whites, and blacks in the 1990s; among females sexually active in the prior three months, only 8.5 percent used no method in 2003 compared to 13 percent in 1991 (Santelli et al. 2006, 108). The Connecticut data from the 2009 YRBS show that

59 percent of sexually actively high school students said they used condoms and 24 percent used birth control pills (Merritt 2010).

29. According to YRBS data, between 1991 and 2003 condom use among high school students increased from 46 percent to 63 percent, then dropped slightly to 61.5 percent in 2007 (Santelli et al. 2009, 26).

30. See Abma, Martinez, and Copen 2010, tables 14 and 15, based on 2006–2008 NSFG data (15 to 19 age group). In 1988, females were most likely to use the pill, but by the 1990s condom use surpassed the pill as the most commonly used method (and many women use both methods simultaneously). Roughly two-thirds of females used condoms the first time they had sex, but only one-half of females who were sexually active used condoms the last time they had sex (table 15). In the 2009 NSSHB, 80 percent of male and 69 percent of female high school students reported using condoms for penile-vaginal intercourse (Fortenberry et al. 2010, 311).

31. Santelli et al. 2006. According the NSFG data (for females age 15 to 19), the use of highly effective injectable contraception such as Depo-Provera and Lunelle doubled from 10 percent to 21 percent between 1995 and 2002 (Abma et al. 2004, 2).

32. NSFG reports a decline between 2002 and 2006–2008 in the use of injectables (21 percent to 17 percent), and oral contraceptives (61 percent to 55 percent), but an increase in periodic abstinence (11 percent to 17 percent) and withdrawal (55 percent to 58 percent) for sexually experienced females 15 to 19 (Abma, Martinez, and Copen 2010, figure 8).

33. Abma, Martinez, and Copen 2010. Among females age 15 to 24, for those who reported they did not use contraception the first time they had sex, the probability of having a child before age 20 was .37 compared to .20 for those who used contraception, and only .07 for those who used more than one form of contraception the first time they had sex (table 17).

34. See Miller 2002 for an overview of studies that look at family influences on contraceptive behavior. See also Zabin and Hirsch 1992; Luster and Small 1994; Rodriguez and Moore 1995; Corcoran, Franklin, and Bennett 2000; Hacker et al. 2000; Hogan, Sun, and Cornwell 2000; Kirby 2002.

35. Rhode 1993–1994, 663; Abma et al. 2004, figures 9, 10; Santelli et al. 2006, 110.

36. Luster and Small 1994; Kowaleski-Jones and Mott 1998; Kirby 2002.

37. For an excellent discussion, see Walkerdine, Lucey, and Melody 2001, chapter 8.

38. According to YRBS 2003 data, 21 percent of sexually active female Hispanic students reported using no method compared to 12 percent of black and 8.5 percent of white students. Whites were twice as likely to use the pill, blacks more likely to use condoms (59 percent) compared to whites (55 percent) and Hispanics (51 percent); and Hispanic and white females were more likely to use withdrawal (12 percent) than blacks (7 percent) (Santelli et al. 2006, table 3). According to NSFG 2006–2008 data, black females 15 to 19 are most likely to report using condoms all the time (65 percent), compared to whites (50 percent) and Hispanics (39 percent) (Abma, Martinez, and Copen 2010, table 16, supplement).

39. Title X provided almost one-quarter of the funding for 4,261 clinics in 2006, and Medicaid provided 30 percent. Almost all of these clinics provide birth control pills, most provide condoms, injectables, and emergency contraceptive pills, and one-quarter of their clients were teenagers (Guttmacher Institute, "Facts on Publicly Funded Contraceptive Services in the United States," May 2010). Edin and Kefalas (2005) also found that poor women in their study had access to birth control through nearby Planned Parenthood clinics, hospitals, or medical clinics.

40. Nathanson 1991, 203, italics in original.

41. Luker (1996) refers to "transitional babies" conceived after the couple broke up and the woman stopped using birth control pills. Edin and Kefalas (2005) found women used condoms at the beginning of a relationship but less often when they became an "exclusive pair" because it would suggest distrust. Garcia also reported that asking a committed partner to use a condom could be a sign of mistrust (2012, 132).

42. See Sanders et al. (2001) for a discussion on oral contraceptive use.

43. Payment for contraception is entangled with political and corporate interests—for example, the controversial debates over the "morning-after" pill (Shear 2013) and insurance payments for contraception in the Affordable Health Care Act (Bronner 2013). As of 2013, 20 states had restrictions on contraception for minors (www.guttmacher.org/statecenter/spibs/spib_OMCL.pdf). In Connecticut, at the time of our study, girls under age 18 needed parental consent for a prescription for hormonal contraception (www.guttmacher.org/pubs/tgr/08/4/gr080406.pdf), but after 2008, minors could obtain birth control without parental consent (www.ct.gov/dcf/lib/dcf/child_welfare_services/pdf/legal_rights_of_teens.pdf).

44. In the NSFG 2006–2008 data (for teens 15 to 19), 96 percent of women reported that they "appreciate" it if a new partner used a condom; and 86 percent of men thought a new partner would appreciate it, and few found condoms embarrassing (10 percent of women and 8 percent of men) (Abma, Martinez, and Copen 2010, table 20). Yet, only 52 percent of females used condoms every time compared to 71 percent of males (Abma, Martinez, and Copen 2010, table 16).

45. In a 2010 survey, 76 percent of adults believed that it is "very important" that "teens be given a strong message that they should not have sex until they are at least out of high school" (Albert 2010, 15).

46. See Tolman 2002, 9–12; Furstenberg 2007, 101; Schalet 2011, 56–66, 73–74.

47. Schalet 2011. She argues that the United States espouses an "adversarial individualism" (the individual exists *apart from* others), while the Netherlands developed "interdependent individualism," where freedoms come from being *a part of* a family and nation. As a result, in Dutch households, longer periods of dependence on the family and early degrees of sexual independence are nurtured; sleepovers are allowed, there are more open conversations about sex and contraception, and the Dutch report being more in control of their first sexual experience and finding it more pleasurable compared to teens in the United States.

48. Tolman 2002, 179. Garcia (2012) found that Latinas hid condoms in their lockers or got a Depo-Provera shot so their mothers would not find their

birth control pills, but she also found that some Latino parents did provide sexual guidance to their daughters (see chapter 1), arguing that the Latino population is not monolithically silent on topics of sex. And yet, a lack of communication between Latino parents and their children is one reason given for the high rate of Latina births, and it became the basis for the program Families Talking Together, sponsored by The National Campaign (Guilamo-Ramos, Lee, and Jaccard 2012).

49. Families vary in their willingness to have these conversations. Kaplan found that parents did not talk to their daughters about these issues because they worried that the discussion itself would encourage sexual activity (1997, 38–39). Freeman and Rickels (1993) found that teens who did not get pregnant had more accurate reproductive health knowledge and were more likely to have learned about birth control from their mothers. See also Rodriguez and Moore 1995; Fay and Yanoff 2000; Ryan, Franzetta, and Manlove 2007.

50. Kaye, Suellentrop, and Sloup 2009, 11. According to NSFG 2002 data, two-thirds of students had received some sex education in school before age 18 (Abma et al. 2004, table 26). And yet, there is no consistent evidence that sex education programs influence sexual behavior, contraceptive use, or chance of pregnancy (Scher 2008; Furstenberg 2007). The only program that has shown some promise is the Carrera approach, which is expensive and labor intensive (McKay 2002).

51. The Human Growth and Development Curriculum provides a set of guidelines for age-appropriate education, but each school district decides its own curriculum and parents have the right to take their children out of school when the sex education curriculum is taught. www.cga.ct.gov/2008/TOB /H/2008HB-05591-R01-HB.htm.

52. See *Blueprint* 2010. Information also comes from a conversation Mary had with the NBHS nurse practitioner on October 21, 2010. NBHS had roughly 2,700 students in the 2010–2011 school year. In a one-month period in 2010, five students tested positive for chlamydia.

53. www.wfsb.com/story/19560387/controversy-over-giving-teens-condoms-at-new-britain-high-school.

54. The 2009 YRBS in Connecticut found that high school students relied more on one another for information about sexual health than their parents or the school-based programs (Merritt 2010). See also Kaye, Suellentrop, and Sloup 2009, which shows that most information comes from the media and much of it is inaccurate.

55. In a national survey of unmarried adults ages 18 to 29, of those who had used birth control pills, 44 percent thought that they should not use them all year long; among those who had used periodic abstinence (also known as rhythm), 40 percent did not know the most common fertile time of the month; among those using condoms, 47 percent thought it was okay to use petroleum jelly; and 18 percent believed douching prevented pregnancy (Kaye, Suellentrop, and Sloup 2009). See also Balassone 1989; Lawson 1993; Buckingham and Derby 1997; Kaplan 1997.

56. Albert 2010, 27. See also Kaye, Suellentrop, and Sloup 2009.

57. Luker, 2006, chapter 8. In 1921, Sweden established sex education in secondary schools and has since developed age-appropriate, comprehensive sex

education for all levels. In contrast, in France, sex education is limited to after-school programs that were not started until the late 1980s. Despite these differences, both countries have lower teen births rates than the United States.

58. Luker 2006. Schalet also found that the Dutch initiate sexual activity at about the same age, but the United States has significantly higher rates of teen pregnancies and births (2011, 77, table 1.2, p. 226).

59. Luker 2006. She also makes this point in her earlier work *Dubious Conceptions*.

60. Luker 2006, 258.

61. Tolman 2002. Tolman interviewed 30 girls, asking them directly about their sexual desires (not behaviors), yet never found the "secret life of sexuality" she presumed was there. Even though the teens had agreed to be interviewed about sexual desire, some of the girls went mute, others talked about sex without intimacy, and one respondent called Tolman a "pervert" (2002, 36). Fine (1988) also identified the missing discourse of desire and the negative consequences this had for young women.

62. Tolman 2002, 44–45. Tolman and Szalacha found that while most girls adopted a male narrative of desire—with the body and pleasure at the center—they also questioned "their entitlement to their own sexual feelings" and expressed "doubt about the possibility of acting directly on their own desire and then being considered good and normal" (1999, 15–16).

63. Tolman and Szalacha 1999, 16.

64. Tolman (2002) interprets this "it just happened" response to mean "I can't acknowledge desire" and argues that there is probably more agency in their sexual relations than they expressed. See also Sutherland 2002–2003, 334; Bettie 2003, 69; Furstenberg 2007, 101.

65. For example, when Roxanne said she "came up pregnant," the interviewer did not flesh out details. In general, interviewers readily asked follow-up questions about work, school, the father of the baby, and state resources, and they were even eager to probe about domestic violence, incarceration, and corporal punishment, but they did not encourage mothers to talk about sex (neither sexual abuse nor sexual desire).

66. In a qualitative study of 120 teenagers, Fay and Yanoff (2000) found that sex occurred without a lot of discussion about birth control, and the discussion was almost never at the time of sexual activity because they were worried about what their partners would think, and because they were often intoxicated.

67. Tolman 2002. See Tolman's (2002) story of Jenny pp. 60–65, as well as pp. 78–79.

68. Rhode 1993–1994, 657. Kaplan found teen mothers "valued the spontaneity and romance," which "would have been compromised by planning for sex" (1997, 41). Hacker et al. (2000) found that not expecting to have sex was why teens did not use contraception. See also Horowitz 1995, 116, and Furstenberg 2007, 101.

69. Starkman and Rajani 2002; Furstenberg 2007, chapter 4.

70. Lawson 1993, 112–116; Tolman 2002, chapter 5.

71. Lawson writes: "Young women blame themselves for their male partners' sexual feelings (simultaneously denying their own) and take responsibility

for placating him. . . . She does not hold him responsible for arousing her; he is not expected to take responsibility for pleasing her" (1993, 114).

72. Garcia notes that even "the simple act of opening the door to a health center requires girls to negotiate their own understanding of their sexuality, as well as to reckon with what others expect of them or think of their sexuality" (2012, 3). See also Stepp (2013) who discusses the problem of buying condoms in small towns.

73. See Oberman 1994. Kaplan writes, "sexual naiveté is advantageous since a knowledgeable girl may be labeled as being 'too smart for her own good,' and only 'bad' girls develop strategies about sexual activity" (1997, 43). The double standard holds true in Britain, where girls are called "slags" and "tarts" (Walkerdine, Lucey, and Melody 2001, 194).

74. Horowitz found that girls wanted to be considered attractive and having a boyfriend was an indication they were attractive (1995, 116). Tolman asked one teen what "feeling sexy" feels like, and she answered by describing how she would appear beautiful to others who would be thinking, "Oh my gosh, she must have 30 boyfriends outside of school" (2001, 137). One study found girls took longer to feel secure in their physical attractiveness than did boys (Lawson 1993, 112). In a 2010 survey, 63 percent of teens (and 72 percent of adults) agreed that boys are "expected to have sex" and 71 percent of teens (and 77 percent of adults) agreed that girls "receive the message that attracting boys and looking sexy is one of the most important things they can do" (Albert 2010, 6).

75. Rhode and Lawson 1993, 7.

76. Young et al. (2001) found that girls who became pregnant were more likely to have an external locus of control and a poor sense of personal efficacy. See also Orenstein 1995; Pipher 1998; and Miller et al. 1999 for a discussion of self-esteem. In contrast, Robinson and Frank (1994) found no relation between self-esteem, sexual activity, and virginity, and no difference in self-esteem between pregnant and nonpregnant teenagers. And yet, Kowaleski-Jones and Mott found differences between sexually active men and women, with young men feeling "in control of their environment," and young women being depressed and having "feelings of failure and lack control" (1998, 168).

77. Tolman writes that not being aware of their own desire "renders them vulnerable by undermining the credibility of their resistance to unwanted sex" (2002, 79).

78. According to the 2006–2008 NSFG, for those who had sexual intercourse before age 20, only 43 percent of females but 62 percent of males reported they "wanted" their first sexual experience when it happened (Abma, Martinez, and Copen 2010, figure 4).

79. We should note that Schalet found that teen boys also express ambivalence and misgivings around sexual experience and that they do value romantic relationships (2011, 12, 22).

80. Garcia found that even girls who expressed strong feelings of self-esteem and agency nonetheless had difficulties talking with their partners about using condoms (2012, 116–117).

81. Tolman found that because girls wanted to be seen as "good" they did not tell their mothers they were having sex (2002, 179). Schalet talks about how being

a "good daughter" in the United States is incompatible with being sexually active so they keep it a secret (2011, 21–24). See Goffman 1963 for a discussion of the distinction between discredited (known) and discreditable (not yet known) stigmas.

82. Rhode 1993–1994, 641 (and only 1 percent of black teens chose adoption). See also Fessler 2006 for an excellent book on mothers who surrendered their children to adoption in the 1950s and 1960s. Being white, Catholic, and doing well in school are associated with choosing adoption (Ryan and Dunn 1988; Remez 1992; Luker 1996; Hope, Wilder, and Watt 2003).

83. See Horowitz 1995, 153; Kaplan 1996, 434; Lipper 2003, 69, 284; Edin and Kefalas 2005, 43; Jones, Frohwirth, and Moore 2008.

84. The Catholic teen mothers that Coles (1997) interviewed defined abortion as "killing," and derided the hypocrisy of their parents for wanting them to have an abortion at the same time that they were attending mass and professing faith in a religion that condemns abortions.

85. Luttrell discusses agency as being about "connection" and "responsibility" and "taking the consequences"—it is about what they do after they get pregnant and not about what they might have done to prevent the pregnancy (2003, 127).

86. Rhode 1993–1994, 646. Poor, young, and minority women were most at risk for illegal and unsafe abortions.

87. Between 1972 and 1978, abortion rates for teens 15 to 19 rose from 19.1 to 39.7; for teens 15 to 17, the rate stayed around 30 abortions per 1,000 during the 1980s (Guttmacher Institute 2006, table 2.2). Abortions are often underreported in surveys (Landale and Hauan 1996; Kaufman et al. 1998, 1145).

88. The 1976 Hyde amendment restricted federal funding for abortions except for when the mother's life was threatened or in cases of rape or incest, required parental notification of and permission for teenagers in some states, and created the so-called squeal rule, which mandated that clinics receiving Title X funds notify the parents of teens under age 18. Not all states followed these federal guidelines. In 1992, 17 states allowed Medicaid payments for abortions, including Connecticut, and, not surprisingly, there are fewer teen births in states where public funding is available to low-income women (Harris 1996, 130, chapter 5; Boonstra 2007). Abortion restrictions created barriers mostly for poor women and teens (Ginsberg 1989; Lundberg and Plotnick 1990; Rhode 1993–1994, 309–310, 648; Ehrlich 2006, 164–172) and criminalized reproduction (Paltrow 2013). Abortions began moving out of hospitals and into clinics in the 1970s and, by 2006, 90 percent of all abortions were performed in clinics, which become targets for antiabortion activism that included murdering doctors who perform abortions (Bazelon 2010). The erosion of reproductive rights continued into 2013, as Arkansas, North Dakota, Ohio, and Texas all passed legislation that reduced access to abortions.

89. Kost, Henshaw, and Carlin 2010, table 1. From 1979 to 1989, rates remained relatively stable at around 42 abortions per 1000 teens age 15 to 19.

90. For discussions of abortion among Latinas, see Finer and Henshaw 2006; Ventura et al. 2008; and Garcia 2012, 88–90.

91. Zabin, Hirsch, and Emerson 1989; Cooksey 1990; Plotnick 1992, Freeman and Rickels 1993; Walkerdine, Lucey, and Melody 2001; Hope, Wilder, and Watt 2003; Ventura et al. 2004; Ventura et al. 2008; Kaminer 2011.

92. See Ellis and Bochner 1992 for an auto-ethnographic account that illustrates the complexity of feelings that both women and men have about abortion.

93. Bazelon 2010.

94. In 2000, the national abortion rate for teens 15 to 17 was 14.5 compared to 20.7 in Connecticut (Guttmacher Institute, 2006, table 3.6). For additional statistics on abortion see Kost, Henshaw, and Carlin 2010, tables 2.2. and 2.3.

95. In 2000, for teens 15 to 17, the percent of pregnancies aborted was 49 percent in Connecticut and 30 percent in the United States (Guttmacher Institute 2006, table 3.2).

96. In Connecticut, in 2005 there were 52 providers (47 in 2008) and 95 percent of women lived in a county with a provider (www.guttmacher.org/pubs /sfaa/connecticut.html).

97. For discussion on abortion and religion, see Coles 1997 and Petersen 2001. Religiosity was more strongly related to abortion attitudes of whites than Hispanics or blacks (Gay and Lynxwilner 1999; Boggess and Bradner 2000). Ortiz and Nuttell (1987) found in their study of Puerto Ricans that family support was more important than religious beliefs. For the influence of family and friends on the abortion decision, see Brazzell and Acock 1988; Henshaw and Kost 1992; Freeman and Rickels 1993.

98. In a study of 1,500 teenagers who had abortions, 68 percent had decided to abort within two weeks of discovery (Henshaw and Kost 1992).

99. See Trad 1999 and Buckingham and Derby 1997.

100. Although she does not mention her religion when discussing abortion, she was raised Roman Catholic.

101. Harding 2007.

102. White male attitudes toward abortion became more conservative in the 1990s (Boggess and Bradner 2000).

CONCLUSION

1. Ventura, Curtin, and Abma 2012, table 2.

2. Singh, Darroch, and Frost 2001.

3. This is Luker's (1996) main thesis. Edin and Kefalas (2005), who focus on single mothers, not just teen mothers, argue that the incentives and disincentives for childbearing are different for poor and middle-class women. See also Brewster 1994; Bickel et al. 1997; Coles 1997; Havemen, Wolfe, and Wilson 1997; Bissell 2000; Corcoran, Franklin, and Bennett 2000; and Bettie 2003.

4. Geronimus argues: "It is not far-fetched to think that people who frequently witness the deaths of loved ones of all ages, who lose the active involvement of others through disability, and who are themselves transformed from dependents to caregivers at very young ages could be profoundly influenced by their experience in many ways, including as an incentive toward early childbearing" (1992, 246).

5. Black, Erdmans, and Dickinson 2004.

6. Olds et al. 2002; Leventhal 2005; Peterson et al. 2007; Kirkland and Mitchell-Herzfeld 2012.

7. Ross 2013.

8. Adding fuel to the fire, it was also reported that an officer responsible for implementing sexual assault prevention programs had been charged with sexual assault two days before the report was released (Steinhauer 2013).

9. The film, produced by Amy Ziering and directed by Kirby Dick, won awards at the Sundance Film Festival, the Human Rights Watch Film Festival, and the Seattle, Provincetown, and Dallas film festivals. Both the documentary and the Pentagon report are a reminder that patriarchy affects both women and men, as both were victims of sexual violence perpetrated as a form of power and domination. Women, however, bear the larger burden—the film asserts that 20 percent of active-duty female soldiers are sexually assaulted in the military, with one-half of them being between 18 and 21 years of age. See *The Invisible War* website at www.notinvisible.org/the_movie. Of survey respondents in the Pentagon study, 6.1 percent of women and 1.2 percent of men indicated they had been victims of sexual assault in 2011.

10. Despite an initiative launched by the state of Connecticut in 2004 to cut statewide poverty in half by 2014, the state child poverty rate in Connecticut grew from 10.5 percent in 2004 to 14.9 percent in 2011 (Connecticut Voices for Children 2012).

11. Farmer 2005.

12. To hear the interview, go to www.yourpublicmedia.org/content/profile /featured/mary-erdmans-phd.

13. Furstenberg 2007, 166.

14. In 2013, 59 percent indicated that money and wealth should be more evenly distributed, 52 percent felt that the rich should be more heavily taxed to achieve this, and only one-third believed that the current distribution was fair (Newport 2013).

15. In 2013, $8.25 per hour was the third highest minimum wage among states in the country, one dollar higher than the federal minimum wage.

16. As we bring our book to a close, the Fair Minimum Wage Act of 2013 is being considered by Congress to increase the minimum wage to $10.10 over a two-year period and thereafter to tie future increases to the Consumer Price Index.

APPENDIX A

1. Quoted in Kovach 2005, 27.

2. Forty of the 47 partners were the biological fathers of the children, and 26 of the 47 were the partners of the teen mothers. The interviewers were black, white, and Latino men and they were part of the research team that met weekly.

3. See Pillow 2003 for an excellent discussion of reflexivity, positionality, and co-constructed narratives. See also Fine 1994; Fine and Weis 1996; Hertz 1997; Fine et al. 2000; Gergen and Gergen 2000; Fontana and Frey 2005; Olesen 2005.

4. Feminist social scientists have dismissed the rigid separation between the researcher and the researched and have embraced a more humanist relationship that is not troubled by closeness. See Anderson et al. 1990; Cook and Fonow

1990; Alpern et al. 1992; Reinharz 1992; Chafetz 1997; Erdmans 2004; Fontana and Frey 2005; Olesen 2005.

5. Describing her study of 30 girls talking (or not) about sex and sexual desire, Tolman writes that "worrying about the extent to which these reports mirror reality misses the point; what I was trying to learn was how girls themselves make sense of their own feelings and experiences" (2002, 40).

6. Abel 1947; Bertaux 1981; Chalasinski 1981; Geiger 1986; Denzin 1989; Chanfrault-Duchet 1991; Atkinson 1998. In the contemporary era of postmodernism, life stories and other interpretive methods have experienced a resurgence because they help to address the crises of representation, serve as a critique of positivism, and challenge the myth of objectivity (Denzin and Lincoln 2003; Berger and Quinney 2005; Erdmans 2007).

7. This software was designed and developed in Australia, 2002, QSR International Pty Ltd.

8. See Atkinson who argues that "life stories should be read first and foremost as a whole ... the meaning of the story is in the whole, not the parts" (1998, 67).

9. Denzin 1989, 22, 70–72. Like Denzin, we use the terms "turning points," "epiphanies," and "pivotal events" interchangeably as things that altered a life trajectory.

10. Grele 1985, 136–137.

11. See Chanfrault-Duchet's interpretive model of life stories that attends to the textual dimensions of the story form (1991, 79–80).

12. The "listening method" analyzes interviews looking for larger patterns, emergent themes, and "various voices" or multiple meanings to a story (Belenky et al. 1986 [1997]; Fine 1988; Tolman 2002, 38–40; Luttrell 2003).

13. For an excellent set of articles about interpretive methods, see Tolman and Brydon-Miller 2001.

14. See Grele's interview with Studs Terkel (Grele 1985, 33–35).

15. Pillow 2003.

16. Mills 1959.

References

Abel, Theodore. 1947. "The Nature and Use of Biograms." *American Journal of Sociology* 53 (2): 111–118.

Abma, Joyce, Anne Driscoll, and Kristin Moore. 1998. "Young Women's Degree of Control over First Intercourse: An Exploratory Analysis." *Family Planning Perspectives* 30 (1): 12–18.

Abma, Joyce C., Gladys M. Martinez, and Casey Copen. 2010. "Teenagers in the United States: Sexual Activity, Contraceptive Use, and Childbearing, National Survey of Family Growth 2006–2008." *Vital Health Statistics* 23 (30). Washington, DC: National Center for Health Statistics.

Abma, Joyce C., Gladys M. Martinez, William Mosher, and Brittany S. Dawson. 2004. "Teenagers in the United States: Sexual Activity, Contraceptive Use, and Childbearing." *Vital Health Statistics Reports* 23 (24). Hyattsville, MD: National Center for Health Statistics.

Acosta-Belén, Edna, and Carlos E. Santiago. 2006. *Puerto Ricans in the United States: A Contemporary Portrait.* Boulder, CO: Lynne Rienner.

Afable-Munsuz, Aimee, and Claire D. Brindis. 2006. "Acculturation and the Sexual and Reproductive Health of Latino Youth in the United States: A Literature Review." *Perspectives on Sexual and Reproductive Health* 38 (4): 208–219.

Alan Guttmacher Institute. 1994. *Sex and America's Teenagers.* New York: Alan Guttmacher Institute.

———. 2002. *Teenage Pregnancy: Trends and Lessons Learned: Sex and America's Teenagers.* New York: Alan Guttmacher Institute.

Albert, Bill. 2010. "With One Voice 2010: America's Adults and Teens Sound Off about Teen Pregnancy." *National Campaign to Prevent Teen and Unplanned Pregnancy,* December.

Alexander, Karl L., Doris R. Entwisle, and Carrie S. Horsey. 1997. "From First Grade Forward: Early Foundations of High School Dropout." *Sociology of Education* 70 (April): 87–107.

Alexander, Michelle. 2010. *The New Jim Crow: Mass Incarceration in the Age of Colorblindness*. New York: New Press.

Ali, Taby. 2007. *Child Poverty in 2006: How Do Connecticut Cities Measure Up?* September. New Haven, CT: Connecticut Voices for Children.

Allen, Joseph P., Susan Philliber, Scott Herrling, and Gabriel P. Kuperminc. 1997. "Preventing Teen Pregnancy and Academic Failure: Experimental Evaluation of a Developmentally Based Approach." *Child Development* 64:729–742.

Alpern, Sara, Joyce Antler, Elisabeth Israels Perry, and Ingrid Withner Scobie, eds. 1992. *The Challenge of Feminist Biography: Writing the Lives of Modern American Women*. Urbana: University of Illinois Press.

Altimari, Dave. 2008. "Abused Became Abusers in Former Probation Officer's Case." *Hartford Courant*, April 13. http://articles.courant.com/2008-04-13/news/hc-straub0413.artapr13_1_richard-straub-probation-officer-childhood-abuse.

American Psychological Association Zero-Tolerance Task Force. 2008. "Are Zero-Tolerance Policies Effective In The Schools?" *American Psychologist* 63 (9): 852–862.

Anda, Robert F., Alexander Butchart, Vincent J. Felitti, and David Brown. 2010. "Building a Framework for Global Surveillance of the Public Health Implications of Adverse Childhood Experiences." *American Journal of Preventive Medicine.* 39 (1): 93–98.

Anderson, Elijah. 1990. *Streetwise: Race, Class and Change in an Urban Community*. Chicago: University of Chicago Press.

———. 1991. "Neighborhood Effects on Teenage Pregnancy." In *The Urban Underclass,* edited by Christopher Jencks and Paul E. Peterson, 375–398. Washington, DC: Brookings Institution.

———. 1999. *Code of the Street: Decency, Violence and the Moral Life of the Inner City*. New York: W.W. Norton.

Anderson, Kathryn, Susan Armitage, Dana Jack, and Judith Wittner. 1990. "Beginning Where We Are: Feminist Methodology in Oral History." In *Feminist Research Methods: Exemplary Readings in the Social Sciences,* edited by Joyce McCarl Nielson, 94–112. Boulder, CO: Westview Press.

Anderson, Kathryn, and Dana C. Jack. 1991. "Learning to Listen: Interview Techniques and Analyses." *Women's Words: The Feminist Practice of Oral History,* edited by Sherna Berger Gluck and Daphne Patai, 11–26. New York: Routledge.

Astone, Nan Marie, and Sara S. McLanahan. 1991. "Family Structure, Parental Practices and High School Completion." *American Sociological Review* 56 (3): 309–320.

Atkinson, Robert. 1998. *The Life Story Interview*. Thousand Oaks, CA: Sage Publications.

Axinn, William, Greg J. Duncan, and Arland Thornton. 1997. "The Effects of Parents' Income, Wealth and Attitudes on Children's Completed Schooling and Self-Esteem." *Consequences of Growing Up Poor*, edited by Greg J. Duncan and Jeanne Brooks-Gunn, 518–540. New York: Russell Sage Foundation.

Bachu, Amara. 1999. *Trends in Premarital Childbearing: 1930–1994*. Current Population Reports, 23–197. U.S. Census Bureau, Washington, DC.

Balassone, Mary Lou. 1989. "Risk of Contraceptive Discontinuation among Adolescents." *Journal of Adolescent Health Care* 10:527–533.

Basu, Moni. 2009. "Survey Delves into High Birth Rate for Young Latinas." *CNN Health*. May 19. www.cnn.com/2009/HEALTH/05/19/latinas.pregnancy.rate/index.html.

Bazelon, Emily. 2010. "The New Abortion Providers." *New York Times Magazine*, July 18. www.nytimes.com/2010/07/18/magazine/18abortion-t.html?pagewanted = all.

Bearman, Peter S., and Hannah Brückner. 2001. "Promising the Future: Virginity Pledges and First Intercourse." *American Journal of Sociology* 106 (4): 859–912.

Beck, Victoria Simpson, and Stephanie Boys. 2012. "Romeo & Juliet: Star-Crossed Lovers or Sex Offenders?" *Criminal Justice Policy Review*. September 21: 1–21.

Becker, Howard S. 1963. *Outsiders: Studies in the Sociology of Deviance*. New York: New Press.

Beckett, Katherine. 1995. "Fetal Rights and 'Crack Moms': Pregnant Women in the War on Drugs." *Contemporary Drug Problems* 22:587–612.

Belenky, Mary Field, Blythe McVicker Clinchy, Nancy Rule Goldberger, and Jill Mattuck Tarule. 1986 [1997]. *Women's Ways of Knowing: The Development of Self, Voice, and Mind*. New York: Basic Books.

Berger, Ronald J., and Richard Quinney, eds. 2005. *Storytelling Sociology: Narrative as Social Inquiry*. Boulder, CO: Lynne Rienner.

Bertaux, Daniel, ed. 1981. *Biography and Society: The Life History Approach in the Social Sciences*. Beverly Hills, CA: Sage Publications.

Bertaux, Daniel, and Martin Kohli. 1984. "The Life Story Approach: A Continental View." *Annual Review of Sociology* 10:215–237.

Bettie, Julie. 2003. *Women without Class: Girls, Race, and Identity*. Berkeley: University of California Press.

Beutel, Ann M. 2000. "The Relationship between Adolescent Nonmarital Childbearing and Educational Expectations: A Cohort and Period Comparison." *Sociological Quarterly* 41:297–314.

Bickel, Robert, Susan Weaver, Tony Williams, and Linda Lange. 1997. "Opportunity, Community, and Teen Pregnancy in an Appalachian State." *Journal of Educational Research* 90:175–181.

Bissell, Mary. 2000. "Socio-Economic Outcomes of Teen Pregnancy and Parenthood: A Review of the Literature." *Canadian Journal of Human Sexuality* 9:191–204.

Black, Timothy. 2009. *When a Heart Turns Rock Solid: The Lives of Three Puerto Rican Brothers On and Off the Streets*. New York: Pantheon.

Black, Timothy, Meredith C. Damboise, Madelyn Figueroa, Dawn Fuller-Ball, Kevin Lamkins, and Mary Patrice Erdmans. 2006. *Nurturing Families*

Network 2006 Annual Report. June 22. West Hartford, CT: University of Hartford, Center for Social Research.

Black, Timothy, Mary Patrice Erdmans, and Kristina Dickinson. 2004. *Life Stories of Vulnerable Families in Connecticut: An Assessment of the Nurturing Families Network Home Visitation Program.* June 2. West Hartford, CT: University of Hartford, Center for Social Research.

Blake, Barbara J., and Leora Bentov. 2001. "Geographical Mapping of Unmarried Teen Births and Selected Sociodemographic Variables." *Public Health Nursing* 18:33–39.

Blinn-Pike, Lynn. 1999. "Why Abstinent Adolescents Report They Have Not Had Sex: Understanding Sexually Resilient Youth." *Family Relations* 48:295–301.

Blinn-Pike, Lynn, Thomas Berger, Donna Dixon, Diane Kuschel, and Michael Kaplan. 2002. "Is There a Causal Link between Maltreatment and Adolescent Pregnancy? A Literature Review." *Perspectives on Sexual and Reproductive Health* 34 (2): 68–75.

Blueprint for Improving the Lives of New Britain's Young Children Birth through Third Grade. 2010. New Britain, CT: New Britain School Board.

Boggess, Scott, and Carolyn Bradner. 2000. "Trends in Adolescent Males' Abortion Attitudes, 1988–1995: Differences by Race and Ethnicity." *Family Planning Perspectives* 32 (3): 118–123.

Boonstra, Heather D. 2007. "The Heart of the Matter: Public Funding of Abortion for Poor Women in the United States." *Guttmacher Policy Review* 10 (1). www.guttmacher.org/pubs/gpr/10/1/gpr100112.html.

Bourdieu, Pierre, and Loïc Wacquant. 2004. "Symbolic Violence." In *Violence in War and Peace: An Anthology,* edited by Nancy Scheper-Hughes and Philippe Bourgois, 272–274. Oxford: Blackwell.

Bourgois, Phillipe. 1995. *In Search of Respect: Selling Crack in El Barrio.* New York: Cambridge University Press.

———. 1998. "Families and Children in Pain in the U.S. Inner City." In *Small Wars: The Cultural Politics of Childhood,* 331–351. Berkeley: University of California Press.

———. 2001. "The Power of Violence in War and Peace: Post-Cold War Lessons from El Salvador." *Ethnography* 2 (1): 5–37.

———. 2009. "Recognizing Invisible Violence: A Thirty-Year Ethnographic Retrospective." In *Global Health in Times of Violence,* edited by Linda Whiteford and Paul Farmer, 18–40. Santa Fe, NM: School of Advanced Research Press.

Bourgois, Philippe, and Jeff Schonberg. 2009. *Righteous Dopefiend.* Berkeley: University of California Press.

Boyer, Deborah, and David Fine. 1992. "Sexual Abuse as a Factor in Adolescent Pregnancy and Child Maltreatment." *Family Planning Perspectives* 24 (1): 4–12.

Brazzell, Jan F., and Alan C. Acock. 1988. "Influence of Attitudes, Significant Others, and Aspirations on How Adolescents Intend to Resolve a Premarital Pregnancy." *Journal of Marriage and the Family* 50 (2): 413–425.

Breckenridge, Jan, and Eileen Baldry. 1997. "Workers Dealing with Mother Blame and Child Sexual Assault Cases." *Journal of Child Sexual Abuse* 6 (1): 65–80.

Brewster, Karin L. 1994. "Race Differences in Sexual Activity among Adolescent Women: The Role of Neighborhood Characteristics." *American Sociological Review* 59 (1): 408–424.

Bridgeland, John M., John J. Dilulio, and Karen Burke Morison. 2006. *The Silent Epidemic: Perspectives of High School Dropouts.* Washington, DC: Civic Enterprises.

Briere, John, and Marsha Runtz, 1987. "Post Sexual Abuse Trauma: Data and Implications for Clinical Practice." *Journal of Interpersonal Violence* 2 (4): 367–379.

Bronner, Ethan. 2013. "A Flood of Suits Fights Coverage of Birth Control." *New York Times,* January 26.

Brooke, James. 1996. "An Old Law Chastises Pregnant Teen-Agers." *New York Times,* October 28. www.nytimes.com/1996/10/28/us/an-old-law-chastises-pregnant-teen-agers.html.

Brown, David W., Robert F. Anda, Vincent J. Felitti, Valerie J. Edwards, Ann Marie Malarcher, Janet B. Croft, and Wayne H. Giles. 2010. "Adverse Childhood Experiences are Associated with the Risk of Lung Cancer: A Prospective Cohort Study." *BMC Public Health.* www.biomedcentral.com/1471-2458/10/20.

Brown, Elizabeth. 2008. "Special Ed Inequalities Leaving Many Kids Behind." *Hartford Courant,* February 17.

Brown, Jocelyn, Patricia Cohen, Henian Chen, Elizabeth Smailes, and Jeffrey G. Johnson. 2004. "Sexual Trajectories of Abused and Neglected Youths." *Journal of Developmental & Behavioral Pediatrics* 25 (2): 77–82.

Brown, Sarah S., and Katherine Suellentrop. 2009. "What Is to Be Done about the Rise in Teen Childbearing?" *Journal of Adolescent Health* 45:1–2.

Brown, Tina. 2008. "On the Road Back: Nick Carbone Says He's No Victim." *Hartford Courant,* June 25.

Buckingham, Robert W., and Mary P. Derby. 1997. *I'm Pregnant, Now What Do I Do?* Amherst, NY: Prometheus Books.

Bumiller, Kristin. 2008. "In an Abusive State: How Neoliberalism Appropriated the Feminist Movement against Sexual Violence." Durham, NC: Duke University Press.

Burgard, Matt. 2007. "Drifting Students Get Help to Turn Around." *Hartford Courant,* February 3.

Burton, Linda. 1990. "Teenage Childbearing as an Alternative Life-Course Strategy in Multigeneration Black Families." *Human Nature* 1 (2): 123–143.

Burton, Linda M., and Keith E. Whitfield. 2006. "Health, Aging, and America's Poor: Ethnographic Insights on Family Co-Morbidity and Cumulative Disadvantage." In *Aging, Globalization and Inequality,* edited by Jan Baars, Dale Dannefer, Chris Phillipson, and Alan Walker, 103–122. Amityville, NY: Baywood.

Butler, Amy. 1992. "The Changing Economic Consequences of Teenage Childbearing." *Social Science Review,* March: 1–31.

Butler, Janice, and Linda Burton. 1990. "Rethinking Teenage Childbearing: Is Sexual Abuse a Missing Link?" *Family Relations* 39 (1): 73–80.

Campbell, Susan. 2008. "Taking Care of the Victims of Sexual Assault." *Hartford Courant,* April 2.

Canny, Priscilla, and Douglas Hall. 2003. *Census Connections: Child Poverty and Poverty Measures in Connecticut.* November. New Haven, CT: Connecticut Voices for Children.

Canny, Priscilla, Douglas Hall, and Shelley Geballe. 2002. *Child and Family Poverty in Connecticut: 1990 and 2000.* New Haven, CT: Connecticut Voices for Children.

Carr, Patrick J., and Maria J. Kefalas. 2009. *Hollowing Out the Middle: The Rural Brain Drain and What It Means for America.* Boston: Beacon.

Carter, Prudence L. 2005. *Keeping It Real: School Success Beyond Black and White.* New York: Oxford University Press.

Chafetz, Janet Saltman. 1997. "Feminist Theory and Sociology: Underutilized Contributions for Mainstream Theory." *Annual Review of Sociology* 23:97–120.

Chalasinski, Jozef. 1981. "The Life Records of the Young Generation of Polish Peasants as a Manifestation of Contemporary Culture." In *Biography and Society: The Life History Approach in the Social Sciences,* edited by Daniel Bertaux, 119–132. Beverly Hills, CA: Sage Publications.

Chandy, Joseph, Robert W. Blum, and Michael Resnick. 1996. "Female Adolescents with a History of Sexual Abuse: Risk Outcomes and Protective Factors." *Journal of Interpersonal Violence* 11 (4): 503–518.

Chanfrault-Duchet, Marie-Francoise. 1991. "Narrative Structures, Social Models, and Symbolic Representation in the Life Story." In *Women's Words: The Feminist Practice of Oral History,* edited by Sherna Berger Gluck and Daphne Patai, 77–92. New York: Routledge.

Chase-Lansdale, P. Lindsay, Jeanne Brooks-Gunn, and Roberta L. Paikoff. 1991. "Research Programs for Adolescent Mothers: Missing Links and Future Promises." *Family Relations* 40 (4): 396–403.

Chen, Edith, W. Thomas Boyce, and Karen A. Matthews. 2002. "Socioeconomic Differences in Children's Health: How and Why Do These Relationships Change with Age?" *Psychological Bulletin* 28 (2): 295–329.

Cherry, April L. 2007. "The Detention, Confinement, and Incarceration of Pregnant Women for the Benefit of Fetal Heath." *Columbia Journal of Gender and Law* 16:147–197.

Clark, M. Diane, Hanno Petras, Sheppard G. Kellam, Nicholas Ialongo, and Jeanne M. Poduska. 2003. "Who's Most at Risk for School Removal and Later Juvenile Delinquency: Effects of Early Risk Factors, Gender, School /Community Poverty, and Their Impact on More Distal Outcomes." *Women & Criminal Justice* 14:89–116.

Clayton, Eva. 1996. U.S. Congress. House of Representatives. *Weaving the Fabric of a Strong Community Means Devoting More Resources to Preventing Teen Pregnancy.* 104th Congress, 2nd Session, May 30.

Cocca, Carolyn E. 2002. "From 'Welfare Queen' to 'Exploited Teen': Welfare Dependency, Statutory Rape, and Moral Panic." *NWSA Journal* 14:56–79.

———. 2004. *Jailbait: The Politics of Statuary Rape Laws in the United States.* Albany: State University of New York Press.

Coles, Robert. 1997. *The Youngest Parents.* New York: W.W. Norton.

Collins, Patricia H. 2000. *Black Feminist Thought: Knowledge, Consciousness, and the Politics of Empowerment.* New York: Routledge.

Collins, Randall. 2008. *Violence: A Micro-Sociological Theory.* Princeton, NJ: Princeton University Press.

Comas-Diáz, Lillian. 1995. "Puerto Ricans and Sexual Child Abuse." In *Sexual Abuse in Nine North American Communities,* edited by Lisa Aronson Fontes, 31–66. Thousand Oaks, CA: Sage Publications.

Conger, Rand D., Katherine Jewsbury Conger, and Glen H. Elder, Jr. 1997. "Family Economic Hardship and Adolescent Adjustment: Mediating and Moderating Processes." In *Consequences of Growing Up Poor,* edited by Greg J. Duncan and Jeanne Brooks-Gunn, 288–310. New York: Russell Sage Foundation.

Connecticut Registration Report. 1998–2010. "Connecticut Resident Births: Births to Teenagers, Low Birthrate Births, and Prenatal Care Timing and Adequacy, for Counties, Health Districts and Towns by Mother's Race and Hispanic Ethnicity." Table 4. Hartford, CT: Department of Public Health, Office of Vital Records.

Connecticut Voices for Children. 2012. *Poverty, Median Income, and Health Insurance in Connecticut: Summary of 2011 American Community Survey Census Data.* New Haven, CT. www.ctvoices.org/sites/default/files/econ12 censuspovertyacs.pdf.

Contreras, Randol. 2013. *The Stickup Kids: Race, Drugs, Violence and the American Dream.* Berkeley: University of California Press.

Cook, Judith A., and Mary Margaret Fonow. 1990. "Knowledge and Women's Interests: Issues of Epistemology and Methodology in Feminist Sociological Research." In *Feminist Research Methods: Exemplary Readings in the Social Sciences,* edited by Joyce McCarl Nielson, 69–93. Boulder, CO: Westview Press.

Cooksey, Elizabeth. 1990. "Factors in the Resolution of Adolescent Premarital Pregnancies." *Demography* 27 (2): 207–218.

Corcoran, Jacqueline. 1998. "Consequences of Adolescent Pregnancy/Parenting: A Review of the Literature." *Social Work in Health Care* 27 (2): 49–67.

Corcoran, Jacqueline, Cynthia Franklin, and Patricia Bennett. 2000. "Ecological Factors Associated with Adolescent Pregnancy and Parenting." *Social Work Research* 24:29–39.

Corcoran, Mary, and James Kunz. 1997. "Do Unmarried Births among African-American Teens Lead to Adult Poverty?" *Social Service Review,* June: 274–287.

Crane, Jonathan. 1991. "The Epidemic Theory of Ghettos and Neighborhood Effects on Dropping Out and Teenage Childbearing." *American Journal of Sociology* 96 (5): 1226–1259.

Dahinten, V. Susan, Jennifer D. Shapka, and J. Douglas Williams. 2007. "Adolescent Children of Adolescent Mothers: The Impact of Family Functioning on Trajectories of Development." *Journal Youth Adolescence* 36:195–212.

Danziger, Sandra K., and Naomi B. Farber. 1990. "Keeping Inner-City Youths in School: Critical Experiences of Young Black Women." *Social Work Research & Abstracts* 26:32–39.

Darroch, Jacqueline E., Jennifer J. Frost, Susheela Singh. 2001. *Teenage Sexual and Reproductive Behavior in Developed Countries: Can More Progress Be Made?* Occasional Report 3. New York: Alan Guttmacher Institute.

Darroch, Jacqueline E., and Susheela Singh. 1999. *Why Is Teenage Pregnancy Declining? The Roles of Abstinence, Sexual Activity and Contraceptive Use.* Occasional Report 1. New York: Alan Guttmacher Institute.

Dash, Leon. 1989. *When Children Want Children: An Inside Look at the Crisis of Teenage Parenthood.* New York: Penguin.

Debold, Elizabeth, Lyn Mikel Brown, Susan Weseen, and Geraldine Kearse Brookins. 1999. "Cultivating Hardiness Zones for Adolescent Girls: A Reconceptualization of Resilience in Relationships with Caring Adults." In *Beyond Appearance: A New Look at Adolescent Girls,* edited by Norine J. Johnson, Michael C. Roberts, and Judith Worell, 181–203. Washington, DC: American Psychological Association.

Delgado, Richard. 1996. "Statutory Rape Laws: Does It Make Sense to Enforce Them in an Increasingly Permissive Society? No: Selective Enforcement Targets 'Unpopular' Men." *American Bar Association Journal* 82:87.

Denzin, Norman. 1989. *Interpretive Biography.* New York: Sage Publications.

Denzin, Norman K., and Yvonna S. Lincoln. 2003. "Introduction: The Discipline and Practice of Qualitative Research." In *Collecting and Interpreting Qualitative Materials,* 2nd ed., edited by Norman K. Denzin and Yvonna S. Lincoln, 1–46. Thousand Oaks, CA: Sage Publications.

Dolgen, Lauren. 2011. "Why I Created MTV's '16 and Pregnant.'" CNN, May 4. http://articles.cnn.com/2011-05-04/entertainment/teen.mom.dolgen_1_teen-pregnancy-teen-mom-teen-mothers?_s = PM:SHOWBIZ.

Donovan, Patricia. 1996. "Can Statutory Rape Laws Be Effective in Preventing Adolescent Pregnancy?" *Family Planning Perspectives* 29 (1): 30–34, 40.

Dougherty, Jack. 2012. "Part 4: Challenges of Desegregation & Choice." In *On The Line: How Schooling, Housing, and Civil Rights Shaped Hartford and Its Suburbs.* http://ontheline.trincoll.edu/preview-chapter/part-4/.

Douglas, Emily M., and David Finkelhor. 2005. *Child Sexual Abuse Fact Sheet.* Durham, NH: University of New Hampshire Crimes against Children Research Center.

Downs, William R. 1993. "Developmental Considerations for the Effects of Childhood Sexual Abuse." *Journal of Interpersonal Violence* 8 (3): 331–345.

Drobac, Jennifer Ann. 2013. "Wake Up and Smell the Starbucks Coffee: How Doe v. Starbucks Confirms the End of 'The Age of Consent' in California and Perhaps Beyond." *Boston College Journal of Law & Social Justice* 33 (1): 1–45.

Duncan, Greg J., and Jeanne Brooks-Gunn, eds. 1997. *Consequences of Growing Up Poor.* New York: Russell Sage Foundation.

Duncan, Greg J., and Saul D. Hoffman. 1991. "Teenage Underclass Behavior and Subsequent Poverty: Have the Rules Changed?" In *The Urban Underclass,* edited by Christopher Jencks and Paul E. Peterson, 155–174. Washington, DC: Brookings Institution.

Duncan, Greg J., W. Jean Young, Jeanne Brooks-Gunn, and Judith R. Smith. 1998. "How Much Does Childhood Poverty Affect the Life Chances of Children?" *American Sociological Review* 63 (3): 406–423.

Dunlap, Eloise, Andrew Golub, and Bruce D. Johnson. 2003. "Girls' Sexual Development in the Inner City: From Compelled Childhood Sexual Contact to Sex-for-Things Exchanges." *Journal of Child Sexual Abuse* 12 (2): 73–96.

East, Patricia L., and Marianne E. Felice. 1996. *Adolescent Pregnancy and Parenting: Findings from a Racially Diverse Sample.* Mahwah, NJ: Lawrence Erlbaum Associates.

Eaton, Susan. 2007. *The Children in Room E4: American Education on Trial.* Chapel Hill: Algonquin Books of Chapel Hill.

Edin, Kathryn, and Maria Kefalas. 2005. *Promises I Can Keep: Why Poor Women Put Motherhood before Marriage.* Berkeley: University of California Press.

Edsall, Thomas Byrne, and Mary D. Edsall. 1991. *Chain Reaction: The Impact of Race, Rights, and Taxes on American Politics.* New York: W.W. Norton.

Edwards, S. 1992. "Daughters of Teenage Mothers More Likely to Have a Teenage Birth than Daughters of Older Mothers." *Family Planning Perspectives* 24:186–187.

Ehrlich, J. Shoshanna. 2006. "From Age of Consent Laws to the 'Silver Ring Thing': The Regulation of Adolescent Female Sexuality." *Health Matrix* 16:151–181.

Eitle, Tamela McNulty, and David J. Eitle. 2002. "Just Don't Do It: High School Sports Participation and Young Female Sexual Behavior." *Sociology of Sport Journal* 19:403–418.

Elder, Glen H., Jr., Cynthia Gimbel, and Rachel Ivie. 1991. "Turning Points in Life: The Case of Military Service and War." *Military Psychology* 3 (4): 215–231.

Elders, M. Joycelyn, and Alexa E. Albert. 1998. "Adolescent Pregnancy and Sexual Abuse." *Journal of the American Medical Association* 280 (7): 648–649.

Elliott, Diana M., and John Briere. 1995. "Posttraumatic Stress Associated with Delayed Recall of Sexual Abuse: A General Population Study." *Journal of Traumatic Stress* 8:629–647.

Ellis, Carolyn, and Arthur P. Bochner. 1992. "Telling and Performing Personal Stories: The Constraints of Choice in Abortion." In *Investigating Subjectivity: Research on Lived Experience,* edited by Carolyn Ellis and Michael G. Flaherty, 79–101. London: Sage Publications.

Elo, Irma T., Rosalind Berkowitz King, and Frank F. Furstenberg Jr. 1999. "Adolescent Females: Their Sexual Partners and the Fathers of Their Children." *Journal of Marriage and Family* 61 (1): 74–84.

Elstein, Sharon G., and Noy Davis. 1997. "Sexual Relationships between Adult Males and Young Teen Girls: Exploring the Legal and Social Responses." October. American Bar Association Center on Children and the Law.

Entwisle, Doris R., and Karl L. Alexander. 1992. "Summer Setback: Race, Poverty, School Composition, and Mathematics Achievement in the First Two Years of School." *American Sociological Review* 57 (1): 72–84.

Erdmans, Mary Patrice. 2004. *The Grasinski Girls: The Choices They Had and the Choices They Made.* Athens: Ohio University Press.

———. 2007. "The Personal Is Political but Is It Academic?" *Journal of American Ethnic History* 26 (4): 7–23.

———. 2012a. "Title IX and the School Experiences of Pregnant and Mothering Students." *Humanity & Society* 36 (1): 50–75.

———. 2012b. "Life Stories of Adolescent Mothers: Speaking against the Master Narrative." Oral History Association, October 11, Cleveland.

Erdmans, Mary Patrice, and Timothy Black. 2008. "What They Tell You to Forget: From Child Sexual Abuse to Adolescent Motherhood." *Qualitative Health Research* 18 (1): 77–89.

Erikson, Erik. 1968. *Identity: Youth and Crisis*. London: Faber & Faber.

Fagan, Patrick F. 1999. *How Broken Families Rob Children of Their Chances for Future Prosperity*. Washington DC: Heritage Foundation. http://downloads.frc.org/EF/EF08H28.pdf.

———. 2001. Testimony before the House Subcommittee on Empowerment, July 16, 1998. In *Teen Pregnancy and Parenting*, edited by Helen Cothran, 35–38. San Diego: Greenhaven Press.

Fallis, R. Kirk, and Susan Opotow. 2003. "Are Students Failing School or Are Schools Failing Students? Class Cutting in High School." *Journal of Social Issues* 19 (1): 103–119.

Farmer, Paul. 2005. *Pathologies of Power: Health, Human Rights, and the New War on the Poor*. Berkeley: University of California Press.

Farrar, Eleanor, and Robert L. Hampel. 1989. "Social Services in High Schools." In *Dropouts from School: Issues, Dilemmas, and Solutions*, edited by Lois Weis, Eleanor Farrar, and Hugh G. Petrie, 97–111. Albany: State University of New York Press.

Fay, Joe, and Jay M. Yanoff. 2000. "What Are Teens Telling Us about Sexual Health? Results of the Second Annual Youth Conference of the Pennsylvania Coalition to Prevent Teen Pregnancy." *Journal of Sex Education and Therapy* 25:169–177.

Feagin, Joe R. 2006. *Systemic Racism: A Theory of Oppression*. New York: Routledge.

Felitti, Vincent J., and Robert F. Anda. 2009. "The Relationship of Adverse Childhood Experiences to Adult Medical Disease, Psychiatric Disorders, and Sexual Behavior: Implications for Healthcare." In *The Impact of Early Life Trauma on Health and Disease: The Hidden Epidemic,* edited by Ruth A. Lanius, Eric Vermetten, and Clare Pain, 77–87. West Nyack, NY: Cambridge University Press.

Felitti, Vincent J., Robert F. Anda, Dale Nordenberg, David F. Williamson, Alison M. Sptiz, Valerie Edwards, Mary P. Koss, and James S. Marks. 1998. "Relationship of Childhood Abuse and Household Dysfunction to Many of the Leading Causes of Death in Adults." *American Journal of Preventive Medicine* 14 (4): 245–258.

Fentiman, Linda C. 2009. "In the Name of Fetal Protection: Why American Prosecutors Pursue Pregnant Drug Users (and Other Countries Don't)." *Columbia Journal of Gender and Law* 18:647–669.

Ferguson, Thomas, and Joel Rogers. 1986. *Right Turn: The Decline of the Democrats and the Future of American Politics*. New York: Hill and Wang.

Fergusson, David M., John L. Horwood, and Michael T. Lynskey. 1997. "Childhood Sexual Abuse, Adolescent Sexual Behaviors and Sexual Revictimization." *Child Abuse & Neglect* 21 (8): 789–803.

Fergusson, David M., and Lianne J. Woodward. 2000. "Teenage Pregnancy and Female Educational Underachievement: A Prospective Study of a New Zealand Birth Cohort." *Journal of Marriage and the Family* 62 (1): 147–161.

Fernandez-Kelly, M. Patricia. 1994. "Towanda's Triumph: Social and Cultural Capital in the Transition to Adulthood in the Urban Ghetto." *International Journal of Urban and Regional Research* 18 (1): 88–111.

"Fertility of American Women, June 2002." 2003. Current Population Reports. Census Bureau. October. US Department of Commerce, Economics and Statistics Administration.

Fessler, Ann. 2006. *The Girls Who Went Away: The Hidden History of Women Who Surrendered Children for Adoption in the Decades Before Roe V. Wade.* New York: Penguin.

Fine, Michelle. 1988. "Sexuality, Schooling, and Adolescent Females: The Missing Discourse of Desire." *Harvard Educational Review* 58 (1): 29–53.

———. 1991. *Framing Dropouts: Notes on the Politics of an Urban Public High School.* Albany: State University of New York Press.

———. 1994. "Working the Hypens: Reinventing Self and Other in Qualitative Research." In *Handbook of Qualitative Research,* edited by Norman K. Denzin and Yvonna S. Lincoln, 70–82. Thousand Oaks, CA: Sage Publications.

Fine, Michelle, Rosemarie Roberts, and Lois Weis. 2000. "Refusing the Betrayal: Latinas Redefining Gender, Sexuality, Culture, and Resistance." *Review of Education/Pedagogy/Cultural Studies* 22 (2): 87–119.

Fine, Michelle, and Lois Weis. 1996. "Writing the 'Wrongs' of Field Work: Confronting Our Own Research/Writing Dilemmas in Urban Ethnographies." *Qualitative Inquiry* 2:251–74.

———. 1999. *The Unknown City: The Lives of Poor and Working-Class Young Adults.* Boston: Beacon.

Fine, Michelle, Lois Weis, Susan Weseen, and Loonmun Wong. 2000. "For Whom? Qualitative Research, Representations and Social Responsibilities." In *Handbook of Qualitative Research,* 2nd ed., edited by Norman K. Denzin and Yvonna S. Lincoln, 107–131. Thousand Oaks, CA: Sage Publications.

Fine, Michelle, and Nancie Zane. 1989. "Being Wrapped Too Tight: When Low-Income Women Drop Out of High School." In *Dropouts from School: Issues, Dilemmas and Solutions,* edited by Lois Weis, Eleanor Farrar, and Hugh G. Petrie, 23–54. Albany: State University of New York Press.

Finer, Lawrence B. 2010. "Unintended Pregnancy among U.S. Adolescents: Accounting for Sexual Activity." *Journal of Adolescent Health* 47 (3): 312–314.

Finer, Lawrence B., and Stanley K. Henshaw. 2006. "Disparity in Rates of Unintended Pregnancy in the United States, 1994–2001." *Perspectives on Sexual and Reproductive Health* 38 (2): 90–96.

Finkelhor, David. 1986. *A Sourcebook on Child Sexual Abuse.* Beverly Hills, CA: Sage Publications.

———. 1994. "Current Information on the Scope and Nature of Child Sexual Abuse." *Future of Children* 4 (2): 31–53.

Finkelhor, David, and Angela Brown. 1986. "Initial and Long-Term Effects: A Conceptual Framework." In *A Sourcebook on Child Sexual Abuse*, edited by David Finkelhor, 180–198. Beverly Hills, CA: Sage Publications.

Finkelhor, David, and Jennifer Dzuiba-Leatherman. 1994. "Children as Victims of Violence: A National Survey." *Pediatrics* 94 (4): 413–420.

Finkelhor, David, Lisa M. Jones, and Anne Shattuck. 2010. *Updated Trends in Child Maltreatment*. Durham, NH: Crimes against Children Research Center. www.unh.edu/ccrc/pdf/Updated_Trends_in_Child_Maltreatment_2009.pdf.

Fiscella, Kevin, Harriet J. Kitzman, Robert E. Cole, Kimberly J. Sidora, and David Olds. 1998. "Does Child Abuse Predict Adolescent Pregnancy?" *Pediatrics* 10 (4): 620–624.

Fischer, Rachel C., Joseph B. Stanford, Penny Jameson, and M. Jann DeWitt. 1999. "Exploring the Concepts of Intended, Planned, and Wanted Pregnancy." *Journal of Family Practice* 48:117–128.

Flores-Gonzalez, Nilda. 2002. *School Kids/Street Kids: Identity Development in Latino Students*. New York: Teachers College Press.

Fontana, Andrea, and James H. Frey. 2005. "The Interview: From Neutral Stance to Political Involvement." In *The Handbook of Qualitative Research*, 3rd ed., edited by Norman K. Denzin and Yvonna S. Lincoln, 695–728. Thousand Oaks, CA: Sage Publications.

Fontes, Lisa A. 1993. Disclosures of Sexual Abuse by Puerto Rican Children: Oppression and Cultural Barriers. *Journal of Child Sexual Abuse* 2 (1): 21–35.

Forste, Renata, and Marta Tienda. 1992. "Race and Ethnic Variation in the Schooling Consequences of Female Adolescent Sexual Activity." *Social Science Quarterly* 73 (1): 12–30.

Fortenberry, J. Dennis, Vanessa Schick, Debby Herbenick, Stephanie A. Sanders, Brian Dodge, and Michael Reece. 2010. "Sexual Behaviors and Condom Use at Last Vaginal Intercourse: A National Sample of Adolescents Ages 14 to 17 Years." *Journal of Sexual Medicine* 7 (supplement 5): 305–314.

Foster, John Bellamy. 2006. "Aspects of Class in the United States: An Introduction." *Monthly Review* 58 (3): 1–28.

Foucault, Michel. 1980. *Power/Knowledge: Selected Interviews and Other Writings, 1972–1977*. Edited by Colin Gordon. New York: Pantheon.

Frahm, Robert A., and Matthew Kaufman. 2007. "A Punishing School Debate." *Hartford Courant*, May 2.

Franke, Todd Michael, Jo Ann Isken, and Michelle T. Parra. 2003. "A Pervasive School Culture for the Betterment of School Outcomes: One School's Approach to Student Mobility." *Journal of Negro Education* 72 (1): 150–157.

Franklin, Karen. 2004. "Enacting Masculinity: Antigay Violence and Group Rape as Participatory Theater." *Sexuality Research and Social Policy* 1: 25–40.

Freeman, Ellen W., and Karl Rickels. 1993. *Early Childbearing: Perspectives of Black Adolescents on Pregnancy, Abortion, and Contraception*. Newbury Park, CA: Sage Publications.

Friedrich, William N., Anthony J. Urquiza, and Robert Beilke. 1984. "Behavioral Problems in Sexually Abused Young Children." *Journal of Pediatric Psychology* 11 (1): 47–57.

Furstenberg, Frank F., Jr. 2007. *Destinies of the Disadvantaged: The Politics of Teenage Childbearing*. New York: Russell Sage Foundation.

Furstenberg, Frank F., Jeanne Brooks-Gunn, and S. Philip Morgan. 1987. *Adolescent Mothers in Later Life*. New York: Cambridge University Press.

Furstenberg, Frank F., Jr., Thomas D. Cook, Jacquelynne Eccles, Glen H. Elder Jr., and Arnold Sameroff. 2000 [1999]. *Managing to Make It: Urban Families and Adolescent Success*. Chicago: University of Chicago Press.

Gandara, Patricia, and Frances Contreras. 2009. *The Latino Education Crisis: The Consequences of Failed Social Policies*. Cambridge, MA: Harvard University Press.

Gans, Herbert J. 1995. *The War against the Poor: The Underclass and Antipoverty Policy*. New York: Basic Books.

Garcia, Eugene E. 2001. *Hispanic Education in the United States: Raices y Alas*. New York: Rowman & Littlefield.

Garcia, Lorena. 2009. "'Now Why Do You Want To Know About That?': Heteronormativity, Sexism, and Racism In The Sexual (Mis)Education Of Latina Youth." *Gender & Society* 23 (2): 520–541.

———. 2012. *Respect Your Self, Protect Your Self: Latina Girls and Sexual Identity*. New York: New York University Press.

Garey, Anita Ilta. 1999. *Weaving Work and Motherhood*. Philadelphia: Temple University Press.

Garfield, Gail. 2005. *Knowing What They Know: African American Women's Experiences of Violence and Violation*. New Brunswick, NJ: Rutgers University Press.

Gay, David, and John Lynxwilner. 1999. "The Impact of Religiosity on Race Variations in Abortion Attitudes." *Sociological Spectrum* 19:359–377.

Gee, James P. 1985. "The Narrativization of Experience in Oral Style." *Journal of Education* 4:9–35.

Geiger, Susan N. 1986. "Women's Life Histories: Method and Content." *Signs* 11 (2): 334–351.

George, Robert M., Allen Harden, and Bong Joo Lee. 2008. "Consequences of Teen Childbearing for Child Abuse, Neglect, and Foster Care Placement." In *Kids Having Kids: Economic Costs and Social Consequences of Teen Pregnancy*, edited by Saul D. Hoffman and Rebecca A. Maynard, 257–288. Washington, DC: Urban Institute Press.

Gergen, Mary M., and Kenneth J. Gergen. 2000. "Qualitative Inquiry: Tensions and Transformations." In *Handbook of Qualitative Research*, 2nd ed., edited by Norman K. Denzin and Yvonna S. Lincoln, 1025–1046. Thousand Oaks, CA: Sage Publications.

Geronimus, Arline. 1987. "On Teenage Childbearing and Neonatal Mortality in the United States." *Population and Development Review* 13 (2): 245–279.

———. 1992. "Teenage Childbearing and Social Disadvantage: Unprotected Discourse." *Family Relations* 41 (2): 244–248.

———. 1996. "Black/White Differences in the Relationship of Maternal Age to Birthweight: A Population-Based Test of the Weathering Hypothesis." *Social Science & Medicine* 42 (4): 589–597.

———. 1997. "Teenage Childbearing and Personal Responsibility: An Alternative View." *Political Science Quarterly* 112 (3): 405–426.

———. 2003. "Damned If You Do: Culture, Identity, Privilege, and Teenage Childbearing in the United States." *Social Science & Medicine* 57 (5): 881–893.

Geronimus, Arline T., and Sanders Korenman. 1992. "The Socioeconomic Consequences of Teen Childbearing Reconsidered." *Quarterly Journal of Economics* 107:1187–1214.

Geronimus, Arline T., Sanders Korenman, and Marianne M. Hillemeier. 1994. "Does Young Maternal Age Adversely Affect Child Development? Evidence from Cousin Comparisons in the United States." *Population and Development Review* 20 (3): 585–609.

Gershenson, Harold P., Judith S. Musick, Holly S. Ruch-Ross, Vicki Magee, Katherine K. Rubino, and Deborah Rosenberg. 1989. "The Prevalence of Coercive Sexual Experience among Teenage Mothers." *Journal of Interpersonal Violence* 4 (2): 204–219.

Gest, Scott D., Joseph L. Mahoney, and Robert B. Cairns. 1999. "A Developmental Approach to Prevention Research: Configurable Antecedents of Early Parenthood." *American Journal of Community Psychology* 27:543–565.

Gilder, George. 1981. *Wealth and Poverty*. New York: Basic Books.

Gilligan, Carol. 1982. *In a Different Voice*. Cambridge, MA: Harvard University Press.

Ginsburg, Faye D. 1989. *Contested Lives: The Abortion Debate in an American Community*. Berkeley: University of California Press.

Glamour Magazine. 2009. "Let's Stop the New Teenage Mom Craze." October 1. www.glamour.com/magazine/2009/09/lets-stop-the-new-teenage-mom-craze.

Gleason, Philip, and Mark Dynarski. 2002. "Do We Know Whom to Serve? Issues in Using Risk Factors to Identify Dropouts." *Journal of Education for Students Placed at Risk* 7:25–41.

Goffman, Erving. 1963. *Stigma: Notes on the Management of a Spoiled Identity*. Englewood Cliffs, NJ: Prentice-Hall.

Gordon, Linda. 1990. *Woman's Body, Woman's Right: Birth Control in America*. Revised and updated. New York: Penguin.

———. 1999. *The Great Arizona Orphan Abduction*. Cambridge, MA: Harvard University Press.

Gottlieb, Rachel. 2004. "Preaching the Wisdom of Protected Sex." *Hartford Courant*, March 3.

Grele, Ronald. 1985. *Envelopes of Sound: The Art of Oral History*. New York: Praeger.

Grogger, Jeffrey. 2008. "Consequences for Teen Childbearing for Incarceration among Adult Children: Approach and Estimates through 1991." In *Kids Having Kids: Economic Costs and Social Consequences of Teen Pregnancy*, edited by Saul D. Hoffman and Rebecca A. Maynard, 290–310. Washington, DC: Urban Institute Press.

Guilamo-Ramos, Vincent, Jane Lee, and James Jaccard. 2012. "Families Talking Together: Creating Healthy Conversations to Prevent Teen Pregnancy: A Community Health Worker Curriculum." www.thenationalcampaign.org.

Guttmacher Institute. 2006. *U.S. Teenage Pregnancy Statistics: National and State Trends and Trends by Race and Ethnicity.* New York: Guttmacher Institute.

——. 2010. *Facts on Publicly Funded Contraceptive Services in the United States.* New York: Guttmacher Institute.

Guttman, Matthew C. 1996. *The Meanings of Macho: Being a Man in Mexico City.* Berkeley: University of California Press.

Hacker, Jacob S., and Paul Peterson. 2010. *Winner-Take-All Politics: How Washington Made the Rich Richer—and Turned Its Back on the Middle Class.* New York: Simon & Schuster.

Hacker, Karen A., Yared Amare, Nancy Strunk, and Leslie Horst. 2000. "Listening to Youth: Teen Perspectives on Pregnancy Prevention." *Journal of Adolescent Health* 26:279–288.

Hagan, John, and Holly Foster. 2001. "Youth Violence and the End of Adolescence." *American Sociological Review* 66 (6): 874–699.

Hagan, John, and Blair Wheaton. 1993. "The Search for Adolescent Role Exits and the Transition to Adulthood." *Social Forces* 71(4): 955–979.

Hall, Douglas J. 2005. *Connecticut Family Asset Scorecard, 2005.* May. New Haven, CT: Connecticut Voices for Children.

Hall, Douglas J., and Shelley Geballe. 2006. *Pulling Apart in Connecticut: Trends in Family Income, 1981–2002.* January. New Haven, CT: Connecticut Voices for Children.

Hamby, Sherry, David Finkelhor, and Heather Turner. 2012. "Teen Dating Violence: Co-Occurrence with Other Victimizations in the National Survey of Children's Exposure to Violence." *Psychology of Violence* 2 (2): 111–124.

Hamer, Jennifer. 2001. *What It Means to Be Daddy: Fatherhood for Black Men Living Away from Their Children.* New York: Columbia University Press.

Hamilton, Brady E., Joyce A. Martin, and Stephanie J. Ventura. 2007. "Births: Preliminary Data for 2006." *National Vital Statistics Reports* 56 (7), December 5. Hyattsville, MD: National Center for Health Statistics.

——. 2012. "Births: Preliminary Data for 2011." *National Vital Statistics Reports* 61 (5), October 3. Hyattsville, MD: National Center for Health Statistics.

Hamilton, Brady E., and Stephanie J. Ventura. 2012. *Birth Rates for U.S. Teenagers Reach Historic Lows for All Age and Ethnic Groups.* NCHS Data Brief 89. Hyattsville, MD: National Center for Health Statistics.

Harding, David J. 2003. "Counterfactual Models of Neighborhood Effects: The Effect of Neighborhood Poverty on Dropping Out and Teenage Pregnancy." *American Journal of Sociology* 109 (3): 676–719.

——. 2007. "Cultural Context, Sexual Behavior, and Romantic Relationships in Disadvantaged Neighborhoods." *American Sociological Review* 72 (3): 341–364.

Hareven, Tamara K., and Kanji Masaoka. 1988. "Turning Points and Transitions: Perceptions of the Life Course." *Journal of Family History* 13 (3): 271–289.

Harner, Holly M. 2005. "Childhood Sexual Abuse, Teenage Pregnancy, and Partnering with Adult Men: Exploring the Relationship." *Journal of Psychosocial Nursing & Mental Health Services* 43 (8): 20–28, 48–49.

Harris, Irving B. 1996. *Children in Jeopardy: Can We Break the Cycle of Poverty?* New Haven, CT: Yale University Press.

Haveman, Robert, and Barbara Wolfe. 1995. "The Determinants of Children's Attainments: A Review of Methods and Findings." *Journal of Economic Literature* 33 (4): 1829–1878.

Haveman, Robert, Barbara Wolfe, and Elaine Peterson. 2008. "Consequences of Teen Childbearing for the Life Chances of Children, 1968–88." In *Kids Having Kids: Economic Costs and Social Consequences of Teen Pregnancy,* edited by Saul D. Hoffman and Rebecca A. Maynard, 324–341. Washington, DC: Urban Institute Press.

Haveman, Robert, Barbara Wolfe, and James Spaulding. 1991. "Childhood Events and Circumstances Influencing High School Completion." *Demography* 28 (1): 133–157.

Haveman, Robert, Barbara Wolfe, and Kathryn Wilson. 1997. "Childhood Poverty and Adolescent Schooling and Fertility Outcomes: Reduced Form and Structural Estimates." In *Consequences of Growing Up Poor,* edited by Greg J. Duncan and Jeanne Brooks-Gunn, 419–460. New York: Russell Sage Foundation.

Henshaw, Stanley K. 1998. "Unintended Pregnancy in the United States." *Family Planning Perspectives* 30 (1): 24–29, 46.

Henshaw, Stanley K., and Kathryn Kost. 1992. "Parental Involvement in Minors' Abortion Decisions." *Family Planning Perspectives* 24 (5): 196–208.

Hertz, Rosanna. 1997. "Introduction." In *Reflexivity and Voice,* edited by Rosanna Hertz, vii–xviii. Thousand Oaks, CA: Sage Publications.

Hertzog, C. Jay, and P. Lena Morgan. 1999. "Making the Transition from Middle Level to High School." *High School Magazine* 6 (4): 26–30.

Hofferth, Sandra L., Lori Reid, and Frank Mott. 2001. "The Effects of Early Childbearing on Schooling over Time." *Family Planning Perspectives* 33 (6): 259–267.

Hoffman, Saul. 1998. "Teenage Childbearing Is Not So Bad after All . . . Or Is It? A Review of the New Literature." *Family Planning Perspectives* 30 (5): 236–239, 243.

———. 2006. "By the Numbers: The Public Costs of Teen Childbearing." Washington, DC: National Campaign to Prevent Teen Pregnancy.

Hoffman, Saul D., and Rebecca A. Maynard, eds. 2008. *Kids Having Kids: Economic Costs and Social Consequences of Teen Pregnancy.* Washington, DC: Urban Institute Press.

Hogan, Dennis P., and Evelyn M. Kitagawa. 1985. "The Impact of Social Status, Family Structure, and Neighborhood on the Fertility of Black Adolescents." *American Journal of Sociology* 90 (4): 825–855.

Hogan, Dennis P., Rongjun Sun, and Gretchen T. Cornwell. 2000. "Sexual and Fertility Behaviors of American Females Aged 15–19 Years: 1985, 1990, and 1995." *American Journal of Public Health* 90:1421–1425.

hooks, bell. 1993. *Sisters of the Yam.* Cambridge, MA: South End Press.

———. 1995. *Killing Rage: Ending Racism.* New York: Henry Holt.

Hope, Trina L., Esther I. Wilder, and Toni Terling Watt. 2003. "The Relationships among Adolescent Pregnancy, Pregnancy Resolution, and Juvenile Delinquency." *Sociological Quarterly* 44:555–576.

Horowitz, Ruth. 1995. *Teen Mothers: Citizens or Dependents?* Chicago: University of Chicago Press.

Hotz, V. Joseph, Susan Williams McElroy, and Seth G. Sanders. 2005. "Teenage Childbearing and Its Life Cycle Consequences." *Journal of Human Resources* 40 (3): 683–715.

———. 2008. "Consequences of Teen Childbearing for Mothers through 1993." In *Kids Having Kids: Economic Costs and Social Consequences of Teen Pregnancy*, edited by Saul D. Hoffman and Rebecca A. Maynard, 52–73. Washington, DC: Urban Institute Press.

Hughes, Marcia, Meredith C. Damboise, Mary Patrice Erdmans, Kevin Lamkins, and Timothy Black. 2008. *Nurturing Families Network 2008 Annual Report.* June 30. West Hartford, CT: University of Hartford, Center for Social Research.

Hunt, Kevin. 2008. "Reardon Victim Goes Public, Blasts St. Francis Hospital." *Hartford Courant,* June 1.

Isaacs, Julia B., Isabell V. Sawhill, and Ron Haskins. 2008. *Getting Ahead or Losing Ground: Economic Mobility in America.* February. Washington DC: Pew Charitable Trust and the Brookings Institute.

Jarrett, Robin. 1995. "Growing Up Poor: The Family Experience of Socially Mobile Youth in Low-Income African-American Neighborhoods." *Journal of Adolescent Research* 10:111–135.

———. 1997. "African-American Family and Parenting Strategies in Impoverished Neighborhoods." *Qualitative Sociology* 20:275–288.

Jencks, Christopher. 1991. "Is the American Underclass Growing?" *The Urban Underclass,* edited by Christopher Jencks and Paul E. Peterson, 28–100. Washington DC: Brookings Institute.

Johnson, Earl S., Ann Levine, and Fred C. Doolittle. 1999. *Father's Fair Share: Helping Poor Men Manage Child Support and Fatherhood.* New York: Russell Sage Foundation.

Jones, Lisa M., David Finkelhor, and Kathy Kopiec. 2001. "Why Is Sexual Abuse Declining? A Survey of State Child Protection Administrators." *Child Abuse & Neglect* 25 (9): 1139–1158.

Jones, Nikki. 2010. *Between Good and Ghetto: African American Girls and Inner-City Violence.* New Brunswick, NJ: Routledge.

Jones, Rachel K., Lori F. Frohwirth, and Ann M. Moore. 2008. "'I Would Give My Child, Like, Everything in the World': How Issues of Motherhood Influence Women Who Have Abortions." *Journal of Family Issues* 29 (1): 79–99.

Kaminer, Ariel. 2011. "Abortion: Easy Access, Complex Everything Else." *New York Times,* January 23.

Kaplan, Elaine Bell. 1996. "Black Teenage Mothers and Their Mothers: The Impact of Adolescent Childbearing on Daughter's Relations with Mothers." *Social Problems* 43 (4): 427–443.

———. 1997. *Not Our Kind of Girl: Unraveling the Myths of Black Teenage Motherhood.* Berkeley: University of California Press.

Kasinitz, Philip, John H. Mollenkopf, Mary C. Waters, and Jennifer Holdaway. 2008. *Inheriting the City: The Children of Immigrants Come of Age.* New York: Russell Sage Foundation.

Katz, Michael B. 1986. *In the Shadow of the Poorhouse: A Social History of Welfare in America*. New York: Basic Books.

———. 1989. *The Undeserving Poor: From the War on Poverty to the War on Welfare*. New York: Pantheon.

Kaufman, Phillip, Jin Y. Kwon, Steve Klein, and Christopher D. Chapman. 2000. "Dropout Rates in the United States: 1999." *National Center for Education Statistics*. Washington, DC: US Department of Education.

Kaufmann, Rachel B., Alison M. Spitz, Lilo T. Strauss, Leo Morris, John S. Santelli, Lisa M. Koonin, and James S. Marks. 1998. "The Decline in US Teen Pregnancy Rates." *Pediatrics* 102:1141–1147.

Kawachi, Ichiro, and Bruce P. Kennedy. 2002. *The Health of Nations*. New York: New Press.

Kaye, Kelleen, Katherine Suellentrop, and Corinna Sloup. 2009. *The Fog Zone: How Misperceptions, Magical Thinking, and Ambivalence Put Young Adults at Risk for Unplanned Pregnancy*. Washington, DC: National Campaign to Prevent Teen and Unplanned Pregnancy.

Kearney, Melissa S., and Phillip B. Levine. 2014. "Media Influences on Social Outcomes: The Impact of MTV's 16 and Pregnant on Teen Childbearing." Working Paper 19795. Cambridge, MA: National Bureau of Economic Research.

Kelly, Deirdre M. 2000. *Pregnant with Meaning: Teen Moms and the Politics of Inclusive Schooling*. New York: Peter Lang.

Kelly, Joan B. 1998. "Marital Conflict, Divorce, and Children's Adjustment." *Child Adolescent Psychiatry Clinic of North America* 7 (2): 259–271.

Kenney, Janet W., Cindy Reinholtz, and Patti Jo Angelini. 1997. "Ethnic Differences in Childhood and Adolescent Sexual Abuse in Teenage Pregnancy." *Journal of Adolescent Health* 21:3–10.

Kimmel, Michael. 2008. *Guyland: The Perilous World Where Boys Become Men*. New York: Harper Collins.

Kimmel, Michael S., and Michael A. Messner. 2012. *Men's Lives*. 9th ed. Upper Saddle River, NJ: Pearson.

Kirby, Douglas. 2002. "Antecedents of Adolescent Initiation of Sex, Contraceptive Use, and Pregnancy." *American Journal of Health Behavior* 26:473–485.

Kirkland, Kristen, and Susan Mitchell-Herzfeld. 2012. "Evaluating the Effectiveness of Home Visiting Services in Promoting Children's Adjustment in School." May 31. Albany, NY: New York State Office of Children and Family Services.

Kishiyama, Mark M., W. Thomas Boyce, Amy M. Jimenez, Lee M. Perry, and Robert T. Knight. 2008. "Socioeconomic Disparities Affect Prefrontal Function in Children." *Journal of Cognitive Neuroscience* 21 (6): 1106–1115.

Koon-Magnin, Sarah, Derek A. Kreager, and R. Barry Ruback. 2010. "Partner Age Differences, Educational Contexts and Adolescent Female Sexual Activity." *Perspectives on Sexual and Reproductive Health* 42 (3): 206–213.

Kost, Kathryn, Stanley Henshaw, and L. Carlin. 2010. "U.S. Teenage Pregnancies, Births and Abortions: National and State Trends and Trends by State and Ethnicity." Guttmacher Institute. www.gutmacher.org/pubs/USTPtrends .pdf.

Kovach, Ronald. 2005. "Gay Talese on the Art of Creative Nonfiction." *Writer Magazine,* January: 24–28.

Kowaleski-Jones, Lori, and Frank L. Mott. 1998. "Sex, Contraception and Childbearing among High-Risk Youth: Do Different Factors Influence Males and Females?" *Family Planning Perspectives* 30 (4): 163–169.

Kristof, Nicholas. 2005. "Bush's Sex Scandal." *New York Times,* February 16.

Krugman, Paul. 2009. *The Conscience of a Liberal.* 2nd ed. New York: W.W. Norton.

Lamont, Michèle, and Mario L. Small. 2008. "How Culture Matters: Enriching Our Understanding of Poverty." In *The Colors of Poverty: Why Racial and Ethnic Disparities Persist,* edited by David Harris and Ann Lin, 76–102. New York: Russell Sage Foundation.

Lanctot, Nadine, and Carolyn A. Smith. 2001. "Sexual Activity, Pregnancy, and Deviance in a Representative Urban Sample of African American Girls." *Journal of Youth and Adolescence* 30:349–371.

Landale, Nancy S., and Susan M. Hauan. 1996. "Migration and Premarital Childbearing among Puerto Rican Women." *Demography* 33 (4): 429–442.

Landry, David J., and Jacqueline Darroch Forrest. 1995. "How Old Are U.S. Fathers?" *Family Planning Perspectives* 27 (4): 159–161, 165.

Lareau, Annette. 2003. *Unequal Childhoods.* Berkeley: University of California Press.

Lawlor, Debbie A., and Mary Shaw. 2002. "Too Much Too Young? Teenage Pregnancy Is Not a Public Health Problem." *International Journal of Epidemiology* 31:552–554.

Lawrence v. Texas, 539 U.S. 558 (2003).

Lawson, Annette. 1993. "Multiple Fractures: The Cultural Construction of Teenage Sexuality and Pregnancy." In *The Politics of Pregnancy,* edited by Annette Lawson and Deborah L. Rhode, 101–125. New Haven, CT: Yale University Press.

Leadbeater, Bonnie J. 1996. "School Outcomes for Minority-Group Adolescent Mothers at 28 to 36 Months Postpartum: A Longitudinal Follow-Up." *Journal of Research on Adolescence* 6:629–648.

Leadbeater, Bonnie J. Ross, and Niobe Way. 2001. *Growing Up Fast: Transitions to Early Adulthood of Inner-City Adolescent Mothers.* Mahwah, NJ: Lawrence Erlbaum Associates.

Lefkowitz, Bernard. 1997. *Our Guys.* New York: Vintage.

Leitenberg, Harold, and Heidi Saltzman. 2000. "A Statewide Survey of Age and First Intercourse for Adolescent Females and Age of Their Male Partners: Relation to Other Risk Behaviors and Statutory Rape Implications." *Archives of Sexual Behavior* 29:203–215.

Lerman, Evelyn. 1997. *Teen Moms: The Pain and the Promise.* Buena Park, CA: Morning Glory Press.

Leventhal, John M. 2005. "Getting Prevention Right: Maintaining the Status Quo Is Not an Option. *Child Abuse & Neglect* 29 (3): 209–213.

Levin-Epstein, Jodie. 1997. *State TANF Plans: Out-of-Wedlock and Statutory Rape Provisions.* Washington, DC: Center for Law and Social Policy.

Levine, Judith A., Harold Pollack, and Maureen E. Comfort. 2001. "Academic and Behavioral Outcomes among the Children of Young Mothers." *Journal of Marriage and the Family* 63 (2): 355–369.

Levy, Don, Orlando Rodriguez, and Wayne Villemez. 2004. *The Changing Demographics of Connecticut, 1990 to 2000. Part 2: The Five Connecticuts.* May. Storrs, CT: University of Connecticut, Connecticut State Data Center.

Lewis, Susan K., Catherine E. Ross, and John Mirowsky. 1999. "Establishing a Sense of Personal Control in the Transition to Adulthood." *Social Forces* 77:1573–1599.

Lieberman, Joseph. US Congress. Senate. 1996. *Electronic Benefit Transfer Systems and Welfare Reform.* 104th Congress, 2nd Session, July 12.

Linares, L. Oriana, Bonnie J. Leadbeater, Pamela M. Kato, and Leslie Jaffe. 1991. "Predicting School Outcomes for Minority Group Adolescent Mothers: Can Subgroups Be Identified?" *Journal of Research on Adolescence* 1:379–400.

Lindberg, Laura Duberstein, Freya L. Sonestein, Leighton Ku, and Gladys Martinez. 1997. "Age Differences between Minors Who Give Birth and Their Adult Partners." *Family Planning Perspectives* 29 (2): 61–66.

Lipper, Joanna. 2003. *Growing Up Fast.* New York: Picador.

Little, Craig B., and Andrea Rankin. 2001. "Why Do They Start It? Explaining Reported Early-Teen Sexual Activity." *Sociological Forum* 16:703–729.

Livingston, Gretchen, and D'Vera Cohn. 2012. *U.S. Birth Rate Falls to a Record Low; Decline Is Greatest among Immigrants.* November. 29. Washington, DC: Pew Research Center.

Lohman, Judith. 2004. "Dropout Rates: 1999–2002." OLR Research Report, April 8. www.cga.ct.gov/2004/rpt/2004-R-0391.htm.

Luhby, Tami. 2011. "Global Income Inequality: Where the U.S. Ranks." *CNN Money,* November 8. http://money.cnn.com/2011/11/08/news/economy/global_income_inequality/index.htm.

Luker, Kristin. 1996. *Dubious Conceptions: The Politics of Teenage Pregnancy.* Cambridge, MA: Harvard University Press.

———. 2006. *When Sex Goes to School: Warring Views on Sex—and Sex Education—since the Sixties.* New York: W. W. Norton.

Lundberg, Shelly, and Robert D. Plotnick. 1990. "Effects of State Welfare, Abortion and Family Planning Policies on Premarital Childbearing among White Adolescents." *Family Planning Perspectives* 22 (6): 246–251, 275.

Luster, Tom, and Stephen A. Small. 1994. "Factors Associated with Sexual Risk-Taking Behaviors among Adolescents." *Journal of Marriage and the Family* 56 (3): 622–632.

Luttrell, Wendy. 2003. *Pregnant Bodies, Fertile Minds: Gender, Race and the Schooling of Pregnant Teens.* New York: Routledge.

Lynch, Mona. 2012. "Theorizing the Role of the 'War on Drugs' in US Punishment." *Theoretical Criminology* 16 (2): 175–199.

Mac Donald, Heather. 2006. "Hispanic Family Values?: Runaway Illegitimacy Is Creating a New Underclass." *City Journal.* www.city-journal.org/html/16_4_hispanic_family_values.html.

Males, Mike, and Kenneth S. Y. Chew. 1996. "The Ages of Fathers in California Adolescent Births." *American Journal of Public Health* 86 (4): 565–568.

Malone, Matthew J. 2007. "Age Gap in Teenage Sex Continues to Stir Debate." *New York Times*, June 24.

Manlove, Jennifer. 1998. "The Influence of High School Dropout and School Disengagement on the Risk of School Age Pregnancy." *Journal of Research on Adolescence* 8:187–220.

Manlove, Jennifer, Elizabeth Terry, Laura Gitelson, Angela Romano Papillo, and Stephen Russell. 2000. "Explaining Demographic Trends in Teenage Fertility, 1980–1995." *Family Planning Perspectives* 32 (4): 166–175.

Manlove, Jennifer S., Elizabeth Terry-Humen, Lisa A. Mincieli, and Kristin A. Moore. 2008. "Outcomes for Children of Teen Mothers from Kindergarten through Adolescence." In *Kids Having Kids: Economic Costs and Social Consequences of Teen Pregnancy*, edited by Saul D. Hoffman and Rebecca A. Maynard, 161–220. Washington, DC: Urban Institute Press.

Marini, Margaret Mooney. 1984. "Women's Educational Attainment and the Timing of Entry into Parenthood." *American Sociological Review* 49 (4): 491–511.

Martin, Joyce A., Brady E. Hamilton, Paul D. Sutton, Stephanie J. Ventura, T.J. Mathews, and Michelle J.K. Osterman. 2010. "Births: Final Data 2008." *National Vital Statistics Reports* 59 (1), December 8. Hyattsville, MD: National Center for Health Statistics.

Martin, Joyce A., Brady E. Hamilton, Paul D. Sutton, Stephanie J. Ventura, Fay Menacker, and Sharon Kirmeyer. 2006. "Births: Final Data for 2004." *National Vital Statistics Report* 55 (1), September 29. Hyattsville, MD: National Center for Health Statistics.

Martin, Joyce A., Brady E. Hamilton, Paul D. Sutton, Stephanie J. Ventura, Fay Menacker, Sharon Kirmeyer, and T.J. Mathews. 2009. "Births: Final Data for 2006." *National Vital Statistics Report* 57 (7), January 7. Hyattsville, MD: National Center for Health Statistics.

Martin, Joyce A., Brady E. Hamilton, Paul D. Sutton, Stephanie J. Ventura, Fay Menacker, Sharon Kirmeyer, and Martha L. Munson. 2007. "Births: Final Data 2005." *National Vital Statistics Report* 56 (6), December 5. Hyattsville, MD: National Center for Health Statistics.

Martin, Joyce A., Brady E. Hamilton, Paul D. Sutton, Stephanie J. Ventura, Fay Menacker, and Martha L. Munson. 2003. "Births: Final Data 2002." *National Vital Statistics Report* 52 (10), December 17. Hyattsville, MD: National Center for Health Statistics.

Martin, Joyce A., Brady E. Hamilton, Stephanie J. Ventura, Michelle J.K. Osterman, and T.J. Mathews. 2013. "Births: Final Data for 2011." *National Vital Statistics Reports* 62 (1), June 28. Hyattsville, MD: National Center for Health Statistics.

Martin, Joyce A., Brady E. Hamilton, Stephanie J. Ventura, Michelle J.K. Osterman, Elizabeth C. Wilson, and T.J. Mathews. 2012. "Births: Final Data for 2010." *National Vital Statistics Reports* 61 (1), August 28. Hyattsville, MD: National Center for Health Statistics.

Mason, Alex, Laura Zimmerman, and William Evans. 1998. "Sexual and Physical Abuse among Incarcerated Youth: Implications for Sexual Behavior, Contraceptive Use, and Teenage Pregnancy." *Child Abuse & Neglect* 22 (10): 987–995.

Mauer, Marc, and Ryan S. King. 2007. *Uneven Justice: State Rates of Incarceration by Race and Ethnicity*. June. Washington DC: Sentencing Project.

Mayer, Susan E. 1991. "How Much Does a High School's Racial and Socioeconomic Mix Affect Graduation and Teenage Fertility Rates?" In *The Urban Underclass*, edited by Christopher Jencks and Paul E. Peterson, 321–341. Washington, DC: Brookings Institution.

Maynard, Rebecca A., and Saul D. Hoffman. 2008. "The Costs of Adolescent Childbearing." In *Kids Having Kids: Economic Costs and Social Consequences of Teen Pregnancy*, edited by Saul D. Hoffman and Rebecca A. Maynard, 359–402. Washington, DC: Urban Institute Press.

McCargar, Laura. 2011. *Invisible Students: The Role of Alternative and Adult Education in the Connecticut School-to-Prison Pipeline*. Hartford, CT: A Better Way Foundation.

McDermott, Elizabeth, and Hilary Graham. 2005. "Resilient Mothering: Social Inequalities, Late Modernity and the 'Problem' of 'Teenage' Motherhood." *Journal of Youth Studies* 8 (1): 59–79.

McGuffey, C. Shawn. 2005. "Engendering Trauma: Race, Class, and Gender Reaffirmation after Child Sexual Abuse." *Gender & Society* 19 (5): 621–643.

———. 2008. "'Saving Masculinity:' Gender Reaffirmation, Sexuality, Race, and Parental Responses to Male Child Sexual Abuse." *Social Problems* 55 (2): 216–237.

McIntosh, Kent, K. Brigid Flannery, George Sugai, Drew H. Braun, and Krysta L. Cochrane. 2008. "Relationships between Academics and Problem Behavior in the Transition from Middle School to High School." *Journal of Positive Behavior Interventions* 10 (4): 243–255.

McKay, Alexander. 2002. "Sex Research Update." *Canadian Journal of Human Sexuality* 11:51–57.

Mead, Lawrence M. 1986. *Beyond Entitlement: The Social Obligations of Citizenship*. New York: Free Press.

Megan, Kathleen. 2012. "Hartford Students in Regional Magnets and 'Open Choice' Outperform Kids in City Schools." *Hartford Courant*, October 25. http://articles.courant.com/2012-10-25/news/hc-magnet-school-scores-20121025_1_hartford-host-magnet-schools-open-choice-hartford-students.

Menacker, Fay, Joyce Martin, Marian F. MacDorman, and Stephanie J. Ventura. 2004. "Births to 10–14 Year-Old Mothers, 1990–2002: Trends and Health Outcomes." *National Vital Statistics Reports* 53 (7), November 15. Hyattsville, MD: National Center for Health Statistics.

Menjívar, Cecilia. 2011. *Enduring Violence: Ladina Women's Lives in Guatemala*. Berkeley: University of California Press.

Merritt, Deborah Jones. 1996. "Ending Poverty by Cutting Teenaged Births: Promise, Failure, and Paths to the Future." *Ohio State Law Journal* 57 (2): 441–467.

Merritt, Grace E. 2010. "Youth Risk Behavior Survey: 70% of High School Seniors Have Had Sex." *Hartford Courant*, August 16. www.courant.com/health/hc-teen-sex.

Miller, Brent. 2002. "Family Influences on Adolescent Sexual and Contraceptive Behavior." *Journal of Sex Research* 39 (1): 22–26.

Miller, Jody. 2008. *Getting Played: African American Girls, Urban Inequality and Gendered Violence*. New York: New York University Press.

Miller, Kathleen E., Donald F. Sabo, Michael P. Farrell, Grace M. Barnes, and Merrill J. Melnick. 1999. "Sport, Sexual Behavior, Contraceptive Use, and Pregnancy among Male and Female High School Students: Testing Cultural Resource Theory." *Sociology of Sport Journal* 16:366–387.

Mills, C. Wright. 1959. *The Sociological Imagination.* New York: Oxford University Press.

Mizelle, Nancy B., and Judith L. Irvin. 2000. "Transition from Middle School into High School." *Middle School Journal* 31 (5): 37–61.

Mollborn, Stefanie, and Janet Jacobs. 2012. "'We'll Figure a Way': Teenage Mothers' Experiences in Shifting Social and Economic Contexts." *Qualitative Sociology* 35 (1): 23–46.

Mongan, Philip, and Robert Walker. 2012. "'The Road to Hell Is Paved with Good Intentions': A Historical, Theoretical, and Legal Analysis of Zero-Tolerance Weapons Policy in American Schools." *Preventing School Failure* 56 (4): 232–240.

Moore, Kristin A., Brent C. Miller, Barbara W. Sugaland, Donna Ruane Morrison, Dana A. Glei, and Connie Blumenthal. 1995. "Beginning Too Soon: Adolescent Sexual Behavior, Pregnancy, and Parenthood: A Review of Research and Interventions." http://aspe.hhs.gov/HSP/cyp/xsteesex.htm.

Moore, Kristin Anderson, and Nancy O. Snyder. 1991. "Cognitive Attainment among Firstborn Children of Adolescent Mothers." *American Sociological Review* 56 (5): 612–624.

Moore, Kristin A., and Barbara W. Sugland. 1999. "Piecing Together the Puzzle of Teenage Childbearing." *Policy and Practice of Public Human Service* 57 (2): 36–43.

Moore, Kristin Anderson, Christine Winquist Nord, and James L. Peterson. 1989. "Nonvoluntary Sexual Activity among Adolescents." *Family Planning Perspectives* 21 (3): 110–114.

Moynihan, Daniel Patrick. 1965. *The Negro Family: The Case for National Action.* Washington DC: US Department of Labor Office of Policy Planning and Research.

Mullen, Paul E., Judy L. Martin, Jessie C. Anderson, Sarah E. Romans, and G. Peter Herbison. 1994. "The Effect of Child Sexual Abuse on Social, Interpersonal, and Sexual Function in Adult Life." *British Journal of Psychiatry* 165:35–47.

Murray, Charles. 1984. *Losing Ground: American Social Policy, 1950–1980.* New York: Basic Books.

Musick, Judith S. 1993. *Young, Poor, and Pregnant: The Psychology of Teenage Motherhood.* New Haven, CT: Yale University Press.

Nagy, Stephen, Ralph DiClemente, and Anthony G. Adcock. 1995. "Adverse Factors Associated with Forced Sex among Southern Adolescent Girls." *Pediatrics* 96 (5): 944–946.

Nathanson, Constance A. 1991. *Dangerous Passage: The Social Control of Sexuality in Women's Adolescence.* Philadelphia: Temple University Press.

National Institute of Child Health and Human Development. 1998. "Strong Schools, Family Ties Protect Teens from Violence, Drugs, Suicide, and Early Sex." *Research on Today's Issues* 8, August.

Neild, Ruth Curran, and Robert Balfanz. 2006. *Unfulfilled Promise: The Dimensions and Characteristics of Philadelphia's Dropout Crisis, 2000–2005.* www.pyninc.org/downloads/Unfulfilled_Promise_Project_U-turn.pdf.

Neubeck, Kenneth J., and Noel A. Cazenave. 2001. *Welfare Racism: Playing the Race Card against America's Poor.* New York: Routledge.

Newman, Barbara M., Brenda J. Lohman, Philip R. Newman, Mary C. Myers, and Victoria L. Smith. 2000. "Experiences of Urban Youth Navigating the Transition to Ninth Grade." *Youth & Society* 31:387–416.

Newport, Frank. 2013. "Majority in U.S. Want Wealth More Evenly Distributed." www.gallup.com/poll/161927/majority-wealth-evenly-distributed.aspx.

Ng, Allison Stewart, and Keleen Kaye. 2013. "Teen Childbearing in Rural America." www.thenationalcampaign.org/resources/pdf/ss/ss47_teenchild-bearinginruralamerica.pdf.

Nieto, Sonia. 1992. *Affirming Diversity: The Sociopolitical Context of Multicultural Education.* New York: Longman.

Noll, Jennie G., Chad E. Shenk, and Karen T. Putnam. 2009. "Childhood Sexual Abuse and Adolescent Pregnancy: A Meta-Analytic Update. *Journal of Pediatric Psychology* 34 (4): 366–378.

Noll, Jennie G., Penelope K. Trickett, William W. Harris, and Frank W. Putnam. 2009. "The Cumulative Burden Borne by Offspring Whose Mothers Were Sexually Abused as Children: Descriptive Results from a Multigenerational Study." *Journal of Interpersonal Violence* 24 (3): 424–449.

Noll, Jennie G., Penelope K. Trickett, and Frank W. Putnam. 2000. "Social Network Constellation and Sexuality of Sexually Abused and Comparison Girls in Childhood and Adolescence." *Child Maltreatment* 5 (4): 323–337.

Oakes, Jeannie. 2005. *Keeping Track: How Schools Structure Inequality.* 2nd ed. New Haven, CT: Yale University Press.

Oberman, Michelle. 1994. "Turning Girls into Women: Reevaluating Modern Statutory Rape Law." *Journal of Criminal Law and Criminology* 85:15–78.

———. 1996. "Statutory Rape Laws: Does It Make Sense to Enforce Them in an Increasingly Permissive Society? Yes: The Risk of Psychological Harm to Girls Is Too Great." *American Bar Association Journal* 82:86–87.

———. 2000. "Girls in the Master's House: Of Protection, Patriarchy, and the Potential for Using the Master's Tools to Reconfigure Statutory Rape Law." *DePaul Law Review* 50:799–826.

O'Connor, John. 2010. "Marxism and Three Movements of Neoliberalism." *Critical Sociology* 36 (5): 691–715.

Ohlemacher, Stephen. 1997. "Campaign Gives Men a Warning: Statutory Rape Will Not Be Tolerated." *Hartford Courant,* October 8, A3.

Olds, David L., JoAnn Robinson, Ruth O'Brien, Dennis W. Luckey, Lisa M. Pettitt, Charles R. Henderson Jr., Rosanna K. Ng, Karen L. Sheff, Jon Korfmacher, Susan Hiatt, and Ayelet Talmi. 2002. "Home Visiting by Paraprofessionals and by Nurses: A Randomized, Controlled Trial." *Pediatrics* 110 (3): 486–96.

Olesen, Virginia L. 2005. "Early Millennial Feminist Qualitative Research: Challenges and Contours." In *The Handbook of Qualitative Research,* 3rd ed., edited by Norman K. Denzin and Yvonna S. Lincoln, 235–278. Thousand Oaks, CA: Sage Publications.

Oliveri, Rigel. 2000. "Rape Law Enforcement in the Wake of Welfare Reform." *Stanford Law Review* 52 (2): 463–508.

Omi, Michael. 1991. "Shifting the Blame: Racial Ideology and Politics in the Post–Civil Rights Era." *Critical Sociology* 18 (3): 77–98.

Orenstein, Peggy. 1995. *Schoolgirls: Young Women, Self-Esteem and the Confidence Cap.* New York: Doubleday.

Ortiz, C.G., and Ena Vazquez Nuttall. 1987. "Adolescent Pregnancy: Effects of Family Support, Education, and Religion on the Decision to Carry or Terminate among Puerto Rican Teenagers." *Adolescence* 22 (88): 897–917.

Otterman, Sharon. 2013. "Hasidic Therapist Sentenced to 103 Years in Sexual Abuse Case." *New York Times*, January 22, A17.

Owens, David. 2012. "Shenkman Sentenced to 70 Years in Prison." *Hartford Courant,* January 4. http://articles.courant.com/2012-01-04/news/hc-shenkman-sentence-0105-20120104_1_richard-shenkman-claim-of-mental-illness-prosecutor-vicki-melchiorre.

Owens, David, and Christine Dempsey. 2009. "Desperate Pleas for Help: Murder-Suicide." *Hartford Courant,* June 30.

Pachter, Lee M., and Cynthia García Coll. 2009. "Racism and Child Health: A Review of the Literature and Future Directions." *Journal of Developmental and Behavioral Pediatrics* 30 (3): 255–263.

Pagani, Linda, Bernard Boulerice, and Richard E. Tremblay. 1997. "The Influence of Poverty on Children's Classroom Placement and Behavior Problems." In *Consequences of Growing Up Poor,* edited by Greg J. Duncan and Jeanne Brooks-Gunn, 311–339. New York: Russell Sage Foundation.

Paltrow, Lynn M. 2013. "*Roe v. Wade* and the New Jane Crow: Reproductive Rights in the Age of Mass Incarceration." *American Journal of Public Health* 103 (1): 17–21.

Peckinpaugh, Janet. 2010. "Former News Anchor Peckinpaugh Shares Story of Abuse, Stalking." *Hartford Courant,* April 18. http://articles.courant.com/2010-04-18/news/hc-peckinpaugh-abuse-stalking.artapr18_1_stalking-anchor-second-night.

Peet, Richard. 2009. *Unholy Trinity: The IMF, World Band and WTO.* 2nd ed. New York: Zed Books.

Peleikis, Dawn E., Arnstein Mykletun, Alv A. Dahl. 2004. "The Relative Influence of Childhood Sexual Abuse and Other Family Background Risk Factors on Adult Adversities in Female Outpatients Treated for Anxiety Disorders and Depression." *Child Abuse & Neglect* 28 (1): 61–76.

Perales, Nina. 1999. "Cultural Stereotypes and the Legal Response to Pregnant Teens." In *Mother Troubles: Rethinking Contemporary Maternal Dilemmas,* edited by Julia E. Hanigsberg and Sara Ruddick, 81–96. Boston: Beacon.

Peters, H. Elizabeth, and Natalie C. Mullis. 1997. "The Role of Family Income and Sources of Income in Adolescent Achievement." In *Consequences of Growing Up Poor,* edited by Greg J. Duncan and Jeanne Brooks-Gunn, 340–381. New York: Russell Sage Foundation.

Peters, Stephanie Doyle, Gail Elizabeth Wyatt, and David Finkelhor. 1986. "Prevalence." In *A Sourcebook on Child Sexual Abuse,* 15–59. Beverly Hills, CA: Sage Publications.

Petersen, Larry R. 2001. "Religion, Plausibility Structures, and Education's Effect on Attitudes toward Elective Abortion." *Journal for the Scientific Study of Religion* 40:187–205.

Peterson, Carla A., Gayle J. Luze, Elaine M. Eshbaugh, Hyun-Joo Jeon, and Kelly Ross Kantz. 2007. "Enhancing Parent-Child Interactions through Home Visiting: Promising Practice or Unfulfilled Promise?" *Journal of Early Intervention* 29 (2): 119–140.

Pew Research Center Publications. 2010. "The Decline of Marriage and Rise of New Families." http://pewresearch.org/pubs/1802/decline-marriage-rise-new-families.

Phoenix, Ann. 1993. "The Social Construction of Teenage Motherhood: A Black and White Issue?" In *The Politics of Pregnancy,* edited by Annette Lawson and Deborah L. Rhode, 74–97. New Haven, CT: Yale University Press.

Pickett, Kate E., Jessica Mookherjee, and Richard G. Wilkinson. 2005. "Adolescent Birth Rates, Total Homicides, and Income Inequality in Rich Countries." *American Journal of Public Health* 95 (7): 1181–1183.

Pierre, Natalie, Lydia A. Shrier, S. Jean Emans, and Robert H. DuRant. 1998. "Adolescent Males Involved in Pregnancy: Associations of Forces Sexual Contact and Risk Behaviors." *Journal of Adolescent Health* 23 (6): 364–369.

Pillow, Wanda S. 2003. "Confession, Catharsis, or Cure? Rethinking the Uses of Reflexivity as a Methodological Power in Qualitative Research." *International Journal of Qualitative Studies in Education* 16 (2): 175–196.

———. 2004. *Unfit Subjects: Educational Policy and the Teen Mother.* New York: Routledge.

Pipher, Mary. 1998. *Reviving Ophelia: Saving the Selves of Adolescent Girls.* New York: Ballantine Books.

Piven, Francis Fox, and Richard A. Cloward. 1985. *The New Class War: Reagan's Attack on the Welfare State and Its Consequences.* 2nd ed. New York: Pantheon.

Plotnick, Robert D. 1992. "The Effects of Attitudes on Teenage Premarital Pregnancy and Its Resolution." *American Sociological Review* 57 (6): 800–811.

Polit, Denise, Cozette Morrow White, and Thomas D. Morton. 1990. "Child Sexual Abuse and Premarital Intercourse among High-Risk Adolescents." *Journal of Adolescent Health Care* 11 (3): 231–34.

Pollin, Robert, and Stephanie Luce. 1998. *The Living Wage: Building a Fair Economy.* New York: New Press.

Prater, Loretta P. 1992. "Early Pregnancy and Academic Achievement of African-American Youth." *Exceptional Children* 59:141–149.

Putnam, Frank. 2003. "Ten-Year Research Update Review: Child Sexual Abuse." *Journal of the American Academy of Child and Adolescent Psychiatry* 42 (3): 269–276.

Putnam, Frank, and Penelope K. Trickett. 1997. "Psychobiological Effects of Sexual Abuse: A Longitudinal Study." *Annals of the New York Academy of Science* 821:150–159.

Quadagno, Jill. 1994. *The Color of Welfare: How Racism Undermined the War on Poverty.* New York: Oxford University Press.

Rainey, David Y., Catherine Stevens-Simon, and David W. Kaplan. 1995. "Are Adolescents Who Report Prior Sexual Abuse at Higher Risk for Pregnancy?" *Child Abuse & Neglect* 19 (10): 1283–1288.

Raj, Anita, Jay G. Silverman, and Hortensia Amaro. 2000. "The Relationship between Sexual Abuse and Sexual Risk among High School Students: Findings from the 1997 Massachusetts Youth Risk Behavior Survey." *Maternal & Child Health Journal* 4 (2): 125–135.

Ream, Robert K. 2005. "Toward Understanding How Social Capital Mediates the Impact of Mobility on Mexican American Achievement." *Social Forces* 84 (1): 201–224.

Records, Kathryn A. 1993. "Life Events of Pregnant and Nonpregnant Adolescents." *Adolescence* 28:325–338.

Reed, Adolph, Jr. 1991. "The Underclass Myth." *Progressive* 55:18–21.

———. 1999. *Stirrings in the Jug: Black Politics in the Post-Segregation Era.* Minneapolis: University of Minnesota Press.

Reich, Robert B. 2010. *After-Shock: The Next Economy and America's Future.* New York: Knopf.

Reinharz, Shulamit. 1992. *Feminist Methods in Social Research.* New York: Oxford University Press.

Remez, L. 1992. "Adoption vs. Parenting: No Difference in Short-Term Effects on Young Mothers." *Family Planning Perspectives* 24 (5): 238–239.

Rhode, Deborah L. 1993. "Adolescent Pregnancy and Public Policy." In *The Politics of Pregnancy,* edited by Annette Lawson and Deborah L. Rhode, 301–335. New Haven, CT: Yale University Press.

———. 1993–1994. "Adolescent Pregnancy and Public Policy." *Political Science Quarterly* 108:635–669.

Rhode, Deborah L., and Annette Lawson. 1993. "Introduction." In *The Politics of Pregnancy: Adolescent Sexuality and Public Policy,* edited by Annette Lawson and Deborah L. Rhode, 1–19. New Haven, CT: Yale University Press.

Rios, Victor M. 2011. *Punished: Policing the Lives of Black and Latino Boys.* New York: New York University Press.

Rivera-Batiz, Francisco, and Carlos E. Santiago. 1994. *Puerto Ricans in the United States: A Changing Reality.* Washington DC: National Puerto Rican Coalition.

Roberts, Ron, Tom O'Connor, Judy Dunn, Jean Golding, The ALSPAC Study Team. 2004. "The Effects of Child Sexual Abuse in Later Family Life: Mental Health, Parenting and Adjustment of Offspring." *Child Abuse & Neglect* 28 (5): 525–545.

Robinson, Rachel B., and Deborah I. Frank. 1994. "The Relation between Self-Esteem, Sexual Activity, and Pregnancy." *Adolescence* 29:27–35.

Rodriguez, Cleo, Jr., and Nelwyn B. Moore. 1995. "Perceptions of Pregnant /Parenting Teens: Reframing Issues for an Integrated Approach to Pregnancy Problems." *Adolescence* 30:685–706.

Romano, Elisa, Mark Zoccolillo, and Daniel Paquette. 2006. "Histories of Child Maltreatment and Psychiatric Disorder in Pregnant Adolescents." *Journal of the American Academy of Child and Adolescent Psychiatry* 45 (3): 329–336.

Ronai, Carol Rambo. 1995. "Multiple Reflections of Child Sex Abuse." *Journal of Contemporary Ethnography* 23 (4): 395–426.

Roosa, Mark W., Jenn-Yun Tein, Cindy Reinholtz, and Patricia Jo Angelini. 1997. "The Relationship of Childhood Sexual Abuse to Teenage Pregnancy." *Journal of Marriage and the Family* 59 (1): 119–130.

Ross, Winston. 2013. "CNN Feels Sorry for Steubenville Rapists; World Can't Believe Its Ears." *The Daily Beast: U.S. News*. March 18. www.thedailybeast .com/articles/2013/03/18/cnn-feels-sorry-for-steubenville-rapists-world-can-t-believe-its-ears.html.

Rubin, Valerie, and Patricia L. East. 1999. "Adolescents' Pregnancy Intentions: Relations to Life Situations and Caretaking Behaviors Prenatally and 2 Years Postpartum." *Journal of Adolescent Health* 24:313–320.

Rumbaut, Ruben G. 2005. "Turning Points in the Transition to Adulthood: Determinants of Educational Attainment, Incarceration, and Early Childbearing among Children of Immigrants." *Ethnic and Racial Studies* 28 (6): 1041–1086.

Russell, Diana E.H., and Nicole Van de Ven, eds. 1976. *The Proceedings of the International Tribunal on Crimes against Women*. Millbrae, CA: Les Femmes.

Ryan, Ione J., and Patricia C. Dunn. 1988. "Association of Race, Sex, Religion, Family Size, and Desired Number of Children on College Students: Preferred Methods of Dealing with Unplanned Pregnancy." *Family Practice Research Journal* 7:153–161.

Ryan, Suzanne, Kerry Franzetta, and Jennifer Manlove. 2007. "Knowledge, Perceptions, and Motivations for Contraception: Influence on Teens' Contraceptive Consistency." *Youth & Society* 39 (2): 182–208.

Sabo, Donald, F., Kathleen E. Miller, Michael P. Farrell, Merrill J. Melnick, and Grace M. Barnes. 1999. "High School Athletic Participation, Sexual Behavior and Adolescent Pregnancy: A Regional Study." *Journal of Adolescent Health* 25:207–216.

Saewyc, Elizabeth M., Leanne Magee, and Sandra Pettingell. 2004. "Teenage Pregnancy and Associated Risk Behaviors among Sexually Abused Adolescents." *Perspectives on Sexual and Reproductive Health* 36 (3): 98–105.

Sanday, Peggy Reeves. 1990. *Fraternity Gang Rape: Sex, Brotherhood, and Privilege on Campus*. New York: New York University Press.

Sanders, Stephanie A., Cynthia A Graham, Jennifer L. Bass, and John Bancroft. 2001. "A Prospective Study of the Effects of Oral Contraceptives on Sexuality and Well-Being and Their Relationship to Discontinuation." *Contraception* 64 (1): 51–58.

Santelli, John S., Brian Morrow, John E. Anderson, and Laura Duberstein Lindberg. 2006. "Contraceptive Use and Pregnancy Risk among High School Students, 1991–2003." *Perspectives on Sexual and Reproductive Health* 38 (2): 106–111.

Santelli, John S., Mark Orr, Laura D. Lindberg, and Daniela C. Diaz. 2009. "Changing Behavioral Risk for Pregnancy among High School Students in the United States, 1991–2007." *Journal of Adolescent Health* 45:25–32.

Santorum, Rick. US Congress. Senate. 1996. *Personal Responsibility, Work Opportunity, and Medicaid Restructuring Act of 1996*. 104th Congress, 2nd Session, July 18, 1996.

Sawhill, Isabel V. 2002. "Issues in TANF Reauthorization: Building Stronger Families." Testimony before the Senate Finance Committee. May 16.

Sawhill, Isabel V., and John E. Morton. 2007. *Economic Mobility: Is the American Dream Alive and Well?* May. Washington, DC: Pew Charitable Trust and the Brookings Institute.

Schalet, Amy T. 2011. *Not under My Roof: Parents, Teens, and the Culture of Sex*. Chicago: University of Chicago Press.

Scheper-Hughes, Nancy, and Philippe Bourgois. 2004. "Introduction: Making Sense of Violence." In *Violence in War and Peace: An Anthology*, edited by Nancy Scheper-Hughes and Philippe Bourgois, 1–27. Oxford: Blackwell.

Scher, Lauren Sue. 2008. "What Do We Know about the Effectiveness of Programs Aimed at Reducing Teen Sexual Risk-Taking?" In *Kids Having Kids: Economic Costs and Social Consequences of Teen Pregnancy*, edited by Saul D. Hoffman and Rebecca A. Maynard, 403–433. Washington, DC: Urban Institute Press.

Scher, Lauren Sue, and Saul Hoffman. 2008. "Consequences for Teen Childbearing for Incarceration among Adult Children: Updated Estimates through 2002." In *Kids Having Kids: Economic Costs and Social Consequences of Teen Pregnancy*, edited by Saul D. Hoffman and Rebecca A. Maynard, 311–322. Washington, DC: Urban Institute Press.

Schmidt, Marian. 1995. "Anglo Americans and Sexual Child Abuse." In *Sexual Abuse in Nine North American Communities*, edited by Lisa Aronson Fontes, 156–175. Thousand Oaks, CA: Sage Publications.

Seccombe, Karen. 2000. "Families in Poverty in the 1990s: Trends, Causes, Consequences, and Lessons Learned." *Journal of Marriage and Family* 62 (4): 1094–1113.

Settersten, Richard A., Jr. 2011. "Becoming Adults: Meanings and Markers for Young Americans." In *Coming of Age in America: The Transition to Adulthood in the Twenty-First Century*, edited by Mary C. Waters, Patrick J. Carr, Maria J. Kefalas, and Jennifer Holdaway, 169–190. Berkeley: University of California Press.

Shear, Michael D. 2013. "Judge Refuses to Drop His Order Allowing Morning-After Pill for All Ages." *New York Times*, May 11, A11.

Sheff v. O'Neill. 1996. 238 Conn. 1, 678 A.2d 1267, 111 Ed. Law Rep. 360. www.sheffmovement.org/pef/sheff1996decision.pdf.

Sidel, Ruth. 2006. *Unsung Heroines: Single Mothers and the American Dream*. Berkeley: University of California Press.

Simms, Margaret C. 1993. "Adolescent Pregnancy among Blacks in the United States: Why Is It a Policy Issue?" In *The Politics of Pregnancy*, edited by Annette Lawson and Deborah L. Rhode, 241–256. New Haven, CT: Yale University Press.

Simpson, Stan. 2007. "Let's Focus on Early Grades." *Hartford Courant*, December 8, B1.

Singh, Susheela, Jacqueline E. Darroch, and Jennifer J. Frost. 2001. "Socioeconomic Disadvantage and Adolescent Women's Sexual and Reproductive

Behavior: The Case of Five Developed Countries." *Family Planning Perspectives* 33 (5): 251–289.

Smith, Alicia, Brad Powell, and Mary Patrice Erdmans. 2013. "*16 and Pregnant*: Managing a Spoiled Identity in the Media." Paper presented at the annual meeting of the Society for the Study of Social Problems, August, New York, NY.

Smith, Judith R., Jeanne Brooks-Gunn, and Pamela K. Klebanov. 1997. "Consequences of Living in Poverty for Young Children's Cognitive and Verbal Ability and Early School Achievement." In *Consequences of Growing Up Poor*, edited by Greg J. Duncan, and Jeanne Brooks-Gunn, 132–189. New York: Russell Sage Foundation.

SmithBattle, Lee. 2007. "Legacies of Advantage and Disadvantage: The Case of Teen Mothers." *Public Health Nursing* 24 (5): 409–420.

Solomon-Fears, Carmen. 2011. "Teenage Pregnancy Prevention: Statistics and Programs." *Congressional Research Service*, February 3.

Stack, Carol B. 1974. "All Our Kin: Strategies for Survival in a Black Community." New York: Harper & Row.

Starkman, Naomi, and Nicole Rajani. 2002. "The Case for Comprehensive Sex Education." *AIDS Patient Care and STDs* 16:313–318.

Starr, Jerold. 1994. "Peace Corps Service as a Turning Point." *International Journal of Aging and Human Development* 39 (2): 137–161.

State of Connecticut. 2005. "Child Poverty Council Initial Plan." Hartford, CT: Office of Policy and Management. www.ct.gov/opm/LIB/opm/HHS/CPC/CPCFinalPlan.pdf.

Stearns, Elizabeth, and Elizabeth J. Glennie. 2006. "When and Why Dropouts Leave High School." *Youth & Society* 38 (1): 29–57.

Stein, Rob. 2007. "As 'Abstinence' Programs Falter, States Opt Out." *Hartford Courant*, December 16, A11.

Steinhauer, Jennifer. 2013. "Sexual Assaults in Military Raise Alarm in Washington." *New York Times,* May 7. www.nytimes.com/2013/05/08/us/politics/pentagon-study-sees-sharp-rise-in-sexual-assaults.html?pagewanted = all.

Stepp, Laura Sessions. 2013. "Rural America Has a Teen Pregnancy Problem." www.cnn.com/2013/02/27/opinion/stepp-teenage-pregancies/.

Stevens-Simon, Catherine, and Elizabeth McAnarney. 1994. "Childhood Victimization: Relationship to Adolescent Pregnancy Outcome." *Child Abuse & Neglect* 18 (7): 569–575.

Stevens-Simon, Catherine, and Susan Reichert. 1994. "Sexual Abuse, Adolescent Pregnancy, and Child Abuse: A Developmental Approach to an Intergenerational Cycle." *Archives of Pediatrics and Adolescent Medicine* 148:23–27.

Stevenson, Wendy, Kenneth I. Maton, and Douglas M. Teti. 1998. "School Importance and Dropout among Pregnant Adolescents." *Journal of Adolescent Health* 5 (22): 376–382.

Stock, Jacqueline L., Michelle A. Bell, Debra K. Boyer, and Frederick A. Connell. 1997. "Adolescent Pregnancy and Sexual Risk-Taking among Sexually Abused Girls." *Family Planning Perspectives* 29 (5): 200–203, 227.

Sun, Yongmin. 2001. "Family Environment and Adolescents' Well-Being before and after Parents' Marital Disruption: A Longitudinal Analysis." *Journal of Marriage and the Family* 63 (3): 697–713.

Sutherland, Kate. 2002–2003. "From Jailbird to Jailbait: Age of Consent Laws and the Construction of Teenage Sexualities." *William & Mary Journal of Women and the Law* 9:313–349.

Sykes, Gini. 1997. *8 Ball Chicks: A Year in the Violent World of Girl Gangs.* Norwell, MA: Anchor.

Sylvester, Kathleen, and Kathleen Reich. 2002. *Making Fathers Count: Assessing the Progress of Responsible Fatherhood Efforts.* Baltimore: Annie E. Casey Foundation.

Taborn, John M. 1990. "Adolescent Pregnancy: A Medical Concern." In *Teenage Pregnancy: Developing Strategies for Change in the Twenty-First Century,* edited by Dionne J. Jones and Stanley F. Battle, 91–100. New Brunswick, NJ: Transaction Publishers.

Tapia, Javiar. 2004. "Latino Households and Schooling: Economic and Sociocultural Factors Affecting Students' Learning and Academic Performance." *International Journal of Qualitative Studies in Education* 17 (3): 415–436.

Teachman, Jay D., Kathleen M. Paasch, Randal D. Day, and Karen P. Carver. 1997. "Poverty during Adolescence and Subsequent Educational Achievement." In *Consequences of Growing Up Poor,* edited by Greg J. Duncan, and Jeanne Brooks-Gunn, 382–418. New York: Russell Sage Foundation.

Tolman, Deborah L. 2001. "Echoes of Sexual Objectification: Listening for One Girl's Erotic Voice." In *From Subjects to Subjectivities: A Handbook of Interpretive and Participatory Methods,* edited by Deborah L. Tolman and Mary L. Brydon-Miller, 130–144. New York: New York University Press.

———. 2002. *Dilemmas of Desire: Teenage Girls Talk about Sexuality.* Cambridge, MA: Harvard University Press.

Tolman, Deborah L., and Mary L. Brydon-Miller, eds. 2001. *From Subjects to Subjectivities: A Handbook of Interpretive and Participatory Methods.* New York: New York University Press.

Tolman, Deborah L., and Laura A. Szalacha. 1999. "Dimensions of Desire: Bridging Qualitative and Quantitative Methods in a Study of Female Adolescent Sexuality." *Psychology of Women Quarterly* 23:7–39.

Torre, Carlos, Hugo Rodriguez Vecchini, and William Burgos, eds. 1994. *The Commuter Nation: Perspectives on Puerto Rican Migration.* Rio Pedras: University of Puerto Rico Press.

Trad, Paul. 1999. "Assessing the Patterns That Prevent Teen Pregnancy." *Adolescence* 34 (133): 221–240.

Trent, Katherine, and Kyle Crowder. 1997. "Adolescent Birth Intentions, Social Disadvantages, and Behavioral Outcomes." *Journal of Marriage and the Family* 59 (3): 523–535.

Upchurch, Dawn M., and James McCarthy. 1990. "The Timing of First Birth and High School Completion." *American Sociological Review* 55 (2): 224–234.

Urban Institute. 1997. "Tougher Statutory Rape Laws Expected to Have Limited Impact on Teen Childbearing." Press Release, April 15.

US Department of Health and Human Services. 2008. *Child Maltreatment, 2008.* Children's Bureau, Administration for Children and Families, Washington, DC. www.acf.hhs.gov/programs/cb/pubs/cm08/chapter3.htm#race.

Ventura, Stephanie J. 2009. "Changing Patterns of Nonmarital Childbearing in the United States." NCHS Data Brief 18. Hyattsville, MD: National Center for Health Statistics.

Ventura, Stephanie A., Joyce C. Abma, William D. Mosher, and Stanley K. Henshaw. 2004. "Estimated Pregnancy Rates for the United States, 1990–2000: An Update." *National Vital Statistics Reports* 52 (23), June 14. Hyattsville, MD: National Center for Health Statistics.

———. 2008. "Estimated Pregnancy Rates by Outcome for the United States, 1990–2004." *National Vital Statistics Reports* 56 (15), April 14. Hyattsville, MD: National Center for Health Statistics.

Ventura, Stephanie J., Sally C. Curtin, and Joyce C. Abma. 2012. "Estimated Pregnancy Rates and Rates of Pregnancy Outcomes for the United States, 1990–2008." *National Vital Statistics Reports* 60 (7), June 20. Hyattsville, MD: National Center for Health Statistics.

Ventura, Stephanie J., T. J. Mathews, Sally C. Curtin. 1998. "Declines in Teenage Birth Rates, 1991–97." *National Vital Statistics Reports* 47 (12), December 17. Hyattsville, MD: National Center for Health Statistics.

Ventura, Stephanie J., T. J. Mathews, Brady E. Hamilton. 2001. "Births to Teens in the United States, 1940–2000." *National Vital Statistics Reports* 49 (10), September 25. Hyattsville, MD: National Center for Health Statistics.

Wacquant, Loïc. 2000. "The New Peculiar Institution: On the Prison as Surrogate Ghetto." *Theoretical Criminology* 4 (3): 377–389.

———. 2001. "Deadly Symbiosis: When Ghetto and Prison Meet and Mesh." *Punishment and Society* 3 (1): 95–133.

———. 2002. "From Slavery to Mass Incarceration: Rethinking the 'Race Question' in the U.S." *New Left Review* 13 (January-February): 41–60.

———. 2008. *Urban Outcasts: A Comparative Sociology of Advanced Marginality.* Malden, MA: Polity Press.

———. 2009. *Punishing the Poor: The Neoliberal Government of Social Insecurity.* Durham, NC: Duke University Press.

Waldman, Hillary. 2008. "Questions Haunt Two of Reardon's Earliest Victims." *Hartford Courant,* October 19.

Walkerdine, Valerie, Helen Lucey, and June Melody. 2001. *Growing Up Girl: Psychosocial Explorations of Gender and Class.* New York: New York University Press.

Wallach, Lorraine B. 1997. "Helping Children Cope with Violence." In *Marriage and the Family,* 23rd ed., 165–170. Guilford, CT: Dushkin/McGraw-Hill.

Waller, Maureen R. 2002. *My Baby's Father: Unmarried Parents and Paternal Responsibility.* Ithaca, NY: Cornell University Press.

Wasserman, Gail A., Virginia A. Rauh, Susan A. Brunelli, Maritza Garcia-Castro, and Belkis Necos. 1990. "Psychosocial Attributes and Life Experiences of Disadvantaged Minority Mothers: Age and Ethnic Variations." *Child Development* 61:566–580.

Waters, Mary C., Patrick J. Carr, Maria J. Kefalas, and Jennifer Holdaway, eds. 2011. *Coming of Age in America: The Transition to Adulthood in the Twenty-First Century.* Berkeley: University of California Press.

Weinstein, Megan. 1998. "The Teenage Pregnancy 'Problem': Welfare Reform and the Personal Responsibility and Work Opportunity Reconciliation Act of 1996." *Berkeley Women's Law Journal* 13:117, 127–139.

Weis, Lois, Eleanor Farrar, and Hugh G. Petrie, eds. 1989. *Dropouts from School: Issues, Dilemmas, and Solutions*. Albany: State University of New York Press.

Wells, Amy Stuart, and Robert L. Crain. 1997. *Stepping Over the Color Line: African American Students in White Suburban Schools*. New Haven, CT: Yale University Press.

Whittier, Nancy. 2009. *The Politics of Child Sexual Abuse: Emotion, Social Movements, and the State*. New York: Oxford University Press.

Widom, Cathy, and Joseph B. Kuhns. 1996. "Childhood Victimization and Subsequent Risk for Promiscuity, Prostitution and Teenage Pregnancy: A Prospective Study." *Public Health* 86:1607–1612.

Williams, Brett. 1994. "Babies and Banks: The 'Reproductive Underclass' and the Raced, Gendered Masking of the Debt." In *Race*, edited by Steven Gregory and Roger Sanjek, 348–365. Camden, NJ: Rutgers University Press.

Williams, John Michael. 2010. *The Gloucester 18*. Sperling Interactive.

Wilson, William J. 1987. *The Truly Disadvantaged: The Inner City, the Underclass, and Public Policy*. Chicago: University of Chicago Press.

Wolfe, Barbara, and Emilie McHugh Rivers. 2008. "Children's Health and Health Care." In *Kids Having Kids: Economic Costs and Social Consequences of Teen Pregnancy*, edited by Saul D. Hoffman and Rebecca A. Maynard, 221–256. Washington, DC: Urban Institute Press.

Wolfe, David A., Christine Wekerle, Deborah Reitzel-Jaffe, and Lorrie Lefebvre. 1998. "Factors Associated with Abusive Relationships among Maltreated and Nonmaltreated Youth." *Development and Psychopathology* 10:61–85.

Wyatt, Gail. 1988. "The Relationship between Child Sexual Abuse and Adolescent Function in Afro American and White American Women." *Annals of New York Academy of Sciences* 528:111–122.

Yampolskaya, Svetlana, Eric C. Brown, and Paul E. Greenbaum. 2002. "Early Pregnancy among Adolescent Females with Serious Emotional Disturbances: Risk Factors and Outcomes." *Journal of Emotional & Behavioral Disorders* 10:108–115.

Young, Leslie. 1992. "Sexual Abuse and the Problem of Embodiment." *Child Abuse & Neglect* 16 (1): 89–100.

Young, Tamera M., Sue S. Martin, Michael E. Young, and Ling Ting. 2001. "Internal Poverty and Teen Pregnancy." *Adolescence* 36:289–304.

Zabin, Laurie S., and Marilyn B. Hirsch. 1992. "To Whom Do Inner-City Minors Talk about Their Pregnancies? Adolescents' Communication with Parents and Parent Surrogates." *Family Planning Perspectives* 24 (4): 148–155.

Zabin, Laurie Schwab, Marilyn B. Hirsch, and Mark R. Emerson. 1989. "When Urban Adolescents Choose Abortion: Effects on Education, Psychological Status and Subsequent Pregnancy." *Family Planning Perspectives* 21 (6): 248–255.

Index

Abma, Joyce, 198
abortion decisions, 207–15; and accessibility, 211, 281n96; and antiabortion discourse, 208–9, 280n88; and family reactions to pregnancy, 45, 213–14, 281n97; and family support, 56, 250n23; and fathers of babies, 113, 211, 212–13, 214–15, 281n102; "good" girls, 180, 185–86, 190, 193, 207–15; and illegal abortion, 208, 280n86; and Latina teen mothers, 58, 250–51nn23,30, 281n97; in life-story narratives, 12, 42, 45, 79, 113, 150, 180, 185, 186, 187; and multiple messages, 213–15; need for openness about, 215; and race/ethnicity, 209, 210tab, 281n97; and religion, 209, 280nn82,84; and responsibility narrative, 207–8, 280nn84,85; timing of, 180, 211, 281n98. *See also* abortion rates
abortion rates, 188, 189*fig.*, 272n2, 280n89; and antiabortion discourse, 209; Connecticut, 209, 281nn94,95; decline in, 13, 14*fig.*, 46*fig.*, 209, 240n3; illegal, 208, 280n86; and race/ethnicity, 210tab.; and *Roe v. Wade,* 208, 280n87; teens, 281nn94,95
Abstinence Education Block Grant, 241n18
abstinence programs, 19, 20, 197–98, 241n18, 242n49, 274n27
Acosta-Belén, Edna, 160

Adolescent Family Life Act (AFLA) ("chastity bill") (1981), 19, 20, 22
adoption decisions, 110, 206–7, 280n82
adult status, 168–73, 271nn64–67, 272n69
AFDC (Aid to Families with Dependent Children). *See* welfare
AFLA (Adolescent Family Life Act) ("chastity bill") (1981), 19, 20, 22
African-American teen mothers. *See* black teen mothers
AGI report (*Sex and America's Teenager*), 63, 252nn60,63
Aid to Families with Dependent Children (AFDC). *See* welfare; welfare reform
Akin, Todd, 221
Alisha (life story of), 77–80, 86, 95
Allie (life story of), 164–65
Anderson, Elijah, 124, 244n70, 253n66
at-risk designation, 37, 248n121
Atkinson, Robert, 283n8
attractiveness, 205
Auletta, Ken, 17

Baldry, Eileen, 261n44
Becker, Howard S., 154–55, 253nn65,69
Bethany (life story of), 94, 105–10, 135
Bettie, Julie, 269n51, 271n66
Between Good and Ghetto (Jones), 124
Billion Women Rising, 221
birth control, 197–206; and abstinence programs, 197–98, 274n27; condoms,

birth control *(continued)*
198, 199, 204, 254n82, 275nn29,30, 276nn41,44, 279n80; and education, 156; and eugenics, 18; extent of use, 198, 274–75n28; and first sexual experience, 198, 275n33; funding for, 198, 276nn39,43; "good" girls, 188; and intention to become pregnant, 26; and "it just happened" narrative, 202–6, 278nn66,68, 279n80; in life-story narratives, 1, 44; misinformation about, 201, 277nn54,55; need for openness about, 199–202, 276–77nn44,48,49; and patriarchy, 197, 204, 278–79nn71,72; and politics of blame/gain narrative, 18, 19, 201–2, 276n43; and race/ethnicity, 198, 275n38; and transitional babies, 199, 276n41; types of, 198, 275nn29–32
birth rates. *See* teen birth rates
black matriarchy, 18, 247n112
black teen mothers: birth rates, 23–25, 59; education, 157, 267nn28,29; "good" girls, 193–95; life-story narratives, 40–45, 77–80, 110–14, 143–45, 194–95; young young mothers, 40–45, 51–52. *See also* black teen mothers as social problem; race/ethnicity
black teen mothers as social problem, 2–3; and intention to become pregnant, 25; and out-of-wedlock births, 14, 247n112; and politics of blame/gain narrative, 17–20; and racism, 34; and underclass narrative, 16, 17. *See also* racism
Blair, Tony, 242n47
Bloomberg, Michael, 192, 193
Booysen, Anene, 220
Bourgois, Phillipe, 256n110, 262n2
Breckenridge, Jan, 261n44
Bridget (life story of), 204, 205, 209
Brown, Angela, 97
Brown, Sarah, 193, 240–41n15, 265n11
Burton, Linda, 33, 244n75
Bush, George W., 242n49

Caitlyn (life story of), 169–70
Carbone, Nick, 12, 17
Carla (life story of), 66
Carr, Patrick J., 271n63
Carter, Jimmy, 255n93
Carter, Prudence, 270–71n61
Cassandra (life story of), 90, 99–100, 123–24, 125–27
Catholicism, Roman, 209, 213, 280nn82,84, 281n100

Celina (life story of), 70, 255n101
Center for Latino Adolescent and Family Health, 250n19
"chastity bill" (Adolescent Family Life Act) (AFLA) (1981), 19, 20, 22
chastity laws, 19, 20, 22, 247n112, 251n40
Chery (life story of), 193–94, 214
child care, 33–34, 174
child sexual abuse, 77–104; disclosure /silence, 99–101, 103, 260nn41,43, 261n44; early birth trajectories, 91–96; institutional perpetration of, 87, 103, 257nn6,7; and life-story methodology, 85–86, 89–91, 259n22; in life-story narratives, 8, 77–84, 91–94, 102–3, 105–6, 111; and life trajectories, 2; and partner violence, 95, 97, 260n32; and patriarchy, 73–74, 97–98, 104, 261n44, 261n59; prevalence/incidence, 88–89, 257–58nn10–14,17; prosecution for, 101, 102, 261n46, 261n54; and psychological disturbance, 94, 95–96, 259n26; and race/ethnicity, 89, 99, 100, 258n17; recovery from, 98–99, 101–3, 260n39; and residential mobility, 159; sample characteristics, 89–90, 99–100, 259n21; skepticism about, 87–88; and statutory rape laws, 64, 66, 95, 251n44; and teen sexual activity, 97, 259–60n29; therapy for victims of, 101–3, 261n56; trauma of, 96–98, 259n28
child support, 22, 247n112
childbirth timing. *See* fertility timing
circular migration, 159–61, 162
Civil Rights Movement, 17, 18, 118
Clark, Tena, 115
class: and abortion decisions, 209; and birth control, 198; and child sexual abuse, 102; and fertility timing, 26, 28–29, 33, 245nn86,89; and out-of-wedlock births, 14–15; sample characteristics, 37–38, 47. *See also* economic opportunity /inequality; poverty
Clayton, Eva, 62, 76
Clinton, Bill, 20, 22
Coalition for Domestic Violence, 117
Cocca, Carolyn, 62, 70, 257n120
Codes, Laura, 100
Coles, Robert, 244n70
Collins, Patricia Hill, 242n37
Collins, Randall, 262n5
Community-based Abstinence Education Program, 242n49

condoms, 198, 199, 204, 254n82, 275nn29,30, 276nn41,44, 279n80. *See also* birth control

Connecticut: abortion rates and accessibility, 209, 281nn94–96; economic opportunity/inequality, 36, 37, 59, 121–22, 247–48n119,120; education, 152, 162, 164, 165–66, 265n5, 269nn46–48, 270n60; poverty, 36, 59, 122, 247–48nn119,120, 263nn18,21, 282n10; race/ethnicity, 36, 37, 58–59, 247n115, 248n120; racial segregation, 37, 152, 157, 165–66, 248n120; sex education, 200–201, 277n51; statutory rape laws, 61–62, 251nn43,44, 253n72; teen birth rates, 36, 247n115; young young mothers, 46, 59

consequences of early childbirth, 28, 29–32; as distraction, 31–32, 247nn97,103,105; and economic opportunity/inequality, 32, 246–47n104; and education, 29, 31, 151–55, 245n93, 246nn100,102, 264nn1,2, 265nn8,10–14; and "good" girls, 38; and motherhood as starting over, 31, 246n98; and poverty, 29–30, 245–46nn93,96

contraception. *See* birth control

Contreras, Frances, 268n38

Cordelia (life story of), 71–72

Cosby, Bill, 12–13

counseling. *See* therapy

crack cocaine laws, 65, 253n70

Crain, Robert L., 270n61

Crowder, Kyle, 26

cultural-norm stereotypes, 53–54, 56, 57–58, 75, 250n25, 255n94. *See also* culture-of-poverty thesis; racism

culture-of-poverty thesis: and economic opportunity/inequality, 28–29, 245n86; and intention to become pregnant, 25–26, 28–29, 244nn70,75, 245n89; and underclass narrative, 17. *See also* cultural-norm stereotypes

Damaris (life story of), 196

Danielle (life story of), 54–57, 165

Dankowsky, John, 222

Dash, Leon, 23, 25, 244n75, 253n66, 260n41

David, George, 256–57n116

Davis, Noy, 68

Deirdre (life story of), 80–84, 85, 86, 94, 99

Delgado, Richard, 76

Delores (life story of), 85, 95

Democratic Leadership Council, 27

Democratic Party, 19, 20, 27

Denzin, Norman, 234, 239n10, 283n9

depression, 167, 168, 271n62

desegregation, 165–67, 270–71nn60,61

desire. *See* sexual desire; teen sexual activity

Diane (life story of), 1–2

Dilemmas of Desire (Tolman), 202

Dolgen, Lauren, 241n16

domestic violence: in white families, 117, 130–31, 262n7, 264n36. *See also* domestic violence in family of origin; partner violence

domestic violence in family of origin, 118; and education, 158–59, 268n36; in life-story narratives, 43, 78, 110–11, 119, 120–21, 123, 130–31, 146, 158–59; sample characteristics, 46–47, 115, 118, 119, 119*tab.*, 249n6; white teen mothers, 130, 131; young young mothers, 43, 46–47, 249nn5,6

double standard, 68, 204, 279n73

Douglas, Emily M., 89

Douglas-David, Marie, 256–57n116

drinking. *See* substance abuse

Drobac, Jennifer, 67, 254n86

dropping out. *See* education

drug trade, 44, 73, 83, 108, 109, 112, 123–24, 126–27, 257n1

drug use. *See* substance abuse

Dubious Conceptions (Luker), 30

Dukakis, Michael, 20

East, Patricia L., 271n68

economic opportunity/inequality, 27–29; Connecticut, 36, 37, 59, 121–22, 247–48n119,120; and culture-of-poverty thesis, 28–29, 245n86; and education, 157, 161–65, 168, 174–75; international comparisons, 32, 245n88, 246–47n104; and violence, 116–17, 121–22. *See also* poverty

Edin, Kathryn, 26, 244n76, 276n41, 281n3

education, 143–75; and abortion decisions, 209; and absent parents, 156, 266n24; and adult status, 168–73, 271nn64–67, 272n69; and child sexual abuse, 93, 94; Connecticut, 152, 162, 164, 165–66, 265n5, 269nn46–48, 270n60; and consequences of early childbirth, 29, 31, 151–55, 245n93, 246nn100,102, 264nn1,2, 265nn8,10–14; desegregation, 165–67, 270–71nn60,61; disengagement patterns, 155–58,

education *(continued)*
265–66n16, 266nn19,21, 267n33; and
domestic violence in family of origin,
158–59, 268n36; and economic
opportunity/inequality, 157, 161–65,
168, 174–75; extracurricular activities,
156, 266n22; and fertility timing, 56–57,
143, 152–53, 154–55, 265nn8,10,
266nn18,20; GED certificate, 154,
265n13; "good" girls, 180–82, 183–84,
187, 193, 194–95; and institutional
failure, 161–65, 168, 268nn42–44,
269n45,47–50, 270nn52–54; intervention programs, 161–62, 174–75, 183–84,
269n46, 272n74; Latina teen mothers,
157, 159–61, 162, 163, 167, 267nn27–
29, 269n51; and poverty, 152, 160,
264–65n3, 267n25; and race/ethnicity,
156–57, 267nn27–29; and residential
dislocation, 158–61; and special needs,
156, 162, 163, 266n23; and substance
abuse, 107; suspension practices, 164,
270nn52,53; and teen mothers as social
problem, 173–74, 193; and young young
mothers, 41, 43, 47, 55, 56–57. *See also*
education in life-story narratives;
education in sample characteristics; sex
education
education in life-story narratives, 9–10, 83,
93, 143–51; and adult status, 169–72;
desegregation, 166–67; "good" girls,
180–82, 183–84, 194–95; young young
mothers, 41, 43, 55
education in sample characteristics, 154*tab.*;
Advance Placement classes, 157,
267n26; disengagement patterns, 155,
156–57, 157*tab.*, 266nn19,21; family of
origin, 37, 38, 156; Latina teen mothers,
157, 267n27; race/ethnicity, 156–57,
267nn27,28; and special needs, 266n23;
young young mothers, 47
ELL (English Language Learners), 160, 162,
268nn38,40
Elo, Irma T., 256n116
Elstein, Sharon, 68
emasculation. *See* masculinity
employment, 11–12, 169, 171, 172, 271n64
English Language Learners (ELL), 160, 162,
268nn38,40
epiphanies (turning points), 6, 234, 239n10,
283n9
Erdmans, Mary Patrice, 222, 272n70
Erica (life story of), 85
eugenics, 18, 28–29, 245n89

Fagan, Patrick, 27, 28
Fallis, R. Kirk, 269n45
False Memory Syndrome Foundation, 87
Families Talking Together, 277n48
family of origin: education, 37, 38, 156;
"good" girls, 189, 190; incarceration in,
77–78, 82, 83, 159, 163; sample
characteristics, 37–38, 47, 119*tab.*, 156,
189, 190, 248n123; substance abuse in,
77–78, 118, 119, 119*tab.*, 122, 159;
support for teen mother, 12, 55–56,
250n23; violence in, 118–19, 119*tab.*,
122; young young mothers, 43, 46–47,
249n6. *See also* child sexual abuse;
domestic violence in family of origin;
parenting style in family of origin
family planning policies, 18. *See also* birth
control
family reactions to pregnancy, 11, 110, 125,
145, 263n30; and abortion decisions,
45, 213–14, 281n97; and cultural-norm
stereotypes, 56; "good" girls, 179, 180,
186, 190, 193, 194, 195–96, 273n16;
and motherhood as respectability, 125;
young young mothers, 42, 43, 44–45,
56, 250n24
Family Support Act (FSA) (1988), 22
Farmer, Paul, 212
fathers of babies, 10, 79–80, 83–84; child
support, 22, 247n112; "good" girls,
178–80, 184–85, 186–87, 191, 195;
incarceration, 10, 92, 94, 131; infidelity,
122, 126; interviews, 282n2; and
life-story methodology, 282n2; and
masculinity, 125–26; and motherhood as
starting over, 139–40; as partners,
65–66, 73, 253n78, 254–55nn80,92,
256n116; and patriarchy, 73, 247n112;
and symbolic violence, 128; and young
young mothers, 42, 44, 45, 47, 54–56.
See also fathers of babies reactions to
pregnancy; partner violence; statutory
rape laws
fathers of babies reactions to pregnancy, 80,
107, 110, 113–14, 145; and abortion
decisions, 113, 150, 211, 212–13,
214–15, 281n102; "good" girls, 179–80,
186; and motherhood as starting over,
151; partner violence, 84, 133; and
young young mothers, 45, 55
Fay, Joe, 278n66
Feagin, Joe, 57
Federal Office of Child Support Enforcement, 22

Fergusson, David M., 266n20
Fernandez-Kelly, M. Patricia, 264n38, 267n26, 271n67
fertility timing: and adult status, 172–73, 271n65; class norms, 26, 28–29, 33, 245nn86,89; and education, 56–57, 143, 152–53, 154–55, 265nn8,10, 266nn18,20; and poverty, 30, 244n75; rural areas, 33, 169, 271n63; and stigmatization, 196
Fine, Michelle, 130, 268n42,43
Finkelhor, David, 87–88, 89, 97, 258n14, 261n54
Fiscella, Kevin, 261n56
fornication laws, 61, 252n48
Forste, Renata, 267n29
Foucault, Michel, 245n89
Frank, Deborah I., 279n76
Friedman, Milton, 243n52
FSA (Family Support Act) (1988), 22
Furstenberg, Frank F., Jr., 14, 16, 30, 197, 223, 246nn96,103, 249–50n17, 256n116, 265n12

Gail (life story of), 190–91, 200, 209
Gandara, Patricia, 268n38
gangs, 82, 114, 122, 123, 125, 137. See also neighborhood conditions
Gans, Herbert, 17
Garcia, Lorena, 250–51n30, 254n82, 276nn41,48, 279nn72,80
Garey, Anita Ilta, 34
Garfield, Gail, 116, 262n5
GED certificate, 154, 169, 172, 265nn13,14
gender inequality. See patriarchy
Geronimus, Arline, 26, 30, 31, 33, 245n86, 246n97, 281n4
Gershenson, Harold P., 259n22
Gilligan, Carol, 73
Gladys (life story of), 40–42, 51–52
glamorization. See media
Glorimar (life story of), 160
Gloucester, 18, 25
Goffman, Erving, 192, 273n12
Goldwater, Barry, 19
"good" girls, 176–97, 215–16; and abortion decisions, 180, 185–86, 190, 193, 207–15; and adoption decisions, 206–7, 280n82; and consequences of early childbirth, 38; family of origin, 189, 190; life-story narratives, 176–87, 194–95; and life trajectories, 2; and responsibility narrative, 206, 207; sample characteristics, 189, 191, 273n7;

and stigmatization, 191, 192–97, 273nn12,16,17; and teen mothers as social problem, 192–93; and teen sexual activity, 203, 279–80n73,81; terminology, 192–93, 273n12. See also birth control
Gordon, Linda, 17, 18, 32, 240n8, 243n62
government programs/legislation, 3; abortion, 208, 280n88; abstinence, 19, 20, 197–98, 241n18, 242n49, 274n27; chastity laws, 19, 20, 22, 247n112, 251n40; child support, 22, 247n112; current prevention efforts, 16, 241n18; fornication laws, 61, 252n48; and neoliberal narrative, 22; and politics of blame/gain narrative, 18, 19. See also statutory rape laws
grade retention, 164–65, 270n54
Great Society, 17, 21

Hacker, Karen A., 278n68
Hammer, Harry, 165
Harding, David, 213
Hayek, Friedrich von, 243n52
Haylee (life story of), 182–87, 213–14
Herger, Wall, 27, 31
Heritage Foundation, 27
Hispanic teen mothers. See Latina teen mothers
Hoffman, Saul D., 244–45n84, 246n96
home-visitation program, 5–6, 220, 227, 228; at-risk designation, 37, 248n121. See also intervention programs
homelessness, 73
Horowitz, Ruth, 265n14, 272n69, 279n74
Hotz, V. Joseph, 152–53, 246nn97,98
humanist interview practices, 231–32, 282n4
Hyde amendment (1976), 280n88

illegitimacy. See out-of-wedlock births
immigration, 47, 51–52, 53, 75, 265n10
incarceration: Connecticut, 248n120; in family of origin, 77–78, 82, 83, 159, 163; fathers of babies, 2, 10, 69, 92, 94, 122, 131; partners of teen mothers, 113, 127, 132, 133, 134; and race/ethnicity, 248n120
inequality. See economic opportunity/ inequality; poverty
Ingram, John G., 103
intention to become pregnant: and cultural-norm stereotypes, 53; and culture-of-poverty thesis, 25–26, 28–29,

intention to become pregnant *(continued)*
244nn70,75, 245n89; and education,
173, 271n68; extent of, 26,
244nn73,74,76; and "it just happened"
narrative, 279nn78,79; and media, 25,
244n72; and motherhood as respectability, 125, 126; and statutory rape laws,
253n66. *See also* motherhood as
respectability; motherhood as starting
over
international comparisons: economic
opportunity/inequality, 32, 245n88,
246–47n104; out-of-wedlock births, 14;
politics of blame/gain narrative, 242n47;
teen birth rates, 13–14, 23–24, 201–2,
240n5, 243n62, 277n58; teen mothers
as social problem, 240n5, 242n47; teen
sexual activity, 200, 276n47, 278n58,
279n73
intervention programs, 161–62, 174–75,
183–84, 220, 269n46, 272n74
The Invisible War, 221, 282n9
Iris (life story of), 199, 205
"it just happened" narrative, 202–6,
278nn66,68, 279–80nn77–81
Ivalesse (life story of), 8–12, 35–36, 51

Jackie (life story of), 99, 100, 119–20,
139–40
Jackson, Jesse, 20
Jacobs, Janet, 263n30
jail. *See* incarceration
Jailbait (Cocca), 62
Janisa (life story of), 162
Jencks, Christopher, 17, 242n30
Jesenia (life story of), 99
Jones, Nikki, 124
Julie (life story of), 170–71

Kaplan, Elaine, 190, 273n12, 277n49,
278n68, 279n73
Kate (life story of), 91–94, 96
Kawachi, Ichiro, 247n104
Kefalas, Maria J., 26, 244n76, 271n63,
276n41, 281n3
Keisha (life story of), 259n21
Kelly, Deirdre M., 265–66n16
Kelly (life story of), 120–21, 163
Kennedy, Bruce P., 247n104
Kennedy, Ted, 20
Keynesian economics, 21, 243nn51,52
Kim (life story of), 100
Kimmel, Michael, 124
King, Rosalind Berkowitz, 256n116

Korenman, Sanders, 246n97
Kowaleski-Jones, Lori, 279n76

Lamb, Wally, 259n26
language issues, 160, 162, 268nn38,40
Lark (life story of), 195–96, 202
LaRonda (life story of), 99, 159
Latina teen mothers: and abortion decisions,
58, 250–51nn23,30, 281n97; and birth
control, 276–77n48; birth rates, 24–25,
58–59, 243nn64,65, 250nn26,28,29;
and child sexual abuse, 100; education,
157, 159–61, 162, 163, 167, 267nn27–
29, 269n51; and family support, 56,
250nn23,24; "good" girls, 176–82, 205,
211, 215; life-story narratives, 8–12,
54–57, 80–84, 119–20, 123–24, 125–27,
146–51, 166–67, 212–13; poverty, 160,
268n40; residential dislocation, 159–61.
See also Latina teen mothers as social
problem; race/ethnicity
Latina teen mothers as social problem, 2–3,
47, 53–60, 250nn19,21; and cultural-
norm stereotypes, 53–54, 56, 57, 58, 75,
250n25, 255n94; and statutory rape
laws, 68, 255n94; and white racial
frame, 57–60. *See also* racism
Laura (life story of), 94, 131–35
Lauren (life story of), 164–65
Lawson, Annette, 205, 278–79n71
legislation. *See* government programs/
legislation
Lieberman, Joe, 61, 62, 64, 76
life-story methodology, 5–7, 35, 227–35;
analysis, 233–35, 283nn8,9,12;
anonymity, 239n1; and child sexual
abuse, 85–86, 89–91, 259n22; and
domestic violence, 130–31; and
education, 269n45; humanist interview
practices, 231–32, 282n4; interview
process, 229–33, 259n22, 282–83nn4,5;
motifs in, 98; and parenting style,
249n16; partner interviews, 282n2; and
postmodernism, 283n6; and race/
ethnicity, 38, 229, 248n124; racial
terminology, 239n2; and teen mothers as
social problem, 38; and teen sexual
activity, 203, 278n65; and trust, 228–29;
turning points in, 6, 234, 239n10,
283n9; voice in, 6–7, 38–39, 234,
283n12; and white racial frame, 86,
257n4, 264n36. *See also* Connecticut;
sample characteristics; *specific life
stories*

Lilly (life story of), 73–74, 95, 122
Limbaugh, Rush, 221
Lina (life story of), 189–90
Linares, L. Oriana, 271n62
Lindberg, Laura Duberstein, 63
Lipper, Joanna, 260n43
Liz (life story of), 171–72
Luanne (life story of), 42–45, 46, 71, 72, 74,
    205, 207–8
Lucey, Helen, 273n12
Luker, Kristin, 26, 30, 31, 153, 201,
    246n104, 266n20, 267n29, 276n41
Luttrell, Wendy, 280n85

Mac Donald, Heather, 53–54, 57, 58, 59
Maggie (life story of), 67
Males, Michael, 63
mandated reporting, 61, 65, 69, 70, 252n49,
    253n72, 255n97
Manlove, Jennifer, 246n102, 266n20,
    267n29
Marcelina (life story of), 211–12
Marisol (life story of), 212–13
marriage, 15, 240n12. See also out-of-wed-
    lock births
Martin, Alice, 262n7
masculinity: and fathers of babies, 125–26;
    and politics of blame/gain narrative, 18;
    and sexual predation, 71–72; and teen
    sexual activity, 205; and violence,
    117–18, 124, 126, 129. See also
    patriarchy
Maynard, Rebecca A., 244–45n84
McCargar, Laura, 162, 164
McCarthy, James, 272n70
McElroy, Susan Williams, 246nn97,98
media: and child sexual abuse, 261n52; and
    intention to become pregnant, 25,
    244n72; and prevention, 15–16,
    241nn16,17; and teen mothers as social
    problem, 15–16, 240–41n15
Melody, June, 273n12
Menjivar, Cecilia, 262n13
Messner, Michael, 124
Mexican teen mothers, 57, 243n64,
    250nn21,25. See also Latina teen
    mothers
Michelle (life story of), 98, 99, 102
Mills, C. Wright, 235
minimum wage, 282nn15,16
miscarriage, 106, 133, 135, 153, 246n97
mobility. See economic opportunity
    /inequality
Mollborn, Stefanie, 263n30

Mollie (life story of), 102
Mondale, Walter, 20
Monique (life story of), 143–45, 166
moral entrepreneurs, 64, 76, 253nn65,69
motherhood as respectability, 129, 138; and
    family reactions to pregnancy, 125; and
    fertility timing, 29; and intention to
    become pregnant, 125, 126; and
    poverty, 218–19, 281n3; and racism,
    122, 128; young young mothers, 56
motherhood as starting over, 134–35, 219,
    281n4; assessment of, 264n39; and
    consequences of early childbirth, 31,
    246n98; in life-story narratives, 114,
    151; and poverty, 264n38; and violence,
    120, 138–40, 142
Mott, Frank L., 279n76
Mourdock, Richard, 221
Moynihan, Daniel Patrick, 18
Musick, Judith, 97, 101
Myrdal, Gunnar, 16–17

Nathanson, Constance A., 197, 199,
    245n86
National Campaign to Prevent Teen and
    Unplanned Pregnancy, 2, 193,
    241nn15,16, 250n19, 265n11
National Fatherhood Initiative, 247n112
nativism, 53. See also racism
Navarro, Valerie Small, 76
neighborhood conditions, 11; and
    motherhood as starting over, 139; and
    parenting style, 51, 249–50n17;
    violence, 112, 121, 122, 123–24, 126,
    263n22; young young mothers, 51, 75
neoliberal narrative, 20–22, 54,
    243nn51,52,55,57
New Deal, 21, 243n52
Nixon, Richard M., 19, 243n51
Nona (life story of), 52
Not Under My Roof (Schalet), 200

Oakes, Jeannie, 269n50
Obama, Barack, 16
Oberman, Michelle, 60, 67, 68, 72, 73,
    255n100
Oliveri, Rigel, 243n57, 253n69, 254n80
Open Choice program, 166, 270n60
Opotow, Susan, 269n45
opportunity structure. See economic
    opportunity/inequality
out-of-wedlock births: international
    comparisons, 14; and patriarchy, 34,
    247n112; and politics of blame/gain

out-of-wedlock births *(continued)*
narrative, 27, 242n46; public opinion, 15, 240n13; rates of, 14, 15*fig.*, 240n10; and teen mothers as social problem, 14, 27, 34, 240nn8,9, 247n112

Palin, Bristol, 29
Pamela (life story of), 176–82, 205, 211, 215
Pandey, Jyoti Singh, 220
parental reactions to pregnancy. *See* family reactions to pregnancy
parenting style in family of origin: and birth control, 200, 276–77nn48,49; and child sexual abuse, 96; and education, 266n24; "good" girls, 182; and immigration, 47, 51–52, 53; and life-story methodology, 249n16; in life-story narratives, 8–9, 40–41, 43, 52, 143–44; and neighborhood conditions, 51, 249–50n17; young young mothers, 40–41, 43, 47, 50–53, 75, 249–50nn16,17
parents of teen mothers. *See* family of origin; family reactions to pregnancy; parenting style in family of origin
partner violence: and child sexual abuse, 93, 94, 95, 97, 260n32; and life-story methodology, 233; in life-story narratives, 2, 45, 73, 79, 84, 107–8, 113, 120–21, 132, 133, 178; and patriarchy, 73; and poverty, 122; prevalence of, 115; white teen mothers, 132, 133; young young mothers, 45, 73
patriarchy: and attractiveness, 205; and birth control, 197, 204, 278–79nn71,72; and child sexual abuse, 73–74, 97–98, 104, 261n44, 261n59; and intention to become pregnant, 29; invisibility of, 32; and out-of-wedlock births, 34, 247n112; and personal responsibility narratives, 36; and sex education, 202; and sexual predation, 71–73, 256nn105,107,108,110; and statutory rape laws, 47, 50, 71–73, 247n112, 256nn105,107,108,110; and street code, 124, 125, 126; systemic nature of, 33–34; and teen mothers as social problem, 34, 247n112; and teen sexual activity, 204–5, 247n112, 279nn74,76; and violence, 115–16, 124, 125, 220–21, 282nn8,9
Peckinpaugh, Janet, 117
Perales, Nina, 255n94

Personal Responsibility and Work Opportunity Reconciliation Act. *See* welfare reform (1996)
Personal Responsibility Education Program (PREP), 241n18
personal responsibility narratives, 35–36, 206, 207–8, 280nn84,85
Peters, Ellen, 165
Phoenix, Ann, 23
Pillow, Wanda, 19–20, 235
Pistorius, Oscar, 220
Planned Parenthood, 192, 276n39
Plotnick, Robert D., 272n74
police, 112, 127, 136–37
politics of blame/gain narrative, 17–20; and birth control, 18, 19, 201–2, 276n43; and fertility timing, 28, 245n86; international comparisons, 242n47; and out-of-wedlock births, 27, 242n46; and racism, 18, 20, 242n37; and statutory rape laws, 63–64, 76, 253nn65,69, 257n120
The Politics of Pregnancy (Phoenix), 23
postmodernism, 283n6
poverty: and child sexual abuse, 100; Connecticut, 36, 59, 122, 247–48nn119,120, 263nn18,21, 282n10; and consequences of early childbirth, 29–30, 245–46nn93,96; and economic opportunity/inequality, 27–29, 218, 245nn86,88; and education, 152, 160, 264–65n3, 267n25; extent of, 36, 59, 251n36; Latina teen mothers, 160, 268n40; in life-story narratives, 11, 73–74, 120, 123–24, 125–27; and motherhood as respectability, 218–19, 281n3; and motherhood as starting over, 264n38; need for social change, 222–23, 282n14; and parenting style, 47, 51, 249–50n17; and personal responsibility narratives, 35–36; Puerto Rican teen mothers, 160, 268n40; and race/ethnicity, 248n120, 251n36; sample characteristics, 38; and statutory rape laws, 65, 253n69; systemic nature of, 32–33; and taxpayer costs, 245n84; teen birth rate correlation, 24–25, 30, 59, 251n36; and teen sexual activity, 50, 249nn9,13; and violence, 121–29, 126. *See also* class; culture-of-poverty thesis; economic opportunity/inequality
predatory man thesis, 47, 249n7. *See also* statutory rape laws
pregnancy rates. *See* teen pregnancy rates

prenatal care, 3, 45, 181, 195, 248n1
prostitution. *See* sex work
PRWORA (Personal Responsibility and
Work Opportunity Reconciliation Act).
See welfare reform (1996)
psychological disturbance, 94, 95–96,
259n26
Puerto Rican teen mothers: abortion
decisions, 281n97; and child sexual
abuse, 100; education, 157, 159–61,
162, 163, 167, 267nn27–28; life-story
narratives, 8–12, 54–57, 80–84, 119–20,
123–24, 125–27, 146–51, 166–67;
poverty, 160, 268n40; residential
dislocation, 159–61. *See also* Latina teen
mothers
Putnam, Frank, 89

race/ethnicity: and abortion decisions, 209,
210*tab.*, 281n97; and birth control, 198,
275n38; and child sexual abuse, 89, 99,
100, 258n17; Connecticut, 36, 37,
58–59, 247n115, 248n120; and
education, 156–57, 164, 267nn27–29,
269n51; language issues, 160, 162,
268nn38,40; and life-story methodology, 38, 229, 248n124; and poverty,
248n120, 251n36; racial segregation,
37, 152, 157, 165–66, 248n120; sample
characteristics, 36; school desegregation,
165–67, 270–71nn60,61; and teen birth
rates, 23–24, 24*fig.*, 25, 36, 243nn63–
65, 247n115; and varying experiences of
violence, 135–38; and young young
mothers, 47. *See also* racism
racial segregation, 37, 152, 157, 165–66,
248n120. *See also* desegregation
racial terminology, 239n2
racism: and attractiveness, 205; and child
sexual abuse, 100; and cultural-norm
stereotypes, 53–54, 57–58, 250n25,
255n94; and culture-of-poverty thesis,
25; and education, 165–67; and
eugenics, 18; and "good" girls, 193; and
motherhood as respectability, 122, 128;
and neoliberal narrative, 21; and politics
of blame/gain narrative, 18, 20, 242n37;
and sexual predation, 74; and statutory
rape laws, 50, 64, 68, 255nn93,94;
systemic nature of, 34–35; and teen
mothers as social problem, 2–3, 20, 34,
57–60, 250n25; and underclass
narrative, 16–17, 18, 29; and violence,
86, 116–18, 122, 127; white racial

frame, 57–60, 86, 116, 235, 257n4,
264n36. *See also* racial segregation
rape, 73, 78, 79, 90, 111, 115, 132, 133. *See
also* child sexual abuse; violence
Reagan, Ronald, 19–20, 21
Reardon, George, 87
Reed, Adolph, 16, 27
residential dislocation, 158–61
responsibility narrative, 35–36, 206, 207–8,
280nn84,85
Rhode, Deborah L., 205, 272n74
Robinson, Rachel B., 279n76
Rockefeller Foundation, 242n31
Roe v. Wade, 208, 280n87
Rojana, Ramon, 64
Roman Catholicism, 209, 213, 280nn82,84,
281n100
Ronai, Carol Rambo, 100–101, 260n39
Rowland, John, 62, 165
Roxanne (life story of), 187, 202–3
Rubin, Valerie, 271n68
Rumbaut, Ruben G., 250n21, 265n10
rural teen mothers, 33, 36, 169, 171,
271n63

sample characteristics, 236–38*tab.*; at-risk
designation, 37, 248n121; child sexual
abuse, 89–90, 99–100, 259n21; class,
37–38, 47; domestic violence in family
of origin, 46–47, 115, 118, 119,
119*tab.*, 249n6; education, 37, 38, 47,
154*tab.*, 156, 157*tab.*, 266nn19,21,23,
267nn26–28; family of origin, 37–38,
47, 119*tab.*, 156, 189, 190, 248n123;
"good" girls, 189, 191, 273n7; poverty,
38; program eligibility, 37,
248nn121,122; race/ethnicity, 36; and
statutory rape laws, 46; substance abuse,
118, 119, 119*tab.*; young young
mothers, 46–47, 48–49*tab.*, 59–60,
249n5. *See also* education in sample
characteristics
Sanders, Seth G., 246nn97,98
Sandusky, Jerry, 257n7
Sandy (life story of), 163–64
Santiago, Carlos, 160
Santorum, Rick, 14, 62
Sara (life story of), 206–7
Schalet, Amy, 200, 276n47, 279–80nn79,81
Schonberg, Jeff, 262n2
school. *See* education
self-esteem/self-worth, 72–73, 74, 98, 134,
204–5, 256n113, 279n76
self-harm, 79, 94, 95, 114

Settersten, Richard, Jr., 271n65
Sex and America's Teenager (AGI), 63
sex education, 200–202, 277–
78nn50,51,57; abstinence programs, 19,
20, 197–98, 241nn18, 242n49, 274n27
sex work, 73, 108–9, 111–12, 120, 137–38
sexism. *See* patriarchy
sexual activity. *See* teen sexual activity
sexual desire, 202, 205–6, 278nn61,62,64.
See also teen sexual activity
sexually transmitted diseases, 201, 277n52
Sheff, Milo, 165
Shenkman, Richard, 117
Sidel, Ruth, 34
Simms, Margaret C., 175, 272n74
single mothers. *See* out-of-wedlock births
16 and Pregnant, 15–16, 25, 241nn16,17
SmithBattle, Lee, 267n25
social context, 3–4, 217–18. *See also*
patriarchy; poverty; racism; violence
Social Science Research Council, 242n31
social support for teen mothers, 3, 223–24,
282nn15,16. *See also* intervention
programs
special needs, 156, 162, 163, 266n23
Spur Posse, 71, 72, 256nn107,108
starting over. *See* motherhood as starting
over
statutory rape laws, 22, 60–75; age of
consent in, 60–61, 251n41; age-span
provisions in, 61, 251nn42,43; and
chastity laws, 251n40; and child sexual
abuse, 64, 66, 95, 251n44; and data
misuse, 62–64, 76, 252–53nn60,62–64;
and definitions of consent and
predation, 67, 70–72, 254nn86–88,
255–56n101; and fathers as partners,
65–66, 68, 253n78, 254–55nn80,92,96,
256n116; and fornication laws, 61,
252n48; importance of, 66, 254nn81,82;
and intention to become pregnant,
253n66; and leniency, 70, 255n100; in
life-story narratives, 69–70; and
mandated reporting, 65, 69, 253n72,
255n97; and patriarchy, 47, 50, 71–73,
247n112, 256nn105,107,108,110; and
politics of blame/gain narrative, 63–64,
76, 253nn65,69, 257n120; and poverty,
65, 253n69; and predatory man thesis,
47, 249n7; and racism, 50, 64, 68,
255nn93,94; and sample characteristics,
46; selective enforcement of, 64–65,
253nn69,73,75–77; and taxpayer costs,
62, 64; and teen mothers as social

problem, 61, 62, 64, 68, 75–76, 251n45,
252nn48,52, 255n94, 257n120; and
teen sexual activity, 67–70, 257n117;
and welfare reform, 22, 61, 62, 76,
251–52nn46,47
Steenkamp, Reeva, 220
stigmatization, 3, 23; and "good" girls, 191,
192–97, 273nn12,16,17; and violence,
116. *See also* teen mothers as social
problem
Straub, Richard, 257n6
street code, 124, 125, 126
substance abuse: in family of origin, 77–78,
118, 119, 119*tab.*, 122, 159; by fathers
of babies, 131; and life-story methodology, 232–33; and residential mobility,
159; by teen mothers, 106, 107, 108,
109, 112, 119, 119*tab.*, 133, 135–36
Susan (life story of), 69–70
suspension practices, 164, 270nn52,53
Sutherland, Kate, 67, 196–97, 204, 247n112
symbolic violence, 128, 263n32
Szalacha, Laura A., 278n62

Talese, Gay, 227
Tameka (life story of), 94, 110–14, 128
taxpayer costs, 244–45n84; and consequences of early childbirth, 31; and
neoliberal narrative, 21, 22; and
out-of-wedlock births, 27; and statutory
rape laws, 62, 64; and welfare reform,
62, 252n55
teen birth rates, 13*fig.*, 14*fig.*, 63*tab.*, 188,
189*fig.*, 217; and birth control, 188;
Connecticut, 36, 247n115; and
cultural-norm stereotypes, 57; decline
vs. teen mothers as social problem, 13,
23; international comparisons, 13–14,
23–24, 201–2, 240n5, 243n62, 277n58;
Latina, 24–25, 57, 58, 243nn64,65,
250nn26,28,29; poverty correlation,
24–25, 30, 59, 251n36; and race/
ethnicity, 23–24, 24*fig.*, 25, 36,
243nn63–65, 247n115; and sex
education, 201–2, 277–78n57; young
young mothers, 46, 46*fig.*, 58–59, 75,
249nn3,5
Teen Mom, 15–16, 25
teen mothers as social problem, 12–13, 47,
221, 250nn19,21; and child sexual
abuse, 85; and consequences of early
childbirth, 29–32, 245–46n93; and
cultural-norm stereotypes, 53–54, 56,
57, 58, 75, 250n25, 255n94; culture-of-

poverty thesis, 17, 25–26, 28–29, 244nn70,75, 245n86, 245n89; and education, 173–74, 193; and "good" girls, 192–93; international comparisons, 240n5, 242n47; and life-story methodology, 38; and media, 15–16, 240–41n15; neoliberal narrative, 20–22, 54, 243nn51,52,55,57; and out-of-wedlock births, 14, 27, 34, 240nn8,9, 247n112; and patriarchy, 34, 247n112; politics of blame/gain narrative, 17–20, 27, 76, 242nn37,46,47, 257n120; and racism, 2–3, 20, 34, 57–60, 250n25; in spite of declining teen birth rates, 13, 23; and statutory rape laws, 61, 62, 64, 68, 75–76, 251n45, 252nn48,52, 255n94, 257n120; and taxpayer costs, 21, 22, 27, 31, 62, 64, 244–45n84, 252n55; underclass narrative, 2, 16–17, 25, 29, 47, 54, 58, 242nn30,31; and violence, 116; and welfare reform, 3

teen pregnancy rates: and birth control, 197, 274n26; decline in, 13, 14*fig.*, 240n4, 274n23; middle teenagers, 188, 189*fig.*; unintended, 188, 272n1; young young mothers, 46, 46*fig.*

teen sexual activity: attitudes toward, 50, 196–97, 200, 249n8, 274n21, 276n45; and birth control, 197, 200; and child sexual abuse, 97, 259–60n29; double standard, 68, 204, 279n73; and education, 148; international comparisons, 200, 276n47, 278n58, 279n73; "it just happened" narrative, 202–6, 278nn66,68, 279–80nn77–79,81; and life-story methodology, 203, 278n65; need for openness about, 199–202, 205–6, 216, 219, 276n47, 278nn61,62, 279n77; and patriarchy, 204–5, 247n112, 279nn74,76; and politics of blame/gain narrative, 19; and poverty, 50, 249nn9,13; rates of, 50, 188, 197, 249nn9,13, 272–73nn4–6, 274n25; and statutory rape laws, 67–70, 257n117

Terese (life story of), 130–31

Terkel, Studs, 235

Thatcher, Margaret, 222, 242n47

therapy, 101–3, 134, 261n56

Tienda, Marta, 267n29

timing. *See* fertility timing

Tita (life story of), 146–51, 159–60, 164, 167, 208, 256n101

Title IX, 174, 272n70

Title X, 18, 198, 280n88

Tolman, Deborah L., 202, 203, 278nn61,62, 279nn74,77,81, 283n5

Trent, Katherine, 26

turning points, 6, 234, 239n10, 283n9

twixter generation, 271n65

underclass narrative, 16–17, 29, 242nn30,31; and intention to become pregnant, 25; and Latina teen mothers as social problem, 2, 47, 54, 58

unmarried mothers. *See* out-of-wedlock births

Upchurch, Dawn M., 272n70

Urban Institute, 63

va y ven (circular migration), 159–61, 162

Victims of Child Abuse Laws (VOCAL), 87

Victoria (life story of), 191

violence, 140–42; and economic opportunity/inequality, 116–17, 121–22; in family of origin, 118–19, 119*tab.*, 122; and hierarchy matrix, 115, 116, 125, 262nn2,5; institutional perpetration of, 220–21, 256n105, 282nn8,9; interpersonal, 115, 262n5; in life-story narratives, 73–74, 105–14, 119–21, 123–24, 125–27, 130–35; and masculinity, 117–18, 124, 126; and motherhood as starting over, 138–40; and patriarchy, 115–16, 124, 125, 220–21, 282nn8,9; and poverty, 121–29, 126; prevalence of, 115; and race/ethnicity, 135–38; sample characteristics, 115, 118, 119, 119*tab.*; and street code, 124; symbolic, 128, 263n32; and white racial frame, 86; and white teen mothers, 129–38, 264n36. *See also* child sexual abuse; domestic violence in family of origin; partner violence

Violet (life story of), 158–59

virgin-whore continuum, 196–97, 204. *See also* stigmatization

Walkerdine, Valerie, 273n12

Wanda (life story of), 195, 200, 203, 211

War on Poverty, 18, 19

Weis, Lois, 130

welfare: and neoliberal narrative, 21, 22, 243n55; and politics of blame/gain narrative, 18–19, 20, 76, 242n46. *See also* welfare reform (1996)

welfare mother narrative, 18, 19–20. *See also* politics of blame/gain narrative

welfare reform (1996): and abortion decisions, 188; and neoliberal narrative,

welfare reform (1996) *(continued)*
22, 243n57; and out-of-wedlock births,
27; and politics of blame/gain narrative,
20; and statutory rape laws, 22, 61, 62,
76, 251–52nn46,47; and taxpayer costs,
252n55; and teen mothers as social
problem, 3; and underclass narrative, 29
Welfare Reform Act (1996). *See* welfare
reform (1996)
Welfare Rights Movement, 18
Wells, Amy Stuart, 270n61
When Children Want Children (Dash), 23,
25
When Sex Goes to School (Luker), 201
white racial frame, 57–60, 86, 116, 235,
257n4, 264n36. *See also* racism
white teen mothers: birth rates, 24; and
child sexual abuse, 91–94, 102;
domestic violence in family of origin,
130, 131; education, 156–57, 267n28;
"good" girls, 187; and intention to
become pregnant, 25, 244n72; life-story
narratives, 69–70, 91–94, 105–10,
120–21, 130–35, 169–72; and statutory
rape laws, 69–70; and violence, 120–21,
129–38, 264n36
Whittier, Nancy, 104

Wilson, Genarlow, 255n93
Wilson, Mary Margaret, 76
Wilson, Pete, 253n65
Woodward, Lianne J., 266n20

Yajaira (life story of), 166–67
Yanoff, Jay M., 278n66
young young mothers, 40–60, 75–76; birth
rates, 46, 46*fig.*, 58–59, 75, 249nn3,5;
family of origin, 43, 46–47, 249n6;
family reactions to pregnancy, 42, 43,
44–45, 56, 250n24; and Latina teen
mothers as social problem, 53–59;
life-story narratives, 40–45, 52, 54–57;
and parenting style, 40–41, 43, 47,
50–53, 75, 249–50nn16,17; and
poverty, 59–60; prenatal care, 45,
248n1; sample characteristics, 46–47,
48–49*tab.*, 59–60, 249n5; and teen
sexual activity, 50. *See also* statutory
rape laws
Yousafzai, Malala, 220

Zane, Nancie, 268n43
zero-tolerance policies, 270n53
Zina (life story of), 194–95, 207